KU-538-960

Counselling Adult Survivors of Child Sexual Abuse

Second edition

Christiane Sanderson

Jessica Kingsley Publishers
London and Bristol, Pennsylvania

All rights reserved. No paragraph of this publication may be reproduced, copied or transmitted save with written permission or in accordance with the provisions of the Copyright Act 1956 (as amended), or under the terms of any licence permitting limited copying issued by the Copyright Licensing Agency, 33-34 Alfred Place, London WC1E 7DP. Any person who does any unauthorised act in relation to this publication may be liable to criminal prosecution and civil claims for damages.

The right of Christiane Sanderson to be identified as author of this work has been asserted by her in accordance with the Copyright, Designs and Patents Act 1988.

First published in the United Kingdom in 1991 by
Jessica Kingsley Publishers Ltd
116 Pentonville Road
London N1 9JB, England
and
1900 Frost Road, Suite 101
Bristol, PA 19007, U S A

Second edition 1995

Copyright © 1995 Christiane Sanderson

Library of Congress Cataloging in Publication Data
A CIP catalogue record for this book is available from the Library of Congress

British Library Cataloguing in Publication Data
A CIP catalogue record for this book is available from the British Library

ISBN 1-85302-252-7

Printed and Bound in Great Britain by
Biddles Ltd., Guildford and King's Lynn

29N
STL

Acc.no S20/cav.

95/0002818
£15.95

T.

10 0337401 5

RY
LLEGE
OF NURSING AND
MIDWIFERY

WITHDRAWN

Counselling Adult Survivors
of Child Sexual Abuse

Second edition

**Books are to be returned on or before
the last date below.**

22 SEP 1995
11 DEC 1995
28 FEB 1997
19 DEC 1997
30 JAN 1998
24 FEB 1998
-6 MAR 1998
20 OCT 1998
DER

UNIVERSITY LIBRARY
14 JAN 2000
DER
UNIVERSITY OF NOTTINGHAM
17 JUL 2008
UNIVERSITY LIBRARY
24 AUG 2011

GE
ND

LIBREX —

Books of related interest

Counselling – The Deaf Challenge
Mairian Corker
ISBN 1 85302 223 3

The Listening Reader
Fiction and Poetry for Counsellors and Psychotherapists
Ben Knights
ISBN 1 85302 266 7

Shakespeare as Prompter
The Amending Imagination and the Therapeutic Process
Murray Cox and Alice Theilgaard
ISBN 1 85302 159 8

Love After Death
Mary Jones
ISBN 1 85302 287 X

Learning and Teaching in Social Work
Towards Reflective Practice
Edited by Margaret Yelloly and Mary Henkel
ISBN 1 85302 237 3

Good Practice in Supervision
Statutory and Voluntary Organisations
Edited by Jacki Pritchard
ISBN 1 85302 279 9

Dedication

To Michael and James
without whom this book could
not have been written.

Acknowledgements

The idea for this book came out of setting up the Incest Survivors Network and the many enquiries I got from both survivors and health professionals. There seemed to be insufficient resources available to either survivors or professionals on the long term effects of child sexual abuse and what therapeutic intervention was most beneficial to survivors.

I would like to thank all the survivors who have attended the support groups run by ISN and my clients. Their shared experiences of the reality and trauma of child sexual abuse form a major contribution to this book. Without them I would not have been able to understand the deeply wounding effects of child sexual abuse and the consequences of this trauma in their adult lives. I would like to thank them for allowing me to accompany them on their journey of healing, and also to validate their courage in reclaiming their childhood.

My thanks also go to family and friends who supported me throughout the writing of the book. My special thanks go to Sharon, Chris and Steve, Carol and Chris, Mrs Doyle, Susanne and my parents-in-law for giving me the space to write in their house. I would also like to thank Denise Rodricks and Jill Sullivan for all their help and wealth of experience, and Liz Kelly, SCOSAC and Henry Plotkin for developing my level of analysis. Jessica Kingsley deserves a huge thank you for believing in me and my ideas.

Finally, my thanks go to my husband and my young son who, despite my long absences at the word processor, supported me willingly without complaint, especially in times of stress and despondency. Their love, understanding and constant support spurred me on to the final page. I hope they like the result.

Contents

List of tables

Preface to the Second Edition

Since the publication of the first edition *Counselling Adult Survivors of Child Sexual Abuse* in 1990 there have been a number of controversial debates about the nature of child sexual abuse, its prevalence, the existence of satanic and ritual abuse, the apparent increase of female sexual abusers, and the validity of childhood memories pertaining to child sexual abuse. These debates have serious implications not only for the victims and survivors of child sexual abuse, but also for those mental health professionals working with them.

This revised edition includes new information and data on the incidence of child sexual abuse and looks more closely at the complexities of sexual abuse by female abusers, in particular at the emotional impact of this type of abuse on the victim, to enable counsellors and therapists to develop a greater understanding when working with survivors of female sexual abuse.

The controversy surrounding satanic and ritual abuse are outside the scope of the new edition. However, the reader will be alerted to coverage of this in other publications which specifically address this highly controversial phenomenon (see Sinason, 1994) both in terms of theory and practice.

Perhaps the bitterest controversy concerns the truthfulness and authenticity of reports of child sexual abuse and the apparent increase in false allegations of abuse leading to counter claims of false accusations. This heated debate has divided clinicians and academics alike, especially in relation to the new diagnostic syndrome which proposes that false memories may be iatrogenically induced during the process of therapy as result of individual clients' heightened suggestibility and disreputable therapeutic practices.

In order to evaluate the usefulness and validity of the concept of 'False Memory Syndrome' an entirely new chapter is included in this edition which aims to present both clinical and scientific arguments pertaining to the retrieval of memories, as well as analysing the impact of the application of this syndrome not only on victims and survivors, but also on therapists and society as a whole.

In preparing the second edition I would like to thank the following for their generous help and support. Dr David Oakley for his time, energy and support, Roger Scotford from the British False Memory Society, Marjorie Orr for much invaluable material, Childline and the NSPCC for providing more recent British statistics, Christine Feigen for many useful discussions, Melanie Partington for her inimitable help, Michael and James, and baby Max who was there throughout.

CHAPTER 1

Introduction

Increasing public awareness of incest and child sexual abuse through media coverage, documentaries, films, studio discussion programmes and the setting up of Childline in the United Kingdom has focused attention on the many children who suffer from the unwanted sexual attentions of fathers, mothers, stepfathers, grandfathers, grandmothers, brothers, aunts, uncles, cousins, friends of the family, neighbours or youth leaders, as well as other male and female authority figures. Well publicised cases of child sexual abuse that have been brought to the attention of social services or the courts, including the lengthy inquiry into Cleveland, have ensured that incest and child sexual abuse is kept to the forefront of public consciousness.

The emphasis is on the plight of the children and much of the available resources are being poured into the training of social workers, mental health professionals and police to provide effective intervention when sexual abuse is disclosed or reported. Of necessity, the priority is on helping those children that are currently being sexually abused. Resources are limited and not all children who have disclosed are provided with the type of support and therapeutic intervention which will ameliorate the possible long term effects associated with the sexual abuse and its disclosure. Although increasing numbers of children appear to be disclosing their abuse, there are probably many more children who do not and, as a consequence of not disclosing, continue to be sexually assaulted.

While this concentration of resources and focus on children is necessary and of fundamental importance, it is sometimes ignored by both professionals and the public that children who are currently, or until relatively recently, being abused will eventually grow up into adults. Those children that have benefited from positive therapeutic intervention may have been able to repair much of the damage resulting from child sexual abuse so that they are able to lead healthy and well adjusted adult lives, but those children who were not provided with positive therapeutic intervention, or who never disclosed the secret of their abuse, may remain deeply scarred. The hidden scars of incest may stay with these children throughout their lives.

The scars of incest and child sexual abuse are often deeply buried, or hidden, and cannot be seen on the surface. They often penetrate deep inside the psyche of child where they have the propensity to influence and direct behaviour both in childhood and adulthood. This often results in destructive behaviour patterns which inhibit the survivor from being able to live a free, mentally healthy or satisfying life. Many survivors feel permanently scarred and damaged by the abuse, and believe themselves to be unable ever to heal from the experiences, much less lead a happy or normal life.

Yet survivors can heal, even in adulthood. Although little research has been specifically directed at retrospective treatment intervention with adult survivors of child sexual abuse, researchers and clinicians in America have begun to recognise the importance of treatment intervention with adult survivors and have reported high efficacy and considerable success rates (Briere, 1989; Courtois, 1988; Gil, 1988; Jehu, 1988). In addition, several therapists have written self help manuals with survivors that not only provide valuable information and healing exercises for survivors, but also courage and the hope that it is possible to heal from their scars to lead more healthy, satisfying and fulfilled lives (Thornton & Bass, 1989).

Research on treatment interventions with adult survivors of child sexual abuse is slowly filtering through to the continent and Britain but to date there has been a paucity of literature available to the mental health professional, or the survivor, which specifies the possible long-term psychological effects of child sexual abuse, the diverse treatment approaches available, and the types of techniques that can be used in treatment.

Counselling Survivors of Child Sexual Abuse aims to redress this imbalance, by providing an overview of the literature to date, not only of the theories which attempt to account for the occurrence of child sexual abuse, but which also explain the traumagenic impact of child sexual abuse, how to ameliorate these effects, and how to facilitate the healing of the adult. Treatment techniques and the role of the counsellor in employing these techniques are also discussed in such a way that the counsellor can utilise the book not only as a theoretical review of the literature, but also as a practical handbook for use with any clients who may be adult survivors of child sexual abuse.

Historical background

Research into child sexual abuse and incest is still in its infancy and our knowledge base is still in the process of development. Although the taboo against incest is deeply engendered in most cultures, the historical incidence of incestuous and non-incestuous sexual abuse against children does not necessarily reflect the myriad of cultural sanctions against its practice (Rush, 1980). Arguably, the taboo is not one of incest but rather the taboo of keeping the sexual abuse of children secret and hidden. This taboo of secrecy is still much in evidence today whereby children are still reluctant to disclose their abuse experiences, while adult survivors have only just begun to emerge to tell their stories, often as many as thirty, forty or fifty years after the event.

Incestuous and non-incestuous sexual abuse has been practised over the centuries but has never really been a central focus for scientific inquiry which has warranted specific research interest. At the most, the literature has presented anecdotal accounts based on observed characteristics and individual clinicians interpretations. When psychiatrists, clinicians or psychoanalysts did report cases involving alleged child sexual abuse or incest it was argued that this was an extremely rare occurrence, with as few as between one and two cases per million (Weinberg, 1955) children encountering such an experience. This is despite reports that over 9,000 children between the ages of four and twelve were raped in Paris between 1858 and 1869. Disclosures of sexual abuse often met with reactions of shock or disbelief, and were almost unanimously relegated to the realm fantasy or fiction as the unconscious expression of incestuous desires by the daughter for her father (Freud, 1933). This conceptualisation gave birth to the notion of the child as seductress, whose active initiation of her sexual fantasies rendered the father powerless, thereby making him a passive victim of his daughter's sexual appetite.

The child as sexual aggressor prompted many clinicians to lay the blame and responsibility for the sexual abuse on the child while exonerating the abuser. Further blame has also been apportioned to the mother for not performing her conjugal duties in making herself sexually available, thereby increasing her husband's vulnerability to his daughter's sexual advances. From these beliefs, clinicians began to argue that, when these rare cases of incest presented in their consulting rooms, what they were witnessing was not only the sexual fantasies of daughters but also a representation and manifestation of underlying family dysfunction. Moreover, it was argued that such family dysfunction needed to be treated not by focusing on the symptoms such as incest, but rather by focusing on the family as a whole by exploring underlying family dynamics on an interpersonal level rather than by treating the child victim or attempting to ameliorate the myriad of elements suggestive of intrapsychic trauma.

The 1960s and 1970s saw a resurgence of interest in child sexual abuse. This was partly a natural progression following increased awareness and discussion of the physical abuse of children, but also reflected a shift in focus on the role of women in society. Feminism provided a vehicle in which women were encouraged to share feelings and ideas about their experiences. Consciousness-raising among women facilitated the discussion of women's status in society, while exploring such issues as domestic violence in the family, and rape. From this exchange of information and the sharing of experiences it became evident that child sexual abuse was a common rather than an isolated experience which many women had experienced and suffered from.

This recognition and acknowledgement allowed women to speak out about their sexually abusive experiences and prompted researchers and clinicians to reassess the state of knowledge about incestuous and non-incestuous child sexual abuse. Feminists and other researchers began to reinterpret earlier findings, and with improved research methodology, to conduct more sophisticated empirical research not only to assess the incidence of child sexual abuse but also to develop intervention and prevention strategies, including treatment models for both child and adult intervention.

Although there has been much progress in recent years in the collection and analysis of data, there are still a number of problems associated with empirical validation. This is especially the case when assessing the impact and psychological effects of sexual abuse, and in evaluating the most efficacious treatment models. There are also severe difficulties with the definition of incest and what constitutes child sexual abuse and, as a corollary to its definition, in analysing and verifying incidence rates.

Definition

There have been numerous attempts at defining incest and child sexual abuse, many of which incorporate severe limitations and shortcomings. The legal and anthropological definition of incest focuses on the consanguinity of the individuals in the relationship and the nature of the sexual act, which must include actual sexual intercourse. This has limitations in that much sexual abuse is conducted within the family structure without there necessarily being a blood relationship. This is primarily so in the case of stepfathers, the mother's sexual partner or boyfriend, friends of the family, or close neighbours. The abused child in the presence of such family constellations often has the same emotional investment and dependency needs as the child who is incestuously abused by her father, grandfather or brother.

To ignore the child's emotional dependency for guidance and protection by adults and her vulnerability to being abused, is to ignore much of the type of sexual abuse that does occur. According to Finkelhor (1984) only one third of reported cases of child sexual abuse are incestuous in legally defined terms, while two thirds consist of powerful and important adult figures in the child's life, on whom she depends for nurturance, protection and guidance without there being a blood relationship. Childline in the United Kingdom report that in 95 per cent of sexual abuse cases reported to them the abuser comes from the child's circle of family and acquaintances, with natural fathers being responsible in 51 per cent of the cases relating to girls and 31 per cent to boys (Childline, 1990). The latest NSPCC figures from 1988–89 show that natural fathers accounted for 24 per cent of all sexual abuse cases, siblings were implicated in 28 per cent of the cases, and 23 per cent constituted father substitutes while in 14 per cent of cases other relatives were implicated. In 15 per cent of cases 'others' (i.e. mothers' boyfriends, neighbours etc) were cited as having been abusers. The incidence figures for natural mothers was two per cent and three per cent for both parents (NSPCC, 1992). These figures suggest that the legal and anthropological definition is only able to account for a small proportion of the total range of intrafamilial child sexual abuse.

A further limitation to many accepted definitions is their focus on the nature and content of the sexual abuse. The focus in the legal definition of incest is exclusively on penile penetration and sexual intercourse and ignores the full range of sexually abusive acts that have been reported, which nevertheless violate the child's boundaries and persona. The spectrum of sexually abusive acts is wide ranging and does not always include full intercourse, but does incorporate non-touching behaviours as well as physical contact behaviours.

Of the non-touching behaviours the most commonly reported include exhibitionism, voyeurism, nudity, verbal innuendos, genital exposure, the use of pornography, and the taking of sexualised photographs. Physical contact behaviours include fondling of the breast or genital area of the child, kissing, masturbation, fellatio, cunnilingus, digital penetration of the anus, sodomy, digital penetration of the vagina, penile penetration of the vagina, 'dry intercourse' in which the abuser rubs his penis against the child's genital area, inner thighs or buttocks, and in some cases bestiality.

Given the wide range of sexually abusive behaviours involved in the sexual abuse of children, definitions which focus exclusively on whether sexual intercourse took place or not are severely limiting. The definition of incest and child sexual abuse has been attempted by a number of researchers and clinicians without any real consensus on what should be subsumed or contained in the definition. Until a comprehensive and commonly adopted definition is formulated, researchers will need to rely on the use of a working definition that best expresses their own orientation and beliefs.

The working definition of child sexual abuse employed in this book is broadly based, to incorporate the full range of intrafamilial and extrafamilial child sexual abuse and the complete spectrum of sexually abusive acts committed against children. Child sexual abuse is therefore defined as the involvement of dependent children and adolescents in sexual activities with an adult, or any person older or bigger, in which the child is used as a sexual object for the gratification of the older person's needs or desires, and to which the child is unable to give consent due to the unequal power in the relationship. This definition excludes consensual sexual activity between peers.

Incest is defined as a sexual act imposed on a child or adolescent by any person within the family constellation who abuses their position of power and trust within the family. It includes all sexual encounters where there is a difference of age and power, and all types of sexual behaviours ranging from pornography, voyeurism, exhibitionism, fondling, masturbation through to penile penetration. Most importantly, this definition includes all family members who have power over, and an investment of trust from, the child. To this effect it includes stepfathers, resident male friends of the family, uncles, brothers, grandfathers, cousins, as well as mothers, female relatives or female family friends.

The term 'incest' as defined above will be used throughout the book to denote the full range of intrafamilial child sexual abuse, while the term 'child sexual abuse' denotes both intra- and extrafamilial abuse. Thus, the terms 'incest' and 'child sexual abuse' may be used interchangeably. This usage reflects not only the working definition employed, but also illustrates the full range of abuse experiences disclosed by adult survivors in counselling. No differentiation is made in terms of what the blood relationship is to the abuser, as the impact and long term psychological effects are the same irrespective of consanguity.

Similarly, treatment models as a whole do not distinguish between consanguity or the nature of the sexually abusive act. What is of prime importance in treatment is to explore the meaning that the sexually abusive act had for the child and later adult, and how it was experienced as intrusive or exploitative. Whether penetration, touching or physical contact took place is of secondary importance. The focus of treatment is on how these experiences were perceived by the child, and how they have affected her both in childhood and in adulthood. For this reason the counsellor needs to be wary of constructing hierarchies in terms of severity of the sexual act, or the nature of the relationship, which may render some types of abuse less severe in impact than others.

Specific types of sexually abusive acts may require specific therapeutic focus, or attention, or the use of specific treatment techniques. However, in general, treatment approaches do not make distinctions between the content of the sexual activity but focus on the individual needs of the survivor. Flexibility in approach and techniques employed are more valuable and efficacious in treating adult survivors of child sexual abuse than the use of abuse hierarchies relating to the sexual practice involved, or the relationship of the survivor to the abuser. Thus children who are consistently raped by their stepfathers may be as traumatised as the daughter who is regularly orally masturbated by her father.

Although the focus of the book is primarily on the full range of intrafamilial sexual abuse, this does not deny the existence of extra-familial sexual abuse which includes neighbours, youth leaders, teachers, religious instructors, nursery workers, or the child molester who is a stranger. It also does not deny the high incidence of child sex rings, ritualistic abuse, and the more recently reported increase in child pornography and the use of children in the tourism and travel industry. It appears that ritualistic and the satanic sexual abuse of children is currently under-reported (Scan, 1989) with little or no research available to date on the long term psychological effects of this type of abuse, or whether it warrants more specific treatment requirements. That such ritualistic abuse is cause for serious concern is reflected in the setting up of a working party, funded by the Department of Health, to look at the possibility of creating a national expert team to focus specifically on issues and problems related to ritualistic abuse (SCOSAC, 1990).

Although La Fontaine's (1994) investigative study on satanic and ritualistic abuse generated very little conclusive evidence, suggesting that the prevalence and existence of satanic abuse is over-estimated and over-dramatised, more recent clinical accounts (see Sinason, 1994) do point to the existence of such abuse. Sinason and her collaborative authors attempt to provide a framework within which to view satanic and ritualistic abuse, while highlighting specific clinical issues and useful techniques and interventions when working with children and adult survivors of such abuse. For those readers wishing to familiarise themselves with these issues and clinical intervention, Valerie Sinason's *Treating Survivors of Satanist Abuse* is an excellent resource and reference guide (Sinason, 1994).

While there has been some research in America on the operation of child sex rings and their use of child pornography (Burgess, 1984; Burgess and Grant, 1988) which suggests that such rings are fairly wide spread, data on such rings is still limited in Britain. Equally there have been a number of investigative accounts published in America on organised sexual abuse of children (Finkelhor, 1989; Hollingsworth, 1986) to date there are few verifiable accounts available of such cases in the UK. This does not mean that they do not exist or that children are not suffering from such abuse, it merely suggests that such reports are under-investigated and under-reported. What is clear is that there has been an increase in media reporting on child sex rings and paedophiles and their part in the manufacture and distribution of child pornography, especially videos involving sexual acts with children. It is hoped that with heightened awareness of the activities of child sex rings this type of sexual abuse will be further investigated.

The latest NSPCC figures on organised abuse in the UK for the years 1990–1991 suggest that organised abuse is prevalent (Creighton, 1993). In canvassing NSPCC child protection teams throughout England, Wales and Northern Ireland, Creighton found that there were at least 19 cases of organised abuse with which the NSPCC were actively involved, which represented 43 known families and involved 61 children. However, the number of children suspected of involvement in organised abuse was 239, while the number of suspected adult perpetrators was 91. This would seem to suggest that organised abuse is much more frequent than at first thought and that much organised abuse remains hidden. Arguably, the known cases only really represent the tip of the iceberg; the majority are hidden.

In investigating the incidence of organised abuse, the NSPCC protection teams identified three main categories: networks in which children are exchanged sexually; organised Ritual abuse, and pornography rings. Each of these categories differed in the profile of the children involved. In the case of network abuse the children were more likely to be boys (60%), slightly older than the other two categories, with a mean age of 13.7, and generally speaking unrelated to the perpetrator(s). These children were often lured into the network by an older peer with promises of rewards. The networks consisted of 20 children with two or three adults.

In the ritual abuse category the children were predominantly girls (83%) and much younger, with a mean age of 7.2. The adults involved in ritual abuse were often members of either the immediate or the extended family, with an average of seven adults and 13 children per group. The data for the pornography category was limited in that the sample size was very small, but in this study consisted entirely of female children with a mean age of 12.3. The perpetrators in this group were strangers to the children's families, but not necessarily strangers to the children. Some of the perpetrators already had criminal records, many of which were for sexual offences against children.

Detective Inspector Michal Hames of the Obscene Publications Branch at New Scotland Yard has argued that child pornography rings not only exchange offensive and pornographic material, but may also be involved in passing children around between them (Hames, 1993). More disturbingly, Hames has found that there is a trend for the pornographic material to feature increasingly violent sexual assaults on children as a

'... response to the demand for ever more depraved material or as a result of increased success at detection' (Hames, 1993).

As a result of increased detection of child pornographic material it has been established that there are a number of countries that are known haunts for paedophiles either to buy children, or pornographic material. This is particularly true in Thailand where many families, due to extreme poverty, sell their children into prostitution, while Portugal, and Amsterdam in Holland, are regarded as 'safe' places in which to buy explicit child pornographic material.

Such recognition has resulted in an increased awareness about the world-wide sexual exploitation of children, especially through international travel and tourism. Paedophiles are known to travel to developing countries such as Thailand, the Philippines and Sri Lanka for ease of access to children for sexual purposes. According to Kevin Ireland of The Save the Children Fund, the organised sexual exploitation of children is worldwide, but is particularly prevalent in developing countries which suffer from high levels of poverty, which forces some parents to sell their own children into prostitution to supplement the family income (Ireland, 1993).

Ireland argues that, while the majority of abusers using children for sexual purposes are known paedophiles, some tourists become involved in sex with young children due to their availability, and that some men, while away from home, are more likely to give way to repressed paedophilic tendencies (Ennew, 1986; Ireland, 1993). Another factor is that an assumption is made that a young child prostitute may be less likely to have AIDS. The reality for many of these children is that they soon contract AIDS, at which point they are sent back to their families, who often reside in more rural parts of the country, to die.

That perpetrators from the UK are involved in such sexual exploitation is known, but what is not known is how many 'situational' abusers return home who may then go on to act out their experience of sex with young children in their country of origin. Obviously, if some do go on to abuse young children in their country of origin this puts increasingly more children at risk.

Ireland argues that to control, or indeed diminish, the sexual trafficking of children, remedial action needs to be taken on three levels. First, in the country where the exploitation takes place, second in the country in which the tourist originated, where the perpetrator could be prosecuted in their own country for offences committed abroad, and third in the international arena, where a concerted effort should be made by all countries involved to minimise the availability of children for such exploitation (Ireland, 1993).

Incidence

The definition of what constitutes incest or child sexual abuse has had considerable influence on the collection, presentation, and analysis of available data on incidence rates and the prevalence of incest and child sexual abuse. Research studies have used different definitions both of relationship to the abuser, the age difference between abuser and child, and the nature of the sexual activity. This has resulted in highly divergent incident rates, depending upon the definition employed. Finkelhor's (1984) survey of the then published research literature demonstrated that between 12 per cent and 38 per cent of women are sexually abused as children, while between 2.5 per cent and 9 per cent of men are sexually abused as boys.

Available data from these studies also vary because of the population sample surveyed, the sensitivity of the questions asked, the type of questionnaires used, and biases in the analysis and interpretation of the data collected. Despite these deviations in the incidence rates, what is clear is that sexual abuse does occur to an alarming extent in childhood. A more recent survey in Los Angeles (*Los Angeles Times*, 1985) reported that 22 per cent of all adults had been sexually abused as children, of which 27 per cent were female and 16 per cent were male. The most recent research figures for Britain are 12 per cent for girls and eight per cent for boys (Baker and Duncan, 1985). The NSPCC, on the basis of the number of children registered with them, estimate that the national incidence in England and Wales of child sexual abuse for children under 14 years of age is 5,850 and 6,600 for children under the age of 16 (NSPCC, 1990). Of the registered sexual abuse cases 78 per cent involve female children and 22 per cent involve male children. The NSPCC report that on average more boys are being registered for child sexual abuse, particularly among five to nine year olds, currently 31 per cent, compared to 25 per cent in the birth to four-year-old age group and 15 per cent in the 10–16 year-old group (NSPCC, 1990).

Childline figures for 1993 show that in 94 per cent of cases the perpetrator comes from within the family. In the sexual abuse of female children, the father is implicated in 38 per cent of cases, with stepfathers responsible in 10 per cent and brothers in 12 per cent of cases. Mothers or other female relatives are implicated in only 2 per cent of cases. In the case of sexual abuse of male children, the father is implicated in 31 per cent of cases, followed by the mother in 18 per cent of cases, while in 11 per cent of cases a female relative such as a stepmother, sister or aunt is implicated.

The apparent difference between incidence rates for male and female children and their alleged vulnerability to abuse also needs to be reassessed. It has been argued that the incidence rate for males is underreported because males find it more difficult to disclose their abuse histories (Finkelhor, 1984). This may also reflect a research bias in which attention has been focused almost exclusively on female victims while ignoring male victims. Arguably, increased awareness and the recognition that boys are also highly vulnerable to being sexually abused as children, may encourage more boys and adult male survivors to disclose their abuse experiences in the future (Lew, 1988; Hunter, 1990).

An increase in research focusing on male victims would be welcome in supplying more accurate data on its incidence, and any specific treatment or intervention requirements. It would also shed more light on the notion that child sexual abusers were themselves abused as children, and the possibility that their abuse lies at the root of the putative notion of a cycle of inter-generational abuse. This has ramifications for our understanding of the dynamics of incest and of how this cycle may be arrested, and ultimately prevented.

One overwhelming finding is that 91–97 per cent of abusers are male (Finkelhor, 1984) and that the incidence of female abusers is much less common. The most recent figures in the UK suggest that only 9 per cent of females sexually abuse children (Childline, 1992). Again, this may reflect a bias in under-reporting among female abusers themselves and their victims. Increasingly, more studies are being conducted that suggest that female abusers are not as uncommon as previously noted. Some American studies purport to show that female abusers are implicated in up to 13 per cent of cases where female children are involved and 25 per cent of cases where male children are involved (Hunt, 1990). While the incidence figures for female abusers may be hidden and therefore higher than currently reported, it is important to look more closely at the available data.

Women as Perpetrators of Child Sexual Abuse

Until 1990 the incidence of child sexual abuse by women seemed largely hidden, with very little discussion or research conducted in this area. It was believed by many professionals that less than 2 per cent of child sexual abusers were female and in these rare cases that women were not the initiators of the sexual abuse, but were coerced through threat of punishment and violence to collude and participate with a male partner. In those cases where a woman did initiate sexual contact with a child it was assumed that the child was male, and that this was in some way a healthy initiation of an eager, and more than willing adolescent boy, into the delights of sexual intimacy with an older woman, reminiscent of the film 'The Graduate'. The reality is quite different.

Finkelhor and Russell as early as 1984 were beginning to question the incidence of female child sexual abusers and estimated that as many as 13 per cent of child sexual abusers were in fact female (Finkelhor and Russell, 1984). Similarly, Childline found in their statistics of callers reporting child sexual abuse during 1990–1991, that while 91 per cent of perpetrators were identified as male, nine per cent were female. These figures were in stark contrast to the longstanding NSPCC and Home Office figures which indicated that no more than 2–3% of child sexual abuse was perpetrated by females, and only then under threat or coercion of a male partner.

O'Connor (1987; 1988), while studying a group of female sex offenders, found that in nearly all of the cases of child sexual abuse involving female perpetrators, the women were coerced into aiding and abetting a male committing the offence. More important, O'Connor argues that 'sexual gratification was never noted as a motivation for the women involved in sex offences with a victim.'

From this finding it is possible to argue that, in cases involving females sexually abusing children, the women are rarely the instigators of the sexual abuse but rather are in some way forced into or controlled by a male abuser to participate in the gratification of his needs to abuse. Thus the woman's involvement may range from procuring victims to actual participation in any sexual act. It would seem likely that she may be dependent on the male abuser, who has power and control over her, so that she feels she has no choice but to comply with his demands in the sexual abuse.

However, this finding does not seem to apply in the case of adolescent females; a number of researchers have found that adolescent female sexual offenders often sexually abuse children in a babysitting context, in the absence of any coercion by a male (Scavo, 1989; Allen, 1990). Arguably, these adolescent females, being given power over a younger child, may be acting out their own sexual abuse experiences on their charges.

To redress the balance of these divergent findings and to explore and understand female sexual abuse, Michelle Elliot of Kidscape attempted to organise the world's first conference on Female Sexual Abusers in London in 1992. Somewhat surprisingly, she, and some of her guest speakers, were met with open hostility, particularly in the press, from feminists who saw this as part of a feminist backlash and an excuse to blame mothers, yet again. Many of these feminists argued that, in looking at female perpetrators of child sexual abuse, the focus was being shifted from the majority of abusers who are male to a tiny number who happened to be female, thus denying the reality of child sexual abuse in the majority of cases as a male act of power and dominance over female child victims.

While it is undeniable that the majority of child sexual abusers are male, it cannot be ignored that some women also abuse children sexually. No matter how small the percentage is, it exists and is significant. To deny that females sexually abuse children is to deny the experiences of those child victims and adult survivors who were abused by women.

That such denial is common was demonstrated by Michelle Elliot's study of survivors who were sexually abused by females in childhood, in which 78 per cent reported that, when they sought help, no-one, including professionals, believed them, or felt able to help them (Elliot, 1993). Often their disclosures were met with shock, disbelief, and denial, and relegated to the realm of fantasy, or Oedipal wishes, very much as the early disclosures of child sexual abuse in the 1960s and 1970s were dismissed. Ironically, some survivors had to pretend that their abusers were male in order to be acknowledged and heard.

Elliot (1993) also found that, of 127 victims who contacted her with a sexual abuse history by a female perpetrator, 33 per cent were male and 67 per cent were female. In 75 per cent of all cases of abuse the female acted alone, often with no man in the family. Mothers were the sole perpetrators in 50 per cent of all female victims and 75 per cent of the male victims. The remaining female abusers ranged from stepmother, aunt, grandmother, babysitter, friends of family and other female authority figures such as teacher and nun.

The kind of abuse reported included oral sex, penetration of both vagina and anus with not only fingers but also objects, such as bottles, rose stem and sticks, enforced sucking of the perpetrator's nipples, forced mutual masturbation, and full intercourse. In some cases there was a combination of physical and sexual abuse (Elliot, 1993). In over 50 per cent, for both male and female victims, the abuse started before the age of five and went on well into adolescence, and in some cases into adulthood.

Arguably, to date it is impossible to quantify the level of child sexual abuse perpetrated by females, especially as such abuse is seen as 'The Last Taboo'. To acknowledge the existence of female sexual abuse will undoubtedly challenge many myths and misconceptions about females, especially in relation to violence, aggression and sexuality and, as such, ultimately threatens to destroy deeply ingrained beliefs about female sexual passivity, lack of aggression, the sanctity of motherhood and the existence of the maternal instinct.

Kirsta (1994) argues that the denial of female sexual abusers relies on the myth of motherhood which is informed by several false assumptions about females and female sexuality. These focus on the premise that because the sexual abuse of children is primarily about male power over females, and as women do not possess a penis, therefore women do not sexually abuse (Kirsta, 1994). Second, as females are seen as not being inherently sexually aggressive, how can they be initiators of sexual abuse? This works on the fallacious assumption that female sexual passivity is the norm, thereby denying women an active role in the expression of their sexuality.

Finally, it challenges the belief that women naturally know how to relate to children and that their natural role is a caring and nurturing one, in which they act as protectors, thereby automatically excluding them from perpetrating abusive acts against children. This is to deny the capacity of women to possess both negative as well as positive qualities in relation to themselves and others, and to deny the full range of female behaviours and feelings in relation to children.

What has emerged is that females do sexually abuse children, sometimes under the auspices of acceptable child rearing practices such as ensuring personal hygiene, or masturbating a male child to sleep, and that because women have traditionally had more access to children, such abuse remains more hidden under the belief that close physical intimacy and contact with children is 'normal' for women. Some feminists have even argued that some children who claim to have been abused by their mothers have misinterpreted such acts of loving care and intimacy as erotic stimulation when in reality they were just normal expressions of caring behaviour. If this same argument were applied to male abusers it would be demolished as denial of actual acts of sexual abuse.

In ascertaining the long term effects of child sexual abuse by female perpetrators, Elliot found that all the female victims who contacted her reported that the abuse caused considerable distress and had adverse effects on their life, ranging from substance abuse, suicidal ideation and suicide attempts, depression, eating disorders, difficulties in inter-personal relationships, unresolved anger, gender identity problems, fear about close physical contact with their own children, and in some cases actual sexual abuse of children. Only four male victims (12%) reported no adverse effects, with 88 per cent reporting similar long term effects to that of the female victims, particularly gender identity problems combined with intense feelings of hatred and violence towards women as a result of their abuse by a female.

In ignoring the fact that females do sexually abuse children other than through threat or coercion, in which the male is assigned full responsibility, many professionals deny the impact of sexual abuse by women. In addition, some professionals prefer to believe that those female sexual abusers that do initiate the sexual contact in the absence of a male, must be suffering from severe mental illness, or indeed be psychotic. However, research both in America and the UK demonstrates that there is in fact a very low incidence of mental illness, and that the majority of female perpetrators are seen as mentally stable, ordinary and likeable. They are certainly not crazed lunatics, cackling crones or witches (Kirsta, 1994).

In comparing male with female abusers, many survivors and professionals report that female sexual abusers are often more violent in their acts, which are accompanied with a greater level of humiliation towards the victim. However, female abusers often feel much more guilt about their abusive acts, which prompts them to admit more easily to the abuse when a disclosure is made. Many female abusers disclose the abuse to the relevant authorities themselves, are often much more contrite about the abuse and are more willing to seek help, and to sustain change.

Nevertheless, the abuse profile of female perpetrators is to date still very sketchy compared to our knowledge about male perpetrators of child sexual abuse. This is primarily because sexual abuse by females has been denied, therefore under-reported and under investigated. In one of the few studies available to date, Mathews et al. (1989) have begun to demonstrate that early childhood experiences do have an impact on later abusive behaviour. As a result of their detailed study of female sexual abusers, they have been able to establish four distinct types of female perpetrators.

The first type of female perpetrator is called the 'Teacher–Lover' offender, in which an older woman sexually seduces young adolescent boys. These perpetrators are characterised as not having been sexually abused in childhood yet feeling inadequate or powerless in relation to adult men. Their sexual abuse of young boys is seen as acting out intense and unexpressed feelings of anger towards all men, and that these feelings are directed, albeit in a sexual way, towards young boys who are seen as a 'safer' target than an adult male. Many of the women in this category fail to acknowledge their behaviour as sexually abusive, or indeed criminal, as they are able to rationalise that the young boy is enjoying what they are doing.

This rationalisation is informed and reinforced by popular culture in which such films as 'The Graduate' appear to depict such liaisons as an accurate representation of the desires and fantasies of all young adolescent boys. Believing that society sanctions such encounters, the female perpetrator then begins to see the child as a more than willing participant, if not the initiator of the sexual intimacy. In reality, most male victims feel betrayed and used, which for many fuels their anger, aggression and negative attitudes towards women, especially when they become adults.

According to Mathews *et al.* (1989), by far the largest category of female perpetrators is represented by what they call the 'predisposed offenders' whose most common characteristic is a history of intra-familial sexual abuse in early childhood, often with multiple abusers who are related to the family. The effect of such early experiences of sexual abuse is that, as adult women, they feel hurt and betrayed by the very people who should have nurtured and protected them. One way of discharging these feelings is to act out their own abuse by sexually abusing their own children, or the child of a close relative. In contrast to the 'Teacher–Lover', these female abusers are often suffused with guilt and remorse, invariably leading them to disclose their abusive behaviour, or try to seek help.

The main characteristics of perpetrators in the third category, called 'Experimenter–Exploiter' abuser, are an apparent lack of knowledge or understanding about sex often due to a rigid or puritanical upbringing in which sex was seen as a taboo subject and never broached. The female abusers in this category are fascinated by sex but, due to their lack of knowledge and understanding, and inexperience, may attempt to experiment with a young child in their care when left alone babysitting. This would account for Scavo's (1989) and Allen's (1990) finding of a reported increase in young women sexually abusing children left in their care.

The women in the last category, that of the 'Male–Coerced' offender, frequently also report a history of early childhood sexual abuse, but more often by strangers or people outside of the family. Such women invariably go on to form unhealthy relationships with abusive men. These female perpetrators possess extremely low self-esteem and suffer from intense self-hatred, frequently seeing themselves as evil. In being in a relationship with an abusive man, these women are often forced by means of threats of violence or sexual abuse, or coerced by their abusive partners, to participate in the sexual abuse of children. Somewhat disturbingly, however, Mathews (1993) reports that 44 per cent of the female abusers in this category who were initially coerced or forced, go on to initiate the sexual abuse of children by themselves without any male coercion.

Research conducted in Leeds in the UK confirms many of these findings (Hanks and Saradjian, 1991). In addition, it has been established that female abusers also suffer from high levels of anxiety and aggression, while being socially and emotionally isolated, resulting in difficulties, in forming healthy adult relationships. Hanks argues that by becoming a 'powerful, controlling perpetrator' through re-enacting their abuse experience, these women not only experience a release from tension but also perceive a level of control which '... becomes a powerful motivator to repeat the abusive behaviour' (Hanks and Saradjian, 1991).

This misuse of power and control has been alluded to by Estela Welldon (1993) who argues that an overwhelming sense of powerlessness, lack of control and low self-esteem

LIBRARY DERBY COLLEGE OF NURSING AND MIDWIFERY

can lead to a need for power and control over others, especially those who are dependent and helpless. The state of motherhood to some extent assigns instant power, authority and control to the mother, which she can misuse in relation to her vulnerable child who is totally helpless and thus dependent on the mother for its physical and emotional survival.

For those mothers who experienced abuse in childhood, or who feel powerless and have no alternative sources for the gratification of their needs, having children can become the 'ultimate power trip' in which they might misuse their power both physically and sexually over their own children in acting out abusive behaviour (Welldon, 1993).

Welldon also proposes that, when a mother abuses her own child, this can be seen as a form of self-destructive behaviour which can be plotted along a continuum of other self-destructive behaviours such as anorexia and self-mutilation. Given that the infant is a part of the mother's body and thus her 'creation', the child may be seen as an extension of the mother. Thus, the mother is seen to be turning her own anger, rage and self-hatred onto her herself in physically or sexually abusing her own child, thereby mutilating and destroying herself.

Other researchers have suggested that, in the case of mothers who abuse male children, this is seen as a way of acting out deeply felt hatred and rage towards all men in which the child sexual abuse becomes a symbolic act of murder, albeit in a psychic sense (Kirsta, 1994; Mathews et al. 1989).

Thus, the current data available on female sexual abusers highlights the fact that the sexual abuse of children by women is not necessarily driven by sexual needs, desires or gratification, but can be construed as an act of power and control. This is not dissimilar to the feminist argument which seeks to explain the motivation of male sexual abusers within the context of power, control and dominance of men over women and children which is engendered and sustained in a culture based on patriarch.

The data also clearly illustrates that not all women are necessarily nurturing and caring protectors of children, or indeed sexually passive, but that, like their male counterparts, also have the capacity to act out their sense of powerlessness, injustice, hurt and anger. It must, however, be clarified that the majority of women do not act out their abusive experiences, due to socialisation factors in which they are taught to 'act in' by internalising their feelings of hurt or anger, and turning them against the self. What the current literature does demonstrate is that females do have the capacity to act out their abuse experiences and that some females do this by sexually abusing children.

To acknowledge this enables us to view women with much more objectivity, enabling us to see both their positive and negative attributes thereby creating a more realistic picture of how women experience the world, how they function in their environment and how they relate to others. Such a picture allows for a wider range and more complex permutations of thinking, feeling and behaving which are not constricted by traditional myths of motherhood and the maternal instinct, which attempt to present women as primarily responsible for the protection and nurturing of their young, thereby rendering them incapable of acting out their aggressive, or indeed sexual urges.

Undoubtedly females can, and do, sexually abuse children but whatever their motivation and level of participation, they remain at present a small minority compared to male sexual abusers. However, in trying to understand the minority, researchers and clinicians alike must guard against being diverted from reality, which is that the majority of child sexual abuse is perpetrated by males.

For this reason, this book will focus primarily on child sexual abuse involving male abusers as this form of abuse is more likely to be encountered by counsellors and clinicians in therapeutic practice. While not denying that there are survivors who experienced sexual abuse by a female, this is likely to be less frequently encountered at the present time.

A further consideration is that if inter-generational abuse is at the root of child sexual abuse we need to ask the question, why if so many more females are abused than males, are there so few female in comparison to male abusers? This may be due to socialisation as a result of which, females are socialised to internalise their feelings of anger, frustration, aggression or pain, while males are actively encouraged to externalise such feelings by venting them on to others. Thus the female survivor internalises, or acts in, her abuse experiences perhaps by indulging in self destructive or self mutilating behaviours, while the male may externalise, or act out, his abuse by abusing others more vulnerable than him.

As the available research literature on male victims, and female abusers, is still inconclusive and by its nature limited, the focus of this book will predominantly be on male abusers and their female victims. This is reflected in the almost exclusive use throughout the text of the 'he' pronoun to denote the abuser, and the 'she' pronoun to denote the victim or survivor. This does not deny the existence of male victims, or female abusers, it merely reflects the availability of research material and my experience of counselling female survivors most of whom were abused by men.

Aim of the book

The aim of *Counselling Survivors of Child Sexual Abuse* is to provide mental health professionals, nurses, social workers, health visitors, doctors, pastoral counsellors, therapists, counselling psychologists and any other counsellors who may come into contact with adult survivors of incest or child sexual abuse with an overview of the the literature available to date on the theories of child sexual abuse, the impact and long term psychological effects on the child and later adult, along with models of treatment which have proven to be useful in ameliorating these deleterious effects. As the book is written for counsellors working on variety of levels, in differing disciplines and in a variety of capacities, without necessarily being trained psychotherapists, the word 'counsellor' is used to include both the trained therapist and the professional who uses counselling skills. To avoid repetition, the words counsellor and therapist may sometimes be used interchangeably within the text.

A fundamental premise of the book is to present an eclectic approach to the treatment of child sexual abuse by encouraging counsellors to adopt a flexible approach to treatment rather than advocating a strict adherence to a rigid or specific therapeutic orientation. Therapeutic intervention needs to be individualised to the needs of each survivor and her presenting difficulties. There are no hard and fast rules for which therapeutic technique to use, but rather an emphasis on the counsellor experimenting with the myriad of available techniques to ascertain which work best for each individual survivor. The counsellor is also advised to adopt a positive prognosis to treatment outcome which emphasises that adult survivors can repair the damage of child sexual abuse and heal from the scars of their abuse experience. For this reason the term 'survivor' is used in preference to the term 'victim'.

Labelling women who were sexually abused in childhood as victims reinforces their adopted victim role and victim behaviours by making the woman feel that she was a passive instrument of her abuse. In contrast, the term survivor highlights the creative coping mechanisms that many such women adopted in childhood to survive their abuse while validating her achievement in having survived her ordeal. In addition, the label 'survivor' fosters a more positive self-image which, through healing, will empower her to make active choices in her life, rather than remaining a victim of her abuse.

A corollary to this is the normalisation of her abuse experience and her coping strategies. To this effect the survivor is not seen as mad, or dangerous to know, but as an essentially normal individual whose psychological functioning has been distorted by her abnormal abuse experiences in childhood. It is the sexual abuse that was abnormal and bad, not the child that was being abused, or indeed the survivor who lived through that experience. Emphasis is placed on acknowledging and reinforcing the belief that in many ways the survivor is remarkably sane and normal, and that her responses to the abuse were normal in the presence of an abnormal experience and her attempts to make sense of it.

The book is organised into three sections. The first section is theoretical in orientation in presenting theories of incest and child sexual abuse; the possible long term psychological effects; and the impact of sexual abuse on the child and adult survivor. The middle section is practical in its approach in presenting the variety of treatment approaches and models that have been adopted with some success by clinicians in the treatment of adult survivors of child sexual abuse. This section also includes a description of how to uncover the abuse, a review of the variety of techniques that are specifically helpful to survivors, the value of group therapy as an adjunct, or alternative to, individual counselling, and a discussion of the recurring themes and topics that are particularly pertinent to survivors.

The last section looks at the role of the counsellor in the therapeutic dyad, and how the counsellor can empower the survivor to take control of her life by relinquishing her dependency on the therapeutic relationship. The final chapter looks to the issues that influence the outcome of treatment in discussing how the counsellor can prepare the survivor in her return to health, by encouraging her to establish support networks outside of therapy.

The appendix includes a resource list of agencies, self help groups and organisations working in the area of child sexual abuse, along with a list of useful books and other materials that counsellors can use to familiarise themselves with the whole topic of child sexual abuse. In addition, a selected bibliography for survivors, containing first hand accounts of survivors' childhood experiences and their healing process, is also appended. To retain confidentiality, the individual accounts of survivors have been changed, including names and specific details that may identify them to others.

CHAPTER 2

Theoretical Approaches to Child Sexual Abuse

Increasing awareness of the prevalence of child sexual abuse has given rise to a number of theoretical approaches which aim to explain its occurrence, while generating and influencing treatment models. Some of these theoretical models are still in the process of development as new research is generated and our understanding of child sexual abuse is augmented. This has led to some of the earlier theoretical approaches (such as the psychoanalytic formulation) being challenged and expanded.

Currently there are five major theoretical approaches, all of which have developed from specific levels of investigation and theoretical orientation. The earliest proposed theory was Freud's psychoanalytic formulation which was rooted in his work on hysteria and the psychosexual development of the personality. This approach has been adopted not only by psychoanalysts but also by many psychotherapists and psychiatrists. The level of investigation underlying this approach is based on Freud's observation of female patients, as victims of child sexual abuse, and his formulation of the Oedipus Complex.

The early 1940s saw the development of 'family dysfunction' theory as an explanation for child sexual abuse. Although this theory had its roots in approaches to family psychiatry, it found an increased resurgence in the 1960s and 1970s with a shift in emphasis in the aetiology of mental disorders such as schizophrenia which became inextricably linked to pathological and skewed family dynamics (Laing, 1965). This approach has since been adopted by a number of researchers (Lustig, 1966; Maisch, 1973; Rosenfeld, 1979) whose level of investigation focuses on the family and its interpersonal dynamics as a unit, rather than the individual victim or abuser. Not surprisingly, this approach advocates treatment for the whole family unit, not for the individual within it. Despite its obvious limitations, family dysfunction theory is probably still by far the most widely adopted approach, especially by statutory agencies.

Psychological formulations of child sexual abuse (Groth, 1979) differ in perspective from both psychoanalytic and family dysfunction approaches in focusing their investigation on the abuser rather than on the victim or family. Psychologists aim to assess levels of functioning of the abuser and attempt to categorise these within the framework of other sexual offenders such as paedophiles, rapists and exhibitionists, to arrive at some level of taxonomic classification. With this in mind, treatment concentrates primarily on changing the abuser's level of functioning, and interest in the desired sexual object. More recently attempts have been made to place the effects of victimisation, such as in child sexual abuse, within a cognitive framework (McCann et al., 1988). This model views the victimisation experience in child sexual abuse in the light of how the victim organises and processes information about the world. To this effect, during cognitive development the child builds up and develops schemas as a means for internally structuring information about events and experiences. These schemas must affect how we understand and interpret events which arouse emotions and behaviour.

The limitations in the above three theoretical approaches has given rise to a feminist re-interpretation of child sexual abuse (Butler, 1978; Nelson, 1982; Rush, 1977) which takes into account power relationships and differential gender socialisation within patriarchal society. In contrast to psychoanalytic and family dysfunction theory, feminist theory firmly places the responsibility for child sexual abuse on the abuser. The focus of investigation has been primarily directed towards the victim's experience of sexual abuse, and how this reflects the broader operation of patriarchy. The treatment focus in this approach is on the survivor of child sexual abuse, not the abuser or other family members.

Although all these four approaches have considered and interpreted some vital aspects of child sexual abuse, they all suffer from some limitations. These limitations indicate a need for a more comprehensive theoretical approach which takes into account and incorporates all the factors that researchers and clinicians have isolated as contributing to child sexual abuse, including psychodynamic factors, family dynamics, as well as socio-cultural factors. Finkelhor (1984) has proposed a multi-causal model which operates on four distinct levels.

Finkelhor's Four-Preconditions Model of Child Sexual Abuse looks at the motivation of the abuser, the need for the abuser to overcome internal inhibitions, plus the need to overcome external inhibitors such accessibility and opportunity, and the role of the victim in offering resistance to the abuse. The model proposes that all four preconditions come into play in a logical sequence before abuse can occur. Although Finkelhor's model has some quite distinct advantages over earlier formulations which will become evident when looking at these approaches in depth, and when evaluating their explanatory power, nevertheless his model is still in the process of development and has not been empirically tested.

The psychoanalytic approach

Freud's early clinical work on hysteria in treating predominantly female clients revealed that the cause of hysteria and neurosis appeared to be not hereditary or biological factors, but rather early childhood sexual abuse, often at the hands of fathers. From this Freud developed his 'seduction theory' (1896) which asserted that the trauma of the stimulation of the genitals during child sexual abuse was the root cause of later psychic damage, in particular hysteria and neurosis. Freud presented this causal relationship between childhood sexual trauma and psychic damage in a group of papers entitled *The Aetiology of Hysteria* in 1896, which cited some eighteen cases of childhood sexual abuse to support his theory of seduction.

Despite the evidence, the seduction theory was poorly received by Freud's peers, and although Freud's patients continued to disclose sexually abusive experiences, Freud never again publicly referred to his seduction theory. A number of writers (Fairtlough, 1983; Krull, 1979; Masson, 1984; Miller, 1984 Rush, 1977) have argued that this was not necessarily due to the reception of the seduction, but was a direct result of Freud's faltering belief in his patient's disclosures, which seemed to him increasingly less credible. These doubts were further augmented by Freud's self analysis, and the exploration of his tangled and complex relationship with his own father, who had recently died, and his family in general, including his relationship with his own daughter.

Krull (1979) argues that, through the analysis of his dreams, Freud recovered childhood memories of being 'sexually instructed' by his nursemaid. Freud's self analysis, and the possibility of his own sexual abuse, may have created strong elements of denial which prompted him to question the validity of his patient's disclosures by relegating their experiences to the realm of fantasy rather than fact. This denial may have contributed to his renunciation of the seduction theory in 1897, which he replaced with his Oedipal theory.

According to Rush (1977), Freud's personal and intellectual conflicts prevented Freud from reconciling the implications of child sexual abuse with '... either his self image or his identification with other men of his class' (Rush, 1977). This led Freud to assert in his *Introductory Lectures on Psychoanalysis* that 'I was driven to recognise in the end that these reports (by his patients) were untrue and so came to understand that the hysterical symptoms are derived from fantasies and not from real occurrences... this fantasy of being seduced by the father (is) the expression of the typical Oedipus Complex in women' (Freud, 1933).

In Freud's Oedipal Complex, the daughter is cast as the active desiring agent, who wishes her father to become her love object, while the father is seen as the passive, innocent object of the daughter's seduction. According to Freud, little girls '... notice the penis of a brother or playmate, strikingly visible and of large proportions, and recognise it as the superior counterpart of their own small inconspicuous organ, and from that time forward fall victim to envy for the penis' (Freud, 1977).

As the daughter realises that as neither she, nor her mother, possesses the 'superior' penis she turns from her mother to her father in the hope of being given a penis. It is the daughter's strong projection of 'penis-envy' and love for her father that creates the fantasy of sexual activity between father and daughter. This theory of the girl child's sexual fantasies about her father came largely to be accepted as fact, and as result was adopted by many psychoanalysts and psychiatrists.

Although some psychiatrists have since questioned the validity of relegating these aspects of child sexual abuse to the realm of fantasy, and have begun to acknowledge that child sexual abuse is indeed lodged in reality, Freud's Oedipal theory nevertheless coloured much of the early psychiatric literature pertaining to incest and child sexual abuse, and how it may best be interpreted. As a result, much of the psychiatric literature still assumes that incest is largely the consummation of the girl acting out her sexual desires and fantasies for her father. Consequently, many survivors are not believed and find that their reality is denied while alternative interpretations are imposed on her in which she is seen as the 'seductress', who is responsible for her own abuse.

This notion is exemplified by Bender and Blau (1937) who suggest that the '... conspicuously charming and attractive personalities of the victims...' make them ready participants and active initiators of the incestuous relationship. The man, in contrast, is seen as weak and powerless in the presence of such seduction, and therefore cannot help but act upon this overtly displayed sexual invitation.

The concept of the child-as-seductress is not only lodged in much of the psychiatric literature, but has also influenced other professionals who comment on the seductive, attractive, precocious or promiscuous behaviour of young female incest victims. This is best illustrated by the following comment made by an American judge when summing up a case in which a five-year-old girl was raped by the mother's lover: '... I am satisfied that we have an unusually promiscuous young lady... I do not put the blame on the child exactly, but I do believe that she was the aggressor' (*Spare Rib*, 1982).

Associated with the concept of the seductive child is the tendency for some psychoanalysts and psychiatrists to view the mother as being responsible for the occurrence of incest. Mothers are often seen as pathological, with their own unresolved Oedipus Complex, who use their daughters as surrogates to act out their own incestuous desires. Gordon (1955) argues that incest is an act of revenge against a cold rejecting mother, a view which is echoed by Rinehart (1961) who asserts that the mother '... acts out her Oedipal wish for father through her daughter... the daughter has learned to turn to men for security and affection because of intense affectional frustration at the hands of her mother. She is placed in the role of surrogate wife in which she can turn to her father to gain satisfaction of her needs... through a sexual channel' (Rinehart, 1961).

A further interpretation views incest as a complex multi-generational model in which incest is passed on from mother to daughter. Kaufman *et al.* (1954) assert that 'These mothers displaced on to the chosen daughter all the hostility really felt for the maternal grandmother. They relinquish their responsibilities as parents so that they, in effect, become daughters again, and the daughter a mother... the mothers... finally created situations where they deserted the fathers, who then became involved in the incestuous relationship with the daughter'. Types of desertion or abandonment by the mother include '... giving birth to a new sibling, turning to the maternal grandmother, or developing some new interest outside the home'.

Thus, the psychoanalytic model denies the reality of incest by asserting that it arises out of fantasy on the part of the daughter who has incestuous desires for her father. Responsibility for these wishes and the manifestation of incest is firmly placed on the child who is seen as the seductress, active initiator and even aggressor, while the father is seen as weak and powerless in the face of such sexual desires. Further responsibility is also placed on the mother in so far as she is perceived to be acting out her own incestuous wishes, while abandoning both her daughter and her husband.

Limitations of the psychoanalytic approach

Despite the apparent wide acceptance of the psychoanalytic model by many psychiatrists, and its influence on much of our understanding of incest, there are several criticisms which challenge its validity. Firstly, recent research has shown that incest and child sexual abuse is much more prevalent than was previously recognised, and that it certainly is not the rare phenomena the psychoanalytic model claims. Current data from America suggests that 27 per cent of female and 16 per cent of male adults have been sexually abused as children (Los Angeles Times Survey, 1985), while Russell (1983) found that 38 per cent of women had been sexually abused before the age of 18. As one survivor commented 'In a street of 100 houses nearly 40 children could be being sexually abused.'

Secondly, the psychoanalytic formulation has explanatory power for the occurrence of father/daughter incest but fails to explain other types of intra- and extra-familial child sexual abuse such as father/son, mother/daughter, mother/son, sibling, uncle, or grandparent incest, or sexual assaults committed by neighbours, teachers or family friends. This is a severe limitation as, according to Finkelhor (1984), father/daughter incest only accounts for less than a third of all child sexual abuse.

A further limitation is the model's narrow focus on the intra-psychic functioning of individuals, which ignores wider social and cultural factors, in particular that sexual abuse is primarily committed by men. As Finkelhor (1984) notes, male abusers account for 95 per cent of sexual assault of girls, and 80 per cent of assaults against boys.

Fourthly, and perhaps more fundamentally, the psychoanalytic model places responsibility for the abuse on the unconscious desires of the 'seductive' child, or the collusive mother, while exonerating the abuser. Thus the mother and victim are seen as active initiators and aggressors, while the abuser is seen as a passive and powerless object manipulated by his wife and daughter's desires. This sets aside not only sexual desire that the father may have for his daughter, but also the power that men are assigned and wield in society.

As a result, a number of writers have attempted a reinterpretation of the psychoanalytic formulation, in particular the Oedipal Complex, which acknowledges the more active participation of the father. Chodorow (1978) observes that the father's sexual desires play an active role in the Oedipalisation of his daughter, and that fathers generally tend to sex type their children along more traditional gender roles to encourage and reinforce feminine heterosexuality.

In contrast, Herman's (1981) reinterpretation of the Oedipal Complex emphasises that

> 'The girl's interest in her father does not develop out of an earlier bond with the father as caretaker. Rather it is a reaction to the girl's discovery that males are everywhere preferred to females... By establishing a special and privileged relationship with her father, she seeks to be elevated into the superior company of men... the father's behaviour towards his daughter thus assumes immense importance. If the father chooses to eroticise the relationship with his daughter he will encounter little or no resistance'. (Herman, 1981)

This interpretation acknowledges the power and status that males have, and can be extended to explain why it is predominantly men that sexually abuse children. Herman's argument also accounts to some extent for why children are vulnerable to being coerced into abusive situations. Both Chodorow and Herman acknowledge the active participation of the father which allows for a shift in responsibility from the child to the adult.

This shift in responsibility represents a fundamental component in the treatment of adult survivors of child sexual abuse. One psychoanalyst who supports this crucial shift is Alice Miller who does not see the disturbance within the child, but more accurately in the 'narcissistic abuse' of the child to satisfy the parent's (father's) emotional needs, without regard for the emotional and developmental needs of the child.

This is especially true for males who traditionally do not perform nurturing and caring roles in relation to their children, and therefore have limited understanding of what needs children have, much less of how these are expressed and best satisfied. Such men often interpret a child's need for physical and emotional affection as a need for sexual attention, or indeed invitation. Yet, this is an adult male interpretation, which does not at all reflect the child's actual needs or desires. In the same way, it is the adult who chooses to act upon his interpretation which is not the consequence of supposed manipulation by the child.

Miller (1985) provides a detailed analysis of how both physical and sexual abuse is passed from generation to generation, from parent to child, because of their own history of abusive experiences. The abuse of children becomes culturally and historically rooted, where it continues to grant permission to abuse without questioning the effect this has on children. This re-analysis of the psychoanalytic model acknowledges the high incidence of sexual abuse, and expands its focus to include socio-cultural factors.

The reinterpretation of the Oedipal Complex does not deny that children do have sexual feelings, or sometimes behave in ways that may be construed by adults as sexual. What is important is the recognition that it is the adult who interprets the child's behaviour as sexual, and that it is the adult who fails to recognise that children are not able to consent to a sexual relationship. Fairtlough (1983) illustrates this point: '... the contention that a girl who plays at driving a car is ready to take a real car onto the road would be considered preposterous'.

Despite the much needed reinterpretation of the psychoanalytic model to explain incest and child sexual abuse, these more recent reformulations are to a large extent still ignored by many psychiatrists. While acknowledging that the phenomenon of child sexual abuse is not rare, and is in reality an alarmingly common occurrence, there has been little substantial revision of the basic assumptions and tenets of Freud's original theory. Some psychiatrists still deny the reality of the experience of incest by attributing it to fantasy and sexual desires on the part of the victim. This attitude has serious implications for treatment which aims to treat incest and child sexual abuse as a 'disturbance' within the victim, and not the abuser.

Despite these limitations, McLeod and Saraga (1988) argue that the most valuable contribution made by psychoanalytic theory is the formulation that emotions of love and hate towards the abuser can exist simultaneously. This is particularly important in therapeutic intervention in allowing the survivor to express both these apparently conflicting emotions, without judging her in any way.

The family dysfunction approach

In contrast to the psychoanalytic model of incest, family dysfunction theory does not argue that the disturbance lies within the individual psyche of the victim, but rather that the family as a unit is dysfunctional. The notion of the 'dysfunctional family' was first proposed in the 1940s as a concept within family systems theory which grew out of the discipline of family psychiatry. Family dysfunction theory benefited from a resurgence in interest in the 1960s and 1970s when there was a shift in emphasis in looking at the underlying aetiological factors influencing such mental disorders as schizophrenia. It was argued that such mental disorders were not necessarily organic in nature but stemmed from pathological, or skewed family dynamics. This shift in emphasis coincided with an increase in research interest in incest, which in combination helped to establish family dysfunction theory as a major force in the explanation of incest and child sexual abuse.

Family dysfunction theory has become the most widely held explanation for the manifestation of incest, and together with its treatment methods, has been adopted by many government and statutory agencies throughout the United Kingdom, America and Australia. The central tenets of the family dysfunction model is that the family as a unit is pathological, and that abnormal behaviour such as incest is not attributed to individual pathology but is seen as a symptom of overall family maladjustment. According to Maisch (1973) incest is viewed merely as one symptom of an already disturbed family.

The family dysfunction model proposes that '... all members of the family are relevant aetiologically, even those that are apparently uninvolved, such as the mother' (Guthell and Avery, 1977). Underpinning this framework is a system of family norms which is used as a yardstick to measure degrees of dysfunction or pathology. Thus, the dysfunctional family unit is seen as not conforming to socially approved goals or values, and is a unit in which 'normal' family hierarchies, based on age and sex, have been destroyed.

In the typical dysfunctional family, incest has been described by researchers as a rationale for maintaining the family's pathology and for ensuring that it is kept secret. Lustig *et al.* (1966) asserts that

> 'The parent's childhood fears, wishes and fantasies are acted out within the dysfunctional family. Many of these impulses which are unacceptable could not be acted out outside the family without jeopardising its stability and even its existence. Thus we propose that incest is a transaction which serves to protect and maintain the family in which it occurs' (Lustig *et al., 1966*).

Such inward looking and socially isolated families, with their pathological fears, utilise incest to reduce tension in order to maintain homeostasis and balance within the family. Other dynamics allegedly common to the dysfunctional family are that the mother does not fulfil her assigned role as sexual provider for the husband, or her nurturing role as a mother, as protector of the children, by absenting herself both emotionally and physically from her children (Cormier, 1962; Forward and Buck, 1977; Justice and Justice, 1979; Lustig et al. 1966).

The mother is seen to fail fundamentally. Firstly, she is seen as a dysfunctional wife who fails to comply with her husband's sexual demands and who is '... committed to pursuing her own desires and wishes rather than caring for her daughters and husband' (Rist, 1979). In addition, it is argued that the mother actively invites incest by absenting herself through hospitalisation, or escape into depression, mental or psychosomatic illness; by being either too dependent and emotionally infantile, or by being too independent in working outside the home, especially if this is at night; that she is sexually either frigid or promiscuous; or that she is emotionally frigid (Justice and Justice, 1979).

Secondly, the mother is seen as a dysfunctional mother who is cold and distant, thereby failing to provide adequate nurturing, care and emotional support to her children. The logical extension of this, according to Forward and Buck (1977) and Lustig *et al.* (1966), is that in the absence of a nurturing mother, the 'seductive' and 'love starved' daughter turns to, and accepts, incestuous advances from her 'sex starved' father as a substitute for her mother's failure to love her.

Thirdly, both the mother and the father are seen as dysfunctional adults and parents who seek '... a role reversal and disintegration of the boundaries between the generations, with the child cast in the role of satisfying the needs of her father and required to assume a protective role towards her mother ' (Lustig *et al., 1966*). Thus the mother supposedly '... engineers the incestuous relationship' (Dietz and Craft, 1980) by placing enormous responsibilities on the daughter such as housework, and child care duties, in addition to her enforced 'wifely duties' towards the father.

In this formulation, the mother is seen to collude with the incest, and it is this collusion which has been considered to be the 'cornerstone of the family pathology' (Fairtlough, 1983). It is argued by many family dysfunction theorists that the mother knows consciously or unconsciously that incest is taking place, but that she chooses to deny it, even when confronted by her daughter, by not taking preventative action to protect her daughter, or by blaming the daughter for the incest (Kempe, 1977).

Justice and Justice (1979) have proposed that the mother's collusion reflects her relief at not having to service her husband sexually, while other writers have argued that the mother's collusion in the incest allows her to satisfy her own incestuous desires for her father (Henderson, 1972), or her daughter (Rist, 1979). Emphasis on the specific pathology of the mother suggests that

> '... the real abuser in an incestuous family is the mother. By frustrating her husband sexually, failing to support her daughter emotionally, or foisting her maternal duties and responsibilities onto her daughter, she engineers the incestuous relationship' (Dietz and Craft, 1980).

Limitations of the family dysfunction approach

Despite its wide acceptance, the family dysfunction model suffers from quite severe limitations. Firstly, like the psychoanalytic model, family dysfunction theory really only has explanatory power for intra-familial sexual abuse, in particular father/daughter incest, while not being able to account for extra-familial child sexual abuse. It thus fails to take into consideration at least two thirds of child sexual abuse which is non-incestuous and extra-familial.

Secondly, as the family dysfunction model regards incest merely as a symptom of pathological family relationships which serves as a functional system to keep the family together, it detracts from the painful and devastating effects incest has, not only upon the family, but more specifically on the child. This has implications for treatment intervention in which the daughter's experience is not only minimised, but more alarmingly, denied. The therapeutic focus is on family dynamics and restoring interpersonal relationships, while the sexual activity and abuse is seen as secondary and much less important.

Thirdly, family dysfunction theory proposes that as the cause of incest is rooted in the dynamics of intra-familial relationships, each family member is seen as equally culpable. However, this is merely an assumption and not a tested theory. Careful analysis of much of the literature suggests that, in reality, responsibility is displaced from the abuser and is at best bestowed on the whole family, or at worst, and probably more frequently, is dumped on the mother. The consequences of such assignment of responsibility is that family members are told that the incest was not really the father's fault, but that they all share equal responsibility for participating in it.

Underscoring this view is the belief that the therapeutic goal of family dysfunction treatment is not to treat the incest, but to realign the family's behaviour into more appropriate behaviours. Thus, the mother is persuaded to become not only the perfect wife by providing sexual satisfaction to her husband, but also the perfect mother by adopting highly elevated nurturing and protective behaviours, and a good housewife by not pursuing any independence outside the home either through leisure pursuits or employment. This realignment aims to reinstate the authority, control and power of the father in the family home.

Some researchers, such as Machotka *et al.* (1967), advocate the non-prosecution of fathers by condemning such action as an '... inappropriate assignment of legal guilt which allows other family members to maintain a destructive denial of their own responsibility'. However, such a lack of assignment of responsibility denies who the actual perpetrator is (i.e. the father), and ignores that he chose to respond actively to family configurations and dynamics by sexually abusing his daughter.

Despite the emphasis on the culpability of all family members, the literature nevertheless concentrates primarily on the pathology of the mother and the daughter, while paying little attention to the father's role. Fathers are seen to have a right to be nurtured and sexually serviced by females. Role reversal between daughter and mother and its impact on incest implies that '... the husband gets confused because he is used to imposing his sexual demands on whoever does the housework and he does not really notice who it is' (Jeffries, 1982).

Fourthly, evidence for the collusive mother who chooses to ignore, or deny the incest, is not supported by more recent literature. Mrazek (1982) found that many mothers do act when incest is disclosed, with 73 per cent reporting the abuse, while Berliner and Conte (1981) report that of their sample of 583 families, 60 per cent of the mothers took immediate preventative action. This is contrary to the argument proposed by much of the family dysfunction literature which argues that mothers actively choose to maintain the incest. The sense of betrayal many survivors express towards their mothers is not necessarily due to collusion, but to the high expectations that children have of mothers to protect and nurture them, which includes an investment of almost magical, omniscient qualities in her which assume that she must know what is happening to her daughter.

Little recognition is shown of the dynamics and circumstances that may prevent the mother from reporting the abuse. Dietz and Craft (1980) found that in 78 per cent of incest families that were known to social workers the mother was also a victim of domestic violence. This has been reported by other researchers (Finkelhor, 1979; Truesdell, McNeil and Deschner, 1986; Tormes, 1968) as have other constraints such as financial and emotional dependence on the husband. These strictures suggest that many mothers have realistic fears for their safety and well being, as well as that of the family, if they disclose the incestuous relationship.

Psychological approaches

Psychological theories of incest focus their perspective on the abuser rather than the family, or the victim. They attempt to locate the abuser in some sort of taxonomic system which allows them to compare child sexual abusers with other types of sexual offenders. Thus, psychologists are principally concerned with the administration and evaluation of psychological tests and assessments, either at the point of prosecution, or on already incarcerated prison populations.

To date, psychologists have approached their study of the child sexual abuser on two levels. The first, and most widely researched, is concerned with the attempt to find a putative 'incestuous personality', while the second aims to isolate the motivations of incestuous fathers. The search for such a personality profile focuses on establishing the existence of fixed and stable personality traits that are predictive of the child sexual abuser, which when compared to other sexual offenders, will show marked differences. The types of sexual offenders that child sexual abusers are most commonly compared to include primarily paedophiles, exhibitionists, and rapists.

Some psychologists have also attempted to compare incestuous fathers with 'normal' fathers in order to '... determine if and how persons convicted of sex offences differ from those that have not been so convicted' (Gebhard et al., 1965). The types of comparisons that Gebhard et al. conducted to generate a personality profile of child sexual abusers included not only demographic data, but also behavioural traits such as masturbatory habits, marriages, homosexual experiences, descriptions of the content of their dreams and fantasies, and criminal activities.

The problem with such studies is that they may be affected by subjective biases of the researcher. To circumvent such biases psychologists administer clinical personality tests such as the EPQ (Eysenck Personality Questionnaire) which isolate degrees of extroversion/ introversion, neuroticism and psychoticism. Other scales used include the MMPI scale which aims to show degrees of social introversion, depression and hysteria, and several tests that assess 'ego integration' such as the Bender-Gestalt test, the Rorschach test, and the Id-Ego-Superego test.

These tests have provided several personality characteristics that have commonly been isolated. Gebhard et al. (1965) and Groth (1979) both found that emotional deprivation including the possibility of sexual assault and chaotic family life, play an influential role in the personality of incestuous fathers. Other researchers, such as Peters (1976), noted that incestuous fathers appeared to be 'inadequate men' who, because of their perceived inadequacy, turned to little girls for the sexual gratification that they felt unable to obtain through adult channels. This was confirmed to some extent by Panton (1979) who found that incestuous abusers feared not being able to function well in adult relationships and were thus highly socially introverted.

One of the outstanding personality characteristics of incestuous fathers has been found to be their need to exercise a highly elevated level of dominance and control over the family (Cromier *et al.*, 1962; Meiselman, 1978; Raphling *et al.*, 1967; Winberg, 1955). This finding fits in with the notion of masculine inadequacy which may be expressed in a need to dominate and control others in the family environment as a mechanism for asserting their putative masculinity.

One commonly reported finding is that incestuous fathers are highly adept at rationalisation and displacing responsibility and blame onto others rather than the self. Weiner found '... evidence of high intelligence and a well integrated system of intellectual defences, indication of paranoid traits... each (has a) considerable capacity for rationalisation' (Weiner, 1962), while Gebhard *et al.* (1965) found that although the range of intelligence was wide, elevated intelligence facilitated increased levels of rationalisation. In contrast, Cavallin (1966) found that abusers are of only average intelligence.

Despite some of the corroborated findings for the existence of an 'incestuous personality', many of the findings are contradictory and therefore still inconclusive. However, it is clear that abusers come from all social backgrounds and are not confined to socially or economically deprived families. In addition, they do not suffer from mental illness (Cavallin, 1966; Lukianowicz, 1972), nor are they criminals. Renvoize (1982) reports that 80 per cent of incest offenders have never had previous dealings with the police.

Sexually incestuous abusers have been found to be either oversexed or undersexed, with some researchers arguing that these men are unconscious homosexuals, while still others argue equally strongly that they are uninhibited heterosexuals (Nelson, 1982). However, child sexual abusers, along with paedophiles, do demonstrate increased sexual arousal to photographic stimuli involving sex with children (Renvoize, 1982).

When analysing types of child sexual abusers, psychologists have found a number of distinguishing features. A common finding is that for some abusers the use of alcohol or alcoholism (Virkkunen, 1974) contributes to a reduction in internal inhibitions to commit incest, so that the act stems from this, rather than from actual sexual feelings towards the child (Fairtlough, 1983). Another finding has been the existence of elevated levels of dependency on the part of the father (Gebhard *et al.*, 1965), while Meiselman (1978) argues that 'The typical incestuous father is not mentally retarded, psychotic or paedophilic, but is characterised by some sort of personality disturbance that interferes with his ability to control his impulses in a situation where the temptation to commit incest exists'.

A further distinction is proposed by Groth (1978) between the fixated and the regressive abuser. The fixated abuser has been conditioned from childhood and adolescence to be primarily sexually attracted to significantly younger children, while the regressive abuser has an adult heterosexual orientation, but in response to acute stress, adopts incestuous sexual relations. The notion of 'regression under stress' endorses current understanding of abusers with 'incestuous personalities' as being socially introverted, overinvested in the family, as suffering from masculine inadequacy, and driven to commit incestuous acts when under economic, emotional, or financial stress. Such stresses either exacerbate already existing inadequacies, or cause such disorientation that normal impulse control is impaired, allowing abuse to occur.

One of the positive outcomes of psychological research into child sexual abusers is that the collection of both demographic and clinical data has helped to dispel many myths and stereotypes, in particular that incest only occurs in poor, rural communities, and that abusers are merely 'dirty old men in raincoats' who hover by the park gate. The data accrued by psychologists emphasises that the child sexual abuser and incestuous father '... is rarely a freak, dangerous criminal or a psychotic... he is often an otherwise law-abiding guy next door' (Forward and Buck, 1978). In the words of Rich Snowdon, who facilitated a weekly counselling group for men who had committed incest,

> 'Who commits incestuous assault? What kind of men are they? Per-
> verts... sickos... deeply-troubled men... psychopaths... monsters... I couldn't
> stop being amazed that they were all regular guys, ordinary working men and
> average pillars of the community. They reminded me of the men I knew growing
> up.' (Snowdon, 1982)

More recently, psychologists have attempted to account for the effects of victimisation within a cognitive framework, using concepts from both attribution theory (Eiser, 1980) and Seligman's (1975) notion of 'learned helplessness' (Osborn, 1990). McCann *et al*.'s (1988) model of victimisation proposes that there are five major schemas, or structures for organising and understanding the world, which are affected through victimisation. These centre on safety, trust, power, esteem and intimacy.

Clinical evidence shows that these schemas are indeed affected by the sexual abuse experience and manifest in most adult survivors. Thus this cognitive model does have some explanatory power for the observed effects of child sexual abuse, but as yet does not enhance our understanding of why child sexual abuse occurs.

Limitations of psychological approaches

Although the psychologists' shift in emphasis to the attributes and personality charac-teristics of the abuser is perhaps more helpful, there are nevertheless several limitations in the proposed theories, not least that much of the evidence is contradictory and must therefore remain inconclusive. Further research on the 'incestuous personality' may redress this, but will not eradicate a major tautological flaw: the abuser commits incest because he has an 'incestuous personality'.

This implies that a natural and normal part of male sexuality is specifically directed at young girls, in particular daughters, and that sexual abuse is only prevented by exercising a level of self control (Waldby, 1985). This implication is also noted by Forward and Buck who propose that the '... aggressors differ from the rest of us only in so far that they are unable to control *very normal impulses*' (Forward and Buck, 1978, our italics).

This appears to limit the possible treatment of child sexual abusers. Abusers may benefit from cognitive restructuring techniques to re-evaluate their attitudes towards women and children, and may master new problem solving and stress management skills to control their 'natural' impulses, but these impulses will always be there, needing to be controlled. Treatment focuses on maintaining self control but does not attempt to change the impulse as this is assumed to be a 'natural' part of the male behavioural repertoire.

Further, psychologists ignore power relationships within the family. Too often the abuser's personality is seen and assessed in isolation, away from the actual social and family milieu in which he operates and where incest occurs. Psychological assessments commonly imply that abusers are rather weak, inadequate, passive and introverted individuals. Yet, in the family environment these men are seen as domineering and overly controlling. Herman (1982) argues that this may be due to abusers being highly sensitive to power structures and remarkably adept at changing their behavioural repertoire depending on who wields power. Thus, in the presence of psychologists, therapists, lawyers and the police who are perceived as being more powerful, the abuser acts in a helpless, confused and somewhat pathetic way.

As Herman asserts 'Face to face with men of equal power or superior authority they become engaging and submissive' (Herman, 1982). In contrast, behind closed doors, in their family home where they assume power over the family, they are able to satisfy their need for domination and control knowing that they will not be challenged. It is only within the patriarchal family that the weak, inadequate male can assert masculine notions of power, domination and control, which he feels unable to achieve in his social interactions with other, more adequate (powerful) males.

A final criticism is one of sample bias in that psychologists conduct most of their assessments with already charged or imminently to be prosecuted abusers, or abusers that are already incarcerated. There may be marked differences between those incestuous fathers, or abusers, who have been reported to the police and those that continue to abuse children in secrecy. Personality profiles and characteristics of as yet undetected abusers will enhance our knowledge of child sexual abuse and promote the development of more sophisticated and practical preventative measures.

The feminist approach

As a result of the many limitations inherent in the psychoanalytic, family dysfunction and psychological approaches to child sexual abuse and incest, there has been a need for considerable reinterpretation. The focus of the feminist reinterpretation is based on two important aspects that have not been extensively addressed and have to some extent been pointedly ignored by other models, namely the role that unequal power relationships play in child sexual abuse, and the abuser's responsibility in initiating and maintaining the abuse.

The feminist analysis of child sexual abuse focuses on male power within the family, including the unequal power relationship between child and adult. These power relationships are further analysed in relation to the manifestation of male power in patriarchal society, and differential gender socialisation, especially male sexual socialisation. This reinterpretation places responsibility for the abuse on the abuser, while focusing on the experiential effects on the victim and the mother.

Examinations of male power within the family show that abusers are often 'family tyrants' (Dietz and Craft, 1980; Finkelhor, 1979; Forward and Buck; Herman and Hirschman, 1977) who see their children as their property to exploit as they wish, including sexually. Incest is thus seen as just one expression of 'normal' male/female relations in a patriarchal society with such assertions as that the incest victim 'bears the quintessence of female oppression' (O'Donnell and Craney, 1982).

Analysis of reported findings of perceived masculine inadequacy and social isolation of incestuous fathers have led to speculations that this prompts abusers to enforce patriarchal rule within the family where it is 'socially acceptable' and where little interference from outside will be encountered. Within the family the abuser is able to reconstruct traditional patriarchal domination of the family in which, by means of threat, physical violence or sexual coercion, he is not only obeyed, but also sexually and emotionally serviced by females (Fairtlough, 1983; Finkelhor, 1979; Herman and Hirschman, 1977).

The conclusions that feminist theory has drawn from these observations is that the sexual assault of daughters and children is inherent in a family system which allows and actively socialises males to assume and wield their power. Herman (1981) argues from this that '... incest represents a common pattern of traditional female socialisation...' in which females are socialised to be submissive, passive and compliant providers of male needs. To this Ward (1984) has added the pervasive fear of rape that all females experience, and asserts that incest should be seen not only as an act of violence but also as an act of rape.

Feminist reinterpretation of power hierarchies within the family focuses not only on the helplessness of the victim, the daughter, but also highlights the powerlessness of the mother within the family dynamics. This deeply entrenched powerlessness exerts pressure on the mother to deny the incest. Although many mothers do act protectively towards their children when incest has been disclosed, it is undeniable that some mothers do not.

This is hardly surprising, given the myriad of problems the mother may face as a result of disclosure. Not only are many women dependent on their husbands financially, but female socialisation, oppression, the threat of physical and sexual violence, along with suppressed childhood memories may prevent mothers from 'seeing' or 'hearing' the incest (Ward, 1981). It is questionable whether mothers really do collude with incest. Herman's analysis appears much more apt 'Maternal collusion in incest, when it occurs, is a measure of maternal powerlessness' (1981). Thus both mother and daughter are victims, equally powerless against the husband/father.

Carol Ann Hopper (1987) further argues that many mothers do act appropriately in the light of disclosure and often have no knowledge of the incest because usually it takes place in her absence, with the child being sworn to secrecy by being threatened with harm either to herself or her mother. Society's expectation of mothers as 'protectors' becomes shattered in the presence of incest and is often seen by professionals as a 'failure to protect' on the mother's part, and that failure makes her responsible for the abuse.

Included in the feminist analysis is a focus on differential male sexual socialisation to account for child sexual abuse. Sexuality contains culturally moulded components which include values, feelings and attitudes, as well as biological drives, which account for stereotypical gender roles in the expression of sexuality. Finkelhor (1984) proposes that there are four distinct features of 'normal' masculine sexual socialisation that predispose men towards child sexual abuse.

Firstly, Finkelhor argues that as men do not generally practice nurturing behaviours they become socialised to express their dependency needs through sex. In the absence of practicing a nurturing role , males fail to acquire a real understanding of the needs that children have, and how best to satisfy these. In addition, physical contact may become sexualised as many males are unable to distinguish between affectionate and sexual touching. Secondly, men tend to need sex as a form of reconfirmation of adequacy when their ego has encountered any form of rebuff. This need for reconfirmation and affirmation outweighs availability of appropriate sexual partners. If the only available sexual partner is a child, then it will be sacrificed in order to bolster ego deficiencies.

Thirdly, many men experience sexual arousal outside the context of a relationship, but are more specifically aroused and stimulated by the genitals of their preferred sexual object. Whether these belong to an adult or child may become largely irrelevant. Availability of partner, rather than age of partner, becomes the criterion for such sexual arousal and its desired satisfaction. Finally, men are socialised to desire sexual partners who are younger and smaller than themselves. Sexual attraction to a young, pre-pubescent child may represent only marginal movement along an already established and accepted continuum.

As male gender identity is more dependent on 'sexual success' (Finkelhor, 1981), the sexually inadequate man may prefer a child as sexual partner to bolster an inadequate ego to an adult. Armstrong (1978) has noted that some survivors felt that their fathers were sexually more at ease with them because of their compliance and because they would not criticise his sexual performance. Such socialisation makes male sexual exploitative behaviour towards women increasingly comprehensible (Herman, 1981).

Impaired nurturing and diminished capacity for displaying affection, along with putative masculine identity, restricts the forming of genuine relationships while encouraging sexual contact only with compliant, submissive women who have inferior status. Lack of understanding of the emotional needs of children when coupled with distorted expressions of affection further diminishes empathy and identification with the victim, and understanding of her perceptions of the sexual act. This serves to reduce further any internal inhibitions towards exploitative and abusive sexual contact.

The masculine sexual domination over females is further linked by some feminists to the patriarchal nature of heterosexual relationships (Ward, 1984) which are embedded within structured power hierarchies within society, in particular the family. The message that females receive through such power structures and female socialisation serve to emphasise women's powerlessness, passivity and their role as victim. When internalised, these messages generate submissive, compliant and self effacing behaviours which offer little, or no protection, against sexual abuse.

Incestuous abusers, in contrast to physical abusers, have been reported to adhere to more rigid sex-role stereotyping, especially for 'femininity', which reinforce passivity and compliance, thereby making it more difficult for their daughters to protect themselves from sexual abuse. The division and allocation of domestic duties in incestuous families reflect these gender stereotypes, with female children expected to perform most household tasks to maintain the desired gender segregation of roles preferred by abusers (Scheurell and Rinder, 1973). This has led Nelson to comment that '... the father, not the mother, is dominant in pushing daughters in the maternal role' (1982).

A fundamental contribution offered by the feminist approach is that it does not focus exclusively on incestuous abuse within the family. In interpreting child sexual abuse as a sexual power relationship, rooted in differential gender socialisation and male power in patriarchal society, it is able to broaden its focus to include the dynamics of extra-familial child sexual abuse as well intra-familial and incestuous abuse, all of which rely on males exerting their sexual power over females.

Included in this more global approach is the analysis of the role of pornography in perpetuating and legitimising child sexual abuse. Densen-Gerber (1980) reports that in 1977 child pornography was a multi-million dollar industry with 264 US magazines depicting sexual acts with children and adults, including instructions on how to achieve intercourse with pre-pubertal children. Furthermore, of 64 video films, 16 depicted incest and 19 involved very young children. Such pornography is often used to reduce inhibition prior to initiating sexual contact. The virulence of child pornography and the increase in child sex rings demonstrate that not only do men exert their sexual power over children, but more fundamentally that men find children erotically desirable (Finkelhor, 1981).

Such analysis provides powerful evidence against the notion that child sexual abuse is not a problem of parenting but a function of masculine socialisation. It also illuminates the overwhelming finding that the majority of abusers are male and demonstrates how men respond differently to victimisation. In addition, unequal power relationships between males and females are embedded in social organisations such as the family, where they become internalised by individuals. Such social construction is considered by feminists to account in part for why society has been so tardy in acknowledging the existence of child sexual abuse, and why it so readily points the finger of blame at the females involved: the mother and the daughter.

Some feminist writers have begun to challenge the notion of 'cycles of abuse' in which sexual abuse is transmitted from generation to generation. Thus, mothers of children who are sexually abused will themselves have been sexually abused in childhood.

Arguments purporting to provide evidence for the 'intergenerational transmission' of abuse are based on the findings that mothers of sexually abused children have often been sexually abused themselves, or form relationships with men who abuse them.

In attempting to account for these findings, researchers have argued that women who have been abused in childhood fail to protect their own children from being sexually abused by 'unconsciously recreating' a sexually abusive situation to resolve their own 'repressed conflicts'. In addition, it is argued that previously abused women actively choose abusive male partners who are either going to abuse them or their children, or both.

Hooper (1987) counters these interpretations by arguing that given the high incidence rates for child sexual abuse, with up to one in four females experiencing sexual abuse in childhood, it is not surprising that there is a connection between previous abuse experiences and vulnerability of the offspring to being abused. This connection is augmented if the father was an abuser and goes on to abuse his granddaughter.

The interpretation that previously abused women fail to protect their own children from sexual abuse is not borne out by clinical observations which suggest that women who were sexually abused in childhood are often more than usually vigilant and aware of the possibility of abuse, and act appropriately to protect the child. Such mothers frequently appear over-protective of their children rather than failing to protect them.

In challenging the notion that previously abused women choose abusive men, Hooper (1987) points out that as to date no specific characteristics of sexually abusive men, other than gender, have been isolated by psychologists and professionals. Given the lack of identifying characteristics, can women really be expected to identify potentially sexually abusive men, something the experts have been unable to do to date?

Limitations of the feminist approach

The feminist approach to child sexual abuse and incest probably comes closer than any of the other interpretations to providing explanations for and suggesting responses to the range of abusing behaviours. It has several structural advantages, not least that it takes into consideration both the social structure of society and differential gender socialisation. It places the responsibility for sexual abuse with the abuser, thereby removing blame from mother and daughter. While this shift in responsibility may be welcome, there is a danger that those survivors who feel abandoned and betrayed by their mothers may be prevented from exploring these feelings in therapy for fear of indulging in 'mother blaming behaviour'. The feminist counsellor must guard against this by giving the survivor permission to explore such feelings without berating or denigrating any negative feelings she may have towards her mother.

Although the mother did not abuse the child, children often believe mothers to be omniscient and omnipotent, and rightly or wrongly expect to be protected by her. When this expectation is not met, the child feels betrayed and abandoned by her mother. To the survivor these are genuine feelings which need to be explored and worked through and not be denied as 'mother blaming behaviour'. Once the survivor has explored and integrated these feelings, then it will be possible to put her mother's behaviour into a more accurate and realistic perspective, enabling her to acknowledge that she was also a victim.

While the feminist perspective goes much further than earlier models in considering the social structure of society, much of the feminist interpretation nevertheless focuses on incest and the relationship between father and daughter, while minimising the sexual abuse of male children. In focusing on the sexual power held by men over women in which all females, little girls and adults alike, feel vulnerable, feminist analysis has little or no explanation for the sexual exploitation of male children (Allen, 1990).

With the increase in disclosures by males about their own childhood sexual abuse, and as more clinical data becomes available about the specific factors pertaining to such abuse, it may be necessary to incorporate such findings without any feminist analysis. In addition, as more information becomes available about the incidence and characteristics of female perpetrators, feminists may need to expand their analysis to account more fully for their involvement in child sexual abuse. Although female perpetrators are very much in the minority, and account for only a minute proportion of child sexual abuse, the fact that some females do sexually abuse children, without being coerced or forced to do so by a male co-offender, may require some interpretation within a feminist perspective.

A further limitation is that the feminist model is essentially sociological in its approach to child sexual abuse, and as such minimises psychological factors and motivations. Although feminist theory acknowledges and validates the survivor's feelings about the abuse, along with its concomitant psychological damage, it nevertheless tends to focus on social structure and socialisation, and not on the psychological aspects.

Feminist theory argues that incest and child sexual abuse is motivated by a desire to control or possess the child, and that this is not primarily motivated by sexual feeling (Fairtlough, 1983). However, this interpretation does not account for the fact that many abusers find children erotically stimulating, as seen in the prevalence of child pornography and its use in reducing inhibitions prior to committing abuse. The proposition is that the desire to control and over-power is predominant and that this control is expressed sexually through sexual fantasy. Arguably, this may be the case for some abusers but it is doubtful that it accounts for all permutations of child sexual abuse.

In emphasising that all females are vulnerable to sexual abuse feminist analysis can be construed as dismissive of the survivor's individual experience. Some survivors are not able to identify themselves with other women, and need to be validated for their unique courage in surviving their abuse. To relegate the survivor's experience as one common to all women denies her specific experience which she needs to resolve first, before she is able to identify with other women.

Associated with this is the assumption that all females are vulnerable, socialised to be compliant, and paralysed to offer any resistance. While this is true for many women, some do resist. Investigating how these children resisted, and how they differ from the non-resisting survivor, will enhance our knowledge of how sexual abuse can be prevented or diminished. Increasing the psychological ego strength of female children through more positive, less prohibitive socialisation may be the first step enabling children to resist child sexual abuse. The assumption that all children are passive and compliant merely serves to reinforce negative messages while denying female strength.

Finally, in focusing on the powerlessness of mothers, feminist analysis may be indulging in a form of stereotyping in which all women are seen as powerless. While many males undoubtedly do try to control females, individual women may themselves not feel powerless, and actively resist such control. In Hooper's words, 'We should be careful not simply to substitute another stereotyped "role" – the powerless mother – for the collusive mother' (Hooper, 1987).

Finkelhor's Four Preconditions Model of child sexual abuse

To bridge the gap between psychological and sociological interpretations, Finkelhor (1984) proposed a multi-factor model which has explanatory power on both levels. In reviewing all the causal factors that researchers and clinicians have isolated as contributing to child sexual abuse, Finkelhor developed a hierarchical model which includes individual factors related to the victim, abuser and the family, as well as social and cultural factors. Finkelhor's Four Preconditions Model of Child Sexual Abuse provides an adaptable and flexible framework which can accommodate new developments and research data to enhance our understanding of child sexual abuse.

Finkelhor's model accounts for both intra- and extra-familial child sexual abuse and as such does not distinguish between the two. This has important implications for treatment which should ideally avoid distinctions between types of abuse to prevent a value laden hierarchy of severity of abuse to become operational in influencing treatment.

Secondly, the model addresses the issue of responsibility by emphasising that sexual abuse only takes place if the man already has sexual feelings for the child. Although Finkelhor includes the child's and the mother's behaviour in his analysis, it is clear that these are only relevant in response to the abuser's manifest sexual interest. This perspective clearly places the responsibility with the abuser.

Thirdly, this model has somewhat more explanatory power than other approaches in that it incorporates both psychological factors such as the motivation of the abuser, the existence of internal inhibitors, and the ego strength of the child, and sociological factors such as male socialisation, pornography, social tolerance of eroticising children, unequal power relationships between males and females, and the patriarchal prerogatives of fathers and men (see Table 2.1). The model also views potential victims as not necessarily passive, but as possessing the power to resist.

Finally, Finkelhor's model provides a vital enhancement to treatment in that it allows for evaluation and intervention on all four levels. Thus, clinicians can evaluate the strength

Table 2.1: Preconditions for sexual abuse

**Precondition I: Factors related
   to motivation to sexually
   abuse**

Emotional congruence

Arrested emotional development.
Need to feel powerful and controlling.
Reenactment of childhood trauma to
   undo the hurt.
Narcissistic identification with self
   as a young child.

Masculine requirement to
   be dominant and power-
   ful in sexual relationship.

Sexual arousal

Childhood sexual experience that
   was traumatic or strongly
   conditioning.
Modelling of sexual interest in children
   by someone else.
Misattribution of arousal cues.
Biologic abnormality.

Child pornography.
Erotic portrayal of children
   in advertising.
Male tendency to sexualise
   all emotional needs.

Blockage

Oedipal conflict.
Castration anxiety.
Fear of adult females.
Traumatic sexual experience with adult.
Inadequate social skills.
Marital problems.

Repressive norms about
   masturbation and extra-
   marital sex.

**Precondition II: Factors
   predisposing to overcoming
   internal inhibitors**

Alcohol.
Psychosis.
Impulse disorder.
Senility.
Failure of incest inhibition mechanism
   in family dynamics.

Social toleration of sexual
   interest in children.
Weak criminal sanctions
   against offenders.
Ideology of patriarchal
   prerogatives for fathers.
Social toleration for deviance
   committed while intoxicated.
Child pornography.
Male inability to identify
   with needs of children.

**Precondition III: Factors
   predisposing to overcoming
   external inhibitors**

Mother who is absent or ill
Mother who is not close to or
   protective of child.
Mother who is dominated or abused
   by father
Social isolation of family.
Unusual opportunities to be alone with
   child.
Lack of supervision of child.
Unusual sleeping or rooming conditions.

Lack of social supports for
Barriers to women's equality.
Erosion of social networks.
Ideology of family sanctity.

**Precondition IV: Factors
   predisposing to overcoming
   child's resistance**

Child who is emotionally insecure or
   deprived.
Child who lacks knowledge about
   sexual abuse
Situation of unusual trust between
   child and offender.
Coercion.

Unavailability of sex
   education for children.
Social powerlessness of
   children

of the four preconditions on an individual and a family level, thereby allowing useful intervention strategies to be developed. Capitalising on the strengths while implementing problem solving techniques to ameliorate the weaknesses may facilitate cessation of abuse and prevent its re-occurrence.

Finkelhor argues that all the known factors contributing to child sexual abuse can be grouped into four pre-conditions which need to be met prior to the instigation of child sexual abuse. The four preconditions are:

1. *Motivation:* The potential abuser needs to have some motivation to sexually abuse a child. Thus, he will need to find children erotically and sexually desirable.

2. *Internal inhibitions:* The potential abuser must overcome internal inhibitions that may act against his motivation to sexually abuse.

3. *External inhibitions:* The potential abuser also has to overcome external obstacles and inhibitions prior to sexually abusing the child.

4. *Resistance:* Finally, the potential abuser has to overcome the child's possible resistance to being sexually abused.

All four preconditions have to be fulfilled for the abuse to commence. The presence of only one condition, such as lack of maternal protection, social isolation or emotional deprivation is not sufficient to explain abuse. This can only be achieved if all four preconditions are met in a logical sequential order.

1. Motivation to sexually abuse

Table 2.1 illustrates some of the factors that operate in the motivation to sexually abuse. Precondition I incorporates some commonly reported observations which are categorised according to whether they manifest themselves on an individual or socio-cultural level.

Finkelhor argues that there are three functional components subsumed under the motivation to sexually abuse children:

(i) *Emotional congruence* in which sexual contact with a child satisfies profound emotional needs;

(ii) *Sexual arousal* in which the child represents the source of sexual gratification for the abuser; and

(iii) *Blockage* when alternative sources of sexual gratification are not available or experienced as less satisfactory.

As these components are not actual preconditions, not all three need to be present for sexual abuse to occur. They are however important in explaining the variety of motivations abusers may have for sexually abusing children. The three components explain not only the instance of abusers who are not sexually motivated but enjoy degrading victims by wielding power, but also the paedophile, and the sexually motivated abuser who looks towards children for variety, even though he has access to other sources of sexual gratification. In some instances elements from all three components may be present to account for whether the motivation is strong and persistent, weak and episodic, or whether the focus is primarily on girls or boys, or both.

2. Overcoming internal inhibitors

To sexually abuse, the abuser needs not only to be motivated but also to be able to overcome his internal inhibitions against acting on his motivation. No matter how strong the sexual interest in children might be, if the abuser is inhibited by taboos then he will not abuse. Arguably, most people do have some inhibitions towards sexually abusing children.

Disinhibition is not a source of motivation, it merely releases the motivation. Thus an individual who has no inhibitions against child sexual abuse, but who is not motivated, will not abuse. The second precondition aims to isolate the factors that account for how inhibitions are overcome, and whether they are temporary or not. The element of disinhibition is an integral part of understanding child sexual abuse.

3. Overcoming external inhibitors

While preconditions 1 and 2 account for the abuser's behaviour, preconditions 3 and 4 consider the environment outside the abuser and child which control whether and whom he abuses. External inhibitors that may restrain the abuser's action include family constellation, neighbours, peers, and societal sanctions, as well as the level of supervision that a child receives.

Although a child cannot be supervised constantly, lack of supervision has been shown in the clinical literature to be a contributing factor to sexual abuse, as has physical proximity and opportunity. External inhibitions against committing child sexual abuse may easily be overcome if the abuser is left alone with a child who is not supervised.

4. Overcoming the resistance of the child

One limitation of much of the research literature is the failure to recognise that children are able to resist, or avoid abuse. The focus in the clinical literature is on children who have been sexually abused, while ignoring those who although approached were able to avoid it or resist. The feminist argument proposes that female socialisation produces passive and compliant victims. Thus, the research literature and many of the theoretical approaches pay scant attention to the fact that children do have a capacity to resist.

This capacity may operate in a very subtle, covert way, and does not necessarily involve overt protestations. Abusers may sense which children are good potential targets, who can be intimidated, and can be exhorted to keep a secret. Abusers report that they can almost instinctively pick out a vulnerable child on whom to focus their sexual attentions, while ignoring those who might resist. Frequently these children may not even be aware that they are being sexually approached, or indeed resisting such advances.

Table 2.1 pinpoints some of the risk factors that inhibit the capacity to resist, such as emotional insecurity and neediness, lack of physical affection, lack of friends, lack of support and interest from parents, age, naivety, and lack of information. Knowing which factors make children vulnerable is essential in formulating prevention programmes. Isolating behaviours that constitute a risk, while emphasising those that enhance resistance or avoidance, can empower children to protect themselves.

This is not to say that children who are not vulnerable do not get abused. Many children may be forced or coerced despite displaying resistance or avoidance behaviours. In such instances the factors overcoming a child's resistance has nothing to do with the child, or the child's relationship with the abuser, but is the result of force, threat or violence. No matter how much resistance is manifested by the child, this may not necessarily prevent abuse.

Precondition 4 has three possible outcomes: (i) the child may resist overtly by saying no and running away, or covertly by presenting a confident assertive demeanour which conveys strong messages to the abuser not to attempt abuse for fear of detection or exposure; (ii) the child may resist but still be abused through the use of force or violence; or (iii) a child may resist but be overcome through coercion.

Acknowledging the child's capacity to resist or avoid abuse enhances our understanding of child sexual abuse. The notion that children can resist, albeit frequently covertly, is a positive one which could usefully generate more empirical research on the content of resistance behaviours, and how these can be incorporated and adopted in preventive programmes which aim to teach children how to avoid sexual abuse.

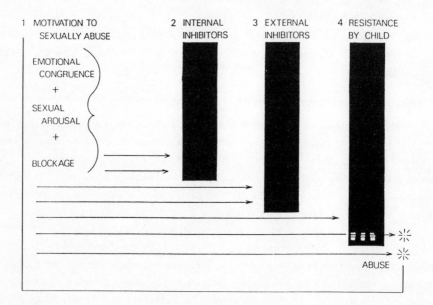

Figure 2.1: Four preconditions of sex abuse

Operation of the model

The four preconditions come into play in a logical, sequence (see Figure 2.1). The potential abuser must firstly have a strong motivation to abuse. To act upon this motivation he will need to overcome any internal inhibitions. When these have been overcome, the potential abuser will need to overcome external inhibitions, such as opportunity and lack of supervision before he can act. Finally, the potential abuser needs to overcome the child's resistance.

Finkelhor's model has considerable explanatory power and also has implications for treatment and evaluation in that it allows each operational level to be assessed separately. Treatment intervention can thus be implemented on each individual level by focusing on specific problem areas rather than relying on generalised, unstructured observations.

Limitations of the Four Preconditions Model of child sexual abuse

Finkelhor's model is a useful framework which integrates all the research and clinical findings available to date on which factors contribute to child sexual abuse. It has tremendous heuristic value in integrating existing knowledge, while remaining flexible enough to adapt to new research data and findings.

Although Finkelhor's model enhances our understanding of child sexual abuse and factors leading up to it, it is nevertheless essentially a descriptive framework which incorporates a range of dissonant theories and observed clinical date. As such, in its present form, it cannot be viewed as a theory until it is tested empirically, in particular in its application to treatment and intervention. Knowledge about child sexual abuse, its effect on the child, and the long term effects on adults, is still limited, especially in formulations of effective treatment and intervention models.

The Four Precondition Model of child sexual abuse presents a comprehensive, multicausal, hierarchical model with both psychological and sociological explanatory power. What needs to be assessed is whether its current formulation is rigorous enough to withstand empirical testing, and its ultimate contribution to treatment intervention. Its synthesis of existing knowledge and its flexibility in incorporating new findings as they become available, provides a valuable description of child sexual abuse.

CHAPTER 3

The Long Term Effects of Child Sexual Abuse

The study of long term effects of child sexual abuse on adult survivors has been beset with problems, not only in terms of the definition of child sexual abuse but also as a result of biases in sampling, and differences in impact between survivors. Consequently, some studies, particularly earlier ones, found no long term effects at all (Lukianowicz, 1972) while more recent studies appear to present a variety of long term effects (Briere, 1985; Browne and Finkelhor, 1985; Jehu, Gazan and Klassen, 1985), with as many as 98.6 per cent of survivors reporting that they have been severely affected by their abuse experience (Walby, 1984).

An additional problem is that it is often very difficult to analyse the effects found. Some are not exclusive to childhood sexual abuse and may reflect other underlying disorders. Also, the occurrence of child sexual abuse is often interwoven with complex family dynamics and a variety of childhood experiences, making it difficult to isolate the root cause as specific to the abuse. Despite the increase in research, and the use of more sensitive psychological measures of possible long term effects, it has not been possible to determine precisely the extent to which problems are a direct result of sexual abuse.

Earlier studies of the long term effects of child sexual abuse concentrated on cataloguing the range and types of problems adult survivors encountered. This has since been supplemented by a 'documentation' phase in which researchers have used increasingly sensitive and recognised measures of psychopathology including statistical procedures to ascertain the relevant contributions to sexual abuse (Finkelhor, 1988). Currently researchers and clinicians are entering a third phase in which they are proposing models to account for and explain why certain long term effects arise (Finkelhor, 1988).

This and the following chapter will present the long term effects observed to date by clinicians and researchers, both in clinical samples and samples from the general population, and assess the current models that have been proposed to explain why these effects occur. It will also consider individual differences in the impact of child sexual abuse by looking at age of onset, relationship to the abuser, length and frequency of abuse, type of sexual acts, and how these affect outcome.

Long term effects of child sexual abuse

One difficulty in assessing the long term effects of childhood sexual abuse is that through the repression of the trauma, or dissociation, survivors may not consciously remember the abuse experience. Clinical observation suggests that many survivors function well without any recollection or intrusive thoughts of the abuse for long periods of time, until an event or experience reactivates the trauma. Events and stimuli that may trigger memories range from watching a television programme or film, reading a book, or talking to someone who discloses their sexual abuse experience.

There are a number of life experiences in the developmental span which may restimulate memories, with specific life events triggering particular types of symptoms.

Actual sexual abuse, or restimulation of trauma in adolescence, may result in running away, delinquency, substance abuse, promiscuity and prostitution. In addition, the adolescent may indulge in self-mutilatory behaviour or enter into an early marriage to escape the abuse.

Some survivors report a trouble-free adolescence but may encounter problems during their first stable relationship. Frequently survivors find that any close intimacy with a partner recapitulates the abuse trauma, causing them to have intrusive flashbacks of the abuse, impaired sexual arousal, and an inability to differentiate between love and sex. Some of these symptoms may not occur until the survivor gets married, shortly after the honeymoon phase is over.

The next life event, or developmental milestone, which has been reported by many survivors, is pregnancy or the birth of their first child, particularly if their first child is female. During pregnancy survivors may worry that they are in some way gynaecologically abnormal and that the child may be damaged in some way, or that they will miscarry. If they do miscarry, or produce a less than healthy offspring, survivors report feeling that they are being punished for their involvement in the abuse experience.

The birth of the child might restimulate childhood memories of vulnerability to abuse. Many survivors become anxious and over-protective towards the child, or distance themselves from it as it reminds them of their own abuse experience. If the child is female, the survivor may overidentify with the child and in some cases develop phobic reactions to the child's genitalia. For some survivors the abuse trauma is not restimulated until their child reaches the age when the mother was abused, resulting in intrusive memories and powerful flashbacks.

Divorce or separation may also trigger abuse memories, particularly in survivors who were abused by step-fathers. They fear divorce or separation in case they choose an inappropriate partner who may go on to abuse their children.

Two other life events that have been reported as restimulating the abuse trauma are the death of the abuser, and/or the death of the mother. These events may result in the survivor facing her conflicting emotions of love, hate, pain and anger. Many survivors feel the need to disclose the abuse to the surviving partner, or the family in order to complete 'unfinished business' and talk through unresolved feelings about her abuse experience.

Adverse long term effects can manifest themselves during any of these life events despite the survivor not having felt any negative effects in the past. Any developmental milestone that is significant for the survivor has the potential to restimulate memories and cause the abuse trauma to resurface.

Although Lukianowicz (1972) found no long term negative effects of child sexual abuse, more recent researchers have highlighted the considerable negative effects child sexual abuse can generate in adult survivors (Finkelhor, 1985; Briere, 1985; Courtois, 1988; Jehu, 1988). These mainly fall into the categories of: (1) emotional effects; (2) interpersonal effects; (3) behavioural effects; (4) cognitive/perceptual effects; (5) physical effects; and (6) effects on sexual functioning (see Table 3.1).

Table 3.1: List of long term effects of child sexual abuse on adult survivors by category

Emotional effects

Depression
Low Self Esteem
Guilt
Anxiety
Obsessive/Compulsive
Anger

Interpersonal effects

Isolation/Alienation
General Social Relationships
Relationships with Men
Relationships with Women
Relationships with Parents
Effects on Parenting
Fear of Intimacy
Revictimisation

Behavioural effects

Self Destructive Behaviours
Self Mutilation
Suicide
Eating Disorders
Alcohol Abuse
Drug Abuse

Cognitive/Perceptual effects

Denial
Cognitive distortions
Dissociation
Amnesia
Multiple personality
Nightmares
Hallucinations

Physical effects

Psychosomatic pains
Sleep disturbances

Sexual effects

Impaired motivation
Phobias/aversions
Impaired arousal
Impaired orgasm
Sexual dissatisfaction
Vaginismus
Dyspareunia
Inability to separate sex from affection
Oversexualisation
Sexual Orientation
Promiscuity
Prostitution

Emotional effects

Emotional effects most commonly experienced by survivors of child sexual abuse focus on depression, problems of guilt, low self-esteem, anxiety, and anger.

Depression

The most commonly reported symptom in the category of emotional effects is that of depression, particularly in the clinical literature, but also in non-clinical samples such as community studies. In a community mental health study of a random sample of 387 women, Bagley and Ramsey (1985) found that women who had a history of child sexual abuse scored more highly in the depressed range on two separate depression scales. Of the abused women, 17 per cent scored in the depressive range on the Centre for Environmental Studies Depression Scale (CES-D) while 15 per cent scored highly on the Middlesex Hospital Questionnaire's measure of depression compared to 9 per cent and 7 per cent respectively of non-abused women. S. Peters (1984) found that women who experienced sexual abuse involving physical contact had a higher incidence of depression, including depressive episodes which necessitated more frequent hospitalisation.

Sedney and Brooks (1984) found that of a sample of 301 college women, 65 per cent of the sexually abused group reported symptoms of depression compared to 43 per cent of the non-abused group, while hospitalisation was necessary for 18 per cent of the abused group and only 4 per cent of the control group. In a further college sample, Briere and Runtz (1985) administered the 72 item Hopkins Symptom Checklist to 278 women students and found that those with a sexual abuse history reported more depressive symptoms in the preceding 12 months than the non-abused women.

Research with clinical populations reflect less distinct differences between abused and non-abused women. This was particularly notable in Meiselman's (1978) study of women with a history of incest in which 35 per cent of the incest group reported depressive symptoms compared with 23 per cent of a comparison group. This difference proved to be statistically non-significant, as did Herman's (1981) finding that 60 per cent of incest survivors reported depression along with 55 per cent of the control group. In contrast, Jehu, Gazan and Klassen (1985) found that of their sample of 22 women with a history of sexual abuse, 82 per cent scored highly on the Beck Depression Inventory. However, this sample was relatively small and was not compared to a control group.

In combination, these findings suggest that there is both clinical and empirical evidence for depression and depressive symptoms, commonly manifested in adult survivors of child sexual abuse.

Low self-esteem

Another commonly observed long term effect is low self-esteem with survivors expressing feelings of inferiority and worthlessness. Courtois (1979) found in her community study that 87 per cent of women who had been sexually abused reported that their self-esteem had been moderately to severely affected. This is consistent with Herman's (1981) finding that 60 per cent of incest victims in psychotherapy indicated a 'predominantly negative self image' compared to 10 per cent of those women with seductive fathers, prompting the observation that 'Many women felt that what had set them apart from others was their own evilness. With depressing regularity, these women referred to themselves as bitches, witches and whores. The incest secret formed the core of their identity' (p.97).

Further evidence of lowered self-esteem comes from Jehu, Gazan and Klassen's (1985) clinical sample using various assessment techniques together with the Battle Self Esteem Questionnaire in which 86 per cent of sexually abused women generated scores indicating low self esteem. Bagley and Ramsay (1985) found in their random sample of 387 women, that 19 per cent of the women with a history of abuse scored in the 'very poor' category of the Coopersmith Self Esteem Inventory, compared to 5 per cent of the control group. In contrast, only 9 per cent of the abused women demonstrated 'very good' levels of self esteem against 20 per cent of the control group.

Guilt

Associated with low self esteem are overwhelming feelings of guilt. Jehu, Gazan and Klassen (1985) provide sound clinical evidence on how widespread feelings of guilt are. In their sample, 82 per cent of survivors indicated on a Belief Inventory that they blame themselves for the abuse, and that this misattribution is often a further source of guilt. Tsai and Wagner (1978) have also reported a high incidence of guilt among adult survivors, and suggest that feelings of guilt are universal among this group of women.

Based on their experience of therapeutic groups for adult survivors, Tsai and Wagner argue that feelings of guilt may be accounted for by three major factors. Firstly, due to the secrecy associated with sexual abuse, the child perceives that these encounters are shameful and should not be revealed to others. Secondly, if the child experiences physical or sexual pleasure during the abuse, including orgasm, this generates substantial guilt feelings. Finally, the child, and later adult, may blame herself for not stopping the abuse and allowing it to continue, or believe that she must have contributed to its continuation in some way by not revealing the secret.

DeYoung (1981) proposes that many incestuous relationships often do not begin with an act of rape, but develop slowly over time. She suggests that in cases where the father is gentle, the father and daughter may enter the incestuous relationship willingly as the sexual contact feels physically and emotionally like an expression of love. Over time, increasing pressure to keep the secret combined with the realisation that the sexual activity is not only illegal but morally reprehensible, feelings of fear and intimidation begin to emerge.

This realisation may not occur until the incestuous relationship has been established for some considerable time. The father now merely needs to remind the daughter of her lack of resistance in the past to trigger already acquired and internalised guilt feelings. When combined with prompts such as 'no one will believe you' or 'people will think that it is your fault', guilt is reinforced and silence ensured.

Anxiety

There is some evidence that women with a history of child sexual abuse suffer from anxiety attacks and tension. Briere (1984) found that 54 per cent of abused women suffered anxiety attacks compared to 28 per cent of non-abused women. Similarly, Jehu, Gazan and Klassen (1985) report that 59 per cent of survivors experienced anxiety and other phobic disorders. These clinical findings are reinforced by two community studies. Sedney and Brooks' (1984) college sample revealed that 59 per cent of abused women suffered from anxiety and nervousness, while 41 per cent suffered from extreme tension, in contrast to 41 per cent and 29 per cent of non-abused women. Bagley and Ramsey's (1985) study further indicated that 19 per cent of abused women suffered somatic anxiety compared to only 9 per cent of non-abused females.

Obsessive/compulsive disorders

Associated with anxiety attacks is the finding by Jehu, Gazan and Klassen (1985) that 27 per cent of their sample of women seeking therapy for histories of child sexual abuse suffered from obsessive/compulsive disorders.

Anger

Clinical observations suggest that most survivors of child sexual abuse experience intense rage and anger. However, this anger is not necessarily directed at the abuser or the mother, but is free floating, diffuse and without focus. Often anger is internalised where it manifests itself in self destructive and self mutilatory behaviours such as eating disorders, the infliction of self injury, and suicide attempts. A vital goal in therapy is to encourage the survivor to express and externalise her anger, and to help her focus and direct it in more appropriate ways to minimise self destruction.

Interpersonal effects

There is considerable evidence that survivors of child sexual abuse experience a variety of interpersonal effects. These are predominantly characterised by feelings of isolation and alienation, feelings of stigmatisation and being different from others, fear of intimacy and avoidance of relationships, and an inability to trust others. These result not only in problems in general social relationships, but also in relationships with men and women, and parents. Problems with partners in a close relationship may also arise, with a high incidence of revictimisation. In addition, there is some evidence that survivors experience problems in their own parenting skills and their relationship with their children.

Isolation / alienation

Empirical evidence that survivors of child sexual abuse suffer from isolation and alienation in adulthood comes mainly from the clinical literature. In her study of 30 incest survivors, Courtois (1979) found that 73 per cent of these women expressed feelings of isolation, alienation and feelings of being different from other people, including elements of mistrust and insecurity. Briere (1984) reported that 64 per cent of survivors suffered from feelings of isolation compared to 49 per cent of the control group. This is echoed in Herman's (1981) sample of incest survivors, all of whom experienced a sense of being branded, stigmatised or marked in some way, and cut off from ordinary human interaction.

General social relationships

A sense of isolation has been found to affect social functioning in many general social relationships, particularly in relationships with women and men, but also in difficulties in relationship with parents, and in the parenting of children.

Relationships with men

Courtois (1979) reports that 79 per cent of her sample of incest survivors experienced severe to moderate problems in relating to men generally, with 40 per cent of them never marrying. Often these women expressed a distinct fear of men. Briere (1984) found that 48 per cent of his clinical sample reported a fear of men compared to 15 per cent of non-abused women. This is more than amply supported by the findings of Jehu, Gazan and Klassen (1985) who noted that 77 per cent of their sample of survivors reported that 'No man can be trusted'.

However, this evidence is at variance with Herman's (1981) study of 40 survivors of father/daughter incest, which found that only 8 per cent of the sample expressed hostility, or fear and avoidance, of men. Herman also reports that the majority of survivors tended to overvalue and idealise men, and that their feelings of anger were predominantly directed towards other women, including themselves.

Relationships with women

Herman (1981) reports that survivors generally feel more hostility towards other women and themselves than they do towards men, and that this often hampers them in establishing and maintaining supportive female friendships. In addition, these women viewed themselves and other women in a contemptuous light as inadequate individuals with very little to offer other than as rivals for male partners. This hostility towards women is corroborated by Briere's (1984) finding that 12 per cent of his abused sample expressed a fear of women compared to only 4 per cent of the non-abused women.

Relationships with parents

It has been noted that most incest survivors appear to direct most of their predominantly negative and hostile feelings towards their mother rather than their abuser. Although most survivors express hostility and dislike of both parents, there is a difference in apportioning these feelings.

Meiselman's (1978) clinical sample of survivors of father/daughter incest reported a dislike for both parents, with 60 per cent expressing a dislike of the mother and only 40 per cent reporting strong negative feelings towards the father, the abuser. This is supported by Herman's (1981) finding that residual feelings of rage and anger were almost exclusively directed towards the mother and DeYoung's (1982) evidence that 79 per cent of her incest survivors expressed hostile feelings towards their mothers, and only 52 per cent hostility towards the abuser.

Why this difference in the expression of hostility should occur is under-reported. However, clinical observation suggests that women feel anger, rage and hostility towards their mother because the mother did not protect the child from sexual abuse, and are therefore to some extent seen as responsible for its occurrence and maintenance.

This is understandable in terms of the child's cognitive development which views parents, particularly the mother, to be omnipotent and omniscient. In addition, subtle messages about the need for men's sexual desires to be met, and the notion that 'men can't help themselves' when seeking sexual gratification, encourages the survivor to excuse the abuser's need to sexually abuse.

Later parenting

Much has been written on the inter-generational cycle of abuse in which it is proposed that abused children grow up to abuse children. To date there is insufficient empirical evidence to indicate that this happens in the case of survivors of child sexual abuse. In their study of mothers in child abuse families, Goodwin, McCarthy and Divasto (1981) found that 24 per cent of the mothers had a history of incest compared to 3 per cent in a non-abusive control group. These researchers argue that previously sexually abused mothers adopt emotional and physical distance from their children, thus providing opportunities to abuse. They further suggest that difficulties in parenting occur when closeness and affection is imbued with sexual meaning or overtones.

An alternative explanation might be that survivors of child sexual abuse have inadequate parental role models, who do not provide the opportunity to differentiate between good and bad parenting, and as such prevent the acquisition of appropriate protective behaviours with which to protect their own children in potentially abusive situations. A corollary to this is that survivors are also vulnerable to revictimisation in choosing potentially abusive partners who may abuse their children.

It would be premature to conclude from this study that all survivors of sexual abuse go on to abuse their children. Clinical observations suggest that many survivors are hypervigilant mothers who assiduously monitor their children's movements and contacts, and actively teach their children how to avoid potentially abusive situations. These mothers are often extremely anxious about their children and their vulnerability to sexual abuse.

There is insufficient data available on what percentage of survivors go on to abuse, and whether there is a difference between male and female survivors in predisposing them to abuse their own or other children. Differences in gender socialisation predicts that male survivors are more likely to externalise their abuse experience by abusing others, whereas female survivors are more likely to internalise their abuse, resulting in self-destructive behaviours. More empirical data on possible sex differences between survivors, and whether the abuse manifests itself as sexual, physical or both would enhance our understanding of inter-generational cycles of abuse. Until such data are available, one must be wary of assuming that a cycle of abuse exists for survivors of sexual abuse.

Revictimisation

When survivors do form close or long term stable relationships they may compulsively attach themselves to unsuitable partners, who frequently resemble the abuser. Russell (1986) found in her community sample that between 38 per cent and 48 per cent of abused women were married to physically violent husbands compared to 17 per cent of non-abused women. This finding concurs with Briere's (1984) study in which 49 per cent of sexually abused survivors were battered by their partners, compared to 18 per cent of the non-survivor group.

Herman (1981) reports that 28 per cent of incest survivors 'repeatedly endured beatings from their husbands or lovers. In many cases, they seemed to feel that they deserved to be beaten.' This is echoed by Meiselman (1978) who notes that 42 per cent of her sample of incest survivors were labelled by their therapists as being 'masochistic' in that the women appeared to seek and passively endure abusive relationships in which they behaved as 'doormats', 'punching bags' and 'dish-rags'. Further corroboration comes from Tsai and Wagner (1978), and Jehu, Gazan and Klassen (1985), who report that 27 per cent of their sample engaged in dissonant relationships in which they felt that 'Only bad worthless guys would be interested in me'.

A number of explanations have been proposed to account for this revictimisation. Tsai and Wagner (1978) argue that the survivor already lacking in self-esteem, selects partners who are worthless and who will not have high expectations of her. This reinforces the survivor's poor self-image in that she believes that she deserves no better, and ensures that she does not have to live up to a high standard.

Both Meiselman (1978) and Herman (1981) suggest that the survivor, because of her childhood abuse, may not have learned the necessary skills either to protect herself adequately, or to assert herself in a relationship. Her expectations of what constitutes a 'good' relationship, and her rights within that, may have become distorted by modelling her mother's passive acceptance role in relation to a dominant father.

In the same way that the mother was unable to protect the child from sexual abuse, she was also unable to model or teach the daughter self-protective and assertive skills. Without an appropriate role model, the survivor is unable to act any differently from her mother, thus leaving herself vulnerable to abuse, and inter-generational victimisation.

In assessing the phenomenon of victimisation, Van der Kolk (1989) argues that trauma can be repeated on behavioural, emotional, physiologic and neuroendocrinologic levels and that the confusion of pain and love may cause individuals to develop strong attachments and emotional ties with people who are physically, emotionally or sexually threatening to them. In the presence of overt threat the survivor may experience a return of the earlier childhood trauma and thus return to primitive and archaic behaviour patterns.

In addition to revictimisation in relationships, there is also considerable empirical evidence that survivors of child sexual abuse are more vulnerable to rape. Russell's (1986) probability sample of 930 women found that between 33 per cent and 68 per cent of survivors were later subjected to rape compared to 17 per cent of the non-abused group. Russell also found that between 40 per cent and 62 per cent of survivors were later sexually assaulted by their husbands compared to 21 per cent of the non-abused group.

These findings are supported by Fromuth (1983) who noted that women who were sexually abused before the age 13 were more vulnerable to rape in adulthood, while Miller *et al.* (1978) report that of those women who had repetitive experiences of rape in adulthood, 18 per cent had a history of incest compared to only 4 per cent of first-time rape victims.

Fear of intimacy

There is some evidence that survivors of sexual abuse have a fear of intimacy and avoid forming close relationships. This can result in a constant search for numerous transient relationships, which involve casual sexual encounters, in preference to more stable and constant relationships. A consequence of this may be promiscuity and prostitution or brief, often unsatisfying and destructive relationships which reinforce the survivor's distrust of others.

Meiselman (1978) notes that 64 per cent of her clinical sample reported conflict with, and fear of, their husband or partner compared to 40 per cent of the non-abused control group. In addition, she found that 39 per cent of her sample had never married. More strikingly, Jehu, Gazan and Klassen (1985) report that 77 per cent of their clinical sample felt that it was '... dangerous to get too close to anyone because they always betray, exploit, or hurt you'.

Fear of intimacy is inextricably linked to inability to trust others, which includes a sense of betrayal together with reactions of fear and hostility. Levay and Kagle (1977) argue that a fear of intimate relationships is an 'intimacy dysfunction' in which individuals find it difficult to enjoy sexual contact within an established close emotional relationship. Jehu, Gazan and Klassen (1985) propose that this may be manifest in survivors of sexual abuse where more intimate relationships serve to recapitulate the abusive relationship she had with the abuser, to whom she was emotionally close.

Behavioural effects

Both the clinical literature and empirical research show that many survivors of child sexual abuse experience negative effects on their adult behaviours. These focus particularly on self destructive behaviours which may become life threatening. The most commonly reported self destructive behaviours include self-mutilatory behaviours, suicide, eating disorders, and substance abuse.

Self-destructive behaviours

An association between childhood sexual abuse and self-destructive behaviour was noted by Bagley and Ramsey (1985) who report that survivors of such abuse display strong suicide ideation, or deliberate attempts at self-harm. Feelings of guilt, shame, blame and anger are often difficult for survivors of sexual abuse to come to terms with in an adaptive way. Many survivors internalise these feelings, generating a negative self-image and low self-esteem. Given their lack of self-worth, these women are unable to protect themselves, or indeed care for themselves, in a healthy manner, believing themselves to be unworthy of nurturing.

This can have severe consequences for their behavioural repertoire in which they seek to destroy themselves either physically, or in socially destructive ways. Most self-destructive behaviour is expressed through self mutilation, suicide, eating disorders, chemical addictions, and substance abuse, but some survivors may also display other self-destructive addictions such as gambling, shoplifting, stealing, or bouts of lavish spending. Gil (1988) argues that in these cases the survivor feels that she is controlled by the addiction, and that the addiction is ego-dystonic.

Self mutilation

Self mutilation is often an attempt to expiate feelings of guilt and shame, or may be the only way available to the survivor to express her confusion of feelings (Carroll *et al.*, 1980; Goodwin, Sims and Bergman, 1979; Grunebaum and Klerman, 1967; Walsh and Rose, 1988). In his community study, Briere (1984) found that 31 per cent of survivors of child sexual abuse exhibited a desire to hurt themselves, compared to only 19 per cent of the non-abused group. This is supported by Sedney and Brooks (1984) who noted that 39 per cent of sexually abused women expressed thoughts of hurting themselves, versus 16 per cent of non-abused women.

During self-mutilation, the woman causes physical damage to her self most commonly by scratching, biting, cutting or piercing parts of her body. According to Gil (1988) the survivor may do this chronically, ritualistically or sporadically, with most women hiding the evidence. Some survivors utilise self-mutilation as a means of drawing attention to themselves through their injuries. The severity of self-mutilation can range from scratching too hard at one area of the skin, to slashing wrists, or to simulating suicide.

Gil (1988) proposes a variety of reasons why survivors of child sexual abuse mutilate themselves. For those survivors who have dissociated from their traumatic experiences in childhood, it is a way of being able to feel concretely that they exist. In dissociation the mind splits from the body in order to avoid the effect of pain, to bring about a sense of unreality, and of not feeling the body. Cutting themselves is a method of proving that they are indeed alive, do have feelings of pain and are flesh and blood. This link between body alienation and self mutilation has also been noted by Rist (1979).

In addition, during child sexual abuse, pain and love may become inextricably linked. This association may result in the survivor inducing pain in order to recreate the love she felt toward the abuser, particularly if the abuser was a parent. Self-mutilation is also closely linked to self-punishment. Survivors internalise many negative feelings about themselves, believing themselves to be irredeemably bad, and as a result they attempt to destroy their body and their soul.

Finally, self-mutilation may express a need for attention. As children, survivors may not have received acknowledgement that sexual abuse was taking place, particularly in the absence of any overt physical signs. In order to gain nurturing attention and to alert others to their trauma and invisible scars, abused children may have learned that to mutilate themselves was the only way to elicit the attention they so desperately needed.

Suicide

There has been considerable clinical and non-clinical evidence linking child sexual abuse to suicide and attempted suicide (Harrison, Lumry and Claypatch, 1984). Clinical studies have found that 37 per cent of survivors of father/daughter incest had histories of attempted suicide (Herman, 1981), while the Jehu, Gazan and Klassen (1985) clinical sample report an even higher percentage of 73 per cent.

These figures are also echoed in the non-clinical literature with Briere (1984) noting that 51 per cent of sexually abused women demonstrated a history of suicide, compared to 34 per cent of non-abused women. Sedney and Brooks (1984) also found that, in addition to thoughts of harming themselves, 16 per cent of survivors of child sexual abuse had attempted suicide at least once, compared to 6 per cent of a non-abused control group.

Eating disorders

Researchers such as Oppenheimer, Howells, Palmer and Chaloner (1986) noted that women with such eating disorders as anorexia nervosa and bulimia also report a high incidence of child sexual abuse. This is not surprising as one of the symptoms which indicate sexual abuse in children is appetitive changes, including eating disorders (Anderson, Bach and Griffith, 1976; Peters, 1984).

It has been proposed that the link between sexual abuse and eating disorders may be due to a disgust with femininity, sexuality and negative body image, leading to anorexia or bulimia (Oppenheimer *et al.*, 1986). Survivors may display negative reactions to bodily manifestations of femininity and sexuality as reminders of their abusive experience, resulting in eating disorders (Calam and Slade, 1986). However, guilt, self-blame and the need for self-punishment may also be operating, particularly in maintaining the disorder.

Calam and Slade (1986) suggest that self-starvation, as in anorexia nervosa, may be a method of punishing or regaining control of the parent who has exploited or failed to protect. As bulimia is often more covert than anorexia, this function would not be fulfilled and is therefore argued to be more closely associated with rape or extra-familial sexual abuse, where the abuser is not subject to control.

Gil (1988) notes a high incidence of both anorexia and bulimia in survivors of sexual abuse, which is not true for obesity which she argues is mainly associated with men. However, some survivors, if not clinically obese, do actively seek to be overweight in order to hide their bodies, and to make themselves sexually unattractive in order to avoid sexual advances of any kind. Others feel that their vulnerability decreases as a function of their body size. The larger they are the better they will be able to protect themselves.

Alcohol abuse

Child sexual abuse and substance abuse are also closely associated, with considerable empirical evidence of a link to alcohol dependency. Peters (1984) revealed that 17 per cent of the sexually abused group had symptoms of alcohol abuse compared to 4 per cent of the non-abused group. This was confirmed by Briere (1984) who found that 27 per cent of survivors of child sexual abuse had a history of alcoholism versus 11 per cent of non-abused women.

The clinical literature supports these findings with Jehu, Gazan and Klassen (1985) reporting that 41 per cent of survivors suffer from alcohol abuse, and Herman (1981) who found that 35 per cent of her sample of incest survivors abused both drugs and alcohol compared to 5 per cent of non-abused women. In stark contrast, Sedney and Brooks (1984) report a low incidence of substance abuse with no significant difference between abused and non-abused women.

Drug abuse

As with alcohol abuse, Peters (1984) found a significant difference in the abuse of drugs between abused and non-abused groups, with 27 per cent of survivors abusing at least one type of drug versus 12 per cent of a control group. Briere (1984) reports an even greater differential of 21 per cent versus 2 per cent respectively with a history of drug addiction, while Jehu, Gazan and Klassen (1985) record that 23 per cent of their abused women displayed a history of drug addiction.

Cognitive/perceptual effects

A number of long term cognitive and perceptual effects have been reported in the literature on survivors of child sexual abuse. These primarily centre around cognitive distortions, denial, dissociation, amnesia, multiple personality, nightmares and hallucinations.

Cognitive distortions

Aaron T. Beck (1979) argues that cognitions are inextricably linked to affect. Thus if cognitive distortions are manifest then it is likely that distortions in affect will also be evident. This link between distorted cognitions and distorted affect has been usefully employed by Jehu, Gazan and Klassen (1985) in their work with adult survivors of child sexual abuse. Survivors have been noted to manifest a myriad of cognitive distortions not only about themselves but also about others and the world around them. Common cognitive distortions include all-or-nothing or dichotomous thinking, magnification, minimisation, overgeneralisation, mislabelling, mental filtering, disqualifying the positive, jumping to conclusions, emotional reasoning, personalisation and making misattributions.

Often these cognitive distortions are rooted in the internalisation of negative or inaccurate messages which were imposed or acquired in childhood. To ameliorate the effects of these cognitive distortions on mood and affect it is necessary to explore the adaptiveness and accuracy of these cognitions. Thus, a crucial component in the treatment of adult survivors of child sexual abuse is the restructuring of cognitive distortions by replacing these with more accurate and realistic cognitions about the self, others and the world. This facilitates an elevation of mood and alleviates negative affect.

Denial

Denial is a defence mechanism that internally and intra-psychically negates unpleasant realities. In order to cope with the trauma of child sexual abuse, many survivors activate denial, by repressing memories and feelings associated with these experiences, as a way of coping and getting on with their lives. The behavioural component of denial is avoidance in which survivors avoid or refuse to encounter situations, objects, or activities because of their relationship to internal problems. This results in survivors not talking about their experiences either in therapy, or to others, thereby reinforcing already potent feelings of isolation, alienation, stigmatisation, and being different from others.

Ellenson (1986) argues that denial in survivors can result in considerable perceptual disturbances. These include minimisation of the abuse and its effects whereby the survivor claims not to have been affected by it at all. More alarmingly, survivors may doubt the validity of their experiences, believing the abuse did not happen but was a figment of their wicked and overactive imagination. If survivors do remember their abuse experiences they may not be able to make a connection between the abuse and their present difficulties.

There is little data on how common denial is in the case of survivors, because often survivors enter therapy for a variety of presenting symptoms. That they were sexually abused in childhood may sometimes not be unearthed in therapy for a considerable period of time, sometimes only after many years, and for some women, never. Thus it is difficult to ascertain precisely how many women who seek therapy have a history of child sexual abuse. What is likely is that denial is relatively common in survivors and that it is manifested in several distinct ways, particularly in dissociation and amnesia.

Dissociation

The *Diagnostic and Statistical Manual of Mental Disorders* (DSM-III-R, 1987) defines dissociative phenomena as '... a disturbance or alteration in the normally integrative functions of identity, memory, or consciousness.' In addition, DSM-III-R categorises three types of dissociative phenomena; (1) multiple personality disorder; (2) depersonalisation disorder; and (3) psychogenic amnesia or fugue. The first two categories are considered to be disturbances in identity, while the latter constitutes a disturbance in memory. In multiple personality the person's identity is temporarily forgotten and a new identity may be adopted, or imposed, while depersonalisation disorder is indicated when the customary feelings of one's own reality is replaced by a feeling of unreality. Psychogenic amnesia, or psychogenic fugue is manifest when memory is impaired, and important events or specific time spans cannot be recalled.

There is a strong link between dissociative phenomena and psychic trauma. Eth and Pynoos (1985) describe psychic trauma as '...when an individual is exposed to an overwhelming event resulting in helplessness in the face of intolerable danger, anxiety and instinctual arousal'. That psychic trauma can occur in child sexual abuse is evident in that children are considerably smaller than the abusing adult, are emotionally dependent on them, and are vulnerable in not being able to escape their abuser.

The emerging empirical and clinical evidence indicates that there is a high correlation between early, severe childhood abuse and the use of dissociation as a defensive strategy (Kluft, 1985). Briere (1984) found that of 152 women seeking crisis counselling, 42 per cent of previously abused women experienced dissociative phenomena ('spacing out') versus 22 per cent of non-abused women. In addition, 21 per cent of survivors reported depersonalisation, while 33 per cent experienced derealisation compared to 11 per cent of the non-abused group.

Several writers have argued that dissociation is a highly innovative, if not creative defence against psychic trauma, which may be highly adaptive as an initial defence against sexual abuse, but which becomes non-adaptive and counterproductive as a defence strategy in adulthood (Gil, 1988; Fraser, 1987) in that it interferes with the woman's ability to cope effectively with reality. Kluft (1986) further proposes that not all survivors of child sexual abuse activate this almost instinctive defensive response. Dissociative phenomena are more likely to occur in the presence of chronic and inconsistent abuse, wherein both love and abuse is present and repeated. In such cases, dissociation is the preferred form of defence in that it is more likely to minimise the perception of trauma (Gil, 1988).

Although some individuals perceive such unpredictable trauma as so overwhelming as to necessitate the activation of dissociation in order to defend themselves, others do not appear to have a capacity to dissociate, but are more likely to adopt denial as their primary psychological defence. From this observation Gil (1988) proposes that there are three types of individuals who are particularly vulnerable to dissociation; (1) those who have suffered chronic physical and sexual abuse; (2) those who were abused by more than one abuser; and (3) those who experienced ritualistic or bizarre abuse.

Amnesia

Dissociative phenomena have the ability to block access to memory, in particular to cognitive, sensory, motoric, and affective memory. This can lead to psychogenic amnesia for certain events and periods of time, and the emotions associated with them. Memory and recall become so impaired that many survivors have no memories at all of their childhood. When these women enter therapy, they do so for a variety of presenting symptoms without knowing that they were sexually abused as a child. Often they may be in therapy for a considerable period of time before memories are recalled. Sometimes this can take years, while for others memory never returns.

It is likely that dissociation and psychogenic amnesia is a very common psychological defence among survivors but that it remains unreported. Maltz and Holman (1986) suggest that as many as 50 per cent of all survivors cannot remember their abuse experiences and as result present dissociative states to some degree. It is essential in the case of psychogenic amnesia to adopt a positive approach to memory work as a therapeutic goal, in order to facilitate recall and the return of memory (see Chapter 8) which can then be integrated with the abuse experience into the adult self.

Multiple personality

There is an increasingly strong correlation between multiple personality disorder (MPD) and a history of child sexual abuse (Gil, 1988) with some writers asserting that '... without abuse, we would have few cases of multiple personality disorder' (Wilbur, 1985). Traditionally, MPD has encountered much scepticism, with many clinicians believing it to be a condition exclusive to hysterical females, or malingerers seeking attention. However, there has been an upsurge of interest in this disorder, with considerable new evidence.

DSM-III-R (1987) proposes the following diagnostic criteria for MPD: (1) The existence within the person of two or more distinct personalities or personality states (each with its own relatively enduring pattern of perceiving, relating, and thinking about the environment and self); and (2) At least two of these personalities or personality states recurrently take full control of the person's behaviour. In addition, people with this disorder have '... unique memories, behaviour patterns and social relationships'.

The number of personalities can vary from two to over a hundred with the transition between personalities often occurring suddenly. Putnam (1985) has identified four distinct types of personalities: (1) Child Personalities who hold or buffer traumatic experiences; (2) Persecutor Personalities who inflict pain or punishment on the natal personality through suicide attempts or self mutilation; (3) Helper Personalities who offer advice or enable the natal personality to accomplish tasks; and (4) Recorder or Memory Personalities who, in contrast to the amnesia inherent in the other personalities, maintain continuous awareness.

The incidence and prevalence of MPD is currently unknown, but a number of recent studies have provided evidence that sexual abuse, in particular incest, is involved in the majority of reported and studied cases (Boor, 1982; Greaves, 1980; Bliss, 1980; Putnam, 1983; Wilbur, 1984; Saltman and Solomon, 1982; Schultz, 1985; Stern 1984) Of these, Putnam (1983) reported that 97 out of every 100 MPD patients had histories of child abuse, while Schultz (1985) notes that of 309 MPD patients, 97.4 per cent were abused in childhood.

Not all survivors of child sexual abuse develop MPD. Sachs (1985) suggests that the major difference between those individuals who do develop MPD and those who do not '... is based on the degree to which the ability to dissociate is available in their biological repertoire'. In addition, the nature of the abuse also plays an important role, especially if the abuse is frequent, unpredictable, inconsistent, sadistic, bizarre or aggressive.

To illustrate the development of personalities Sachs (1985) argues that '... chronic abuse stimulates repeated dissociations which when chained together by a shared affective state, develop into a personality with a unique identity and behavioural repertoire...'. This would suggest that MPD is a highly creative response to a traumatic and painful environment.

The treatment of this disorder may necessitate specialist training which the uninitiated are advised not to attempt. The essential therapeutic goal is the fusion of the personalities (Kluft, 1986). When this fusion persists for more than two years treatment is thought to have achieved a positive outcome.

Perceptual disturbances

Ellenson (1986) argues that survivors of child sexual abuse encounter certain perceptual disturbances which, if they occur with any frequency, may indicate a history of abuse. Along with dissociation, he asserts that survivors are also subject to recurring and unsettling intrusive obsessions. These include strong impulses to harm one's child, feelings that one's child is in danger, or that one's child is being harmed while she, the parent, is absent.

Survivors may also have strong and persistent phobic reactions to being alone, or being in physically compromised situations, in which they may not be able to defend themselves. In addition, Ellenson (1986) notes the incidence of recurring illusions among survivors. These centre particularly around the sensation that there is an evil and malevolent entity, or being, loose in the home, and that they might somehow be entered by this entity.

Hallucinations

Associated with perceptual disturbances are the manifestation of hallucinations which Ellenson (1985) argues are also predictive of a history of child sexual abuse. He proposes several types of common recurring auditory, visual and tactile hallucinations. In the case of auditory hallucinations, survivors report hearing a child or other person crying; sounds of someone breaking into the house or invading their space; or loud booming sounds such as explosions or heavy doors closing.

Survivors who report recurring visual hallucinations experience the movement of objects in their peripheral field of vision; shadowy figures furtively moving around their home, particularly when in bed at night; and the presence of dark, featureless silhouettes. Recurring tactile hallucinations include experiencing physical sensations that range from soft, or light touching, to being physically overwhelmed and pushed over.

Nightmares

There is considerable evidence that survivors of child sexual abuse are subject to recurring nightmares. Briere (1984) found that 54 per cent of abused women suffered from nightmares compared to 23 per cent of the non-abused women, while Jehu, Gazan and Klassen (1985) report that 73 per cent of their sample suffered from nightmares. Ellenson (1985) argues that recurring nightmares, especially those containing specific manifest content, are indicative of a history of child sexual abuse.

The content of these nightmares commonly centre around the following themes: (1) catastrophes that endanger the client, family members, or both; (2) children being harmed or killed; (3) client or family members both being chased by attackers; and (4) scenes of death, or violence, or both. Some survivors also have recurrent nightmares about their abuser and re-experiencing their sexual abuse with him, or their mother discovering the abuse by witnessing the sexual assault.

Physical effects

Psychosomatic pains

Physical complaints are often the only way survivors allow themselves to express their pain. Survivors of child sexual abuse often report a variety of health or physical problems which most commonly include headaches, stomach ailments, bladder infections, cramps, sore throats and skin disorders. Pain may also be localised in certain areas that were subject to abuse such as recurring sore throats in women who were repeatedly forced to perform oral sex. Other survivors recount a history of pelvic or vaginal pain which is often related to the abuse. The incidence of vaginal infections such as thrush, or recurring bouts of cystitis are also commonly reported. As a consequence of such recurring pain, survivors believe that they have in some way been physically and biologically damaged by the sexual abuse.

In addition, many survivors are hypervigilant which prevents them from relaxing, even during sleep, causing inordinate muscle tension and related feelings of pain.

Gil (1988) notes that headaches are almost always migraine headaches which often first commenced shortly after the abuse started. In the case of stomach pains, these are predominantly nervous or acid in nature and as such related to fear and anxiety. Skin disorders include rashes, blemishes and recurring scabs which are exacerbated by anxious scratching. Although these physical effects are not exclusive to survivors of child sexual abuse, research has shown that they are perhaps more common in survivors than non-abused women.

Sleep disturbances

There is also evidence that women with a history of child sexual abuse suffer from sleeping difficulties. Briere (1985) found that 72 per cent of his sample of abused women experienced restless sleeping patterns compared to 55 per cent of non-abused women while Sedney and Brooks (1984) reported that 51 per cent of survivors had difficulty with sleeping versus 29 per cent of a control group. This is echoed by Jehu, Gazan and Klassen (1985) who noted that 73 per cent of their abused women experienced difficulty in sleeping including nightmares.

Effects on sexual functioning

Researchers have paid particular attention to the effects child sexual abuse has on later sexuality. Most studies show that survivors report later problems in sexual adjustment. Often these problems are reflected in a general sexual dissatisfaction including impaired motivation, sexual aversions, impaired arousal, impaired orgasm, vaginismus, and dyspareunia. Additional difficulties are an inability to separate sex from affection, oversexualisation, promiscuity, prostitution, and confusion about sexual orientation.

Effects of child sexual abuse on sexuality are often phasic. Late adolescence and the early twenties are punctuated by seemingly problem free sexual activity, or by considerable promiscuity and the likelihood of prostitution. Casual sexual relations in which the survivor remains in control seem to be the preferred behaviour pattern. For some survivors sexual problems may not manifest themselves until the survivor is in a stable relationship.

Although initially the sexual relationship with a stable partner appears problem-free, due perhaps to novelty and mutual exploration, once the relationship deepens and involves the expression of feelings and emotions other than sex, memories of the childhood sexual abuse may be reactivated causing a confusion of feelings which may affect the relationship and leading to sexual dissatisfaction. This response pattern is referred to as 'intimacy dysfunction' by Levay and Kagle (1977).

Clinical observation also suggests that some survivors do not experience sexual problems until the birth of their first child, particularly if this a daughter. Although hormonal changes may account for some of the manifest sexual problems, other factors may be involved. Carrying the child during pregnancy and giving birth may be the first time in many years that the woman has allowed herself to feel her body, allowing her to become aware of it and its procreative function. This may make the survivor feel extremely vulnerable and may trigger many memories related to her childhood. In addition, the child may remind the survivor of herself as a vulnerable child which may also trigger memories that the survivor has tried to repress for many years.

Sexual adjustment and general dissatisfaction

Many studies using clinical samples have found a high incidence in problems of sexual adjustment, and high levels of sexual dissatisfaction. Meiselman (1978) found that 87 per cent of father–daughter incest survivors reported either a history of, or current, sexual problems including frigidity, promiscuity, and confusion about sexual orientation compared to 20 per cent of non-abused women. Similarly, Courtois (1979) found that 80 per cent of her sample reported severe to moderate problems surrounding sexual activity including a compulsive need for sex, abstention from sex, or an inability to relax sufficiently to enjoy sexual contact.

Herman (1981) notes that 55 per cent of incest victims reported later sexual problems, while Briere (1984) found that 45 per cent of survivors in his clinical sample experienced difficulty in sexual adjustment compared to 15 per cent of non-abused women. Langmade (1983) also reports that women who have a history of child sexual abuse are more sexually anxious, experience more sexual guilt, and report greater dissatisfaction with sexual relationships than the control groups. This is echoed by Jehu, Gazan and Klassen (1985) who found that 59 per cent of their sample of abused women reported sexual dissatis-faction.

Sexual dysfunction was experienced by 64 per cent of women who were sexually abused in childhood compared to 28 per cent of non-abused women in Glasner's (1980) study, while Baisden and Baisden (1979) found that 90 per cent of women seeking counselling for sexual dysfunction had been sexually active at a young age.

Tsai, Feldman-Summers and Edgar (1979) compared three groups of women on sexual adjustment measures. The groups consisted of sexually abused women who sought therapy; sexually abused women who described themselves as 'well adjusted' and had not sought therapy; and a matched control group of non-abused women. There was no difference in terms of sexual adjustment between the 'well adjusted' women and the non-abused control group. However, those women seeking therapy rated themselves to be less sexually responsive, obtained less satisfaction from their sexual relationships, were less satisfied with the quality of their close relationships with men, and were involved with a greater number of sexual partners. One must be cautious in interpreting these results as assignment to the three groups was determined by subjective self-reports of adjustment.

Of the non-clinical studies, Finkelhor (1979) found that survivors of sexual abuse reported significantly lower levels of sexual self-esteem than non-abused individuals. In contrast, Fromuth (1983) found no correlation between sexual abuse and sexual self-esteem, desire for intercourse, or self-ratings for sexual adjustment. Arguably, one reason for the lack of correlation may be that as 96 per cent of the respondents were unmarried with an average age of 19, that they had not formed stable enough relationships to trigger 'intimacy dysfunction' or repressed memories.

Impaired motivation

Becker, Skinner, Abel and Treacy (1982) report that of their sample of incest survivors, 33 per cent experienced impaired motivation for sexual activity, while Briere (1984) found that 42 per cent of abused women experienced a decreased sex drive compared to 29 per cent of the non-abused women. This concurs with Jehu, Gazan and Klassen's (1985) finding that 45 per cent of survivors exhibited impaired motivation.

This is consistent with survivors self-reports which describe little or no interest in sex, and a preference to abstain from sexual contact. Often abused women find abstinence a relief from being overwhelmed with highly arousing emotions, or a confusion of feelings. Other causes for a dysfunction in desire may be conflict between partners, fear of intimacy, and avoidance because sex is only ever experienced as painful, distressing or unsatisfying to the woman (Jehu, 1979; Kaplan, 1979).

Sexual phobias/aversions

Associated with impaired motivation is a fear of sex, which may incorporate sexual aversions. Becker et al (1982) note that 75 per cent of incest survivors experienced a fear of sex, while Jehu, Gazan and Klassen (1985) report that 41 per cent of their sample exhibited phobic/aversive reactions. A possible explanation for this is that sexual activity has the potential for evoking strong phobic reactions in the woman (Kaplan, Fyer and Novick, 1982). In addition, the anticipation of anxiety may be more overwhelming than actual exposure, so that any approach, even innocent, affectionate and non-threatening physical contact may produce an aversive reaction.

Survivors often report that specific features of sexual activity such as being fondled or touched in a particular way, or parts of the body, elicit intense anxiety which may be accompanied by 'flashback memories' of being sexually abused as a child, thereby recapitulating the trauma. These 'flashback memories' are often so pervasive and vivid that they intrude on what is happening in the present with a chosen and desired partner by reactivating the same responses experienced during abuse. Other triggers that may elicit such fear reactions are specific features of foreplay, coming into contact with semen, certain smells such as cigarette smoke or alcohol on the breath, and body alignment and size.

Jehu, Gazan and Klassen (1985) note that for many survivors feelings of anxiety are accompanied by physiological responses such as '... profuse sweating, nausea, vomiting, diarrhoea, or palpitations'. These aversive reactions prevent the woman from relaxing or enjoying the sexual encounter. In addition, this fear of sex induces avoidance of arousal, impairs motivation, restricts foreplay and reduces the number of sexual approaches. When sex is performed, it is often under noticeable pressure from the partner, necessitating psychological preparation ('psyching up'), or the imbibing of alcohol to reduce and inhibit anxiety.

Other factors influencing sexual aversion is loss of control, and fear of experiencing pleasure. Many survivors need to feel that they are in control when initiating and sustaining sexual activity, as any feelings of coercion or force by the partner will recapitulate the earlier abuse experiences causing distress and anxiety. Similarly, feelings of pleasure arising out of sexual activity may be associated with guilt and confusion felt in childhood when the child's body responded to the abuse.

Impaired arousal

Phobic reactions may also be manifest in impaired arousal reported by survivors. Becker *et al.* (1982) note that 42 per cent of incest survivors report arousal dysfunction, while Jehu, Gazan and Klassen (1985) found that 55 per cent of their sample exhibited impaired arousal. As noted above, the sexual encounter may evoke phobic reactions which create excessive anxiety which in turn can disrupt and inhibit arousal. Arousal may also be terminated by aversive physiological responses such as nausea and vomiting.

In addition, phobic reactions may interfere with effective sexual stimulation reducing sexual responses such as vaginal lubrication and swelling, even though these may not be impaired during masturbation. A cognitive component in impaired arousal may be the 'blocking' of all sexual feeling and erotic sensations through dissociation which, in extreme cases, can result in 'genital' or 'sexual anaesthesia'.

Some survivors may only experience arousal if they fantasise about the abuse and the abuser. Although such fantasies facilitate sexual arousal, many survivors find this highly distressing in that it reinforces powerful feelings of guilt, shame and self blame (Deighton and McPeek, 1985).

Impaired orgasm

There is considerable evidence that women who were sexually abused in childhood experience difficulty in reaching orgasm. Becker *et al.* (1982) found that 42 per cent of their incest victims suffered from primary or secondary non-orgasmia, while Jehu, Gazan and Klassen (1985) report that 32 per cent of their sample exhibited impaired orgasm.

More powerful evidence comes from Meiselman (1978) who noted that 74 per cent of her sample of survivors of father/daughter incest experienced orgiastic dysfunction. It is interesting to note that some of the survivors in this sample were only able to reach orgasm in certain situations, such as through masturbation, when under the influence of alcohol, with a new partner, or with an undemanding, non-threatening partner with whom they felt safe.

Not all survivors suffer from impaired orgasm. Indeed, Jehu, Gazan and Klassen (1985) report that some survivors have orgasms 'out of the blue' which are not necessarily related to sexual arousal, but may be related to muscle spasm, lying in a certain position, or the result of a 'flashback'. McGuire and Wagner (1978) note that some survivors can only reach orgasm during intercourse, but not in response to other forms of stimulation by a partner. Often easily attained 'out of the blue' orgasms are reported to be unenjoyable or unsatisfying as they cannot be controlled by the survivor and are not accompanied by any pleasure. Such orgasms are the manifestation of physical responses to sexual stimulation acquired and conditioned at a developmentally immature age (Tsai and Wagner, 1978).

Vaginismus

Sexual phobias are also strongly associated with vaginismus in a eliciting a fear of vaginal penetration. In vaginismus the muscles at the outer third of the vagina and the perineum contract, so that either penetration is prevented entirely, or if penetration is achieved, it is accompanied by extreme pain (Fertel, 1977; Lamont, 1978). The operant phobic reaction is probably acquired during childhood abuse in response to the threat of penetration, thereby eliciting involuntary reflex responses which produce contractions and reflex spasms preventing intromission.

Dyspareunia

Associated with vaginismus is dyspareunia in which women experience pain during intercourse. Gross et al. (1980) report that in their sample of 25 women suffering from chronic pelvic pain, 36 per cent had a history of incest. According to Lamont (1980) and Wabrek and Wabrek (1975) this condition may be caused either by inadequate vaginal lubrication during the arousal phase, or by the muscular contractions manifested in vaginismus.

Oversexualisation

Many survivors of child sexual abuse show a tendency to oversexualise their relationships with men. Jehu, Gazan and Klassen (1985) found that a common response among survivors was that '...no man could care for me without a sexual relationship...' with 71 per cent of survivors agreeing with this statement. Linked to oversexualisation is the inability to separate or distinguish sex from affection, probably due to the confusion of parental love and sexuality in childhood (Meiselman, 1978). Many survivors find it difficult to differentiate sex from affection and feel the two are so entangled as to defy being unravelled. Thus an affectionate hug may be interpreted as a sexual approach, or the sexual act becomes basic and animalistic with no feelings of tenderness, love or affection.

Alternative explanations for oversexualisation suggest that survivors have learned to use sex as an effective means of getting rewards (Herman, 1981), or that because of their feelings of inadequacy and low self-esteem, they have a compulsive need for sex as proof of being loved and an adequate woman (Courtois, 1979). The connection between sex, love and approval may have been conditioned in childhood, during the sexual abuse, and becomes difficult to extinguish in adulthood. The sad consequence of their behaviour is that the women become involved in brief, often unsatisfying, hurtful and frequently destructive relationships.

Promiscuity

Several researchers have noted that there is a strong correlation between child sexual abuse and promiscuity. Herman (1981) reports that 35 per cent of her sample of survivors of father/daughter incest exhibited promiscuous behaviour while observing that they had a '... repertoire of sexually stylised behaviour...' which they used as means of getting attention and affection. To a lesser extent, Meiselman (1978) found that 25 per cent of her sample engaged in promiscuous behaviour, while DeYoung (1982) reported that 28 per cent of her sample engaged in promiscuous activities. Tsai, Feldman-Summers and Edgar (1979) also observed that 43 per cent of abused women who sought therapy displayed promiscuous behaviour, compared to 17 per cent of abused women who reported themselves as 'well-adjusted' and 9 per cent of the control group of non-abused women.

In contrast, Fromuth (1983) found no difference between 482 abused and non-abused women in terms of promiscuity. What was indicated, however, was that a history of child sexual abuse predicted whether women described themselves as promiscuous or not. This is a significant finding in that it suggests that promiscuity may be linked to negative self image and self attributions, and not actual behaviour or number of sexual partners.

Prostitution

There also seems to be a strong link between child sexual abuse and prostitution. James and Meyerding (1977) found that of 136 prostitutes 55 per cent had been sexually abused as children, and that 65 per cent of adolescents in the sample were forced into sexual activity before the age of 16. These findings are echoed in Silbert and Pines's (1981) study of prostitutes which reported that 60 per cent had been abused prior to the age of 16, by an average of two people, for an average of 20 months, with a mean age of onset of abuse of 10.

Although Fields (1981) found that there was no difference in the prevalence of child sexual abuse between a sample of prostitutes matched for age, race and education and a control group of non-prostitutes (45 per cent versus 37 per cent respectively) there was evidence that the prostitutes were abused at an earlier age of 14.5 years than the non-prostitutes whose age was 16.5, and were more likely to have been physically forced into sex.

Sexual orientation

Sexual orientation among survivors of child sexual abuse has also received some attention although to date there is little empirical evidence for a connection between child sexual abuse and homosexuality. Those studies that have provided data appear to be discrepant in their findings.

Meiselman (1978) found that 30 per cent of incest survivors had either adopted a lesbian lifestyle, or had homosexual experiences and feelings, although these did not manifest themselves until after many years of heterosexual experiences. An even higher percentage is quoted by Gundlach (1977) who noted that 55 per cent of women who were molested or raped by a stranger before age 15 were homosexual in adulthood, while 94 per cent of women who were molested or raped by a relative or close friend were homosexual.

Other studies show no association between homosexuality and child sexual abuse (Bell and Weinberg, 1981). Indeed, Herman (1981) observed that only 5 per cent of incest survivors were homosexual and that 7.5 per cent were bisexual in their orientation. The discrepancy in these findings suggests that it would be premature to assume that there is a correlation between child sexual abuse and sexual orientation.

The confusion that survivors have about their sexuality has been noted by Giaretto (1976) who found that an inordinately high percentage of women raped in childhood suffered from rosaphrenia. Rosaphrenia is manifested when an individual cannot accept her own sexuality regardless of how she practices sex. Of 160 women tested for rosaphrenia, 90 per cent were raped in childhood, while 22.5 per cent of these were raped by their father or stepfather. This chilling finding illustrates the confusion that survivors experience in trying to reclaim their sexuality.

To overcome many of the problems associated with confusion about sexuality, some survivors go to extraordinary lengths to choose sexual partners who are physically different from the abuser. These differences may merely be the contrast between fair colouring and dark colouring, or between height, weight and build. Other survivors only feel physically and sexually attracted to partners who come from an entirely different racial or ethnic background in order to minimise reminders of the abuser.

The Impact of Child Sexual Abuse

The previous chapter concentrated on documenting the long term effects of child sexual abuse on adult survivors. This chapter aims to look at the impact of child sexual abuse, and the differential effects it has on survivors. Not all survivors report being adversely affected by their abuse experiences, or manifest chronic or acute symptomatology. To understand why some individuals are more vulnerable than others to severity of trauma, it is necessary to look at the influence of several factors such as age of onset, relationship to the abuser, length and frequency of abuse, and type of sexual abuse to ascertain differential effects on impact and psychological sequelae.

Researchers have recently attempted to integrate research findings on which factors operate in the dynamics of child sexual abuse, and isolate the types of effects that are commonly associated with differences in impact. To date only two models have been proposed to account specifically for the dynamics of child sexual abuse and its impact on the survivor: Post Traumatic Stress Disorder (PTSD) and the Four Traumagenic Dynamics Model of Child Sexual Abuse proposed by Browne and Finkelhor (1988). Both these models will be considered and evaluated in terms of their explanatory power for the impact of child sexual abuse.

Factors influencing differences in impact

There has been considerable empirical research into which factors exert an influence on the severity of impact and differential effects of child sexual abuse. Effects by type of abuse investigated to date include the duration and frequency of abuse, relationship to abuser, sex and age of abuser, type of sexual act, the use of force or violence, age at onset, and the effects of disclosure. Much of the research collected to date is contradictory and largely inconclusive.

Clinical observation suggests that the greatest trauma occurs if the abuse goes on for a long period of time, if the child is closely related to the abuser, if the sexual activity includes penetration, and if it is accompanied by aggression (Groth, 1978). MacFarlane (1978) also noted other factors which appeared to influence severity of impact. These include whether the child participates in the sexual abuse, negative parental reactions to disclosure, and the child's age at onset of the abuse, with older children seemingly more traumatised due to increased cognitive development and awareness of the cultural taboos of incest and child sexual abuse. Despite these observations, the empirical evidence is largely inconsistent, with little consensus among researchers.

Duration and frequency of abuse

Of nine studies looking for an association between duration and frequency of abuse and severity of impact, four studies found evidence for longer duration and increased trauma, three studies reported no correlation whatsoever, while two noted that the longer the abuse continued the less the trauma.

Russell (1986) found that 73 per cent of survivors who were abused for more than five years reported considerable to extreme traumatisation compared to 62 per cent who were molested for between one week and five years, and 46 per cent of those who were only abused once. Tsai *et al.* (1979) reported greater negative effects the longer and more frequent the abuse. Similarly, Bagley and Ramsay (1985) found that the longer the duration the more severe the survivor's mental health status, while Urguiza and Beilke (1986) noted that duration and frequency were predictive of increased traumatisation.

In contrast, Finkelhor (1979) and Tufts (1984) found no association between duration and severity of impact, a finding echoed by Langmade (1983) who noted no difference between long or short duration on measures of sexual anxiety, sexual guilt or sexual dissatisfaction. Even more intriguing are two studies that found reversed results. Courtois (1979) found that the longer the abuse lasted the less the traumatisation, while Seidner and Calhoun (1984) noted that a high frequency of abuse was associated with higher self acceptance but lower social maturity.

Thus, there is little consensus among researchers on the effects of duration and frequency of abuse and severity of impact. Perhaps this is not so surprising as there are a number of other variables associated with this factor which may confound its investigation such as age of onset, relationship to the abuser, and the nature of the sexual activity. It may be that rather than isolating one factor as being predictive, it is the combination of variables which influences psychological sequelae.

Relationship to abuser

Clinical observations indicate that the closer the relationship between abuser and abused, the more traumatic the impact of child sexual abuse. Again there is contradictory evidence with three studies (Landis, 1956; Anderson *et al.*, 1981; Friedrich, 1986) reporting more trauma when the relationship is between close relatives, and four studies finding no difference in impact between closely related abusers and other types of abusers (Finkelhor, 1979; Russell, 1986; Seidner and Calhoun, 1984; Tufts, 1984).

These discrepant findings suggest that the relationship to the abuser is not a constant predictor of severity of trauma. One reason for this may be that closeness of relationship is not necessarily a reflection of degree of betrayal experienced by the abused child. The sense of betrayal from being abused by a trusted adult such as a friend of the family may be considerably greater than abuse by a long distant cousin or blood relation. In addition, the dynamics may be different between a trusted person, such as a family friend or teacher, and a stranger, with the former generating betrayal of trust, while the latter may serve to induce fear.

Evidence concerning abusers who are fathers and step-fathers is more consistent. Both Russell (1986) and Finkelhor (1979) found that greater trauma was associated with father or stepfather abuse compared to other types of abuser. Bagley and Ramsay (1985) also reported that there was a trend for abuse by natural fathers to be more severe in impact than abuse by a stepfather. However, this proved to be non-significant when analysed statistically. In contrast, Tufts (1984) found that children abused by their stepfathers manifested more distress than if the abuser was the natural father. This may be due to the operation of other factors and family dynamics such as pre-abuse experiences including divorce, single parenting, or the absence of father or male role models.

Age and sex of abuser

Very few studies have looked at the age and sex of the abuser as a variable accounting for the differential impact of child sexual abuse. Those that have controlled for this factor have found that the older the abuser, the more traumatic the impact (Finkelhor, 1979; Fromuth, 1983). Finkelhor also noted that the age of the abuser was the second most important factor predicting trauma. Russell's (1986) data are consistent with this finding in reporting lower levels of trauma if the abuser was younger than 26, or older than 50.

There have only been three studies investigating sex of abuser as a factor in the impact of child sexual abuse. Finkelhor (1979) and Russell (1986) both found that sexual abuse by a male was perceived to be more traumatic than abuse by a female. In addition, Seidner and Calhoun (1984) found that survivors who experienced sexual abuse by a male abuser displayed lower self-acceptance but higher social maturity. It is likely that abuse by females is still relatively under-reported, as is abuse directed at male children, which may account for a bias in these findings

Type of sexual activity

The available empirical evidence suggests that there is an association between severity and degree of trauma and type of sexual activity. Russell (1986) found that 59 per cent of survivors who experienced attempted and actual intercourse, fellatio, cunnilingus, analingus and anal intercourse reported severe traumatisation, compared to 36 per cent who experienced digital exploration and touching of genitals and unclothed parts of the body, and 22 per cent who were subject to unwanted kissing and touching while clothed.

Bagley and Ramsay (1985) report that the single most powerful variable predicting severity of mental health impairment was whether the sexual abuse was accompanied by penetration. Several other studies concur with this finding, although they are not quite so clearly differentiated between actual intercourse and genital touching (Landis, 1956; S.Peters, 1984; Seidner and Calhoun, 1984; Tufts, 1984).

Three studies report no consistent relationship between type of sexual activity and degree of trauma (Anderson *et al.*, 1981; Finkelhor, 1979; Fromuth, 1983). This makes the evidence somewhat inconclusive as to whether more intimate contact, in particular penetration, is more traumatic than manual exploration and contact. It may be that as a single variable it is not predictive but needs to be viewed in combination with other factors. More specifically, it is the psychological meaning that the abuse has for the child and later adult that may be more important than actual sexual acts committed. Thus, it may not matter whether the abuse consisted of rape, penile penetration, inappropriate touching, or voyeurism. It is the child's reaction to it and the related traumagenic dynamics which exert an influence on severity of trauma.

Physical force and violence

There seems to be some association between the use of physical force and violence, and severity of trauma. Both Finkelhor (1979) and Fromuth (1983) found that the more force was used, the more negative the outcome. Russell (1986) noted that 71 per cent of survivors subjected to force during the abuse rated themselves as considerably to extremely traumatised compared to 47 per cent who did not experience force. This was also noted by Tufts (1984) who found that physical injury was predictive of the relative degree of behavioural disturbances in children, while Friedrich *et al.*, (1986) reported an association between the use of force and the internalising and externalising of symptoms.

Dissenting evidence comes from Anderson *et al.* (1981) and Seidner and Calhoun (1984) who found little or no association between force and psychological sequelae, while Bagley and Ramsay (1985) found that although force was associated with greater psychological impairment, this proved to be statistically non-significant. MacFarlane (1978) argues that the lack of association may be due to the observation that the more force that is used, the more the child is able to place attribution of blame on the abuser, thereby reducing long term trauma.

It would seem that there is some relationship between force and violence and severity of trauma in child sexual abuse, but more sophisticated empirical investigation is needed.

Age of onset

Perhaps the largest area of controversy focuses on age of onset as a factor in the impact of child sexual abuse. Some clinicians propose that the younger the child the more vulnerable it is to trauma due to impressionability, while others suggest that the naivety of the younger child in some way protects it from stigmatisation. To date the evidence for this notion is still somewhat contradictory.

Meiselman (1978) noted that the younger the age of the child the more seriously disturbed the adult seemed. She found that 37 per cent of survivors whose sexual abuse started prior to puberty were seriously impaired compared to 17 per cent of those experiencing post-pubertal sexual abuse, a finding replicated by Courtois (1979). In contrast, Finkelhor (1979) and Russell (1986) found a small but non-significant trend that showed that the younger the age of onset, the more severe the effects. Langmade (1983) found no difference in sexual activity, sexual guilt or sexual dissatisfaction related to age of onset, as did Bagley and Ramsay (1985), while Tufts (1984) proposes that chronological age is less important than the number of stages of development that the abuse spans.

Thus, there is little clear relation between age of onset and severity of impact, although there seems to be a trend towards the younger the child, the more traumatic the impact and observed effects. Research on multiple personality disorder (MPD) combined with clinical observation suggests that the younger the age of onset, the more likely the survivor is to dissociate and develop psychogenic amnesia (Putnam, 1985). It is likely that a younger child will be unable to integrate her experiences on a cognitive level and thus 'splits off' from her emotional responses to it. In addition, if memory is still relatively unformed then it is difficult to incorporate the abuse experience into memory systems.

Anecdotal evidence suggests that some abusers use this lack of cognitive under-standing and limited memory capacity as a rational for sexually abusing children under the age of five. The arguments for this include: (1) they are too young to understand; (2) they are too young to remember; (3) they are less likely to tell as they do not recognise that this is abnormal behaviour, and (4) because they are so young and won't be able to remember they will not be affected by it. Exploration of the adoption of coping mechanisms and strategies, and their relation to cognitive development would enhance our understanding of how the abuse experience is dealt with at different stages of cognitive development, and to what extent it is integrated or defended against. The implication of such an increase in knowledge would be invaluable in treatment interven-tion, both for children and the adult survivor.

Disclosure

There is an assumption among some researchers that if the sexual abuse is kept secret and not disclosed until adulthood, that there will be greater mental health impairment. Bagley and Ramsay (1985) did find a fragile association for this which disappeared once other factors were taken into account. In contrast, Finkelhor (1979) found no such relationship at all, while Tufts (1984) found that those children who took a long time to disclose displayed least anxiety and hostility.

It would appear that there are other variables involved in disclosure, in particular parental reaction to disclosure. Tufts (1984) notes that mothers who were angry and punitive generated more traumatic impact, while Anderson *et al.* (1981) found that symptoms were two and a half times worse if the parental response was negative. This suggests that negative responses aggravate trauma, although positive responses do not necessarily ameliorate trauma. Institutional responses from statutory agencies, social workers and the police may also play a role in impact, as may removal of the child from the home. Tufts (1984) found an increase in behavioural problems, in particular aggression, when the child was removed from the parental home.

Arguably, some of the factors investigated do play a role in psychological sequelae and severity of trauma. Although the evidence is often contradictory, more sophisticated methodological research using larger sample groups may provide more consistent results enabling a more precise isolation of which factors account for differential effects and severity of trauma in survivors. Further exploration of the dynamics operating in child sexual abuse will also enhance deeper understanding.

Post-traumatic stress disorder and child sexual abuse

In order to account for adverse long term effects, clinicians and researchers have attempted to formulate explanatory models to explain the full range of symptoms and observed effects. An already well established model which mirrors some of the observed effects of child sexual abuse, although originally formulated to account for the trauma of war and its effects on veterans (Trimble, 1985), is that of Post-Traumatic Stress Disorder (PTSD). More recently, several clinicians have begun to note that PTSD also has applicability to both childhood trauma (Benedek, 1985; Eth and Pynoos, 1985) and to the understanding and the treatment of the impact of child sexual abuse (Courtois, 1986; Donaldson and Gardners, 1985; Eth and Pynoos, 1985; Finkelhor, 1988; Frederick, 1986; Gil, 1988; Goodwin, 1985; Lindberg and Distad, 1985).

The Diagnostic and Statistical Manual of Mental Disorders (DSM-III-R, 1987) proposes that the essential feature of PTSD is '...the development of characteristic symptoms following a psychologically stressing event that is outside the range of usual human experience that would be distressing to almost anyone, and is usually experienced with intense fear, terror and helplessness'. The types of stressful event included are rape or assault, kidnapping and hijacking, military combat, accidental disasters such as car accidents, plane crashes, fires, floods, torture, and more recently child sexual abuse. The diagnostic criteria include the following:

1. The experience of a traumatic event that would elicit symptoms of distress in most individuals such as serious threat to one's own life or physical integrity, or that of attachment figures; sudden destruction of one's home or community; or seeing others who are or have been seriously injured or killed as the result of an accident or physical violence.

2. A persistent re-experiencing of the traumatic event through:

    (a) recurrent and intrusive recollections

    (b) recurrent dreams of the trauma

    (c) sudden feelings that the event is recurring including illusions, hallucinations, dissociation and flashbacks

    (d) distress at exposure to traumas that symbolise or resemble the traumatic event

3. Persistent avoidance of stimuli associated with the trauma including numbing of responsiveness, as indicated by at least three of the following:

    (a) avoidance of feelings or thoughts associated with the trauma

    (b) avoidance of activities or situations that elicit recollections of the trauma

    (c) psychogenic amnesia

    (d) diminished interest in significant activities

    (e) feelings of detachment or estrangement from others

    (f) restricted range of affect such as unable to experience feelings of love

    (g) sense of foreshortened future

4. Persistent symptoms of increased arousal as indicated by at least two of the following:

    (a) difficulty falling or staying asleep

    (b) irritability or outbursts of anger

    (c) difficulty concentrating

    (d) hypervigilance

    (e) exaggerated startle response

    (f) physiologic reaction when exposed to events that symbolise or resemble an aspect of the traumatic event

Although the diagnostic criteria of PTSD account for many of the observed symptoms of child sexual abuse such as flashbacks, psychogenic amnesia, dreams and nightmares, reduced affect and numbing, hypervigilance, isolation, anger, stigmatisation and intrusive recollections of the trauma, it cannot account for the full range of observed symptoms, especially cognitive effects.

Finkelhor (1988) argues that although including child sexual abuse within the framework of PTSD has been an important step forward in understanding its impact, it nevertheless has some limitations. On the positive side, subsuming child sexual abuse under PTSD has resulted in the clarification and description of some of the effects that survivors encounter in adulthood. In addition, PTSD enables these effects to be viewed as a syndrome with a core aetiology, rather than just a catalogue of symptoms.

This puts child sexual abuse into a broader context by highlighting similar dynamics that are seen in other trauma, which may generate further understanding of child sexual

LIBRARY
DERBY COLLEGE
OF NURSING AND

abuse by not viewing it in isolation. This has prompted renewed interest in child sexual abuse and stimulated further research.

Including child sexual abuse in the PTSD framework has also increased the recognition of the impact of child sexual abuse as a major psychological stressor which may serve to reduce some of the stigma attached to it. Some observers have argued that the trauma of child sexual abuse is exclusive only to those with a hysterical predisposition and that it is a self inflicted trauma (Freud, 1897). This notion may now be challenged by viewing child sexual abuse as a PTSD stressor akin to other devastating and uncontrollable traumas such as wars or hijacking.

Limitations of the PTSD Model

On the negative side, Finkelhor (1988) argues that there are several problems with the PTSD formulation which impose severe limitations in its application to the impact of child sexual abuse. These limitations mainly focus on the fact that PTSD cannot adequately account for all the observed symptoms. In concentrating its focus on affect the PTSD formulation ignores many of the cognitive effects observed in survivors of child sexual abuse. In addition, the PTSD model applies only to some victims, not all, and it is limited in not being able to account for the dynamics of sexual abuse that lead to observed symptomatology.

Although the trauma of child sexual abuse shares many elements with PTSD there are qualitative differences in symptomatology which the PTSD model cannot explain. The model emphasises intrusive imagery, nightmares, and numbing of affect as essential symptoms, all of which are indeed seen in some survivors of sexual abuse, but it does not include other symptoms that are commonly observed. Major symptoms that fall outside the PTSD framework include fear, depression, self blame, guilt, and sexual problems as well as self destructive behaviours such as suicide, substance abuse and revictimisation (Briere and Runtz, 1988).

In focusing almost entirely on affect as the location of trauma, the PTSD model is in danger of obscuring or minimising other vital factors such as cognitions. This is inconsistent with observations of the impact of child sexual abuse in which many of the symptoms are located in cognitive processes which lead to distorted beliefs about the self and others, self blame, sexual misinformation and confusion. These distorted cognitions, often acquired during the abuse experience in childhood are related to affect in activating mood disturbances such as guilt and low self esteem in adulthood (Jehu, Gazan and Klassen, 1985).

A further problem with the PTSD framework is that many of the required symptoms are not present in survivors. A study by Kilpatrick et al. (1986) which evaluated PTSD symptomatology in 126 female survivors of child sexual abuse found that these were currently present in only 10 per cent, and ever present in only 36 per cent. Yet these women presented other common symptoms, in particular depression, substance abuse and sexual difficulties which are not subsumed in the PTSD diagnostic criteria.

Given these obvious limitations, caution needs to be exercised in subsuming child sexual abuse into the PTSD framework without including the full range of observed effects and symptomatology. Exaggeration of PTSD symptomatology may lead to assumptions that survivors without PTSD are not diagnosed as having a history of sexual abuse, or that they are less traumatised than those that do. A further inference might be that expert witnesses may testify that child victims or survivors may not have been abused because they lack the relevant PTSD symptoms. As a result of these limitations, Finkelhor strongly argues for '... the notion that sexual abuse trauma be kept distinct from PTSD' (Finkelhor, 1988).

In terms of theory, the PTSD model is further limited in providing an explanation of how observed symptoms develop and the dynamics of sexual abuse trauma. Pynoos and Eth (1985) argue that symptoms manifest themselves through '... helplessness in the face of intolerable danger, anxiety and instinctual arousal.' This has limited explanatory power in cases of child sexual abuse, which are not always necessarily accompanied by danger, threat or violence.

Several researchers (Armstrong, 1978; Finkelhor, 1979; De Young, 1982) have noted that much sexual abuse, especially intra-familial abuse is not necessarily a single event but rather a process, which often starts with normal, discreet affectionate behaviour and gradually evolves over time culminating in increasingly more overt sexual activity. Children often only realise in retrospect that they have in fact been abused in the light of increasing awareness and cognitive understanding of appropriate and inappropriate touching and sexual behaviour.

Thus, the trauma of sexual abuse stems not solely from potential physical danger, threat, or an overwhelming event, but may also be lodged in the dynamics of a relationship involving the betrayal of trust, the meaning allotted to the behaviour, and feelings of guilt.

To fully understand the dynamics of the PTSD model and their influence on the impact of trauma, several researchers have employed Horowitz's (1976) 'completion tendency' theory which proposes that if the psyche is unable to integrate a traumatic experience into existing 'schemata', then the memories will remain active and tend to interfere with normal functioning. Although this approach would account for the nightmares, repetitions and numbing of affect as a defence against the trauma, it nevertheless still cannot explain the common symptoms of anger, worthlessness and self blame observed in survivors.

According to Finkelhor (1988), survivors actually tend to 'overintegrate' their abuse experiences by applying the behaviours learned through that experience indiscriminately and inappropriately. While this may be true, it can be argued that survivors are not necessarily consciously aware of this 'overintegration' and often do not connect their current, maladaptive behaviour patterns to their abuse experience. A major goal in the treatment of adult survivors is to integrate their childhood and abuse experiences in a conscious way in which they understand the source of their behavioural repertoire, and learn to choose which behaviours to adopt adaptively, rather than being directed by the behaviours they have unconsciously integrated and internalised.

This is especially true for survivors who have 'split-off' or dissociated from their abuse experiences. Making repressed memories conscious and re-experiencing the trauma allows the split-off parts of the self and personality to become more fully integrated as a whole. In addition, many survivors do dissociate from feelings and affect and do not 'overintegrate' their emotions, but suppress them.

A more powerful explanation of PTSD, which incorporates cognitive processes, comes from Janoff-Bulman (1985) who suggests that PTSD occurs as a result of the shattering of assumptions when experiencing a traumatic event. Assumptions that the world is a safe place, or that the individual is a good person, may be shattered by a traumatic event causing the individual to believe herself to be bad. The consequent disequilibrium is manifested by intense stress and anxiety and symptoms observed in PTSD.

Despite accounting for some of the observed cognitive symptoms, there are two fundamental shortcomings to Janoff-Bulman's explanation. Firstly, children may hold different assumptions of the world to adults. This raises doubts about the applicability of PTSD to children, particularly as the original formulation was specific to adults. Secondly, Janoff-Bulman's interpretation, while incorporating some of the cognitive processes which can lead to distortions observed in survivors, is still unable to account for many of the sexual problems, particularly inappropriate sexual behaviour. It is more likely that such behaviours are acquired through learning or conditioning rather than disequilibrium arising out of the shattering of assumptions.

The obvious limitations inherent in the present formulation of PTSD to explain the impact of child sexual abuse have led a number of researchers to recommend that, rather than subsuming child sexual abuse under a model lacking in explanatory power, it would be more constructive to delineate a separate and distinct syndrome more specific to sexual trauma (Briere and Runtz, 1988; Corwin, 1985; Finkelhor, 1988; Summit, 1983). While certain concepts and dynamics may be used from the PTSD formulation, the focus should be on sexual trauma, and the dynamics that generate the unique yet commonly observed symptoms that survivors experience. Such a formulation may prevent the PTSD model from becoming so broad as to be meaningless.

The Traumagenic Dynamics Model of child sexual abuse

A more comprehensive alternative to the PTSD model has been formulated by Finkelhor and Browne (1985), which proposes four traumagenic dynamics to explain the impact of child sexual abuse: (1) traumatic sexualisation; (2) betrayal; (3) stigmatisation; and (4) powerlessness (see Table 4.1). Finkelhor and Browne (1985) define traumagenic dynam-

Table 4.1: The Traumagenic Dynamics Model of child sexual abuse (Finkelhor and Browne, 1985)

1: Traumatic Sexualisation

Dynamics
(a) Child rewarded for sexual behaviour inappropriate to developmental level
(b) Abuser exchanges attention and affection for sex
(c) Sexual parts of child fetishized
(d) Abuser transmits misconceptions about sexual behaviour and sexual morality
(e) Conditioning of sexual activity with negative emotion and memories

Psychological impact
(a) Increased salience of sexual issues
(b) Confusion about sexual identity
(c) Confusion about sexual norms
(d) Confusion of sex with love, care getting and arousal sensations
(e) Aversion to sexual intimacy

Behavioural manifestations
(a) Sexual preoccupations and compulsive sexual behaviours
(b) Precocious sexual activity
(c) Aggressive sexual behaviours
(d) Promiscuity
(e) Prostitution
(f) Sexual dysfunctions: flashbacks, difficulty in arousal, orgasm
(g) Avoidance of, or phobic reactions to, sexual intimacy

2. Stigmatisation

Dynamics
(a) Abuser blames, denigrates victim
(b) Abuser and others pressure child to secrecy
(c) Child infers attitudes of shame about activities
(d) Others have shocked reaction to disclosure
(e) Others blame child for events
(f) Victim is stereotyped as damaged goods

Psychological impact
(a) Guilt, shame
(b) Lowered self-esteem
(c) Sense of differentness from others

Behavioural manifestations
(a) Isolation
(b) Drug or alcohol abuse
(c) Criminal involvement
(d) Self mutilation
(e) Suicide

3. Betrayal

Dynamics
(a) Trust and vulnerability manipulated
(b) Violation of expectation that others will provide care and protection
(c) Child's well-being disregarded
(d) Lack of support and protection from parent(s)

Psychological impact
(a) Grief, depression
(b) Extreme dependency
(c) Impaired ability to judge trustworthiness of others
(d) Mistrust, particularly of men
(e) Anger, hostility

Behavioural manifestations
(a) Clinging
(b) Vulnerability to subsequent abuse and exploitation
(c) Allowing own children to be victimised
(d) Isolation
(e) Discomfort in intimate relationships
(f) Marital problems
(g) Aggressive behaviour
(h) Delinquency

4. Powerlessness

Dynamics
(a) Body territory invaded against the child's wishes
(b) Vulnerability to invasion continues over time
(c) Abuser uses force or trickery to involve child
(d) Child feels unable to protect self and halt abuse
(e) Repeated experience of fear
(f) Child is unable to make others believe her

Psychological impact
(a) Anxiety, fear
(b) Lowered sense of efficacy
(c) Perception of self as victim
(d) Need to control
(e) Identification with the aggressor

Behavioural manifestations
(a) Nightmares
(b) Phobias
(c) Somatic complaints, eating and sleeping disorders
(d) Depression
(e) Dissociation
(f) Running away
(g) School problems, truancy
(h) Employment problems
(i) Vulnerability to subsequent victimisation
(j) Aggressive behaviour, bullying
(k) Delinquency
(l) Becoming an abuser

ics as '...an experience that alters a child's cognitive or emotional orientation to the world and causes trauma by distorting the child's self concept, worldview, or affective capacities.' In turn they view coping with these distortions as giving rise to observed psychological and behavioural effects.

Although the model incorporates some important elements of PTSD, in particular distortions in affect, it proposes other dynamics which have more potent explanatory power to account for the diverse symptomatology and differential effects in impact. In focusing on the role of distortion, the Four Traumagenic Model also includes cognitive distortions and proposes that trauma is not merely the result of the shattering of assumptions (Janoff-Bulman, 1985) but rather the distortion of assumptions.

Finkelhor and Browne (1985) do not see these distortions as a failure of integration, as proposed by Horowitz (1976), but rather as overintegration. They argue that the assumptions and coping mechanisms acquired during the abuse experience have initially a very high adaptive value, but become maladaptive in adulthood, or in situations where sexual abuse is not the norm.

The Traumagenic Dynamics Model presents a descriptive framework with which to account for the variety and diversity of observed effects in the impact of child sexual abuse, including gender differences. In categorising symptomatology into four distinct dynamics, some of which overlap, it is able to improve the level of explanation beyond that of PTSD, and enhance current understanding of the observed effects and differential impact of child sexual abuse, and the specific dynamics which activate specific effects.

1. Traumatic sexualisation

The first dynamic explains how sexuality is shaped, often in an inappropriate and dysfunctional manner, by several processes. Moreover, these dynamics are unique to child sexual abuse and would not occur in other childhood traumas. Included in this process are the use of secondary gains and rewards by the abuser for inappropriate sexual behaviour. As a result of these rewards the child may adopt sexual behaviour in order to manipulate others to obtain gratification.

Depending on the type of sexual activity, certain parts of the child's anatomy may become fetishised and accredited with distorted importance or meaning. In addition, confusion and misconception about sexual behaviour is indoctrinated in the child by the abuser which may result in sexuality becoming associated with trauma through frightening and unpleasant memories.

The effects and symptoms activated by the traumatic sexualisation dynamic are specifically related to sexual difficulties such as aversion to sex, flashbacks during sexual activity, motivation and arousal difficulties, and orgasmic problems (Briere, 1984; Courtois, 1979; Langmade, 1983; Tsai and Wagner, 1978). This dynamic also explains inappropriate sexualisation observed in children of survivors (Gelinas, 1983; Herman and Hirshman, 1977; Justice and Justice, 1979; Steele and Alexander, 1981; Summit and Kryso, 1978). It is argued that because of their inappropriate sexual socialisation, survivors may inappropriately sexualise their children, which may lead to sexual or physical abuse.

2. Betrayal

In the second dynamic, betrayal occurs when the victim discovers that someone they trust and depend on, wishes or causes them harm. This may happen the first time abuse takes place, or may not occur until much later. Betrayal is also dependent on how much the victim feels she has been betrayed, not just on the closeness of the relationship. Thus, betrayal may be much worse in the case of an abusive relationship which started off in an affectionate and nurturing way than one in which there was suspicious behaviour from the outset.

Feelings of betrayal are not exclusively directed towards the abuser, but more commonly against the mother or other caretakers, for not having protected the child appropriately during the abuse, or during disclosure (Herman, 1981). This may stem from the child's belief that parents are omnipotent and omniscient, and thus not only aware of what is happening to the child, but also able to ward off any potential danger.

The dynamic of betrayal can explain such commonly noted symptoms and behaviours as depression resulting from disenchantment and loss of a trusted figure (Adams-Tucker, 1981; Benward and Densen-Gerber, 1975; Browning and Boatman, 1977; Herman, 1981; Peters, 1988), overdependency, and impaired judgment in forming positive relationships resulting in invulnerability to revictimisation (Briere, 1984; DeYoung, 1982; Fromuth, 1986; Herman, 1981; Miller *et al.*, 1978; Russell, 1983).

Other effects associated with betrayal on an interpersonal level are the manifestation of angry and hostile feelings (Briere, 1984; Courtois, 1979; J. Peters, 1976), fear of intimacy, fear of men, fear of women, and relationship difficulties (Courtois, 1979; DeYoung, 1982; Herman, 1981; Meiselman, 1978), many of which are adopted as protection from future betrayals.

3. Stigmatisation

The third dynamic of stigmatisation focuses on the received negative messages operating in the abuse experience. Essentially these include evilness, worthlessness, shamefulness and guilt. These messages may be overtly communicated during the abuse by the abuser as a way of blaming (e.g. 'you seduced me'; 'look what you made me do') or labelling the child as 'bitch', or covertly through the furtiveness and secrecy inherent in much of child sexual abuse. In some cases these messages are received later, especially during disclosure, when moral judgements about the deviancy of their experiences may be communicated by others such as the mother, family members, relatives or professionals.

This can lead to self-labelling such as 'seductress' and 'spoiled goods' (Herman 1981) but may also motivate the survivor to seek an explanation for why it happened to her, believing herself to have been singled out for her evilness or badness. This serves to reinforce already existing negative self-image and create a cycle of stigmatisation, leading to isolation and alienation. When such isolation and stigmatisation is combined with substance abuse and prostitution, the survivor may begin to form affiliations with deviant subcultures (Benward and Densen-Gerber, 1975; Briere, 1984; Silbert and Pines, 1981)

Although the dynamic of stigmatisation can result in the manifestation of a variety effects, in particular the most commonly observed symptoms of low self-esteem and worthlessness, in its severe form it may lead to self-destructive behaviours including self-mutilation and suicide (Bagley and Ramsey, 1986; Briere, 1984; DeYoung, 1982; Herman, 1981).

4. Powerlessness

The dynamic of powerlessness consists of two components; (1) repeated overruling and frustration of desires and wishes, along with reduced sense of efficacy, and (2) the threat of injury and annihilation leading to disempowerment. There are a number of aspects of child sexual abuse that play a central role in the dynamic of powerlessness, not least the repeated and undesired invasion of the body through threat and deceit.

In some instances this may be accompanied by violence, coercion or physical threat which produces the dynamic of 'overwhelming event' seen in the PTSD model. This overwhelming powerlessness may be exaggerated when attempts to terminate the abuse by the child are frustrated. Associated with the dynamic of powerlessness are vulnerability, entrapment, fear and anxiety which may increase as a result of disclosure.

Finkelhor and Browne (1985) propose that there are at least three distinct clusters of effects associated with the dynamic of powerlessness. Fear and anxiety are operant in the first cluster which reflect the inability to control an aversive event which gives rise to nightmares, phobias, hypervigilance, dissociation, somatic complaints, sleep problems and numbing or deadness of affect, all of which have been observed in survivors (Adams-Tucker, 1981; Briere, 1984; Ellenson, 1986; Gelinas, 1983; Goodwin, 1982).

The second cluster of effects result from impaired coping skills which generate a low sense of efficacy, despair, depression, and an inability to protect themselves effectively (DeYoung, 1982; Fromuth, 1986; Herman, 1981; Russell, 1983). The third cluster shows how powerlessness may increase a desire to be powerful in order to compensate for having been powerless. This manifests itself in a desperate need to control or dominate, especially in male survivors (Groth, 1979; Rogers and Terry, 1984), aggressive and delinquent behaviour, or becoming an abuser in adulthood as a way of exerting the power they were denied.

Finkelhor and Browne's Traumagenic Dynamics Model of Child Sexual Abuse (1985) has several advantages. Firstly, the traumagenic dynamics offer an explanation for a much wider and more embracing range of reported symptoms. As such the model includes many of the observed symptoms subsumed under the PTSD formulation, but also includes a wider variety of symptoms which cannot be explained by PTSD.

Secondly, the model proposes that the impact of trauma is related to the extent to which any one of the four dynamics are present, and how they might work in conjunction. This enables the explication of similar effects but with different manifestations. The advantage of this lies in treatment which can be modified depending on whether the symptoms of depression are stigma related, or powerlessness related.

Thirdly, the model conceptualises child sexual abuse more accurately as a process, not simply an event, as in the PTSD formulation. This allows different parts of the process to contribute to a different traumagenic dynamic, and for these to operate before, during and after the sexual activity. Thus, it takes into account the child's life prior to the abuse experience which may have made it vulnerable to sexual abuse, such as elements of betrayal or unstable family relationships. These pre-abuse experiences may compound or ameliorate the operant traumagenic dynamic, to influence the impact of the abuse and post-abuse experiences, and presenting symptoms.

A fourth major advantage of the traumagenic dynamic model is that it allows for variation and individual differences in the manifest effects of child sexual abuse. In the absence of a traumagenic dynamic it is expected that there would be an absence of its associated effects. Thus, one survivor may have experienced a high degree of sexual traumatisation, especially if her body responded to the sexual contact, whereas another survivor may have experienced overwhelming powerlessness, especially if the abuse was accompanied with physical violence and beatings.

The Traumagenic Dynamics Model of Child sexual abuse is able to explain more specifically than any other formulations to date not only the full range of symptomatology observed in survivors of child sexual abuse, but also the dynamics of child sexual abuse and the differential traumatic effects this has on survivors. It is also able to account for why some survivors manifest certain symptoms, while others do not, and also why for some the adverse effects are minimal, while in others they are chronic or acute. This has important implications for treatment in underscoring the need to individualise treatment to each survivor rather than adopt a rigid, therapeutic framework or model.

Finkelhor and Browne (1985) have presented us with a highly workable model of the dynamics and impact of child sexual abuse, which best explains differential effects found among survivors. The model has not been presented as a rigid framework, to be adopted uncritically, but rather encourages rigorous empirical testing which can only enhance our as yet still limited understanding of child sexual abuse, its long term effects, the dynamics which activate these effects, its impact on survivors, and effective treatment models and techniques.

CHAPTER 5

Fact or Fantasy: Making Sense of False Memory Syndrome

The question of how accurate memory really is has perplexed researchers, clinicians, and therapists for the last 100 years, ever since Sigmund Freud reconstructed the experiences and testimony of his patients who claimed to have been sexually seduced in childhood. Rather than seeing these patients as having been innocent victims of their parents' sexual desires, he relegated their memories to the realm of fantasy and designated them incestuous desires on the part of the child. Thus, parents and adults became the blameless victims of the infant's sexual lust. Arguably, in doubting his patients' disclosures, Freud considered their reported memories to be false.

Over the last century the authenticity of memory has dominated psychotherapeutic thought to varying degrees. Most recently it has been resurrected on an international scale. The outcome of this renewed focus on the accuracy of memory has culminated in a specious new medical diagnosis based ostensibly on sound, empirical scientifc research, namely that of False Memory Syndrome (FMS). This new debate threatens to divide both academics and clinicians, and will undoubtedly detract from, and distort, the reality of childhood sexual abuse.

The diagnosis of FMS is being paraded as an indisputable, psychiatrically validated diagnostic syndrome of mental disorder with a distinct set of observable signs and symptoms, which, as a result of mammoth media attention, is filtering into public awareness as fact. In reality, no impartial body of psychologists or psychiatrists have yet been able to substantiate the validity of FMS, or verify the associated symptomatology, to warrant inclusion in either the Diagnostic and Statistical Manual of Mental Disorders-III-R (DSM-III-R) or any other professional manual for mental disorders.

Supporters of FMS postulate that a person, usually female, may recall or, more often, be persuaded by exploitative and dangerous therapists to recall memories of childhood sexual abuse decades after the supposed incident(s) took place. These memories, although having been repressed for decades, are accepted by the adult victim and her therapist to be accurate and authentic recollections of childhood experiences. FMS challenges the validity of these memories by adhering to an underlying assumption that, in the majority of cases involving delayed recall of memories of childhood sexual abuse, the recovered memories are in fact false.

What particularly concerns proponents of FMS is that, as these memories are usually only recalled during the process of therapy, therapists must be implanting these memories into their clients' minds for their own gratification or needs. Futhermore, they argue that the resulting false accusations against parents causes irrevocable distress and damage, and are specifically designed to destroy and undermine the very fabric of family life and family values.

Needless to say, the existence of FMS has generated considerable controversy and division not only among clinicians, but also psychologists, memory researchers, the legal profession, as well as the general public. These divisions have created factions, each of which hold deeply entrenched views, which are subsequently reflected in the growing media attention. Childhood sexual abuse has now become part of 'talk show' culture, with very public, often televised disclosures and accusations, particularly in the USA, where it has been implicated in a number of high profile celebrity disclosures, most notably Roseanne Arnold.

This extreme polarisation among academics and researchers can be seen in the literature on FMS. Both factions cling to their own perspective, with very little objectivity or acknowledgement of impartiality. For the therapist or counsellor attempting to sift fact from fiction, in order to enhance clinical practice, this can prove to be a confusing and confounding task. Yet, in order fully to understand memory and memory processing, it is essential that the therapist be apprised of current scientific evidence in an accurate and neutral way, through objective research, rather than being presented with an array of beliefs and perceptions that have been contaminated by personal biases or hidden agendas.

Therapists and counsellors need to know whether FMS really exists, how it is manifested, what are the observable signs and symptoms, and how it can be verified, to enable them to be most efficacious in their therapeutic practice. In the absence of such data, biases may occur which could contaminate the therapeutic process, thereby potentially invalidating the client's experiences, and impeding a full exploration of the meaning these memories have for them, whether recall is delayed or not.

Invariably, the evidence for FMS is purported to be objective and without bias, and is often presented within a scientific, empirical framework by highly respected academics. On the surface the facts supporting FMS seem highly plausible, almost seductively so, yet in evaluating the literature on FMS it becomes clear that its propositions are often based on anecdotal reports rather than scientific evidence. More disturbing is the way in which conclusions in memory research have been distorted to fit somewhat simplistic beliefs about memory functioning, particularly when extrapolating data from one phenomenon or subject population and applying it without discretion to subjects different from those originally studied.

A clear analysis of the literature surrounding FMS and memory functioning reveals how little is known about memory disruption, especially its sequale in early childhood trauma. Further objective research on traumatic forgetting and functional amnesia following any trauma, not just childhood sexual abuse, may illuminate some of the processes involved in forgetting and delayed recall. Similarly, future research into the probability of suggesting whole memory sequences spanning several years, rather than just a single event, may clarify whether therapists really can implant sexual abuse histories into their clients' minds.

To facilitate greater clarity of the issues involved in FMS it is necessary to look at the rise of the FMS movement and the basic tenets upon which it has been conceptualised. Following from this it is important to evaluate current scientific research and under-standing of memory and the processes and mechanisms involved in forgetting, particu-larly in relation to early childhood trauma. A further consideration is the implication of FMS in clinical practice and a need to ensure that false memories do not become an iatrogenic artifact of therapy. Finally, it is also essential to analyse the impact of FMS on a cultural level whereby it can be seen to permit society's collusion in the denial of childhood sexual abuse.

The Development of False Memory Syndrome

The invention of the term False Memory Syndrome has been largely credited to Ralph Underwager, Ph.D, who together with Pamela Freyd, co-founded the False Memory Syndrome Foundation, Inc (FMSF) in March 1992 '... to aid victims, both primary and secondary, of False Memory Syndrome; to seek reasons for the spread of the False Memory Syndrome; and to work for the prevention of new cases of False Memory Syndrome' (1992). In reality, the FMSF is an advocacy group for parents who claim to have been falsely accused of childhood sexual abuse by their adult children. Indeed, Pamela Freyd is just such a parent whose adult daughter, Jennifer, claims that her father Peter sexually abused her in childhood.

In contrast, Ralph Underwager's interest in co-founding the FMSF has rather more sinister connotations. A former Lutheran pastor, psychologist and co-author of *Accusations of Child Sexual Abuse*, who has testified as an expert witness in over 200 sexual abuse trials, Underwager has frequently been criticised for his lack of impartiality in abandoning objective, scientific criteria in his testimony which is invariably in favour of the defendant. More disturbingly, Underwager has clearly stated that he is permissive of, and indeed an advocate of paedophilia.

In an interview with the *Dutch Journal of Paedophilia, Paidika*, Underwager clearly states that paedophilia is a responsible choice for an individual and that '... paedophilia is an acceptable expression of God's will for love and unity' (*Paidika*, 1993). Since giving this interview there has been much pressure on Underwager to resign from the FMSF

Scientific Advisory Board, to which he has now acquiesced, although his wife still remains an active member.

To date the FMSF represent over 7500 families in the USA alone who claim they are innocent victims of the sexual abuse industry, while in Britain the British False Memory Society (BFMS), which incorporates the helpline Adult Children Accusing Parents (ACAP), are currently involved with over 400 families. While these organisations gather copious data on denials of sexual abuse charges made by parents, they have no way of knowing, or indeed establishing the truth or falsity of any reports they receive. In fact, as David Calof points out, the FMSF '... proceeds a priori from the assumption that the disputed memories are false' (Calof, 1993).

Both the FMSF and BFMS assert that memories of childhood sexual abuse have reached epidemic proportions which threaten to destroy thousands of families. Although they acknowledge that some child sexual abuse accusations are true, they imply that the majority are false, due to FMS. To substantiate these claims of false memory, they cite two main factors that contribute to this percieved epidemic. One is inferior science and the other is disreputable therapy. Both of these assertions have been used to discredit those individuals who believe they were sexually abused in childhood and to undermine the process of psychotherapy and therapists in general, and therefore deserve closer scrutiny.

Inferior Science as a Factor in False Memory Syndrome

The premis of inferior science in FMS is based primarily on the lack of scientific evidence to support the notion of repression, in which a traumatic event or experience is banished from consciousness but can be regained decades later. Proponents of FMS also believe that as memory is not objective but subjective it is therefore liable to gross inaccuracies and inauthentic recollections. Furthermore, it is the malleability of memory that makes it susceptible to reconstruction, fabrication, confabulation and leaves it vulnerable to persuasion and suggestion.

In addition, it is argued by supporters of FMS that, as many clinicians and therapists are not trained in the scientific nature of memory and memory processes, they have an inferior knowledge of memory mechanisms. Often their understanding of memory is seen as dangerously limited in being influenced by outdated concepts, such as repression, which lack any scientific corroboration and yet are adopted as part of mainstream clinical practice. This is also thought to apply to clinicians' beliefs, attitudes and understanding of hypnosis and the accuracy of recovered memories when using this technique, which according to Yapko contain many misconceptions (Yapko, 1994).

Advocates of FMS believe that as there is no concrete scientific evidence for the concept of traumatic forgetting, that the delayed recall of previously buried memories decades later is highly suspect and is therefore automatically relegated to the realm of fantasy and fiction, rather than representative of any truth or fact. They contend that

'... most severe traumas are not blocked out by children but remembered only too well' (McHugh, 1993), and that as '... no-one has ever shown that the memory of repeated abuses can be uncontrollably and completely stripped from a persons consciousness...' (Ofshe, 1993) the concept of traumatic forgetting is both fallacious and an iatrogenic artifact of clinicial intervention.

Clinicans, especially those who work with recovered memories, are therefore seen as scientifically illiterate and unqualified to verify the authenticity of any regained memories. They are also seen to use spurious and unscientific methods to aid memory retrieval such as age regression, hypnosis and sodium amytal (a truth serum), all of which are thought to promote the confabulationf extremely graphic and vivid memories, which in turn become deeply entrenched and rooted in the patient's mind, enhancing their veracity as indisputable fact.

To substantiate these claims, the FMS literature rejects the notion of repression and repressed memories due to lack of scientific evidence, and cites numerous studies which purport to show the subjectivity and inaccuracy of memory, and how easily pseudomemories can be implanted. Presenting this research is thought to be sufficient scientific evidence to invalidate delayed recall of childhood sexual abuse. However, closer analysis of the data reveals that, while the research literature demonstrates the presence of such memory mechanisms, it is certainly not conclusive evidence for the existence of FMS.

Arguably, most academics and clinicians acknowledge that memory is not objective but reconstructive. Memory is not like a camera or videotape, which preserves an exact and pristine replica of past experiences. Rather it is subjective and reconstructive with the capacity for many inaccuracies and distortions, especially in the recollection of specific details. The question, however, remains whether despite these distortions and inaccuracies for detail, memory still contains essential truths.

In the last two decades there has been considerable research which testifies to the inaccuracy of memory. The majority of these studies have used eye witness accounts of crimes or accidents to demonstrate the extent to which inaccuracies can occur. However, inaccuracies of memory in these studies cluster primarily around specific details of the observed event, such as the type and colour of a car, and the speed it was travelling, rather than distortions in whether the actual event took place.

Similarly, research on flashbulb memories also provide evidence for the inaccuracy of memory surrounding key events. For example, Neisser and Harsch (1992) have shown that while many people had inaccurate recall of what they were doing at the time President Kennedy was shot, or how they heard about the Challenger disaster, all of them nevertheless remembered that the President was shot, and that Challenger had crashed and that all the astronauts died.

An interesting finding has been that when individuals are personally involved in a disaster, such as the San Fransisco earthquake, they have almost perfect recall compared to those who only heard about it or experienced it vicariously. This has led some memory researchers to acknowledge '... that aspects of traumatic experiences do apparently persist quite accurately whereas others get altered along the way' (Loftus and Kaufmann, 1992). This finding has been supported by studies that have looked at children's recollections of witnessing the murder and death of one of their parents, ostensibly providing further evidence that severe traumas are not blocked out by children (McHugh, 1993).

These findings certainly raise doubts about whether traumatic memories are re-pressed, and by extension questions the existence of repression as a mechanism in memory, without actually defining the use of the term 'repression'. Richard Ofshe, a leading proponent of FMS contends that 'sixty years of experiments have failed to produce any empirical evidence that repression exists' (Ofshe, 1993). This is further underscored by Underwager's claim that 'repression is a concept devoid of scientific corroboration'. (Underwager, 1993).

As there is no scientific evidence, or laboratory data to demonstrate repression, an assumption is then made that there is no possible mechanism for traumatic forgetting, leading to such fallacious conclusions that the concept of traumatic forgetting must therefore be an invention by therapists to support their non-scientific and sciolistic beliefs. Such assumptions inform the type of rigid thinking displayed by many proponents of FMS that '... there is no room for a middle ground... (and that) the mind either functions in a way therapy demands or it does not... The techniques either uncover repressed memories or they create pseudomemories' (Ofshe and Waters, 1993).

Such rigid views have been challenged by other researchers, most notably Van der Kolk who argues that 'traumatised people do not "repress" in the classic psychoanalytic way, which refers to motivated "forgetting" of memories that evoke unpleasant internal (intrapsychic) conflicts. During trauma, the feelings of what is happening is so terrible and unacceptable that they are blocked off from the logical, sensible conscious self and assigned into a limbo self...' (Van der Kolk, 1993) which can emerge at a later time especially when in the presence of high arousal, or when in an environment in which it is safe to explore past experiences.

This would suggest that when looking at repression or traumatic forgetting the focus should not be entirely on retrieval mechanisms but should include possible disruption at all the stages of information processing involved in memory such as attention, encoding, and storage as well as retrieval. Any disruption at these varying stages of processing may not necessarily be entirely the result of impaired psychological functioning, but may also contain some proportion of disruption attributable to physiological or biological factors.

Arguably, information received for processing when the organism is in a state of severe psychological and physiological distress accompanied by high arousal may be processed differently from information received when in a relatively relaxed state of physiological arousal. Further research on the impact of physiological arousal in information processing and memory storage may prove to be illuminating in clarifying which mechanisms, if any, can become impaired and how they might account for traumatic forgetting not purely as a psychological, defensive mechanism but also due to physiological factors.

While the majority of researchers do not dispute the lack of scientific corroboration for repression, especially in its original Freudian sense of intentionality, most do acknowledge the existence of 'motivation-driven memory failure' (Olio and Cornell, 1993). This concept allows for a variety of memory retrieval failures, such as denial, dissociation and functional amnesia that can result in forgetting. What is also undeniable is the existence of such memory mechanisms as delayed recall and amnesia.

Indeed, one of the leading proponents of FMS appears to contradict himself when he acknowledges that people '... may have selective traumatic amnesia, if the terror of an experience is so great that the normal biological process underlying information storage is disrupted...' (Ofshe, 1993). It is perhaps significant that Ofshe limits himself to specific examples, such as alcohol induced blackouts, rather than seeing repeated sexual brutalisations in childhood as terrifying enough to warrant a disruption of normal biological processes.

Research on Traumatic Forgetting

There is a vast body of literature that demonstrates the long lasting psychological and emotional effects as a result of traumatic experiences, ranging from physical abuse, domestic and criminal violence to war traumas, which can result in complete or partical amnesia as well as other disturbances of memory. Thus, despite weak experimental data on repression there is considerable empirical evidence on traumatic forgetting, particularly following exposure to shocking and horrifying events such as public disasters, the traumatic experiences inherent in wars, as well as the incarceration in concentration camps (Bettelheim, 19). These memory disturbances are well documented and have sufficient validity to warrant inclusion in DSM-III-R (1987) under the category of Post-Traumatic Stress Disorder (PTSD).

The observed symptoms of PTSD share many commonalities with symptoms experienced by those individuals with a history of childhood sexual abuse, with or without memories. The similarities cluster around memory disturbances such as dissociation and partial denial, particularly in minimising the effects of the trauma, post-traumatic flashbacks, sleep disturbances such as nightmares and sleep walking, disturbances of mood along with feelings of numbness, emptiness and unreality, with most individuals not knowing why they felt that way.

It has been suggested by a number of researchers that during trauma victims numb their body and disconnect from the impact of their experience, thereby creating emotional numbness and fragmentation of the self, allowing them to dissociate from the experience by activating such defensive mechanisms as psychogenic amnesia or traumatic forgetting (Kluft, 1985; Eth and Pynoos, 1985; Gil, 1988; Fraser, 1987). More recently it has been suggested that these effects are exacerbated when the traumatic experience is most severe, when it is hidden or denied, is met with silence or indifference, or when there is further assault or abuse, as is invariably the case in childhood sexual trauma (Olio and Cornell, 1993; Orbach, 1994).

However, if the traumatic experience is acknowledged and talked about in an open, supportive environment this may have ameliorating effects. This could account for McHugh's findings that children who observed one of their parents being murdered demonstrated no impaired recall of events (McHugh, 1993). Arguably, such children would have been encouraged to talk about their experience, their thoughts, feelings and have constructed meaning in a safe, supportive environment, something that is all too often denied to children who are being sexually absued.

That traumatic forgetting is implicated in cases of childhood sexual abuse has been demonstrated by a number of studies, suggesting that between 18% and 59% of sexual abuse victims 'forget' memories of these experiences for a period of time. As early as 1987 Herman and Schatzow found that out of 53 adult survivors in group therapy, 64% reported some degree of amnesia, either total or partial, and experienced delayed recall. More important, 75% of these women were later able to obtain corroborating evidence for their sexual abuse experiences.

More recent studies support these findings. Williams and Finkelhor in 1992 found that out of 100 women who were interviewed retrospectively, 38% were amnestic about their abuse experiences, despite clear documentation of a history of sexual abuse filed 17 years earlier. Fullilove (1993) found that 18% of women reporting a history of sexual abuse had forgotten the abuse for a period of time, while Briere and Conte (1994) found that out of 450 adult survivors, considerably more than half, 59%, reported some period of not remembering the abuse.

One of the most conclusive studies, conducted in 1992, found that out of 200 women who had been treated in hospital 20 years earlier for child sexual abuse, one in three did not recall their sexual abuse experiences, despite indisputable, corroborating evidence such as hospital files. In combination, the studies cited above present considerable evidence that traumatic forgetting, or psychogenic amnesia is often a factor in childhood sexual abuse and that recovered memories are neither false or necessarily pseudomemories implanted by exploitative or persuasive therapists.

Research on Pseudomemories

Proponents of FMS often cite the research literature on pseudomemories to substantiate their claim that, due to the malleability of memory, it is possible to implant false memories in an individual's mind. Overall, the evidence obtained through studies on pseudomemory demonstrates that it is certainly possible deliberately to implant an unhappy childhood false memory into experimental subjects (Loftus, 1992). However, the pseudomemories that have invariably been implanted tend to focus on generic memories of a single event such as being lost in a shopping centre, or being woken up in the middle of the night, which is vastly different from being sexually abused.

Closer analysis of studies on pseudomemories highlight a number of fundamental differences between experimental paradigms conducted in a laboratory setting and the reality of child sexual abuse. First, the evidence demonstrates that a false memory of a single event can be implanted but does not provide evidence that a whole memory sequence of events and experiences, including repeated brutalisations, can be implanted. Second, the implanting of such a childhood false memory may be more susceptible to further confabulation by the adult in trying to integrate it into existing schemas. Lastly, it is manifestly ridiculous to compare being lost in a shopping precinct with being sexually abused, raped or beaten in childhood. These experiences are too fundamentally different to allow for any reasonable comparison to be made.

A further limitation to these studies is that they do not provide any evidence that it is possible to implant a history of childhood sexual abuse in a person who was not abused in childhood, and as such does not provide any real evidence of FMS. More important, while studies on pseudomemories quite clearly demonstrate the presence of a mechanism by which a false memory could be implanted, it nevertheless does not prove that recovered memories are false. The existence of such a mechanism merely indicates that some have the potential to be false.

Alternative Explanations for Traumatic Forgetting and Delayed Recall

Arguably, the impact of physiology on memory loss and recall are only beginning to be understood and as such necessitates more detailed research. Most researchers do, however, agree that memories are stored as electrical patterns in neurons in the brain and that over time these patterns are translated into new neural circuitry in different brain areas, creating a record of events. However it is argued that in the presence of an intensely traumatic event in which there is high physiological and emotional arousal, the trauma becomes encoded into memory in fragments. As a result of increased physiological arousal and an upsurge of adrenaline, the neurophsyiological processes in memory functioning may become disrupted to the extent that cognitive memory may become severed from the emotions being experienced (Van der Kolk, 1993).

Van der Kolk further argues that in the case of severe and chronic childhood trauma the neurobiology of memory functioning, especially in relation to the limbic system which filters and integrates emotion, sensation, experience and memory, may become permanently damaged, preventing the integration of cognitive memory and emotional arousal. As Van der Kolk states the 'brain is so overwhelmed so many times by negative stimulation and arousal that it cannot accomodate and integrate all the information. This helps explain the phenomena of flashbacks and body memories in the absence of conscious recollections.' (Van der Kolk,199).

As a result of disrupted integration and storage, the emotional sensations may be remembered differently on a non-verbal level either as visual images in the case of flashbacks and nightmares or as bodily sensations. In subsequent states of high arousal these sensations and images may be triggered with no conscious experience or memory behind them, but with, nevertheless, the same intensity of feelings of fear and terror as when it was first experienced.

It is possible that the greater fragmentation observed in survivors who experienced a very early onset of abuse is due to the lack of integration of cognition and emotion for the above reasons, but can also be seen as a function of the child's developmentally limited cognitive capacity, whose unsophisticated and simplistic schemas are as yet unable to make sense or extract a full range of meaning from the experience. Proponents of FMS often cite experimental data that shows that most people do not recollect childhood experiences below the age of three or four, and therefore automatically dispute individual claims of recovered memories of abuse prior to the age of three. It may be that due to limited cognitive functioning there is no conscious recollection as the child was unable to make sense of the experience, but there are memory traces of the emotional trauma and arousal.

This view is supported by Daignault who proposes that young children '... lack the perspective to place the trauma in the overall course of life events' (Daignault, 1993). Making sense of the abuse is made even more difficult when the abuser is in a position of power and is highly valued. Again, further research may illuminate this point and clarify the validity of traumatic memories experienced in very early childhood.

Another explanation that sheds some light on the pertinence of memory disturbances and traumatic forgetting of memories as a result of childhood sexual abuse is the secrecy and betrayal which surround the abuse experiences. As a result of the secrecy surrounding the sexual abuse, it cannot be discussed or acknowledged and so therefore cannot be fully processed.

As Neisser points out 'To fix a childhood memory so that it is lasts into adulthood requires shaping that event into a story and then rehearsing the narrative, telling the tale. Yet in cases of childhood sexual abuse the events and experiences are rarely confronted, shared, ratified, even adequately described' (Neisser, 1993). Thus it is not surprising that as a result of not being able to process the traumatic experiences the child begins to split off such memories and is denied access to them.

What emerges when evaluating the evidence both in the FMS literature and in wider academic research is that memory functioning is complex and the processes of forgetting are to date little understood. Arguably, given our relatively primitive understanding of all the processes involved in memory encoding, storage and retrieval it is somewhat premature to argue that there is conclusive evidence for the existence of FMS in victims of childhood sexual abuse, or indeed to reject the possibility of such mechanisms as traumatic forgetting.

The research on memory functioning has provided us with evidence of some mechanisms that may be implicated in FMS but it does not establish the existence of the syndrome. Alternative explanations for memory disturbances as a result of childhood sexual abuse are equally valid. What is clear is that future research on memory functioning can only benefit all researchers and clinicians in providing greater clarity and under-standing, so that the existing polarisations can be lessened. What is needed is healthy discourse and a pooling of objective scientific data, not a manipulation of the evidence to suit one particular doctrine.

Finally, it is important to acknowledge that even emotionally healthy people have difficulty in remembering the details of benign or neutral events. This would suggest that the whole debate about the accuracy of memories should not be focused in the highly emotional arena of child sexual abuse but addressed in the much broader context of memory research, to include both clinical and non-clinical populations. This could diminish the pejorative nature of current investigations into the authenticity of abuse-related memories in which victims and survivors are often disbelieved and their experiences invalidated primarily because of their abuse history.

Disreputable Therapy as a Factor in False Memory Syndrome

In questioning the veracity of delayed memories of childhood sexual abuse advocates of FMS have implicated the psychotherapeutic process, in particular techniques used in recovered memory therapies, including the use of hypnosis, as crucial in the creation of false memories. They claim that these memories are fictitious and that they have somehow been implanted into the naive and unsuspecting client's mind by exploitative, manipulative, ill-informed and greedy therapists. In fact, Richard Ofshe, a leading advocate of FMS argues that recoverd memory therapy is one of this '... century's most intriguing quackeries (which) no human society since the dawn of time has ever recorded except a bunch of wacked out psychologists in America' (Ofshe, 1993).

The implication is that as childhood sexual abuse is fashionable and big business, therapists can earn more money from their clients if they diagnose a history of child sexual abuse. Thus, according to Barden they can '... turn a $2,000 eating disorder patient into a $200,000 multiple personality disorder'(Horn, 1993). It is further argued that as a result of recovered memory therapy being so lucrative, it has attracted some very poorly trained and ill-informed individuals who claim to be experts in recovering memories of child sexual abuse.

While there is evidence of some individuals purporting to be 'experts' in this field despite very little specific training, often believing that two or three weekend workshops specialising in hypnosis or recovered memory therapy are sufficient in acquiring therapeutic expertise when working with survivors of child sexual abuse, this is not generally reflective of mainstream practice. Such self-styled 'experts' can be potentially dangerous and need to be monitored in their work to protect their clients, and to ensure ethical and professional standards of therapeutic practice.

Indeed, there have been some recently developed offshoots of traditional therapies which claim that the majority of individuals seeking therapy have been sexually abused in childhood, and that child sexual abuse accounts for a variety of mental disorders as well as being implicated in such syndromes as Sudden Infant Death Syndrome, more commonly known as cot death. An example of this is Primal Cause Analysis (PCA) which is practised using an 'altered state of consciousness', ostensibly to bypass the resistances and defences of the conscious mind.

PCA claims that the majority of humanity, throughout history, has been subjected to sexual trauma in infancy. To support this assertion, PCA has uncovered 39 common 'scenes' of child sexual abuse which it is argued will have been experienced to some degree by most individuals. A perusal of the theoretical formulation from which such conclusions are drawn show gross scientific inaccuracies and limited understanding of mental activity, and a distinct lack of good therapeutic practice. Indeed the zealousness of this type of approach and its therapeutic techniques can be potentially very harmful and damaging to clients.

Such therapies can be dangerous and misleading and should be dealt with by regulating bodies whose aim is to maintain good professional standards of therapy. However, it is unjustifiable to assume, as some proponents of FMS do, that because unethical practices and practioners exist, all therapists and clinicians working in the field of child sexual abuse should be undermined and categorised as ill-informed and incompetent.

That some clinicians are ill-informed and suffer from mis-conceptions related to the authenticity of memory was demonstrated by Yapko (1994) who in a survey of 860 psychotherapists in America found that many were ill-informed in their understanding of information processing and memory, and that nearly half harboured gross misconceptions about the clinical utility of hypnosis in providing accurate recall of true events.

Arguably, clinicians need to ensure that they are well informed and that their knowledge base is updated in line with current research data by reading both academic and clinical texts. In addition, good clinical practice demands that individual therapists are aware of their attitudes and beliefs and any concomitant misconceptions they may have through personal therapy, supervision and by referring to current literature to ensure that they do not contaminate the therapeutic process.

One interesting finding in Yapko's survey was that 79% of respondents were aware that false memories could be introduced through hypnosis and integrated with genuine memories by the client (Yapko, 1994). This would suggest some level of awareness about the limitations of the accuracy of memories recalled under hypnosis and the potential for confabulation. Such awareness can only be beneficial in not misleading clients in terms of the authenticity of memories recalled through hypnosis.

Despite such awareness and evidence of good clinical practice, recovered memory therapists are still nevertheless variously described as dangerous, cruel, opportunistic, zealous, arrogant, foolish, paranoid, hysterical, incompetent, simple-minded, foolish yet with great powers of persuasion (Ofshe and Waters, 1993; Gardner, 1992) by many advocates of FMS. They are seen to tamper with the client's memory, by reconstructing their experiences and, through the process of suggestion, implanting whole new memories containing fabricated truths of childhood sexual abuse designed to turn them against their parents and families.

To illustrate this scenario, Ofshe and Waters describe clients as '... blank canvasses on which therapists cain paint...' histories and memories of brutalisations in childhood that never occurred (Ofshe and Waters, 1993). They further argue that therapists expose their clients to 'unrelenting pressure' to uncover repressed memories of these brutalisation and then encourage them to '... insult, revile, defame, humiliate, and sometimes ruin the reputations and lives of their persecutors' (Ofshe and Waters, 1993)

Thus, clients are seen as naive, hysterical, paranoid, delusional (Gardner, 1992), gullible and highly suggestible, whose therapists have been able to implant and inculcate false and fabricated memory sequences of childhood sexual abuse. Overall, this view is demeaning to the clients undergoing therapy and unjustifiably critical of the majority of clinicians who work with survivors of childhood sexual abuse.

It is also inconsistent with the literature on survivors which demonstrates that many clients are highly resistant to persuasion either on a psychological or rational level. In making these propositions, supporters of FMS are demonstrating a level of naivete of survivors' experiences and making a fundamental error in extrapolating from extreme examples of bad therapy and then applying these to all therapy and therapists, thereby implying that such practices and methods are representative of mainstream practice.

Undoubtedly there are some professionals who are overzealous and exploitative but these are the exceptions rather than the rule. Such therapists, rather than helping their clients to understand their emotional and psychological pain, may well have their own hidden agenda. Such therapists may indeed actively pressurise their clients to confront and make public accusations, or seek justice, as a way of assuaging their own anger and rage. Nevertheless, such therapists are not the norm and the majority of therapists are respectful of therapeutic boundaries and do provide a safe and healthy environment for their clients.

Arguably, there are also many therapists who can and do irreparable damage to their clients by denying their memories and experiences of childhood sexual abuse. This is acknowledged by David Calof who points out that 'Many more therapists do bad therapy by denying or minimizing client's experiences' (Calof, 1993). This view is echoed by Susie Orbach who believes that '... a therapist who is not prepared to consider this possiblity (of childhood sexual abuse) is doing their clients or patients a great disservice' (Orbach, 1994).

Further criticism is mounted against therapists in that they are perceived to seek an easy solution for their client's complex range of psychological and emotional distress as a way of increasing the therapist's sense of efficacy and to stave off any feelings of inadequacy in the absence of being able to provide an instant clinical diagnosis. Furthermore, by giving the client a special identity as a 'survivor', with which she can positively identify, they can make the client feel special.

This sense of specialness is thought to be exacerbated when clients read such books as Bass and Davis *The Courage to Heal* (1987) or when they attend survivor groups where peer pressure becomes so great that many supposed survivors try to match others' experiences by internalising them and making them their own.

Some of these assertions contain fundamental misconceptions of the process of therapy and demonstrate a lack of clinical understanding of working with survivors of childhood sexual abuse. First, many clinicians working with survivors of childhood sexual abuse did not deliberately seek to do so but encountered such clients as part of their general therapeutic practice. As one clinician has graphically pointed out, disclosures of childhood sexual abuse are traumatic for the therapist as well as the client, and many therapists would rather not be party to the pain of such excruciating experiences (Calof, 1993).

Furthermore, many survivors are reluctant to tell their story and often doubt and disbelieve themselves and their memories, while many wish they did not have them at all. As Judith Herman has highlighted 'Survivors are frightened, depressed, ashamed and tormented by doubt' (Herman, 1992). More important, instead of feeling special, the majority of survivors feel stigmatised, often reporting that they feel isolated and alienated because of their childhood experiences. Many report that they feel they have the words 'incest survivor' tattooed or emblazoned on their foreheads and that this is a source of shame, not something to embrace or rejoice in.

Another misconception is that memories of childhood sexual abuse often return only during therapy. The clinical literature simply does not support this assertion. Often such memories can, and do return outside of therapy in totally different contexts. Certainly the therapeutic process can facilitate increased access to memories by enabling clients to lower their defences, thus allowing such memories to re-emerge.

Clients need to be able to tolerate the recall of traumatic memories and experiences in order to explore their content and meaning. Such tolerance may only be achieved by some clients in the safety and consistency of a therapeutic relationship (Herman, 1992). However, this is by no means true for all clients, many of whom recall traumatic memories outside of the therapeutic setting.

Equally common is the re-emerging of memories outside of therapy, especially when the individual has lowered her defences, perhaps through illness or hospitalisation. Life events can also trigger previously buried memories. The most frequently cited life events that seem to have an impact on memory recall are sudden loss, or death, a career change or promotion, the start of a new relationship in which there are deep emotional attachments, the birth of child, a child reaching the age at which the abuse started, or revictimisation.

A related false assumption made by proponents of FMS is that it is the simple recall of such memories of childhood sexual abuse that automatically prompts the clinician to diagnose a history of sexual abuse. This is a far too simplistic assumption. Therapists generally do not make a diagnosis on the basis of a single memory. They invariably look at the constellation of symptoms displayed by the client, which include affective fragmentation, flooding, numbness, denial and dissociation as well as memories that may indicate a history of childhood sexual abuse.

Another misconception in the FMS debate is the nature of the therapeutic process. Psychotherapy is not about directing the client prematurely to seek an answer to her difficulties, it is about letting the client tell her story, enabling her to explore the possible meaning behind her feelings, memories and experiences. As such it is a collaborative process with the therapist empowering the client to find her own answers, establish her own meaning and enabling her to find her own solutions. Therapy does not offer a cure, it merely provides a safe environment for the client to make sense of herself and her experiences.

More important, the therapeutic environment is not a place to establish absolute truths. Therapists are not detectives or indeed lawyers who seek evidence of truth and whose aim is to establish the accuracy of every detail related to the client's experiences. Instead, the therapeutic setting offers a private and confidential sanctuary for clients to piece together their childhood experiences and to explore the meaning of these events and the after effects of their experiences.

To illustrate this, one leading clinician argues that a '…therapist's job is not to advocate any one version of reality but to provide a forum where the client can sit with all aspects of their inner conflicts' (Calof, 1993). Indeed, Calof goes so far as to suggest that clients should not be encouraged to seek external validation from the therapist or others, but rather enabled to form their own conclusions. Calof actively discourages the taking of legal action against abusers as he believes it could be a premature staunching of the wounds and concomitant feelings of loss (Calof, 1993).

A fundamental tenet of any therapeutic training and practice is that bad therapeutic practices are irresponsible and unacceptable in any event, and should be addressed by all clinicians, their supervisors and should be monitored and severely dealt with by their respective professional associations, to prevent any further abuse of clients. There is no denying that some therapists do abuse their clients, yet despite evidence of bad clinical practices there is nevertheless still insufficient evidence to suggest that such practices lead to, or indeed cause, FMS.

Indeed, it is still unclear precisely what does cause FMS other than bad therapeutic practice. In evaluating the FMS literature one begins to wonder exactly what the syndrome in FMS really refers to. Is it a syndrome of the patient or the therapist? To date the FMS literature has been unable to present a clear list of observable and distinguishable signs and symptoms representative of FMS to enable the clinician to make an unequivocal diagnosis of FMS. In focusing on bad therapeutic practice, FMS begins to look like a litany of therapists' behaviours, suggesting the presence of a therapist syndrome rather than a syndrome of the patient.

Perhaps the most disquieting feature of FMS is its potential to distract from, and distort the reality and prevalence of childhood sexual abuse. That the prevalence of childhood sexual abuse is unacceptably high has been established not by exploitative therapists and clinicans but through sound, empirical epidemiological research conducted by academics who do not have a vested interest in expoilting clients. To deny its prevalence through a diagnosis of FMS is to deny the reality of those children who are currently being abused, and the damaging effects sexual abuse has not only on the child but also on the adult survivor.

Advocates of FMS claim that the majority of retrospective accusations of child sexual abuse made by adults are false, yet the clinical research literature highlights the fact that false claims and accusations of childhood sexual abuse are relatively rare and figure in only 2% to 8% of reported cases (Herman, 1992). More important, to date there is still not enough evidence to prevent the conclusion that therefore false memories of childhood sexual abuse are equally rare.

In those cases where clients do fabricate false memories of childhood sexual abuse it is not helpful to adopt a pejorative diagnosis of FMS but rather more important to develop an understanding of the client's psychological and emotional pain which prompts them to indulge in such fabrications in order to legitimise their pain (Orbach, 1994). It is only through the demonstration of such an understanding and the exploration of their pain that such clients can be helped in the most optimal way rather than being labelled as frauds.

Implications of False Memory Syndrome on Clinical Practice

As already stated, it is imperative that clinicians monitor their professional conduct in relation to their clients and guard against any contamination of the client's material through misconceived beliefs and attitudes, or personal hidden agendas. It is a fundamental principle of good clinical practice to not lead or direct the client, or to make a premature diagnosis on behalf of the client without exploring the client's experiences and the meaning they have extracted from these experiences.

The focus of the therapeutic process is primarily to explore the full range of the client's feelings, internal as well as external conflicts, thoughts and experiences in a safe environment within which it is possible for the client to make sense of these and to extract her own meaning. As such its aim is not to establish historical truth and the veracity of the actual event, but to explore the client's feelings and the derived meaning attached to these experiences.

To safeguard the therapeutic relationship, and prevent accusations of bad therapeutic practice, it may be useful for clients to be apprised of the fundamental principles of the therapeutic process at the beginning of therapy so that they do not develop unrealistic curative expectations of therapy. Similarly, a discussion about subjective reality and the authenticity of memories may also be usefully explored, not as a way of denying the client's experiences but to validate her subjective perception and concomitant meaning structures.

For those clinicians who use hypnosis it may be necessary to explain its clinical uses as a therapeutic tool, but to caution against any misconceptions about the veracity or historical validity of memories recalled during hypnosis, emphasising that hypnosis is not a literal re-living of a childhood event but a technique which enables the client to access imagery and affect not normally available to the conscious mind. Clinicians need to inform and equip their clients prior to starting the therapeutic process so that they may become empowered in their exploration of their experiences, rather than look for a radical cure outside of themselves.

As clinicians it may not always be possible to distinguish between the authenticity of memories. This is perhaps best left to forensic scientists, or legal professionals. The very nature of the clinical setting relies on subjective, retrospective self report and should be accepted as such. Rather than focusing on the establishment of absolute truths, clinicians may be more effectively employed in enabling clients to explore their own meaning associated with the event, and their subsequent beliefs about feelings and reality.

To facilitate this they need to create a safe environment for the client to explore the full range of experiences rather than isolating only certain abuse related memories and focusing only on their veracity. The difficulty of retrospective self report is that it is almost impossible definitively to establish cause and effect due to the complexities involved in psychological, physical and emotional development. Often pre-trauma and post-trauma experiences also need to be explored by the client to make full sense of her distress.

Clinicians also need to guard against directing clients in terms of retribution or in making public or legal accusations. Clearly such a decision can only ever be taken by the client and should not be directed by the therapist. The therapist may usefully explore the meaning of such retribution, or public accusation with the client and indeed support the client in her decision, but must guard against influencing the client in any way.

Ultimately, while the rise of FMS has many potentially dangerous and negative implications for clients, clinicians and society in general, one potentially positive effect is that it may prompt clinicians to monitor and improve their professional practice in order to guard against precisely those practices that they stand, albeit unjustifiably, accused of by advocates of FMS. The establishment and maintenance of good professional practice is not only essential but also desirable for the benefit of both clients and clinicians. Only such careful monitoring will ensure that there is no validity to these accusations which have become part of a backlash against therapy.

Implications of False Memory Syndrome on Society's Perception of Child Sexual Abuse

Not surprisingly, many supporters of FMS believe that the increased reporting of childhoood sexual abuse derives from a radical feminist agenda that is politically motivated to undermine the whole infrastructure of traditional family values. Thus, according to such writers as Herman and Orbach, FMS is part of a backlash against feminism which as a movement was largely responsible for bringing childhood sexual abuse to the forefront of public awareness.

It has taken many years to get society to acknowledge the existence of child sexual abuse and to establish appropriate resources to help both victims and adult survivors. The danger of accepting FMS is that it gives the whole arena of child sexual abuse a bad name, and in the words of Anthony Clare 'People then think the whole thing is a hoax, that child abuse does not exist and we can relax' (Clare,1994).

The effect of this is that women, men and children will be further discouraged from coming forward and disclosing their abuse for fear of being disbelieved or branded as a fraud. This will effectively relegate child sexual abuse back into the secrecy that it has been fighting to escape, with professionals and society safe in their belief that child sexual abuse does not exist.

Ultimately, the consequence of unequivocal acceptance of FMS is that sexual offenders can continue to commit their crimes in the safety of the knowledge that the likelihood of being found out, or publicly accused is minimised, and that if any disclosures are made they can easily be undermined within the framework of FMS. Delivering children back into the hands of abusers and making them suffer in silence is untenable and a retrogressive step that must be avoided at all costs, even when it is dressed up as science.

CHAPTER 6

Uncovering the Abuse

Many clients enter therapy or seek counselling without being aware that they have had a sexually abusive experience in childhood. It is not uncommon for women who enter therapy because of depression, anxiety, self-destructive behaviour and sexual problems to have no recollection of early sexual assault. Briere and Runtz (1988) found that only 39 per cent of former abuse victims recognised their abuse experience prior to specific and direct questioning about their sexual history. Not only are these women unaware of their experiences but often the therapist or counsellor does not recognise that there is a link between the presenting symptoms and childhood sexual abuse.

As so many survivors are unable to remember their sexual abuse, often through repression and denial, uncovering the abuse can be extremely complex and difficult. Many survivors have been able to dissociate so skilfully from these experiences that, despite being in therapy for many months, sometimes years, neither they nor the therapist is aware that there has been a history of sexual abuse. Yet, for the therapeutic process to proceed, it is crucial to explore the possibility of any experiences of sexual assault in childhood.

To uncover abuse, it is essential that mental health counsellors and clinicians have some knowledge of the nature, impact, incidence and long term psychological effects of child sexual abuse. In addition, they need to be alert to any possible links between presenting symptoms and sexual abuse, along with an awareness of clinically predictive indicators, in order to approach treatment knowledgeably and effectively.

To obtain a comprehensive clinical picture it may be necessary to implement routine questioning of sexual history, including sexually abusive experiences, at intake. It is extremely difficult for the therapist to uncover possible unresolved trauma in the absence of pertinent data. Without information about sexual abuse having occurred in childhood, the therapist may be tempted to focus treatment solely on the presenting symptoms rather than unresolved trauma. Therapy for depression is unlikely to be successful if unresolved past sexual abuse trauma is its root cause.

Counsellors and therapists need to believe in the incidence of child sexual abuse and acknowledge the often adverse and negative long term psychological effects since 'recognition of sexual abuse... is entirely dependent on the individual's inherent willingness to entertain the possibility that the condition may exist' (Sgroi, 1975). Recognition of sexual abuse is particularly difficult for those survivors who have no memory of the abuse, but it can also present problems for some mental health workers.

Some counsellors and therapists may find it difficult to entertain the notion that sexual abuse may have occurred, especially if they themselves have unresolved feelings and attitudes towards their own sexuality and sexual experiences. Before attempting to counsel adult survivors of sexual abuse it is imperative that the counsellor explore his or her own attitudes towards sexuality and child sexual abuse.

An awareness of the nature and incidence of child sexual abuse, along with a willingness to entertain the possibility of its occurrence, provides the basis from which to identify adult survivors of child sexual assault. In order to uncover the abuse, mental health counsellors and therapists also need to acquaint themselves with the type of presenting problems that might indicate such experiences to allow them to develop a frame of reference from which therapy can proceed.

The linking of presenting symptoms to a history of incest or sexual assault facilitates the exploration of these experiences and their effect on current behaviour by cutting through defence and denial. For this reason therapy should not be confined to symptom relief modalities but should encompass a full exploration of the core experiences which have given rise to the presenting psychological symptomatology.

Identifying survivors of child sexual assault

Faria and Belohlavek (1984) classify female adult survivors into two major groups: those who seek treatment and those who do not. Of those that do not seek treatment they suggest that the incest experience presents no overt problems, or that they are reluctant to seek treatment because of feelings of shame and isolation.

Those women who do seek treatment are further classified into three sub-groups. The first sub-group consists of those women who actively enter therapy because of a history of incest of which they are fully aware. Faria and Belohlavek suggest that the proportion of women who fall into this sub-group is probably only minimal when compared to the other two sub-groups. Arguably, increased media coverage and publicised knowledge of incest and child sexual assault could alleviate the feelings of shame and isolation which may have prevented these women from seeking counselling in the past, thereby prompting more survivors to seek help.

The second, and possibly the largest sub-group, is made up of women who are aware of their sexual assault experience but who seek treatment for entirely different presenting symptoms. Often these women, although aware of their sexual history, do not actually disclose their experiences to the therapist either through shame and guilt, or because they are unable to see any connection between their symptoms and their abuse.

Many survivors are reluctant to volunteer information about their abuse and conse-quently find it difficult and painful to disclose their experiences unless specifically asked about their childhood sexual experiences by the therapist. Initially, questioning should be open-ended with the therapist exercising a high degree of sensitivity in noting all responses, verbal and non-verbal, made by the woman. Providing this is not too stressful for the client, questioning can then proceed to more specific details such as age at which abuse occurred, name of the abuser and the nature and frequency of the abuse. A survivor will respond more positively and volunteer more information as a result of gentle questioning such as 'Was there ever any unwanted or confusing touch that happened between family members?' than if the therapist poses such a forthright question as 'Are you an incest victim?'.

The therapist may need to persevere with this type of questioning over time and should not be afraid to return to the subject. It necessitates a tremendous amount of patience and gentle but firm digging to peel off the layers of defence and denial until the survivor can acknowledge her abuse. As one survivor illustrates:

> 'I had been in individual counselling for one and a half years. Incest never came up during that time. I was having problems with my social life and relating with other people – and we could never figure out why that was. My therapist had asked me early in therapy if I had been molested. Her question wasn't something I paid any attention to at all – it didn't ring any bells. She asked me again after a year and a half of therapy, and my initial reaction again was no, I hadn't been molested. She said she was concerned because a lot of the problems I was having reminded her of the constellation of problems experienced by adults who've been sexually abused as children. The question still troubled me, and that next week I started remembering some stuff with my dad that I had remembered but then thought about in a different way. I said to myself, maybe that stuff he did wasn't quite right, and began dealing with it in therapy from then on. I had no category for sex as a kid so I never filed it as sexual abuse in my mind.' (Maltz and Holman, 1987)

The third and final sub-group consists of survivors who have totally dissociated from their incest experience by repressing all memories pertaining to their abuse (see Chapter 5). Clinical observations and reports cite dissociation as being extremely common among adult survivors of child sexual abuse with some clinicians postulating that as many as 50 per cent of all survivors of child sexual assault are unable to remember their experiences (Maltz and Holman, 1987). Further confirmation is provided by Herman and Schactow's (1986) finding that 62 per cent of adults in an incest survivors group had previously 'forgotten' all or most of their childhood sexual abuse.

Many of the women who have dissociated from their sexual abuse experiences are totally unaware of any history of sexual assault. Rosenfield (1979) found that 33 per cent of all psychiatric patients in his sample who were referred for treatment were survivors of child sexual abuse but were unable to remember that they had in fact been abused. Given their dissociative state, these women are extremely difficult to identify and may be overlooked unless the therapist is alert to possible indicators and is willing and able to explore these with the client.

Possible indicators of history of child sexual assault

Adult survivors of child sexual assault share some common characteristics despite disparate presenting symptoms in the clinical setting. A history of impaired mental health or psychiatric hospitalisation, especially with uncertain diagnosis, is a strong indicator of a history of child sexual assault.

Gail

Gail had been sexually abused from the age of two by her father. She was first admitted into a psychiatric hospital at the age of 15 and was re-admitted and released on a regular basis over the following year. She was extremely uncommunicative and displayed an array of self destructive behaviours including strong suicidal ideation which led to several suicide attempts. Her extremely withdrawn state led to a putative diagnosis of mild schizophrenia. Whenever she was due to be released from hospital she ran away to avoid returning home. When delivered to her home she made attempts on her life to ensure that she would be re-admitted. At the age of 20 she was again hospitalised for a period of time, with a diagnosis of personality disorder. Although on this occasion she attempted to reveal that she had been sexually abused as a child by her father the clinician did not explore this further. Since her release she has had periods of seeking therapeutic help for her presenting symptoms of lack of self confidence and conflict in her interpersonal relationships, in particular with her parents.

In line with the observed long-term psychological effects (discussed in Chapter 3) other common presenting symptoms centre around lack of self-esteem (Courtois, 1979; Herman, 1981), overwhelming feelings of guilt, anxiety, and depression. The depressive symptoms can be severe enough to be accompanied by suicidal ideation which may lead to actual suicide attempts. The research literature attests to the frequency of suicidal attempts by survivors with Briere (1984) reporting that 51 per cent of his sample had a history of attempted suicide while Herman (1981) observed that 37 per cent of survivors of father–daughter incest exhibited such behaviours.

Other self destructive behaviours may also be evident, in particular alcohol and substance abuse. One study conducted in a New York city drug treatment centre found that 44 per cent of all female addicts in the programme had been victims of incest (Benward and Denson-Gerber, 1975). Herman (1981) reports that 35 per cent of her sample of 40 survivors of father–daughter incest had been involved in alcohol or drug abuse, while Muldoon (1978) reports as many as 65 per cent. When alcohol and drug abuse is considered separately, Briere (1984) found that 27 per cent of his sample had a history of alcohol abuse while 21 per cent suffered from drug addiction.

Self-abusing behaviours such as eating disorders (in particular anorexia nervosa and bulimia) are also extremely common among adult survivors of child sexual abuse (Calam and Slade, 1986) as is a history of self-mutilatory behaviours. When these behaviour patterns are manifest, in particular substance abuse, it is crucial that treatment is combined with an attempt to reduce the addictive behaviour. This may necessitate the survivor being persuaded to attend regular meetings of Alcoholics Anonymous in the case of alcohol abuse, or to enrol in a drug treatment programme.

In the case of suicidal ideation it is imperative that the counsellor concentrates on the extent of this ideation and the likelihood of the woman making an attempt on her life. If the counsellor or therapist feels unable to control suicidal tendencies then it is essential to refer the client to another agency more able to help or indeed prevent the realisation of suicidal fantasies. It is inadvisable to proceed with the resolution of sexual abuse trauma without first stabilising overt suicidal ideation. The therapeutic resolution of sexual abuse trauma can generate powerful feelings of anxiety, depression, guilt, and fear which may be counterproductive for those women who are already extremely vulnerable.

A history of sexual problems may also indicate incestuous experiences. Some women report that they are non-orgasmic, but more frequently the manifest problems revolve around inhibited arousal and lack of enjoyment of any sexual or physical contact. Many survivors present phobic reactions to physical intimacy of any kind and are unable to separate sex from affection. To this effect they equate affection with sex and believe that any affectionate act is motivated by sexual desire. Alternatively, many survivors believe that in order to receive affection they need to offer themselves sexually.

Some survivors thus engage in indiscriminate and often inappropriate sexual activity, in which they seek control. This may result in a high degree of promiscuity, and by extension lead to prostitution. A significant association between child sexual abuse and prostitution has been reported by a number of researchers (James and Meyerding, 1977; Silbert and Pines, 1983) with one study reporting that 75 per cent of prostitutes interviewed had been incestuously assaulted (cited in Faria and Belohlavek, 1984).

An array of physical complaints are also thought to be associated with child sexual assault. These include severe headaches, stomach ailments, skin disorders, back aches and other psychosomatic pains. In addition, interpersonal problems are strikingly common, in particular unsatisfactory relationships, fear of intimacy, feelings of isolation and being different, and an inability to trust others or to show affection. Associated with this is the stigmatisation of victim behaviours which may result in a vulnerability to revictimisation in later life, and the formation of abusive relationships in which the woman is unable to defend herself appropriately (Russell, 1984; Briere, 1984).

Phyllis

Phyllis, 56, who had been sexually assaulted by her father throughout her life until he died when she was 53, thought that she would escape his unwanted attentions by marrying young. She married when still in her teens and produced seven children in quick succession. Throughout her marriage, her husband was extremely violent, subjecting her to frequent severe and brutal beatings. Her father, who had always used violence in order to force her to have sex, continued to rape her despite her new status as another man's wife and the mother of young children. Phyllis had fled from one abusive relationship to another in which she was continually victimised without being able to defend herself.

Ellenson (1985) has observed two further classes of symptoms which he considers to be predictive of a history of child sexual abuse. These focus specifically on disturbances of thought content and perceptual disturbances. Under disturbances of thought content Ellenson includes nightmares with manifest content of catastrophes, children being harmed or killed, being chased by attackers and scenes of death or violence.

In addition, clients may suffer from recurring intrusive obsessions such as impulses to harm one's child, or feelings that one's child is in danger of being harmed when absent from the mother. Recurring dissociation has also been observed as common to survivors in which the woman dissociates from her past, believing it to be someone else's past, or feels that her child is not hers and thus totally unrelated to her. Finally, Ellenson suggests that persistent phobias, especially a fear of being alone, are clinically predictive of a history of child sexual assault.

The types of perceptual disturbances noted by Ellenson include recurring illusions such as of an evil entity being present or entering the woman's body; recurring auditory hallucinations such as hearing a child crying, or hearing noises that suggest there is an intruder in her presence; and recurring visual hallucinations including furtive shadows and figures especially when in bed at night. Ellenson also reports the presence of recurring tactile hallucinations ranging from light physical touch to being forced or thrown down.

Ellenson argues that survivors very rarely reveal the presence of these types of symptoms and if questioned about them they universally answer that they have been reluctant to report such perceptual and thought disturbances for fear that they were cracking up and that the therapist would view them negatively or '... because I was afraid I would be thought to be crazy' (Ellenson, 1985).

Given the array of possible indicators of child sexual abuse, some of which are also manifest in other clinical disorders, researchers have found it difficult to identify a syndrome that is clinically predictive of a history of childhood sexual abuse. A number of researchers have postulated that the impact of child sexual abuse is best understood within the framework of Post-Traumatic Stress Disorder (Courtois, 1986; Donaldson and Gardner, 1985; Eth and Pynoos, 1985; Frederick, 1986; Goodwin, 1985; Lindberg and Distad, 1985). Although the PTDS model is a useful one in understanding and treating the impact of sexual abuse, Finkelhor (1988) has pointed out a number of limitations in employing this formulation (see Chapter 4).

Although many of these indicators also have some predictive validity for other clinical disorders, counsellors and therapists should be aware of the likelihood of a sexual abuse history when more than one of the above symptoms are present especially when accompanied by self-destructive behaviour patterns. Even if the therapist is only margin-ally suspicious that the client has been sexually abused in childhood it is still essential to raise the issue with the client. If the therapist has not actively asked routine intake questions about the client's sexual history, then it will be necessary, in the presence of more than one or a combination of indicators, to begin exploring the client's sexual history.

To facilitate this exploration in the most effective way, the therapist or counsellor should proceed sensitively from relatively gentle open-ended questions to more specific questions. Negative responses to any questions should elicit further but persistent questioning. The therapist needs also to be aware of any minimisation of the symptoms on the part of the client. It may be necessary to come back to questions in later sessions to unearth the most severely repressed memories. Positive responses to questions should always be followed by requests for examples to enable the therapist to build up a fuller picture and to facilitate recall in the client.

The emphasis should be at all times on sensitively phrased questions and persistence. The therapist should not be frightened of returning to questions that have previously generated a negative response. In the case of women who do remember their abuse this gives them permission to talk about their experience without feeling that the therapist is shocked or judgmental. With those survivors who are unable to remember their sexual abuse, persistent questioning may gradually facilitate the recall of long repressed memories from which they have dissociated.

Dissociation

Often clients may deny any knowledge of a history of child sexual assault or incest. This may be because she has forgotten her experiences or has dissociated from what happened to her as a child.

Nemiah (1975) has described the aetiology of dissociative hysteria as stemming from situations in which the individual experiences overwhelming grief, despair, or anxiety. One response to this trauma is the total repression of painful memories accompanied by the disappearance of painful effect. The fear and pain of the initial assault along with feelings of abandonment by both parents generate powerful emotions in the child that are so painful and overwhelming that the child must deny their existence by pushing them out of consciousness and forcing them into the unconscious.

This response is quite common to many survivors and may be viewed initially as a coping technique employed by the child as an adaptive way of escaping sensory input during victimisation (Briere and Runtz, 1988). Many survivors report that as children, when being sexually abused, they would completely shut off from what was happening to their body. To this effect they maintained mental awareness but blocked all bodily sensations. Some report that they experienced out of body experiences whereby they felt that they were able to look down on what was happening to them from a great height. Others report that they concentrated on one particular visual point in the room in order to escape any painful affect.

Charlotte

Charlotte, while being abused, would peel at the wallpaper in her room, always at the same area until eventually she had scraped through the lath and plaster to the bare brick work. This still did not deter her and she would continue to pick at that until her finger nails were bloody. She found this less painful than her father forcing his penis into her.

As the child grows through adolescence and into adulthood the adaptive nature of dissociation may become a semi-autonomous symptom which may eventually generalise as a defence to any aversive and anxiety provoking experiences. Briere and Runtz (1988) suggest that this defence has both voluntary and involuntary components. Survivors report that they are able to 'switch off' with remarkable ease whenever they feel threatened or afraid. This may result in dissociating to such an extent that they are unable to respond verbally to questions being asked.

Dissociation may also occur during the therapeutic session when the client is attempting to remember particularly aversive and painful memories. The woman may respond in a totally detached way and give the impression that she is talking about someone else's experiences. She may appear very remote and distant. The therapist will need to encourage the woman to begin to get in touch with these painful emotions while emphasising that by doing so she will be able to regain her memory.

Another form of dissociation occurs when the survivor lives on an exclusively mental level. This involves blocking any emotions or feelings that she may have and living in her thoughts. For healing to progress, the therapist must encourage the survivor to integrate her feelings and emotions with the rest of her mental life. One way to achieve this is by encouraging the survivor to feel her body. Relaxation exercises concentrating on breathing and how her body feels can be helpful.

Another technique is the use of such grounding exercises as when the client is asked to imagine she is a tree and that her legs are part of the root growth which is deeply buried into the earth. It is helpful to explore how the client feels during these exercises and to encourage her to adopt the exercise outside the therapy session whenever the client feels she is beginning to dissociate.

It is also useful to encourage the survivor to become conscious of the times when she feels she is about to dissociate and to keep a record of the feelings that have given rise to this need. By recording these feelings the client is able to become consciously aware of which situations generate such responses. This will be useful in any future situations which may trigger dissociation and should allow the survivor to exercise some control over them. When combined with grounding exercises it will help the client to remain in the present and face emotions rather than repressing them.

Although some therapists believe that bringing repressed material to light may make the client worse, clinical observations suggest that if the repressed material is not brought to the surface and integrated it will continue to give rise to adverse psychological symptomatology (Blake-White and Kline, 1985). The therapist must impress upon the woman that these frightening and powerful emotions are connected to past experiences which do not reflect present reality, and as such will not be harmful to her. This will encourage the survivor to peel off the layers of repressed emotions and to explore their childhood meaning, child while remaining in control in the present reality of adulthood.

Blake-White and Kline (1985) advocate the use of the analogy that within each adult lives the child and that this 'inner child' needs to be accepted and listened to. The client is taught to allow and give permission to the child to tell all her experiences without being judgmental or denying any emotions. The frightening memories and the pain are representative of the child reaching out to her. The client must listen to the child and encourage the child to believe that she is now safe and in touch with current reality.

It is important that the therapist be aware that, as memories of the trauma emerge from the unconscious, they may be so terrifying to the survivor that they have to be further repressed and denied. In this instance it is essential that the woman be encouraged to re-examine the repressed material in the light of adult reality. Much of the material was repressed during childhood in the absence of the cognitive power with which to understand the meaning and concept of these events. It is only by the re-evaluation of these early feelings through adult concepts that the survivor will be able to stop these negative feelings from controlling her life.

Denial

As repressed memories emerge from the unconscious many survivors become terrified about what will happen to them. Many feel that they will be so overwhelmed that they will disintegrate or end up as an amorphous mass with no shape or substance. As one survivor illustrates '...I feel that I will end up like a quivering mass of blubber on the floor, from which I will not be able to reshape myself'.

The recall of painful material may cause further repression and denial. The therapist must be aware of denial as a possible defence mechanism. This will manifest itself as a minimisation of the actual events with the survivor stating that it really wasn't as bad as all that or minimising the nature of the sexual abuse. This is especially likely in the early stages of recovering memories. Often it is easier to remember and talk about the least traumatic events and experiences while denying the existence of deeper repressed memories.

At this stage the therapist will need to facilitate further recall by believing and validating the client. This gives the survivor permission to talk about more painful memories without feeling that she is being judged by the therapist. Further exploration of repressed memories may be helped by asking such questions as 'Is that the first time you experienced these feelings?', 'Was that the only time that happened?' or ' Was that the only person to touch you in such a way?'.

In the case of denial, the woman may feel that the emergence of repressed material into consciousness is so terrifying that she will deny its existence and banish it back into the unconscious. Many survivors feel that they would rather suffer the trauma associated with unresolved child sexual abuse than acknowledge that this actually happened.

Leslie

Leslie came to therapy acknowledging that she had been sexually abused as a child. After several sessions, during which she denied that her experience had affected her in any adverse way, she explained that really she was merely seeking therapeutic help for her lack of confidence. She showed tremendous reluctance to talk in detail about the nature of sexual abuse, resorting to minimising its impact. As exploration became deeper she contacted her therapist in between sessions stating that she had told her a wicked lie about her father and that he had not sexually abused her at all. When asked why she felt the need to make up such a lie, she replied that it was easier to blame all her shortcomings onto her father and his sexual abuse than to acknowledge them as being part of her experience. She said that she felt an overwhelming sense of guilt for what she had done by telling this lie. Yet, she felt this guilt was easier to bear than the guilt that might surface by believing that she had been abused.

Later sessions revealed that she was so distraught at the repressed memories that were emerging which produced so much guilt that it was easier to say that it had never happened. Several months later having explored existing memories in more detail, and learned how to face and deal with their attendant feelings, some of the repressed material again surfaced and Leslie was able finally to acknowledge and believe that she had indeed been abused.

Flight into health

In conjunction with denial, many survivors find that when they have started to remember some of their experiences and explore feelings around these issues they start to feel better. This can lead to a 'flight into health' in which having scratched the surface layers of memory, and brought some of the repressed material into consciousness, the survivor feels that she is now cured. Often women leave therapy at this point believing themselves to have resolved their sexual abuse trauma.

Clinical observations suggest that this may be a form of repression and denial (Maltz and Holman, 1987). Often the most painful memories are so deeply buried and repressed that it necessitates the peeling off of several layers of less painful memories before the survivor actually reaches the most repressed material. The therapist needs to be alert to this and continue to ask questions and facilitate recall in order to ascertain how much repressed material still remains in the unconscious.

Although difficult to force a client to continue with therapy when she feels that she is cured, the therapist will need to be aware that the client may be fleeing from the pain of residual repressed memories and suggest to her that it may be advisable to continue therapy despite her feelings of health. This can be achieved by suggesting to the survivor that it is quite common among adults who have been sexually abused as children to flee into health while repressed material is still to be uncovered.

It is essential also for the therapist at this stage to validate what the survivor has achieved to date. Praise for the amount of material that has been brought into consciousness is vital. It is also worth pointing out that she is feeling better and that any further work, no matter how painful, will result in further positive feelings akin to those that she currently has about herself. This will inject some confidence in the woman to continue and persevere with therapy in order to reveal more painful and traumatic material. Emphasis should be placed on the notion that she has progressed through one stage and is now ready to go onto the next stage of uncovering deeper levels of memory and more severely repressed material.

It is helpful to reinforce the positive feelings she has and to point out that this will continue to happen at each stage of uncovering repressed material until all the painful experiences are brought into consciousness and dealt with. This is particularly valuable during sessions in which the client seems at the point of despair. Reminding her of how she felt before and how much she has achieved to date will provide the survivor with validation of how hard she has worked and what can still be achieved.

A corollary to this is that although much of the concentration in the therapeutic session may surround the exploration of negative and painful experiences, time should also be made available to explore positive aspects of the clients life. This includes positive experiences encountered as a child as well as positive achievements attained in adulthood. This will encourage the survivor to acknowledge the positive side of her experiences and current life circumstances.

More specific techniques and therapeutic approaches which facilitate the resolution of the impact of sexual abuse trauma are discussed in Chapters 8 and 9, which present a number of therapeutic approaches and techniques which have been adopted by clinicians to date. Prior to the discussion of treatment approaches and techniques, the goals and objectives in the treatment of adult survivors of child sexual abuse are considered in the following chapter.

CHAPTER 7

Treatment Objectives

Before looking at the variety of therapeutic approaches and techniques employed in the treatment of adult survivors of child sexual abuse, the goals and philosophy of treatment are considered. Irrespective of therapeutic orientation it is important for counsellors to acquaint themselves with treatment objectives that will facilitate trauma resolution and foster healing and growth. Although many of these objectives do not differ greatly from well established objectives engendered in good therapeutic practice, some are specific to the trauma of child sexual abuse.

Normalisation

A primary objective of treatment is to provide some level of normalisation of the survivor's abuse experience and the effects this has had on her psychological functioning, both historically and currently. Adult survivors of child sexual abuse feel themselves to be 'abnormal' both in having been sexually abused as a child, and in how they reacted to it, both then and now. Often they feel that they must have been 'bad' to have such a thing happen to them and blame themselves. In addition, many survivors are convinced that they are the only individuals to have had such abuse experiences, which result in feelings of shame and isolation.

The objective of normalisation is to emphasise to the survivor that her presenting symptoms are a normal response to an abnormal childhood experience and not a sign of mental illness or abnormality. Many coping strategies adopted by survivors during childhood were adaptive and often creative responses to their trauma, which allowed them to survive their experience. However, some of these responses have become maladaptive in adulthood resulting in a variety of presenting symptoms which limit their interpersonal interactions and psychological functioning.

Encouraging the survivor to recognise that her responses were healthy and normal in the presence of abnormal trauma allows the survivor to see herself as a survivor rather than a victim. It also prevents her labeling herself as neurotic, abnormal or bad for not functioning more adaptively. The normalisation of her presenting symptoms and her experience will foster a more positive self-image about herself which facilitates increase in self esteem and destigmatisation. The counsellor needs to make the survivor aware of how strong, courageous and creative she has been in her survival and in seeking to resolve her trauma.

Education

Educating the survivor about the prevalence and later psychological effects of child sexual abuse helps destigmatisation and increases the survivor's awareness about her abusive experience. Many survivors feel that their experience is unique and that they were singled out to be abused. By providing information on the incidence of child sexual abuse the survivor will feel less isolated.

Information about the lasting effects of child sexual abuse, the types of difficulties and presenting symptoms survivors encounter, and how to cope with these, help the survivor to understand better her behaviour and responses. Such information is available in the form of journal articles, books and videos. First person accounts such as Jacqueline Spring's *Cry Hard and Swim* (1987) and Sylvia Fraser's *My Father's House* (1989) may help the survivor to identify with other survivors, while showing her that it is possible to heal from the trauma of child sexual abuse. This can be very positive for the survivor who may feel so tainted and contaminated that she feels that she will never heal from her abuse.

The counsellor will need to monitor how well the survivor is able to respond to such accounts. Some survivors benefit enormously from such identification, while others find such accounts extremely distressing and may regress after reading such material. The counsellor will need to assess each individual client and evaluate how she might respond, prior to recommending such accounts. Some counsellors only recommend those accounts that are pertinent or similar to the client's own experience.

In addition to first person accounts there are now a number of books that address the whole range of child sexual abuse which are specifically written for survivors. Self-help manuals such as *The Courage to Heal* by Ellen Bass and Laura Davis (1988), and Poston and Lison's *Reclaiming Our Lives* (1989) have proven to be very helpful to many survivors, while Sarah Nelson's book *Incest: Fact and Myth* (1987) helps to broaden the survivor's perspective on child sexual abuse in dispelling many of the myths surrounding incest.

Another source of information is the use of videos. Recently a number of programmes including films, documentaries and discussion programmes with other survivors have been shown on television. The counsellor may find it useful to build up a library of such videos to use in the therapeutic session as some of them have considerable cathartic value. While some personal accounts may be very distressing to the survivor in eliciting powerful reactions, videos serve as a vehicle for releasing emotions, which can then be further explored in therapy.

Networking

A corollary to normalisation and education, facilitating the reduction in stigmatisation and isolation, is encouraging the survivor to network with other survivors in the community. More and more self-help support groups (see Appendix B) are being started throughout the country in which survivors of child sexual abuse can share and explore their experiences with other survivors in a safe environment. Participation in such support groups is a valuable therapeutic component as the survivor begins to validate her experience and is able to talk to others. This is initially very frightening as the closely kept 'secret' is threatened by exposure to others.

Support networks and survivors groups are a useful adjunct to individual therapy and should be a part of the treatment objective. Working with other survivors reduces stigmatisation and isolation and fosters the sharing of the secret with others. This encourages the building up of trust, facilitates learning to trust others and can be the beginning of forming interpersonal relationships with others. The counsellor must evaluate whether the survivor is ready to work in such groups prior to encouraging her to join one. Some survivors do not function well in groups and only feel ready for such exposure when they come to the end of their individual counselling, while others find it easy to join such groups fairly early on in their therapy.

An important advantage of such support networks is that the survivor is able to receive support in between sessions, is able to form friendships, and to benefit from support even after the trauma of child sexual abuse is resolved. Many survivors continue to foster their support networks and survivor group when they leave therapy for support in times of crises which do not necessitate a return to therapy.

Preparing the survivor for the healing process

Once the survivor enters therapy or counselling, it is imperative to prepare her for the healing process. Along with clarification of the particular therapeutic orientation the counsellor advocates, it is helpful if the survivor knows what kind of techniques will be used and what is expected of her in the counselling session. This will include a discussion of the extent of client input such as homework and exercises, and the counsellor's input in terms of level of interpretation and advice giving.

Initially survivors are extremely wary and anxious about the therapeutic process but some of these fears can be allayed by discussing the process of healing with the client. This should include a discussion of the client's motivations and expectations of therapy, and exploration of what it means for her to be in therapy. The counsellor needs to be honest in informing the survivor that the healing process will not be easy, and that there will be times when she is distressed and in more pain than she is in now. Knowing this prepares the client for these difficulties.

The counsellor should emphasise that although the survivor's memories will fade they will always remain part of her and that some of the pain associated with these memories may come back. What the counsellor can do is to get the survivor to acknowledge these childhood memories and their associated pain, assess the influence these have over her behavioural repertoire, and begin to integrate them with her adult self. This integration will allow the survivor to process the memories and pain so that they no longer control her behaviour and responses. She will be able to take control of her life in which she can make informed choices rather than eliciting old, maladaptive behaviour patterns and responses.

Treatment phases

Stages of the healing process may also be explored to prepare the survivor for what she will encounter. The early phase of therapy should focus on the building up of trust between the survivor and the counsellor, which will necessitate making the survivor feel safe in the presence of the counsellor and in the therapeutic environment. At this stage the survivor should be asked to provide information about her past history and her sexual abuse (given that this is acknowledged) which will allow the counsellor to assess which therapeutic techniques might be most beneficial to her. It is essential that the treatment focus is on the abuse experience as well as current presenting symptoms.

In the middle phase of therapy the brunt of the work will be done, which will include the discharge of feelings, exploring unresolved issues, getting in touch with the survivor's inner child, and re-experiencing the trauma of abuse. The aim is to integrate the inner child with the adult self so that they work as a unified whole rather than being split, working against each other. Emphasis should also be placed on cognitive restructuring, educating the survivor and the formation of new coping strategies. This might include the acquisition of new skills through assertiveness training, problem solving skills training, stress management, and improving communication skills.

The last stage of the healing process, the termination phase, is concerned with empowering the survivor to make her own choices and decisions without relying on the counsellor. It includes the survivor's individuation and separation from the counsellor, while establishing support networks outside therapy. These might include self-help groups with other survivors as well as supportive friends, partners and in some cases some members of the family of origin.

It is evident that this can be a lengthy process. Survivors should be under no illusions, once they have decided 'To sort this out once and for all,' that it will happen overnight. Some survivors may take as little as nine months to a year; others will take considerably longer. The duration of therapy will depend on the individual and the survivor should not feel a 'failure' if her progress seems to take longer than average.

In addition, it is useful to point out that even if the survivor appears to be static for a period of time in which there is no therapeutic movement, the healing process may still be active, albeit at an unconscious level. Several survivors have remarked that they felt as though they had reached a stasis in therapy when nothing seemed to happen at all, only to find that a lot of groundwork was being prepared unconsciously.

Such preparatory work takes place in the unconscious where it remains until the conscious is ready to allow it to surface and be expressed. Healing from the trauma of child sexual abuse is an ongoing process, with movement both forward and backward. Survivors should be aware that they may encounter some regressive movement which should be viewed as positive rather than negative as this is an indication of the unresolved therapeutic issues that still need to be addressed.

Individualising the therapeutic process

Counsellors starting to work with survivors of child sexual abuse are advised to individualise treatment to suit each survivor for optimal results. This can be done without necessarily compromising therapeutic orientation. Chapter 9 reviews some of the many techniques that have been shown to be beneficial to many survivors in resolving the trauma of child sexual abuse. Remaining flexible and alert to the individual client's needs allows the counsellor to tailor the therapeutic process to obtain maximum results for the client.

Some survivors will find certain techniques extremely helpful, allowing tremendous progress, while others will not benefit from these techniques at all but will find other techniques more useful. The counsellor needs to have the courage to try a variety of techniques, isolating those that work best for the individual client and which produce the best results. A rigid therapeutic approach which does not allow for fluidity and some level of eclecticism is unlikely to be beneficial when counselling survivors of child sexual abuse.

Validating the survivor

It is crucial that the counsellor validate and affirm the survivor by believing her. This means not only believing her abuse experiences, memories and pain, but also believing in her as an individual who has the capacity to heal. The counsellor must guard against conveying doubts about the veracity of the survivor's childhood experiences. Survivors are hypervigilant to any sign that they are not believed or are being judged. If there is even an imperceptible doubt in the counsellor this must not be expressed in the counselling session, but will necessitate attention during the counsellor's supervisory sessions, or his or her own therapy.

The counsellor will also need to make the survivor feel that, no matter what terrible things she feels she may have done, the counsellor will not judge her behaviour or be critical of it. The counsellor will need rather to convey to the survivor that such acts or behaviours may have been her only course of action, and as such served an important function in her survival. The emphasis should be on evaluating how useful her current coping strategies are and how these may be modified to become psychologically adaptive rather than maladaptive.

Feelings about the abuse will also need to be validated and affirmed by the counsellor. Many feelings may be ambiguous, which will cause confusion in the survivor. In particular, survivors may feel both anger and love for the abuser. The counsellor will need to acknowledge the survivor's feelings and validate them without imposing messages which make the survivor feel that she 'should' not have certain feelings such as love towards the abuser or that she 'should' really hate him.

Truth: fact or fantasy

An essential component of validating the survivor is to believe her and her experiences. The issue of truth is a crucial one in resolving the trauma of child sexual abuse. The counsellor must believe in the truth of the survivor's disclosures, and must not relegate or label these as fantasy, no matter how bizarre. Many counsellors who have no experience of working with survivors of child sexual abuse become overwhelmed by some of the experiences that are disclosed to them, believing them to be so bizarre, strange or evil as to be indicative of an over fertile imagination on the part of the survivor.

If the counsellor finds it difficult to believe some of the disclosed material then it is essential to work on this either in supervision or in their own therapy. In addition, counsellors may need to increase their level of information on the types of experiences associated with child sexual abuse. This is especially the case for survivors who were involved in sex ring abuse, sadistic or ritualistic abuse. Recent reports suggest that even the more bizarre aspects of ritualistic abuse, verging on the satanic, are being corroborated by police investigations (Scan, 1989).

A problem that counsellors may face is that many survivors veer from being extremely sure about their abuse and memories, to doubting that abuse really happened. This is often because the abuse happened at night when many of the survivors pretended to be asleep in order to avoid being assaulted. Often these doubts are psychogenic in origin and need to be explored on this basis.

It is virtually impossible to unearth retrospective, corroborating evidence that child sexual abuse or incest actually took place in childhood, as usually only the abuser and the child were present. Child sexual abuse is almost impossible to prove in a court of law retrospectively, and it is counterproductive for the counsellor even to attempt to establish the truth of such facts. What is more important is for the counsellor to focus on the survivor's truth as she believes it happened and to explore this. It is the survivor's perception and the meaning the abuse has for her that must be the focus of the healing process, not corroboration or factual evidence.

Although corroboration from others such as the abuser's confession, or acknowledgement from the mother or siblings is desirable, it is not always forthcoming. Many abusers when confronted deny what happened, as do other family members. Such denial needs to be explored in therapy, with the survivor being encouraged to believe and trust in her perception and memories even in the face of the abuser's denial. The survivor should familiarise herself with the myriad of reasons underlying abuser denial, and what it means to the family to collude with such denial, at the cost of the survivor's truth. It must be emphasised that such denial does not invalidate the survivor's truth and perceptions.

The continuing objective is for the survivor to believe in her truth and to acknowledge and ensure, even in the face of denial, that her experiences are validated and affirmed. If the survivor firmly believes and trusts her experience of what happened to her she will be able to progress rapidly in the healing process. Doubt on her part or on the part of the counsellor impedes the therapeutic process and prevents the survivor from dealing with her trauma.

Responsibility

Like truth, the issue of responsibility for the abuse needs to be addressed at the beginning of the therapeutic relationship, and if necessary, constantly reinforced. Responsibility for the abuse can only lie with the abuser, and must be placed there by both the counsellor and the survivor. Survivors feel guilty and somehow implicated and responsible for the abuse. As such they believe themselves to have encouraged it by initiating the abuse, perpetuated it by seeking out physical contact, liked it because their body responded to it, and maintained it by not doing anything to prevent it, such as saying 'No' or disclosing the secret.

The counsellor needs to explore these internalised messages with the survivor to find their origin. Often the abuser planted the messages by saying 'I know you like this because your body is responding', 'You must like it because you don't even try to stop me', or 'Look at what you made me do' (as he ejaculates over her). The survivor must be made aware that these are the abuser's rationalisations and excuses for sexually assaulting her, and that she has internalised these messages to such an extent that they now form part of her belief system about herself. The survivor should be encouraged to explore how these messages have affected many of her behavioural responses and how they contribute to her negative self-image and lack of self-esteem.

Many survivors also place responsibility for the abuse on the mother or other family members, for not having protected her and stopped the assaults. While it is important not to deny these feelings, the counsellor should point out that even if her mother did not protect her or was emotionally absent, this does not constitute permission for the father or adult male to sexually abuse the child. Thus, the responsibility for this must lie with him. He knew that what he was doing was wrong, yet he still chose to abuse the child. Although other family members may be implicated in maintaining the abuse, they did not force the abuser to take the decision to abuse.

It is essential that the issue of responsibility be explored and that the survivor feels that the counsellor does not hold her in any way responsible for the abuse. The survivor may question her own feelings of responsibility at times, which generates valuable therapeutic focus and issues, but at no point should she be encouraged to feel that her behaviour was responsible for her sexual assault.

Facilitating the expression of feeling

As a defence against the trauma of child sexual abuse, many survivors have dissociated from the feelings associated with their childhood abuse experience. The expression of feelings is seen by many survivors as extremely frightening, for it may release all the emotions that they have repressed for so long. Many survivors believe that if they express their feelings they will lose control over them and 'explode' or get taken over by them. Another common fear is that releasing emotions will make the survivor vulnerable to being abused and hurt again.

This reaction is understandable in that accessing highly arousing emotions related to the abuse will not only remind the survivor of the abuse but also release the painful and frightening feelings that she had at the time. It is almost as though the survivor is transported back through time to when the abuse happened, making her feel vulnerable and exposed to being abused again as she was in childhood. Although distressing, re-experiencing feelings associated with the trauma of abuse is nevertheless an important part of healing

Such fears are genuine and form a major part of the survivor's defensive repertoire. The counsellor must validate and affirm these feelings while offering support and reassurance to the survivor that she is now safe and that her abuser cannot and will not harm her in the same way again, as she is now an adult who is able better to protect and defend herself.

Emphasis must also be placed on the notion that an integral part of the healing process is bringing to the surface repressed memories and feelings which enable the survivor to work through them. Primitive, repressed feelings exert considerable influence on current psychological functioning, and as such must be made conscious and explored for them to be channelled in a constructive and adaptive way to facilitate growth, rather than allowing them to influence the behavioural repertoire in maladaptive and destructive ways.

Encouraging the survivor to release emotions and feelings in a safe environment will enable her to become less afraid of her emotions, allowing her to release them in a controlled way. This also facilitates desensitisation through which the survivor learns to relax in the presence of increasingly distressing emotional arousal until she is no longer distressed or overwhelmed by her emotions. Such desensitisation fosters the integration of feelings and intellectual rationalisation, creating a balance between both body and mind in which the survivor can move rhythmically and naturally without denying one to the detriment of the other. This reduces the body/mind split that so many survivors encounter as a result of dissociation

Working with the inner child

An adjunct to facilitating the expression of feelings is to encourage the survivor to work with her inner, albeit hidden child. Although the metaphor of the 'inner child' may initially seem somewhat abstract to the survivor, it is essential that the counsellor clarifies what is meant by this. The notion of the inner child is that we all have a 'small child' hiding within our adult self that has needs and desires which must be listened to. In the case of adult survivors of child sexual abuse, especially in the presence of dissociation and 'splitting', this inner child influences and directs much adult behaviour. The survivor's child is often extremely needy and requires much attention and nurturing.

The inner child often emerges by acting out primitive behaviours, including impulsive and sometimes self-destructive solutions to problems, in a child-like way, with developmentally immature and childlike cognitions, particularly black and white thinking, or responding with childhood speech patterns and pronunciation. In more severe cases the inner child may take over as a discrete entity and manifest itself as a separate ego state (as in the case of multiple personality), especially when stimulated by powerful abuse-related memories.

More commonly the inner child displays primitive defences which consistently interfere with adult psychological functioning. The dissociation manifested by most survivors as a defence against the trauma of sexual abuse effectively 'splits off' whole chunks of childhood experiences which become separated from the adult self. However, these childhood experiences are stored in memory in a relatively unaltered form as a primitive behavioural repertoire which has the propensity to influence the survivor's behaviour and responses.

The counsellor needs to clarify the metaphor of the hidden inner child to the survivor and identify which aspects of the survivor's behaviour are controlled and influenced by the inner child. Once inner child behaviours have been identified, the counsellor can encourage the survivor to open a channel of communication with her inner child. This will include allowing the inner child to communicate her needs, fears, anxieties and feelings to the adult. In turn, the survivor will need to reassure the child that the adult will not allow her to be abused again and that she will nurture, care, love and protect her from harm.

This dialogue can be achieved in a variety of ways (see Chapter 9) both through verbal communication in which the survivor talks to her child, or through letter writing (Parke, 1990), along with a number of other techniques and exercises which facilitate communication between adult and child. When communication has been established the survivor may appear to regress into her child by manifesting childlike behaviours and thinking in childlike ways. This should not necessarily be seen as 'regression' but as permitting the inner child to have a voice. Allowing the child to have a voice will enable her to talk about her abuse experiences and what these felt like as a child without being filtered through the adult ego state.

Survivors may feel at this stage that they are 'getting worse' and are losing control by behaving in even more maladaptive ways. This can generate much fear and anxiety on the part of the survivor who feels herself to be helpless and vulnerable. In severe cases the activated primitive behavioural repertoire will resemble a parody of childhood. The counsellor needs to provide complete reassurance that it is necessary to go through this stage of healing so that childhood emotions and feelings can be voiced and explored rather than being denied or repressed.

The survivor herself will also need to reassure her inner child that she will continue to nurture and care for her and not let anything bad happen to her. Emphasis should be placed on the positive effects of working with the inner child which allow the survivor to break through archaic dissociative defences to enable the expression of feelings and memories. Once communication and exploration of the inner child has been established, the adult survivor will be able to integrate repressed childhood memories, affects and cognitions into the adult self.

Desensitisation of primitive and anxiety provoking emotions and feelings enables integration in which the survivor can revise and re-evaluate her archaic perceptions of herself and the abuse with adult understanding. The survivor is thus able to take more control of her behavioural repertoire by reducing the influence of archaic behaviours. The adult self is consequently no longer directed and controlled by repressed childhood responses but is able to make informed choices about behaviour.

Integration

The integration of the inner child and the adult self allows the survivor to nurture and acknowledge her child. Integration may also be viewed as restoring the balance between body and mind, in which each state is equally acknowledged, permitting the survivor to choose which state she wishes to operate in. When these states are split the survivor has no control over them, as she not aware of their origin or their influence on her behaviour.

Through integration, all aspects of the survivor's personality can be explored and affirmed, rather than being limited through operating either in the self, or the child ego state. Many survivors have found that through such integration they have learnt not only to love their child but also to reclaim their childhood. Thus many are finally able to experience child-like joy and pleasure in activities in which they previously were inhibited. A good example is the ability to make time to play and pursue activities for the sheer pleasure of them rather than as something that ought to be done.

Tape recognition

As a result of identifying primitive behavioural responses while working with the inner child, the counsellor can go on to help the survivor to recognise when these primitive behaviours are elicited and how best to deal with them. The analogy of tape recognition focuses on the playing of old cassette tapes as an important element of the behavioural repertoire. Behavioural patterns are established in childhood where, if repressed, they remain unaltered in memory to be played again and again without selection or filtering.

Certain stimuli in childhood elicit specific behavioural responses which become part of the behavioural set which is activated whenever those stimuli are present. Developmentally, these behavioural sets are usually revised in the light of new information, increased knowledge, or self-awareness. For many survivors this does not happen. Their tapes are filed away and, because they are repressed, do not benefit from updating, modification, or re-evaluation. This allows archaic behaviour patterns and responses to re-emerge in the presence of its associated stimuli.

It is essential to learn to recognise when old tapes are being played in advance of eliciting archaic behavioural responses. Ideally, the survivor should become sensitised to her recurring behavioural sets so that she can stop them being activated and modify or replace them with more adaptive behaviours. Learning not to listen to the primitive tapes means that they become fainter and fainter until they are gradually erased. Increasingly, the survivor gains control of whether she wants to switch an old tape on, edit it, erase it, or add to it. Such control allows the survivor to exercise a choice over her behavioural repertoire rather than being directed by it, thereby reinforcing her victim role.

The counsellor should encourage the survivor to monitor the range of tapes she plays and to identify them when they are played. Time should also be spent on assessing how adaptive the tapes are to her current adult status. If the survivor feels that they are maladaptive, alternative, more adaptive behavioural patterns should be sought and explored. The survivor can practice these in the therapeutic session through role playing until they become a natural component of her new, revised behavioural repertoire. This will empower the survivor to choose her behaviour rather than being controlled by it.

Reframing

Once the survivor has begun to identify and establish tape recognition it will be possible for the counsellor to begin to reframe the survivor's cognitions and behavioural patterns. This is commonly achieved by means of cognitive restructuring in which the counsellor pinpoints the survivor's distorted beliefs and perceptions. Many of the beliefs survivors have about themselves and their abuse experience are lodged in deeply distorted childhood messages about the abuse which have been internalised. Included in these messages may be family myths and injunctions about her behaviour which the survivor believes to be true.

These messages become so deeply entrenched that the survivor finds it difficult to distinguish between, or separate, facts from beliefs. Jehu, Klassen and Gazan (1985) argue that beliefs have a significant influence on feelings and actions. If these beliefs are distorted or unrealistic it follows that feelings and behaviour may be equally distorted or inappropriate. The counsellor therefore needs to make the survivor aware of any distortions and help her to substitute these with more accurate and realistic beliefs (see Chapter 9).

The reprocessing of cognitive beliefs allows for the reconceptualisation of behavioural responses. This facilitates a more positive behavioural repertoire in which reactions to stress become more favourable. The new perspective and insight gained from cognitive restructuring provides more adaptive stress responses, which in turn reinforce more accurate cognitions. This cycle has a snowballing effect in increasing the survivor's reattribution of blame, responsibility, and the fostering of a more positive self image.

Coping strategies

An adjunct to reframing and cognitive restructuring is the assessment and evaluation of existing coping strategies. It must be emphasised to the survivor that many of the coping strategies she adopted in childhood were extremely adaptive and often very creative. However, some of these developmentally primitive coping strategies and defence mechanisms have, over time, outlived their usefulness and have become maladaptive and in some cases self-destructive. While affirming the survivor in the coping strategies she adopted in childhood, it is now pertinent to re-evaluate their usefulness.

Some coping strategies may still be adaptive in adulthood while others may necessitate only minimal modification. Other strategies may need to be excised completely from the behavioural repertoire and replaced by new, more favourable and adaptive strategies. To achieve this the counsellor will need to isolate those coping strategies that are maladaptive and explore alternative strategies with the survivor. It helps if these are generated by the survivor herself rather than imposed by the counsellor.

When alternative strategies have been explored, the survivor can be encouraged to rehearse them in the counselling session before attempting to adopt them outside. As the survivor gains confidence and feels more comfortable with these new coping strategies, she can be encouraged to test them between sessions until they become a natural part of her behaviour. If a revised or newly adopted strategy fails, the survivor should not see herself as a failure but rather learn from what went wrong and utilise this in any readjustments that need to be made.

Archaic coping strategies which are still adaptive should be shown as an example to the survivor of how creative and successful she was in adopting such a strategy which enabled her to survive. Affirming these will normalise and legitimise the survivor's abuse experiences and encourage her to view herself in a more positive light. It is not that her coping strategies are wrong but rather that they have outlived their usefulness, and would benefit from some reevaluation.

Grieving

The trauma of child sexual abuse includes powerful and overwhelming elements of loss – loss of the abusing parent, loss of the non-protecting mother, loss of childhood, loss of family and siblings, loss of trust, loss of sexuality, loss of an assumptive world. These multiple losses need to be grieved for. The literature on bereavement (Parkes, 1972) specifies the importance of the grieving process in order to avoid pathological manifestations of grief.

Survivors need not only to grieve for their losses, but to feel that they have a right to grieve and be encouraged to exercise that right. The counsellor must reassure the survivor that it is natural and therapeutic for her to cry and mourn her losses. Until she does she cannot restore an assumptive world in which to live. This new assumptive world may necessitate acknowledging that she can never have her childhood back, or indeed the father or mother that she has so desperately longed for. Until an assumptive world without these key figures is established, the survivor will find it difficult to progress in her healing.

For many survivors this mourning process is often one of the most painful aspects of therapy and the counsellor will need to be compassionate and provide much support to the survivor. Grieving multiple losses also includes relinquishing the need to control things and events that are out of the survivor's control, and accepting and letting go of those losses that she cannot regain. As these multiple losses are processed the survivor will begin to acknowledge that she cannot change her past but she can influence and control her future.

Letting go

A corollary to grieving is letting go. The survivor will come to acknowledge that there are certain losses that she cannot regain which she will need to let go of rather than continue to seek. Many survivors still look for approval and acceptance from their parents in the hope of regaining the 'ideal' childhood they desperately wanted but never experienced. Letting go of the notion of ideal childhood, ideal parents, ideal family can encourage the survivor to see her childhood more realistically and accept the reality of her experiences.

Letting go also involves relinquishing the victim role that many survivors cling to in adulthood. Seeing herself as victim inhibits the survivor from acknowledging her true strength and courage and prevents her from taking control of her life. Many survivors have been so adeptly socialised in the victim role that they are frightened to function without such a label. Victim role behaviours are often deeply entrenched and serve to elicit empathy, sympathy and the care-taking she never experienced in childhood. By letting go of the victim role the survivor can see herself as she truly is, a survivor, and empower herself to continue in her survival.

Resolving the abuse trauma means that the survivor can also let go of her abuse experiences. Survivors sometimes hide behind their abuse experiences and use them as a justification or excuse for their behaviour. Often this involves not wanting to change her behaviour at all but to be validated as an abuse victim who finds it difficult to come to terms with life. Such survivors consistently refer to and relate their behaviours, feelings, ideas and adult experiences to their abuse. This is often counterproductive as they merely reinforce their victim role rather than acknowledging that they have control over their lives and are able to change behaviours and attitudes thereby reducing the influence of their abuse experience.

Although the abuse experience can never be totally excised and will always be a part of the survivor, she can nevertheless let go of it sufficiently for it not to be predominant in her life. Letting go of the abuse means that the survivor sees herself as an individual rather than as a label: survivor or victim. This fosters a more positive and healthy image of herself as a normal individual, who encountered adverse childhood experiences, but is no longer controlled or directed by them. By acknowledging the abuse and letting go of it the survivor can see herself as a strong and healthy woman despite her childhood experiences.

Disclosure and confrontation

Although disclosure of abuse by the survivor is a major objective in the treatment of adult survivors of child sexual abuse, the counsellor should not influence the survivor to disclose or confront others until she feels ready to do so. The choice to disclose outside the therapeutic session, or to confront the abuser or other family members, must remain with the survivor. Some survivors feel that their ultimate goal of healing is to 'come out of the closet' and disclose their sexual abuse publicly, for many others such a goal is abhorrent and not an objective of treatment.

Confrontation is a very powerful therapeutic tool which fosters growth and healing and has benefits for many survivors, although it can be very damaging and destructive for some. The decision to confront should not be imposed upon the survivor but left to her choice. The counsellor should support the survivor in whichever choice she makes and ensure that she is given all the support and reassurance she needs. If the survivor does decide to disclose or confront then this will become a treatment objective which will need to be focused on.

The counsellor will need to prepare the survivor for confrontation by evaluating her motivation and expectations of confronting. The survivor will need to have realistic expectations of what confrontation can achieve, and will need to prepare for any disappointment of these expectations. The counsellor can help the client to prepare through rehearsal and role playing techniques. Some counsellors also lend support by accompanying the survivor to the confrontation.

It is essential that confrontation should not be assumed to be a treatment objective for all survivors. Attitudes and feelings surrounding confrontation need to be explored over time as some survivors initially reject the idea, but may revise this towards the end of therapy. The counsellor should leave all avenues to explore this issue open and return to it throughout the healing process to ascertain the survivor's feelings towards the abuser and confrontation.

In exploring the issues of confrontation it is vital to emphasise at all times that the therapeutic focus is on the survivor and not on reuniting the family. If a survivor has such a treatment objective in mind then the counsellor can suggest that she and the family undertake family counselling or therapy in addition to, but not instead of, her own individual counselling.

Traditionally, family therapy focuses on the interpersonal dynamics within the family and not individual intrapsychic functioning. The choice to undertake reparative family work lies with the survivor and should be respected by the counsellor. While reparative family work can have enormous value, it is, however, necessary to point out and consider the potentially destructive consequences of rebalancing the family in which the survivor may lose out again. To avoid such a potentially detrimental effect the survivor should be encouraged not to terminate her individual therapy in favour of family therapy until much of the groundwork and trauma resolution has been completed.

Skill building

A final part of the therapeutic process is focusing on the building up of skills that the survivor has encountered during therapy and adopting these in her life outside counselling. Survivors were often not given the opportunity to acquire many of the basic skills that children learn during childhood such as how to protect herself, how to communicate clearly and firmly, how to assert herself, how to cope with stress effectively, how to enhance her problem-solving and decision-making abilities, how to resolve conflicts, how to set clear boundaries both for herself and others, how to nurture herself and others, how to establish and maintain intimacy in relationships, how to express her sexuality, and effective and positive parenting skills.

Many of these skills form an important part of developmental learning which most children have access to through positive parental role models. Many survivors did not benefit from such positive role models so need to learn and acquire such skills. The counsellor, in providing a positive role model, can facilitate this by modelling more appropriate, effective and adaptive behaviours and skills which the survivor can practise. These precious skills can be learnt through the therapeutic process, adopted by the adult self, and prove invaluable to the survivor throughout the rest of her reclaimed life.

Empowering the survivor

One of the most focal aspects of trauma resolution when working with adult survivors of child sexual abuse is to empower the survivor to make informed choices and decisions not only about her beliefs and attitudes, but also about her behaviour and responses. In addition, the survivor should be empowered to accept challenges and take risks in establishing a new life in which she is in control. This may include career changes and major lifestyle changes.

The survivor will need to be supported initially in making such choices and accepting new challenges. Gradually the survivor will gain confidence and trust in her power of judgement and her decision-making skills so that these become a natural part of her behavioural repertoire. This empowering process will foster behavioural change away from conditioned patterns of fear, anxiety and guilt to those that reflect the survivor's needs, desires and feelings. She will be able to reclaim the dormant and undeveloped parts of her self to emerge with a new acceptance of herself, her body, her sexuality, and her true self.

Empowerment challenges learned helplessness and facilitates the learning of new roles and behaviour patterns which allow the survivor to establish new and more intimate relationships based on her integrated adult self rather than reflecting the needs of her inner child. This fosters further individuation and separation which reduces her dependency needs, including her dependency on the counsellor.

Counsellors will need to be patient during this process, constantly reaffirming, validating and reinforcing independent behaviour which allows the survivor to separate from the therapeutic dyad. The counsellor will need to recognise the survivor's individuation and enhance her self-efficacy. It is only when the survivor feels comfortable in her empowerment that resolution of trauma can be seen to be complete, and that treatment objectives have been attained. The newly emerged, more independent and powerful individual will continue in her process of empowerment long after therapy has terminated as her attainments become self reinforcing and each new challenge is faced and resolved.

CHAPTER 8

Treatment Approaches

The unique characteristics and dynamics of child sexual abuse and incest demand a unique treatment approach which must be individualised to the survivor. This involves not only the use of a broad range of techniques but also a multimodal and eclectic treatment approach. Although much of the knowledge about treating the adult survivor of child sexual abuse is impressionistic, based on clinical observation rather than on empirical validation, a number of techniques and treatment approaches have been reported as generating ameliorating and reparative effects.

Treatment for survivors of child sexual abuse is still in the process of development and to date there has been little or no systematic evaluation on how effective individual treatment approaches or techniques are. As our knowledge of the effects of child sexual abuse increases, and as more clinicians provide empirical evaluations of treatment modalities, it will become easier to assess the effectiveness of the large repertoire of available treatment techniques.

Many of the reported treatment approaches and techniques, although descriptive and impressionistic, nevertheless have face validity and are theoretically based within established therapeutic traditions. Until more empirical data and evaluations become available, clinicians and counsellors will have to rely on trial and error in implementing diverse techniques, and assess their usefulness for each individual client rather than generalising to all survivors.

The variety of approaches and techniques can be used in combination or separately depending on the needs and requirements of each survivor. As the traumagenic impact of child sexual abuse is unique to each woman, it is essential to take into consideration the individual characteristics and symptomatology of each survivor. To assist this, counsellors are advised to adopt a flexible, eclectic approach to the therapeutic process in which specific tools and techniques are individualised to the client, instead of exercising a rigid adherence to their preferred therapeutic orientation.

Whichever techniques or modalities are employed by the counsellor, they will need to reflect a comprehensive approach which encompasses the emotional, cognitive and behavioural components inherent in the difficulties experienced by individual survivors.

Each of these components represents aspects of the traumagenic impact of child sexual abuse and contribute in varying degrees to the long-term psychological and behavioural effects of the trauma. The relative contribution of each component will depend on the individual survivor and the impact that the sexual abuse has had on her. The counsellor will need to assess the level of contribution from each component and incorporate the corresponding treatment techniques to fit the survivor's requirements.

As all three components are operational in the traumagenic impact of child sexual abuse, each requires therapeutic attention. There is a high level of interaction between the three components with affect influencing cognitions, which in turn influence and direct behaviour. Focusing solely on one component, such as the emotional, to the exclusion of the cognitive or behavioural components impedes the integration of the full range of traumagenic effects associated with the abuse experience. Resolving the trauma of child sexual abuse necessitates a multimodal approach that incorporates treatment of cognitions as well as affect and behaviour in combination rather than in isolation.

This chapter will review some of the therapeutic approaches which have been reported to be effective in the treatment of adult survivors of child sexual abuse. Three of these approaches can be divided into separate categories which reflect not only the components inherent in the long term psychological effects child sexual abuse has on survivors, but also major therapeutic schools. Experiential/exploratory therapies focus on resolving the emotional effects of abuse trauma; cognitive therapy aims to replace distorted cognitions which can ameliorate mood disturbances such as depression; while behavioural therapies desensitise the survivor to the abuse trauma, generate a more adaptive behavioural repertoire, and foster the acquisition of new skills and coping strategies which enhance interpersonal functioning.

More specifically-focused approaches which aim to ameliorate specific deficits and effects are also considered, in particular techniques which aid memory retrieval and sexually focused therapy. As many survivors have memory deficits including selective, partial, or total psychogenic amnesia, retrieval of memory is considered as a separate approach in which the therapeutic focus is on the recall of blocked and repressed memories. Sexually-focused therapy, while incorporating many behavioural techniques, is also considered separately in its specific aim to repair the damage of child sexual abuse on survivors' sexuality.

Prior to discussing the variety of therapeutic approaches, a number of other important aspects of treatment are considered. These include treatment modalities to assess which type of therapy, group, individual, couple, or family, is best suited to adult survivors of child sexual abuse; duration of the therapeutic process and the relative value of time limited therapy and long term therapy; and the pacing and timing of therapeutic sessions throughout the healing process.

Treatment modalities

Counselling adult survivors of child sexual abuse is usually most effective when conducted on an individual or group therapy basis. Individual counselling is probably the most efficacious as many survivors initially feel uncomfortable about participating in a group because they tend to feel vulnerable about disclosing highly emotional and anxiety-provoking material to strangers. There are many advantages to group therapy (for a full consideration of the benefits of group therapy see Chapter 10), but counsellors must be careful to assess whether the survivor is emotionally stable enough to cope in a group environment.

Most survivors initially function best in individual counselling as a first step in the healing process. As the survivor begins to heal and is more able to talk about her abuse, she may benefit from participating in group therapy, or a self-help support group, to resolve interpersonal difficulties such as learning to trust others, reducing social isolation, and destigmatising her abuse experience. Such group participation should be actively encouraged by the counsellor as a valuable adjunct to individual counselling.

Couple or partner therapy can also be of value to some survivors, particularly if they have current relationship problems with their partner, or are experiencing pronounced sexual difficulties. Couple therapy can be extremely useful for both the survivor and her partner in enhancing the partner's understanding of the survivor's difficulties, which fosters increased empathy and support. The focus of couple therapy should remain primarily on the survivor and not shift entirely on to the partner. To balance any shift in emphasis, the survivor may be advised to continue in individual therapy.

Occasionally during individual therapy it may be productive to include the survivor's partner in a some of the sessions, or to see the partner separately. This is particularly indicated when the survivor is re-experiencing the more painful and emotionally arousing aspects of the abuse. Partners may not know how best to support or help the survivor during this distressing time, and would therefore benefit from increased awareness of what the survivor is going through, including constructive suggestions of how to support her.

Partners can be encouraged to increase their knowledge of the impact of child sexual abuse and the therapeutic process to recovery. This not only fosters empathy and support but also prepares the partner for any difficult stages that the survivor may go through. It also helps the partner to come to terms with any personality changes in the survivor. Personality changes can sometimes be quite dramatic and, although positive for the survivor, the partner may view these negatively or feel intimidated and threatened by them. Such feelings can be ameliorated to some degree if the partner is prepared for them, and aware of what it means to the survivor to be able to express her new-found personality.

Family therapy is often used when working with children who are being sexually abused, or who have recently disclosed their abuse. The emphasis of traditional family therapy models is on rebalancing and reuniting the family, by treating interpersonal effects rather than the individual intrapsychic or traumagenic dynamics. Family therapy rarely focuses on the survivor's experience of trauma, but considers every member of the family equally. This emphasis makes family therapy difficult to recommend as the sole treatment modality. If the survivor considers rebalancing the family, or undertaking family reparative work as a major goal in her treatment process, then family work may be indicated, but only if the survivor continues with her own individual counselling, and is able to persuade other family members to seek out individual or group counselling for themselves in addition to family therapy.

Duration of therapeutic process

Treating adult survivors of child sexual abuse can be a long and complex process. As the therapeutic focus is retrospective, often spanning several decades, involving highly complex interactions between affect, cognitions and behaviour, it is important that the survivor recognises that it takes time to unravel the effects her abuse experience has had on her. Comparing the recovery process of child sexual abuse with other recovery processes, such as from alcoholism or severe burns, provides the survivor with some idea of the complexity and length of treatment. It is also pertinent to remind the survivor that her abuse experiences have had serious ramifications over a long period of time which cannot be resolved quickly. Time is also important in building up trust between counsellor and survivor to enable them to form a good therapeutic alliance in which the survivor feels comfortable and safe in exploring painful and distressing material.

Once the survivor recognises that the healing and recovery process requires time and energy, she is able to commit herself more easily to long term treatment, and accept that this could involve at least one to three years. Some survivors are unable to commit themselves to long-term, global therapy and need the security of short-term, time-limited, goal-orientated therapy. The counsellor will need to assess the survivor's needs and requirements at intake and discuss with her which type of therapy she would feel most comfortable with.

In most instances long-term, global, in-depth therapy is indicated. Survivors who have already explored some of their abuse trauma often prefer to enter therapy with specific goals in mind which they wish to resolve within a specified time period. Frequently, these survivors enter therapy whenever an unresolved issue related to their abuse emerges, and when it is resolved, are able to terminate therapy without experiencing any adverse effects.

Following the assessment of the survivor's needs, the counsellor can then present the client with a range of options, both in terms of treatment modality, and duration and focus of therapy. These options, should be explored by the survivor to help her formulate the decision which is most beneficial and productive for her. At this point a contract between survivor and counsellor can be drawn up. The contract may include specific goals which should be attained within a specified time frame, with the possibility of further therapy if desired. Alternatively, the contract may merely state that global, exploratory therapy with no time constraints has been agreed, to be revised as necessary.

Contractual agreements are not only crucial in establishing the content and length of the therapeutic process, but are also invaluable in generating a level of commitment between the survivor and counsellor. Such commitment ensures that the survivor will expend time and energy on the therapeutic process, as well as motivating her to resolve her abuse trauma. The counsellor is committed to providing a safe and comfortable environment to enable the survivor to disclose painful emotions and memories. Confidentiality and trust are paramount in creating a safe atmosphere in which the survivor can entrust her feelings to the counsellor, and not feel shamed by her experiences.

The therapeutic contract should also include procedures for terminating therapy. Some survivors 'flee into health' after a few initial therapeutic sessions believing themselves to be healed once they have disclosed their abuse experiences. Often such flight is reflective of having opened a painful wound which the survivor is not ready or willing to heal and so she bandages it by terminating therapy rather than endure any more pain through disinfecting it. Thus, the survivor restores her defensive strategies in order to avoid further painful affect.

Procedures for terminating therapy should specify that prior to termination the survivor discuss her reasons for leaving with the counsellor. The aim should not necessarily be to dissuade the survivor from her decision, but rather to discuss with her her reasons for termination and to explore the meaning of the therapeutic process for her. Examination of what it is in therapy that has prompted this decision, and what is being defended against to activate denial, may enable the survivor to modulate her decision and acknowledge her psychological defences against the processing of painful material.

Time-limited therapy

Time-limited therapy is specifically focused and goal-orientated. Goals may consist of stabilisation through crisis intervention in which the focus is on restoring pre-crisis functioning levels, or may entail the resolution of a specific aspect of the abuse experience. In short-term therapy, goals and time limits are set at the outset. Goals are focused upon immediately and not subject to global investigation.

Crisis intervention requires the counsellor to contain the crisis and assess the stability of the survivor. If she is very unstable and in danger of harming herself, or others, then the counsellor must either refer her to more appropriate agencies which are better equipped to contain the crisis, or attempt stabilisation within the therapeutic session. Until the survivor is stabilised it will be impossible to restore her to more optimal psychological functioning. Once stabilisation is operational, it will be possible to explore what prompted the crisis and elicited such negative behavioural responses.

Frequently it is survivors who are relatively stable, with considerable ego strength, who present themselves for time-limited therapy. These survivors essentially seek therapy either to explore a newly emerged memory, or to work on a certain issue which has arisen and needs to be resolved. Invariably they already have experience of individual counselling in which they have explored some of the issues associated with their abuse trauma, and possess highly developed coping skills and adaptive levels of psychological functioning. Such survivors are often highly motivated and extremely committed to the therapeutic process and work hard to attain the goals they have set themselves. In contrast, there are many survivors who prefer long-term, global treatment in which they can establish a close therapeutic relationship with the counsellor, to build up trust before revealing painful material. It is significant that time-limited therapy has most commonly been adopted as the preferred treatment modality for group therapy (see Chapter 10).

Long-term therapy

The most commonly indicated and preferred type of therapy for most adult survivors of child sexual abuse is long-term, global therapy which has an average duration time of between nine months and three years, depending on the individual client. Long-term therapy allows for more in depth work to be conducted on both a conscious and an unconscious level, providing a more comprehensive analysis of all the traumagenic components of the abuse experience.

Long-term therapy involves establishing a close therapeutic alliance which includes elements of dependency, transference and counter-transference in which issues of trust, reliability and interpretation are tested. Most of the approaches and techniques reviewed here are ideally suited to long-term therapy, although they also have some application to time-limited therapy.

Timing and pacing of the therapeutic process

If the therapeutic process is too intense and overwhelming, the survivor may find it difficult to resolve the trauma of her abuse as she will be too concerned with what is happening in the here and now, rather than in integrating past feelings and cognitions. For this reason the counsellor will need to be sensitive to the timing and pacing of therapy by adopting a pace that is comfortable to the survivor. Very intense therapeutic sessions should ideally be followed by a less traumatic session as an antidote to the high intensity of the preceding sessions.

Intense and anxiety provoking issues occasionally need to be put 'on hold' for short periods to allow the survivor to focus on less traumatic issues or on the acquisition of more adaptive behavioural skills. Such action does not necessarily encourage blocking or avoidance as the traumatic issues tend to resurface shortly afterwards when the survivor feels psychologically stronger for having worked on other skills, allowing her to deal with the intensity of the material in a much more productive way. This is not only a form of distancing and desensitisation, but is a potent way of demonstrating to the survivor that she is making valuable therapeutic progress rather than feeling overwhelmed by constantly being forced to re-experience the trauma of her abuse.

A corollary to this is to ensure that the therapeutic session does not focus exclusively on the negative aspects of the abuse experience, or the negative consequences it has had on the survivor. The survivor may feel that she had some positive childhood experiences which should not be ignored and can fruitfully be explored. It is also essential to spend some time focusing on those positive attributes and skills of the survivor which helped her to survive. Survivors have many positive skills and abilities which they negate or invalidate. Balancing negative sessions with more positively focused ones enables the survivor to integrate both positive and negative aspects of her abuse experience with her adult self.

It is essential for the counsellor to remain flexible in the therapeutic session to allow for desensitisation. If a particular exercise becomes too painful and distressing, the counsellor should consider switching to a less intense exercise, or alternatively to focus on the acquisition of more adaptive behaviour and skills, which incorporate the survivor's already existing abilities. This will lessen the intensity of the material but still allow the survivor to work on interrelated issues. This validates the survivor's achievements to date and prevents her from feeling that she is regressing or failing in the therapeutic process.

Timing and pacing are valuable skills which counsellors should endeavour to incorporate into their therapeutic repertoire and regularly hone. To assist this, counsellors need to remain sensitive and alert to the survivor's level of psychological processing, ability to cope with highly emotionally charged memories, and assess when it is necessary to keep the survivor focused on painful material. Most important, the counsellor will need to act firmly and decisively by either preventing and minimising avoidance behaviours and encouraging further exploration, or shifting to less intense material, depending on what is therapeutically indicated.

Treatment approaches

Once a history of child sexual abuse or incest has been uncovered the counsellor will need to relate presenting symptoms to their root cause in the abuse experience, and focus the therapeutic process on resolving the trauma of child sexual abuse rather than merely treating individual presenting symptoms. Clinical observation indicates that once the survivor has resolved her feelings about her abuse, that there is marked amelioration of many, if not all presenting symptoms.

Treatment of adult survivors of child sexual abuse incorporates a combination of three fundamental therapeutic approaches which reflect major theoretical schools of therapy: emotional, cognitive and behavioural. Experiential/exploratory therapies focus on accessing of emotions, re-experiencing the trauma of the abuse, and integrating these with the adult self. Cognitive therapy aims to identify the survivor's distorted cognitions of herself and others and attempts to replace these with more accurate and realistic cognitions. Behavioural therapies focus on enhancing the survivor's behavioural repertoire through the acquisition of more adaptive behavioural responses, coping strategies and learning new skills.

Although there is considerable overlap between these three basic therapeutic approaches and their related treatment techniques, each approach has a crucial role to play in resolving the abuse trauma. Throughout treatment, one of these approaches will represent the therapeutic focus and become operational, depending on which aspect of the survivor's trauma is under scrutiny and what she is trying to resolve.

Experiential/exploratory therapies aim to integrate unacknowledged and repressed childhood feelings, experiences and memories with the adult self. Time is devoted to re-experiencing the myriad, complex, and sometimes ambivalent feelings associated with the abuse. Re-experiencing blocked or repressed feelings allows them to return to consciousness, where they can be discharged and explored within the safety of the therapeutic environment. Exploring these early feelings and evaluating them is the first step in the integration of primitive affect and cognitions with the adult self. This integration forms the basis of much of the reparative work exemplified in the experiential/exploratory approach.

Cognitive therapies concentrate on the effects of distorted cognitions and beliefs, and their influence on mood disturbances and behaviour. Survivors of child sexual abuse often hold negative and distorted perceptions about themselves, their family, the abuser, and the world in which they live. Isolating these archaic distorted perceptions, and putting them into the context in which they were first learned and later internalised, allows the survivor to reframe them in the light of adult knowledge and understanding. This enables the survivor to see the world in a more accurate and realistic way, and change her behaviour accordingly.

Behavioural therapies aim to desensitise the survivor to the abuse experience and find ways of enhancing the behavioural repertoire in more effective and adaptive ways. The counsellor focuses on the evaluation and assessment of present coping strategies and skills, and highlights those which need to be replaced or modified by more adaptive strategies. The survivor may also benefit from the acquisition of new skills such as stress and anger management, more effective communication skills, assertiveness training, and parenting skills. Although a large part of the behavioural approach consists of teaching new skills and acquiring knowledge, it also incorporate relaxation methods which aim to desensitise the survivor to overwhelming arousal and feelings of anxiety.

All three therapeutic approaches work in conjunction with each other, and can be used interchangeably. Counsellors are advised not to adhere exclusively to one therapeutic orientation to the detriment of the others. This is essential as feelings, cognitions and behaviour are all interlinked and should not be split off from each other. All three types of therapy need to be operational to prevent the type of dissociation, or splitting off, which survivors already use as a defence mechanism by splitting off feelings and emotions from cognitions. If this type of dissociation is reflected in a bias towards adopting one particular therapeutic approach to the exclusion of others, then the resolution of trauma will be imbalanced and to a large extent negated.

The three therapeutic approaches are inter-related and interact in the sense that desensitisation (behavioural) prepares the survivor for intense arousal and re-experiencing of trauma (experiential/exploratory) by encouraging her to relax so that she can put her discharged emotions and cognitions (cognitive) into a more realistic and accurate context, which in turn fosters more adaptive behavioural change.

Experiential/exploratory therapies

Experiential/exploratory therapies are psychodynamic in orientation, and consist of several techniques, many borrowed from humanistic therapies such as Gestalt and Transactional Analysis, which promote the expression and re-experiencing of feelings and emotions related to the abuse which fosters catharsis and abreaction to the trauma. The underlying rational of these techniques is to cut through denial by dismantling defences in order to encourage the recollection and re-expression of memories and emotions which have been repressed.

Many of the techniques included in the experiential/exploratory approach are highly anxiety provoking and threatening to the survivor. By lowering deeply entrenched defences, the survivor re-experiences feelings of vulnerability akin to those that she felt during her abuse which she has previously successfully defended herself against, and tried to control for many years. Highly emotionally charged material can arouse intense anxiety reactions which sometimes appear to be life threatening to the survivor. Desensitisation can help the survivor to relax in the face of her anxiety (see the section of *Behavioural therapies* later in this Chapter) so that she can begin to explore her trauma.

It is crucial that the techniques used in this approach are introduced with caution as the elicited responses may be unpredictable. Some survivors are able to cope with intensely arousing emotions better than others. The counsellor will need to be gentle and empathic to the survivor's feelings of vulnerability and painful arousal, and proceed at a pace which the survivor feels comfortable with. To hurry the survivor by swamping her with some of the techniques employed in this approach can be counterproductive and destructive.

Intrinsic in experiential/exploratory therapies is establishing a positive therapeutic alliance and close bond between survivor and counsellor. The survivor needs to feel safe with the counsellor so that she can trust her or him not to abandon or reject her as she discloses painful memories and relinquishes her defences. It is essential that the counsellor consistently reassures the survivor by providing tangible support, empathy and affirmation.

Ideally, a strong therapeutic alliance needs to be established prior to employing experiential/exploratory techniques so that the survivor feels safe and secure. Once trust has been generated, experiential/exploratory techniques can be introduced gradually. Techniques which are minimal in their intensity and potential to elicit arousal, and least psychologically threatening techniques, should be introduced initially so as not to flood the survivor emotionally. Once the survivor begins to access emotionally intense memories and repressed feelings, and becomes desensitised to them, it is possible to work through the recovered material, prior to moving on to additional cathartic techniques.

The counsellor will need to assess and monitor consistently to what extent the survivor is processing the material and how she is coping with the intensity of elicited feelings. This will guard against overstimulation which may overwhelm the survivor and reactivate old defences. The counsellor should also be vigilant against the survivor becoming over involved in exploring the abuse experience as she may overwhelm herself by living and breathing incest twenty-four hours a day. This distorts the survivor's reality as she begins increasingly to live in her past while denying present reality. Such denial of reality can be alleviated to some extent by the use of expressive techniques that focus on the present, here-and-now rather than the past. Such techniques include empty chair work, role play and working with the inner child on an adult level.

Cathartic techniques which increase self awareness, and foster the expression of emotion and integration of those parts of the self that the survivor has denied or dissociated from include creative therapies such as art therapy (including painting, sculpture and pottery), the use of dance, music and movement, and psychodrama or dramatherapy. Writing is also a powerful, cathartic technique which encourages the survivor to record her feelings, dreams, memories and current emotional state. Journal keeping, autobiographical writing and poetry generate similar effects on accessing split-off emotions to aid integration (see Chapter 9).

Experiential techniques which focus on the body are often the most distressing and emotionally arousing of all the experiential/exploratory techniques. Such techniques should ideally not be introduced until the survivor has explored a considerable part of her abuse experience, and been sufficiently desensitised to be able to cope with high levels of arousal. Particularly powerful techniques which elicit high arousal include any form of body work such as body awareness, body massage, Rolfing and primal scream techniques. The counsellor should ensure that the survivor is relatively stable and integrated before implementing any such techniques.

Exploratory work includes accessing unconscious memories by making these conscious in order to fully explore their meaning and resolve any trauma associated with them. This can sometimes be very painful for the survivor who has repressed and defended against the content of memory by pushing them out of consciousness. Some therapists argue that it is detrimental to the survivor to access unconscious material as she may regress as a result. Arguably, unless therapy is able to access all cognitions, emotions, feelings and memories associated with the abuse then resolution of trauma will remain incomplete.

Facilitating recall of memory may for many survivors be a crucial requirement of allowing them to ascertain the validity of their beliefs and feelings surrounding the abuse. Many survivors are not able to recall aspects of their abuse, leaving them with overwhelming feelings of doubt about whether it really happened or whether it was pure fantasy. Recalling repressed material validates the survivor's experience, allowing her to acknowledge her abuse while giving her permission to begin dealing with it. As so many survivors suffer from psychogenic amnesia, I have reviewed memory retrieval as a separate therapeutic focus later in this chapter.

Cognitive therapies

Cognitive techniques are particularly effective in restoring self-esteem, reattributing blame, responsibility and guilt, and ameliorating feelings of shame, sadness and mood disturbances. Low self-esteem stems not only from the abuse experience but also reflects the attitudes and behaviour of other family members. The techniques employed in this approach challenge conditioned responses, negative internalised messages about the self, and distorted beliefs by replacing them with more accurate and realistic cognitions about the self, others, and the world.

Distorted perceptions and beliefs contribute not only to low self-esteem, shame, guilt and sadness but also to mood disturbances such as depression. A number of clinicians have proposed that if beliefs are distorted or unrealistic, then feelings and actions are also likely to be distorted, and that the correction of distorted beliefs will be accompanied by an alleviation of mood disturbance (Jehu, Gazan and Klassen, 1985).

Cognitive restructuring is based on the work of Beck (1976) and others who have devised intervention programmes which aim to correct distorted beliefs by replacing or reframing them in a more accurate context thereby alleviating many presenting symptoms (Beck and Emery, 1979; Beck et al. 1979; Burns, 1980). The techniques employed in cognitive restructuring have more recently been applied, with some success, to adult survivors of child sexual abuse by Jehu, Klassen and Gazan (1986).

Although Jehu, Klassen and Gazan report that cognitive restructuring techniques are efficacious in ameliorating many of the symptoms observed in survivors, it would be premature to conclude that these techniques, if used exclusively, would benefit all survivors. Cognitive restructuring undoubtedly plays an important role in the treatment of adult survivors of child sexual abuse, but is most effective and beneficial when used in conjunction with experiential/exploratory and behavioural techniques.

As cognitive restructuring is predominantly verbally orientated, survivors who are already articulate may benefit most from this approach, whereas survivors who are not so verbally accomplished may not show great improvement. A further problem with cognitive restructuring is that survivors who intellectualise their abuse experiences and dissociate from their feelings may continue to do so while ignoring their emotions. To avoid this, cognitive restructuring should not be used to the exclusion of experiential/exploratory techniques which aim to access affect.

Jehu, Klassen and Gazan (1986) propose that there are three major components of cognitive restructuring:

1. identifying beliefs;

2. recognising distortions;

3. the substitution of these with more accurate beliefs.

Prior to implementing cognitive restructuring techniques, the counsellor needs to explain the rational of the techniques used. The central aim of cognitive restructuring is to make the survivor aware of her automatic and habitual beliefs, so that she can see how these occur without actual awareness or scrutiny of their validity. The next step is to identify and make the survivor aware of her distorted beliefs so that they can be replaced with more realistic cognitions.

Common cognitive distortions include all-or-nothing thinking, magnification and minimisation, emotional reasoning, jumping to conclusions, overgeneralisation, disqualifying the positive, mental filtering and mislabelling. To help identify distorted beliefs, Jehu (1988) has developed a belief inventory which specifically aims to elicit beliefs associated with child sexual abuse. Other methods which facilitate the identification of beliefs are role playing, visualisation, and the recording of cognitions that occur prior to feelings of distress.

Once distortions have been identified the counsellor can encourage the survivor to generate alternatives to these distortions. This can be achieved through normalisation of the abuse; providing more accurate information; logical analysis which weighs up the evidence in support of the cognition; distancing whereby the survivor is urged to shift from a subjective to an objective perspective; reattribution of blame and responsibility; decatastrophising which puts the survivor's cognitions into context while demagnifying the consequences; and the use of specific assigned exercises that confirm or disconfirm distortions. For a wider discussion of the techniques employed in cognitive restructuring see Chapter 9.

Behavioural therapies

There are a number of behavioural therapies and techniques such as systematic desensitisation, stress management, stress inoculation, anger management, and relaxation which facilitate behavioural change. Behavioural techniques also operate to some extent in sexually focused therapy and in the acquisition of skills and coping strategies. Techniques intrinsic in the behavioural approach aim to reduce learned helplessness through behavioural rehearsal which allows the survivor to relinquish her passive, victim role and replace it with the stronger, more positive and active role of an individual who has the power to make her own informed decisions and choices.

An important behavioural technique is desensitisation in which the survivor is exposed to her fears and learns not to be overwhelmed by the intensity of emotional arousal. This is achieved through relaxation and breathing exercises which aim to bring the survivor to a stable baseline. When the survivor is subsequently exposed to intensely arousing emotions either through re-experiencing aspects of trauma or through flooding, the survivor is taught to relax and breathe deeply until she becomes desensitised to the strength of the emotional arousal and is returned to a stable baseline. Desensitisation allows the survivor to explore the abuse trauma and painful feelings without overwhelming and crippling anxiety. This is a valuable technique which helps the survivor to face her fears and anxieties without dissociating or splitting off.

Stress management and stress inoculation employ similar principles in which the survivor practices muscle relaxation, breath control, covert and overt role playing, thought stoppage, and guided self-dialogue (Veronen and Kilpatrick, 1983). These techniques emphasise the active participation of the survivor in analysing cognitions along with internal images and dialogue. The survivor is then able to exercise more control and choice over her behaviour and responses, thereby reducing learned helplessness.

Anger management techniques focus on the positive and healthy aspects of releasing anger in appropriate ways. Females are often socialised not to express anger or aggression as these are considered to be inappropriate emotional expressions and therefore not subsumed in the female behavioural repertoire. Such socialisation needs to be rebalanced. The survivor should be validated for the anger she feels about her abuse experience by emphasising that she has every right to be angry. The counsellor will also need to assess how the survivor vents her anger, in order to redirect the discharge in more appropriate ways.

Aware that anger is not a permissible female emotion and should not be discharged, survivors tend to internalise their anger by redirecting it at themselves. This internalisation of anger is aetiologically involved in such presenting symptoms as depression, somatic complaints and self destructive behaviours. It is vital that the survivor recognise the ramifications that the internalisation of anger has both psychologically and behaviourally. From this the survivor can explore ways of discharging and externalising her anger more appropriately and adaptively. Survivors who do externalise their anger often do so by directing it in diffuse ways which most commonly involve being angry with an inappropriate individual or situation. Such inappropriate discharge needs to be explored and the source of anger clarified. Once the source of anger has been traced the survivor can refocus and redirect her anger at the person or situation that she is really angry with.

Survivors are often afraid of their anger and feel that they need to keep tight control over it. A common fear is that if they express even a modicum of anger this would release years of repressed and pent up anger which would become uncontrollable and destructive. Many survivors feel that if they lost control over their anger they would become homicidal and brutally murder the abuser, or any threatening male. Practising the discharge of anger in small doses in a safe, controlled environment such as the therapeutic session, with the support of the counsellor, allows the survivor to recognise that anger can be a positive and healthy release, which can be controlled and will not necessarily overwhelm her.

The survivor can rehearse and increase the discharged dose gradually over time in increasingly more adaptive and appropriate ways. Techniques which release anger include hitting pillows with bats or rackets, pounding furniture such as beds or sofas, and screaming. Assertiveness training also encourages the survivor to discharge her anger and aggression in more effective ways, while self defence training reduces learned helplessness and increases self protective behaviours.

A valuable behavioural focus is desensitising the survivor's fear of physical contact by teaching her to differentiate between positive, caring and nurturing touch and exploitative or abusive touch. Although physical contact can be an important therapeutic focus, touching should not be initiated unless specifically requested by the survivor. Counsellors should also examine their feelings about physical contact, and whether they feel comfortable incorporating such techniques into their therapeutic repertoire.

If counsellors feel uncomfortable with physical contact then they are advised to establish firm boundaries at the outset. Some survivors benefit enormously from physical contact with the counsellor and view it as reassuring, caring and affirming behaviour. The decision to establish physical contact must be taken by the survivor and must not, under any circumstances, be sexualised in any way, either by the survivor or the counsellor. The survivor needs to relearn that physical contact can be positive, healthy and affirming, and that it is not a precursor to a sexually abusive act.

Other behavioural techniques aim to reverse developmental deficits and conditioned responses acquired in childhood. These techniques mainly consist of counter-conditioning learned behaviours that have become maladaptive in adulthood. The emphasis is on rectifying developmental arrest or deficits, and modeling new behavioural responses. Helfer (1978) has designed a programme which ameliorates many of the developmental deficits experienced by survivors. The focus is on reactivating and developing atrophied senses, learning positive self-regard, and more effective interpersonal interaction.

Parenting skills are also a vital acquisition for the survivor as they enable her to reparent her child self as well as her adult self. Inadequate parental role models may have inhibited the learning of normal parenting practices such as caring, nurturing, and protecting the self and others. The adult survivor needs to acquire these skills so that she can nurture herself. Counsellors can provide powerful role models by modelling positive and appropriate parenting skills, and although they can never replace the adverse parenting the survivor may have experienced in childhood, they can offer the survivor the opportunity to learn to parent herself in a positive and nurturing way.

Reparenting focuses on setting clear and firm boundaries, to enable the survivor to nurture and care for herself. Therapeutic exercises encourage the survivor to do something pleasurable for herself each day such as taking a luxurious and lengthy bath, taking time for herself away from family commitments, having a massage or sauna, or buying herself something that gives her pleasure. One survivor bought a small bouquet of flowers every two or three days and spent half an hour each day looking at them, absorbing their perfume. This was not only aesthetically pleasing to her but also made her feel secure and happy while helping her to relax.

Other exercises focus on relaxation and reflection, with the survivor spending time each day, in self affirmation of her positive attributes. Validating and complimenting herself for having achieved or accomplished something with expertise fosters a more positive self-image. Such exercises also enhance self-respect and enable the survivor to value herself more highly. This encourages a reduction of self-deprecating cognitions and behaviours.

Throughout these techniques the counsellor must demonstrate and provide a positive role model by modelling adaptive and appropriate behaviours. Apart from supporting the survivor in learning to reparent and nurture herself, the counsellor should also encourage the survivor to build up support networks outside therapy which will validate her and foster positive interpersonal relationships while reducing her fear of intimacy.

The behavioural and cognitive approaches also incorporate a learning component which focuses on the acquisition of new skills and more adaptive behavioural responses and coping strategies. These aim to replace old archaic responses which, although adaptive in childhood, have outlived their function to become maladaptive in adulthood. Acquiring more adaptive coping strategies necessitates identifying existing coping strategies, assessing their level of adaptiveness, and finding alternative strategies.

Alternative strategies should ideally be generated by both the survivor and the counsellor, and explored and evaluated to see if they are indeed more functional. If the counsellor imposes alternative strategies the survivor may find them more difficult to integrate and adopt. The survivor should choose which strategies she feels most comfortable with, and can most easily adopt. Behavioural and cognitive rehearsal will familiarise the survivor with the new skills which she can integrate into her behavioural repertoire.

Other skills that the survivor may need to acquire include stress management and stress inoculation in which the survivor learns more adaptive ways of coping with stressful or frightening events. Stress management is particularly useful for survivors who experience intrusive symptoms such as flashbacks, sleep disturbances, or recurring nightmares, as well as denial and numbing of affect (Horowitz, 1986).

Behavioural learning techniques can also assist the acquisition of skills which enhance the survivor's interpersonal interactions. Communication skills enable the survivor to express her needs and to ask for what she wants more effectively. Assertiveness training is an excellent procedure for improving communication skills, learning to say 'No', setting boundaries, and increasing self confidence.

Techniques aimed at enhancing problem solving and decision making skills are also invaluable. Many survivors do not know what they want, much less how to attain goals. Encouraging the survivor to identify her needs and goals, and generating workable solutions with which to achieve them, enable the survivor to believe and trust in herself while recognising that she can actively influence her life rather than remaining a passive, victim.

Many of the techniques used in the acquisition of new skills can be adopted in the therapeutic session, and are a useful antidote to the more cathartic techniques in the experiential/exploratory approach. Some survivors may, however, benefit from partici-pating in adjunctive therapies or training programmes. This allows for the building up of support networks in which the survivor can practise her newly acquired skills while reducing her dependency on the counsellor. Focusing on the acquisition of skills enhances the survivor's coping strategies and interpersonal interactions and also enables her to begin to make choices about her life which empower her to fulfill her full potential.

Retrieving memories

Some survivors have little or no memory of their abuse due to repression resulting in psychogenic amnesia. Lack of memory can become an important therapeutic focus for the survivor in therapy. One survivor who 'knew' she had been sexually abused but who had no specific memories became very anxious to confirm that abuse had actually occurred to establish that her accusations were not the result of vengeful imagination.

When counselling a survivor who has considerable memory deficits relating to childhood but who feels that she was sexually abused, it is essential to ratify the survivor's feelings even in the absence of concrete memories. The counsellor should not concentrate on fact finding and establishing the truth about whether sexual abuse actually happened, but should emphasise that it is the survivor's perception that she was abused that is paramount.

The survivor should be encouraged to acknowledge that she has been abused despite her lack of memory of specific incidents. Just acknowledging that abuse has taken place can bring long repressed memories back into consciousness. Validation of feelings and experiences will impress upon the survivor that it is safe to express her diverse emotions and that the counsellor will not be shocked by the disclosure of unpleasant memories.

Before initiating techniques focused specifically on the retrieval of memories, it is essential to evaluate the survivor's expectations, fears, and what it means to her to restore memory (Gil, 1988). If expectations are unrealistic and unattainable, it is imperative to make this clear to the survivor in order to avoid later disappointment. Once this has been clarified it is necessary to determine where the memory deficits occur, and how selective they are. Memory deficits might relate to one or other parent, specific events and incidents, or particular time periods ranging from days to all childhood memories.

Gil (1988) proposes three concepts that are particularly useful in helping survivors to remember. Firstly, the counsellor needs to have an understanding of how children receive and categorise information. Secondly, the counsellor must recognise that visual cues can stimulate the retrieval of information. Finally, the counsellor should be aware that re-experiencing traumatic events and concommitant arousal and helplessness aids retrieval of memories.

The developmentally immature brain in children under five is considerably limited in the cognitive processing of perceptions and how these are registered, communicated and stored. Thus, children have difficulty in ordering, sequencing and interpreting events. They also tend to focus on global details and material that is relevant to their daily lives while ignoring peripheral events (Perry, 1987). These limitations in perception influence not only the way memories are stored but also make them more difficult to retrieve in adulthood.

As retrieval of blocked and repressed memories is impeded, clinicians have had to consider other techniques which facilitate recall. A more general approach is hypnosis and hypnotherapy. Not all survivors make good hypnotic subjects which has made it necessary for clinicians to devise techniques which include sensory cues to trigger memory and recall. These sensory cues can have a potent effect on retrieval of memory, and the counsellor is advised to work with those sensory cues which are most accessible to the survivor. Many of the techniques described below have been proposed by Gil (1988) and the reader is referred to her work for further elucidation.

Recognition tasks

Recognition tasks rely on visual cues to facilitate memory recall. Gil (1988) suggests that the first recognition task is to find photographs of the survivor at as many childhood ages as possible. Once these have been collated the survivor is asked to arrange the photographs in chronological order, and to paste them into a notebook, one per page. This process of collating and sequencing photographs may stir latent memories. The survivor is also asked to bring one photo to the therapeutic session to discuss it with the counsellor, who should record the client's observations and responses.

Gil (1988) recommends asking the following questions: 'Who are the important people in the child's life? How does the child spend her time? Where did the child live? Who is the child closest to? What is the child's favourite activity?'. This procedure is repeated with the survivor bringing a new photograph to each session to discuss any triggered memories.

If the survivor is unable to obtain photographs then she should be encouraged to contact relatives to ask them if they remember specific incidents and events, which may help trigger memories. If the woman has no surviving relatives, or when the photographs have been exhausted and fully explored, the counsellor should proceed to the next recognition task.

This task requires the survivor to draw a sketch of a house she lived in, preferably during the abuse period, or a period which is difficult to remember. The survivor initially draws the outside of the house and gradually constructs a floor plan of the inside rooms. If the survivor feels uncomfortable about drawing the house then the counsellor can sketch it for her while asking her to show her around the house. The survivor should be encouraged to remember colours, furnishings, pictures, and any affect associated with the rooms. Other sensory cues may trigger spontaneous recall, so the survivor should also be asked to recall smells, sounds, tactile sensations as well as non-sensory stimuli.

The counsellor is advised to note any changes in the survivor's affect and emotional responses such as holding her breath, sweating, trembling, gasping, swallowing, or hyperventilating. Physical responses indicative of emotional affect such as pain, clutching, fear, twitches, rapid eye movement, and other signs of distress should also be noted. Responses should be discussed with the survivor along with exploration of spontaneous reactions such as 'I hate this room' or 'I am afraid of this room'.

Although the sketch may be taken home in between sessions to see if they trigger any further memories, the counsellor should be aware that some survivors may not feel comfortable about memories being recalled when alone as these may cause her to feel frightened or distressed. To prevent this, these exercises are initially best conducted within the session.

Familiarity tasks

In familiarity tasks the survivor is encouraged to talk about her memories of school, friends, pets, hobbies and family. Although these may have been covered briefly during intake, they are now discussed in more detail. The survivor is asked to remember certain aspects of childhood such as school. To explore fully all memories associated with school the counsellor should ask about school activities, favourite subjects, teachers, end of term reports, how they got to school, and achievements attained. When remembering friends the emphasis should be on recalling individual names or nicknames, what the people looked like, and what games they played. Questions about the family should encompass specific family activities, family routines such as eating and sleeping, their assigned jobs, types of punishments, holidays, and parent's friends.

Focusing on such details tends to generate memory retrieval and elicit flashbacks which should be explored, particularly if the memories elicit other symptoms associated with the trauma of abuse. Time should also be spent in making the survivor aware of the types of responses which may yet occur such as flashbacks, nightmares, hallucinations or overwhelming feelings of fear, so that she knows what to expect. When these memories and responses occur outside of sessions, the survivor should be encouraged to record all her feelings and the events preceding the memory so that they can be explored further in the therapeutic session.

Incomplete memories

Some survivors may never be able to recall sharp picture memories, but retain tentative, dreamlike and vague memories. The counsellor should guard against making any value judgements on the extent of recalled memories to ensure that the survivor does not make an inordinate investment in the retrieval of detailed memories. If the survivor feels too pressurised to remember she will become increasingly frustrated and this will impede retrieval. When this occurs it is advisable to proceed by focusing on other things such as present reality, or the acquisition of new skills.

Making repressed memories conscious can sometimes cause severe regression which generate frightening levels of helplessness and despair. If this occurs then focusing on the retrieval of memory is counterindicated as it may provoke profound depression, deterioration and confusion. The therapist should guard against going beyond the client's ability to tolerate the pain and confusion that memory retrieval may evoke. Some survivors may benefit from hypnotherapy to aid recall, although choice of hypnotherapist is important. A hypnotherapist who has some experience of child sexual abuse whom the survivor can trust will be more effective for restoring memory.

If a survivor can only recall vague, incomplete memories and seems unlikely to regain full recall, the counsellor must discuss with her how she feels about this. It may be necessary to get the survivor to acknowledge that she was abused despite the absence of memories, and to work on this as a basis. The counsellor can then explore the meaning the abuse has for the survivor and how this relates to her current difficulties.

Another useful technique is to get the survivor to explore her reactions to two alternative possibilities: being abused or not being abused, and how these contrasting possibilities affect her perceptions about herself. Survivors who leave therapy without having full recall should do so in the knowledge that they have not failed nor are they inadequate, but recognise that whatever happened in childhood was so painful that they are unable to remember it.

Anatomically correct dolls

Working with anatomically correct dolls is a technique which is usually employed with children when sexual abuse is first disclosed. Gil (1988) has effectively adopted this technique in the treatment of adult survivors who have memory deficits, or who want to explore specific incidents in more detail. A major advantage of working with anatomically correct dolls is that it accesses and integrates physiological, behavioural, cognitive and emotional responses associated with the event. The use of dolls allows the survivor to discuss her reactions to and interpretations of the abuse thereby illuminating defence mechanisms along with feelings of responsibility and guilt.

This technique requires the counsellor to proceed slowly and gently, and to communicate directly with the survivor's inner child. The survivor may need to reconstruct the same incident over several sessions to ascertain if any new feelings, memories or responses are evoked. Gil (1988) also recommends that the counsellor ask about responses to the reconstructed event in a specific sequence:

1. The survivor is asked to describe what happened in sequential order and specific detail ('You sat on the chair; he put his hand on your knee; what happened next').

2. The sequence is repeated.

3. The survivor is asked to describe physiological reactions at each point ('You sat on the chair; describe what your body did, how did it feel').

4. What behaviours accompanied these physiological responses ('You went limp, tensed up, frowned, held your breath, clenched your fists, clenched your jaws').

5. Next the accompanying cognitions are explored ('You sat on the chair; your legs got heavy and sweaty; what did you say to yourself; what did you think').

6. Then behavioural, physiological and cognitive responses are reviewed by reiterating the survivor's previous statements.

7. Finally the survivor is asked to describe anything else she remembers feeling.

Anatomically correct dolls have several other uses. They may be taken home by the survivor where is each is assigned a role to prompt recall. Alternatively, the dolls can be used to resolve aspects of the abuse that the child was unable to resolve at the time. Thus the dolls can be used as a way of acting out alternative endings to the abuse and rescue scenes by allowing the survivor to behave in more self-protective, assertive or powerful ways. Finally, anatomically correct dolls can increase the survivor's identification with her inner child, allowing her to empathise with her child thereby fostering self-empathy and acceptance.

A corollary to this is that anatomically correct dolls highlight the discrepancy in body mass and size between abuser and abused. Such awareness not only increases empathy but can also elicit memories of how the abuse was initiated and maintained, either through the use of force, coercion, being tricked or emotional bribery. These are vital issues to explore to appropriately balance feelings of blame and responsibility, allowing the survivor to relinquish much of her burden of guilt.

Some survivors may react negatively to working with anatomically correct dolls. This may be due to a variety of reasons, and should be respected by the counsellor. Under no circumstances should the counsellor insist on using this technique if it proves uncomfortable to the survivor. There are alternative techniques that can be fruitfully applied and the counsellor needs to explore these with the survivor to find which method the survivor is most comfortable with.

Sexuality focused therapy

As the trauma and impact of child sexual abuse is resolved some survivors will wish to progress to addressing their sexuality. Resolution of trauma will have resulted in the survivor being able to take control of her life, acquire self-esteem and a more positive body image. If dissociation has been resolved, the survivor may now, for the first time in years, be able to feel her body and enjoy pleasurable sensations without feelings of guilt and confusion. Survivors who have integrated feelings with cognitions may now wish to focus on their body to explore the effects child sexual abuse has had on their sexuality.

Sexuality-focused therapy allows the survivor to integrate her body and sexuality as part of the whole person and not as a part of herself that is irrecoverably damaged. This can be achieved through education in sexuality and its concommitant physiological responses which occur during sexual arousal; learning about relationships and the role of sex within them, and developing skills to protect herself and her body from further abuse.

Although sex therapy usually requires specialist training which incorporates the assessment and treatment of sexual problems in the light of medical, psychological and relationship problems, there are a number of techniques that can be employed with survivors to reclaim their sexuality. If a survivor has specific sexual dysfunctions or severe gynaecological problems, which the counsellor is not equipped to ameliorate, then she should be referred to a trained sex therapist.

More general sexuality issues can be addressed in the counselling session to good effect. Sexuality should be openly discussed in session along with exploration of the types of difficulties the survivor has. The counsellor may then give the survivor exercises to practise at home, either alone or with a partner. Such structured exercises facilitate the acquisition of new behaviours while undoing old conditioned patterns of sexual responses that were elicited during the abuse experience.

There are several sexuality-focused techniques that have been used with some success in the treatment of adult survivors of child sexual abuse. Many of these techniques have been proposed by Maltz and Holman (1987) and the reader is advised to acquaint themselves with their book *Incest and Sexuality* for more detailed descriptions.

Sex education

Many survivors are confused or misinformed about physiological responses associated with sexual arousal. This is particularly evident in manifest guilt feelings associated with the sexual arousal they experienced during the abuse. A common misconception is that because the survivor was sexually aroused during the abuse she must have enjoyed it. The fact that she responded sexually generates powerful feelings of guilt and shame, which cause the survivor falsely to attribute blame and responsibility to herself. Sex education aims to inform the survivor that her sexual arousal and responses were absolutely normal physiological reactions to sexual stimulation. Her body did not know she was being sexually abused and therefore responded as any other would in the presence of sexual stimulation. The counsellor should spend time on discussing female and male sexual response cycles, anatomical functioning, and dispelling myths and misconceptions about sexuality.

Self-exploration and self-awareness

Most of the exercises on self-exploration, which can be carried out at home, focus on increasing self-awareness about the body, anatomy and how it responds. The survivor should be encouraged to keep a record of her feelings prior, during and after the exercise to share with the counsellor at the next session. Self-awareness exercises focus on the survivor getting to know and feel her body. This includes looking at parts of herself in the mirror. Specific parts of the body are chosen from the most comfortable to the least comfortable. Thus, initial exercises focus on the least anxiety provoking parts of the body such as the arms, legs, feet, shoulders and face. Progressively the survivor begins to concentrate on increasingly more distressing parts such as the breasts, and gradually genitalia. These exercises are vital in identifying the survivor's concerns about her body image.

When these exercises have been completed the counsellor can request that the survivor begin to feel parts of her body by touching herself. This should be done gradually starting with looking at her arm, touching it and then gently stroking it. Again the survivor will benefit from recording her feelings at each stage of this self exploration. Progressively the survivor begins to explore all parts of her body including her breasts and genitals. This can include self massage to ascertain which parts of the body elicit pleasurable and unpleasurable sensations or feelings.

When the survivor is comfortable about the sensations that are elicited the counsellor can suggest that she should start to acquaint herself with the look and feel of the sexual arousal areas by feeling comfortable about naming parts, and learning techniques to enhance arousal and orgasm. The survivor should monitor which parts of the body or sexual response cycle evoke anxiety or panic reactions, and at which point in sexual intimacy aversive feelings are elicited. Knowing which sensations and aspects of her arousal pattern are distressing will allow the survivor to pinpoint which responses need to be desensitised, avoided, or circumvented so that they do not inhibit her from enjoying sexual intimacy.

Relaxation and desensitisation

This should be carried out in the therapeutic session with the therapist asking the survivor to visualise images of increasingly overt sexual activity. As soon as the client feels uncomfortable about any images evoked she is asked to relax and breathe deeply until the image is not threatening anymore. Over sessions this relaxation can allow the survivor to visualise full sexual intercourse without feeling frightened or threatened. This technique can also be employed at home when touching those parts of the body that the survivor feels uncomfortable with.

Communication

If the survivor is with a stable partner it is useful for the partner to attend some sessions to learn techniques for discussing sexual likes and dislikes. It is helpful for both the partner and the survivor to be able to express openly what aspect of sexual activity they enjoy and those that they find aversive. It also useful for the partner to know where these may stem from and to learn more appropriate, less threatening or coercive behaviours which allow the survivor to enjoy sexual intimacy. This can help establish clearer boundaries for both partners and make the initiation of sexual intimacy less threatening.

Sensate focus

More effective communication may be aided by a series of at home exercises on sensate focus, in which the couple learns to relate on a physically intimate level without feeling pressurised to have sex. Usually, partners take it in turns to exchange touch in a safe setting without overt sexual activity. It is often useful to ban actual sexual intercourse until all the sensate focus exercises are completed. Gradually touching progresses towards more overt and direct sexual activity.

Sensate focus involves three phases. In phase one the focus is on the giver of touch and how they feel about exploring and touching the receiver's body. During this phase the breasts and genitals are not touched, with the receiver quiet unless the touch is unpleasant. Phase two concentrates on the receiver giving verbal and physical demonstrations to the giver about how they like to be touched. In the final phase the emphasis is on teaching and learning stimulation techniques for the sexually aroused parts of the body.

Sensate focus is a vital part of sexuality focused therapy which has been shown to be very effective with survivors (Maltz and Holman, 1987). McGuire and Wagner (1978) have also identified three important treatment issues that could be resolved through the techniques of sensate focus.

In the first there is an identification and expression of the survivor's repressed anger. During sensate focus feelings of anger and rage may be evoked by the survivor in remembering her sexual violation as a child. As she was never allowed to express this rage as a child it is important for the survivor to be able to do this as an adult as soon as feelings of anger emerge. In order to differentiate between the abuser and her current partner during sexual intimacy, the survivor needs to be encouraged to verbalise her anger about her early experiences and responses. Being made aware of how these feelings can be displaced on to her partner enables her to recognise that her partner is not the abuser.

The second treatment issue is one of control over the initiation and pacing of the sensate focus. Because survivors were not able to control the sexual abuse in childhood and experienced it as an invasion, many women need to feel in control in order to enjoy sexual intimacy. In taking control of the initiation of sensual and sexual intimacy, and by controlling its progression or termination the survivor is able to counteract the sense of helplessness intrinsic to her abuse. By internalising the locus of control during sexual intimacy the survivor is able to express her sexuality and sexual enjoyment in a more positive way.

A corollary to this is 'forewarning' the survivor that sexual intimacy may take place. This gives the survivor the opportunity to 'psyche' herself up for sex and prepares her mentally. Survivors experience this as some sort of control in that they are not taken by surprise but know in advance what will happen. Although this 'forewarning' sounds extremely clinical, it can be achieved with an element of romance through using special code words. One couple always opened a special bottle of wine to signal that they desired sexual intimacy. This not only prepared the survivor for sex but the wine helped her alleviate her sexual inhibitions.

Finally, the third treatment issue surrounds guilt feelings associated with sexual pleasure. The counsellor must be aware and sensitive to expressions of guilt associated with the experience of sexual pleasure by giving support and permission that sex is enjoyable and pleasurable. During sexual abuse the child associates sexual attention and pleasure with guilt. A consequence of this is that the survivor represses all feelings of pleasure in order to reduce the guilt. Sensate focus provides a method for allowing the survivor to experience pleasure and resolving feelings of guilt.

Pleasure for pleasure's sake

A technique, borrowed from experiential/exploratory therapies which can also be employed in sexuality focused therapy, is nurturing the inner child. The counsellor can focus this on the survivor's sexuality by encouraging her to discover and nurture elements of sexual innocence, playfulness and the ability to enjoy and seek pleasure for pleasure's sake. By emphasising that sexuality is about good feelings and pleasure, the survivor learns that sex is about enjoyment.

Reclaiming the body

Some survivors benefit from developing cleansing rituals in which they can reclaim their bodies for themselves. One survivor would regularly take several baths a day in order to feel that she was clean. These rituals may be accompanied with positive affirmations such as 'I am reclaiming this part of my body for myself. It is no longer associated with the abuser and I have nothing to be afraid of any more. I am re-establishing the innocence of my skin, hair, and nerves. I go back to innocence that I had as a baby. My body is mine, strong and pure' (Maltz and Holman, 1987).

Breaking of old associations

Many survivors have certain triggers that automatically evoke associations with the abuser. The survivor can help to break such old associations by establishing new, positive ones. When used in conjunction with relaxation it is possible to gradually desensitise the survivor to old associations.

Many survivors have particular difficulty viewing and touching the penis. This penis fear can be desensitised and the survivor encouraged to view it in a new way by establishing new associations. One survivor achieved this by covering her partner's penis in chocolate mousse which she then consumed. Another technique that has been shown to be useful is using perfumed body cream or aromatic oils. This can overcome old sensory associations such as smell and also tactile sensations. One survivor found that the use of perfumed cream overcame her associations of the smell of sexual secretions and body sweat, while also changing tactile sensations to more gentle feelings of softly creamed body and fingers, rather than hard, callused, dirty hands invading her body.

Many survivors instinctively change old associations by choosing partners who are physically the antithesis of the abuser. They will often choose partners who have a completely different physique, colouring and personality. Some survivors also find they can only entertain a relationship with a partner from a different cultural or ethnic background.

An essential component in sexuality-focused therapy is allowing the survivor to gain control by actively, assertively and creatively changing old associations to new, positive one. Encouraging the survivor to experiment until she finds what she feels most comfortable with, and injecting a level of humour can help the survivor to experience her sexuality and sexual intimacy in a relaxed, fun way.

The counsellor needs to recognise the survivor's special needs and specific sexual problems. Sexuality-focused therapy requires tremendous levels of sensitivity and patience. The process of undoing and changing sexual behaviour patterns that are not only deeply ingrained and highly emotive, but are also often distressing and confusing, is slow and should not be rushed. Many survivors are able to enjoy some aspects of their sexuality. Validating and focusing on these along with identifying those which are distressing enables the survivor to gradually reclaim all aspects of her sexuality.

Sexuality-focused therapy can make the survivor feel extremely vulnerable and evoke many distressing emotions. Progress is often gradual and a balance needs to be maintained between opening up sexually and the need to protect the self. Despite the up-and-down nature of sexual recovery, prognosis is often good and counsellors should proceed with persistence and optimism, while encouraging the survivor also to persevere by validating her progress to date.

The need to remain flexible in the treatment approach and to individualise each approach to the needs of the client frequently requires the counsellor to experiment with available techniques. The emphasis for all approaches or techniques is flexibility rather than adhering to a rigid therapeutic framework. The following chapter looks at the range of techniques that have been employed with some success in the treatment of adult survivors of child sexual abuse. Many of the techniques serve a variety of functions, spanning several therapeutic approaches, and should ideally be used in combination. Although most of the techniques cited are used primarily in individual therapy, some can also be applied to group work.

CHAPTER 9

Treatment Techniques

Treatment for adult survivors of child sexual abuse can be categorised into three major treatment approaches, reflecting the type of psychological effects and functioning. Corresponding treatment techniques are similarly classified: experiential/exploratory techniques; cognitive techniques; and behavioural techniques. This classification is, however, not rigid with considerable overlap between techniques and approaches. Thus, role play techniques may be used to access distorted cognitions, to access feelings in an experiential/exploratory way, and to facilitate behaviour change.

As there is little empirical data on the efficaciousness of each individual approach and its associated techniques, the counsellor will need to experiment and be flexible in choosing the most appropriate technique. Thus, a wide variety of techniques is presented in this chapter to demonstrate the amount of choice available to the counsellor with which to experiment. This allows the counsellor to identify those techniques that he or she finds most comfortable working with, and to assess which are the most beneficial to the individual survivor.

Experiential/exploratory techniques

Many of the techniques in this category are borrowed from psychodynamic and humanistic therapies such as Gestalt and Transactional Analysis. Some of these have been freely adopted from these therapeutic orientations, while others have been modified from a variety of sources to suit trauma resolution work with adult survivors of child sexual abuse.

Telling the story

Survivors can find tremendous relief in relating details of their abuse experience to another person who is accepting and empathic. Disclosure can be difficult for some survivors and the counsellor needs to reassure the client that she can proceed at her own pace, only revealing as much as she is comfortable with. Patience on the part of the counsellor is essential since disclosure may take several, if not many sessions. This may sometimes seem like a jigsaw puzzle as events are not necessarily recalled in any sequential order. Perseverance will allow a final picture to emerge. Some survivors will have no memory of their abuse and will need to focus on the retrieval of memories see Chapter 8, while others, although in possession of intact memories, attach no feeling to them, and appear to be 'dissociated' from their experiences.

Each survivor will proceed at a different speed with some unable to verbalise or articulate their history. Bass and Davis (1988) describe one survivor who could not face her therapist while revealing her history, and so therapy was conducted with the therapist and client sitting back to back. This emphasises the level of flexibility required in letting the survivor lead at her own pace, and adopting techniques which are most beneficial to her.

Re-experiencing the trauma

Once a history of sexual abuse has been disclosed the counsellor will need to encourage the survivor to re-experience 'split off' aspects of the trauma in order to integrate these dissociated cognitions and affect with the adult self. This involves making unconscious memories conscious and breaking through the survivor's defence of denial and repression. Although this can be hard and arduous work, the counsellor needs to pursue it firmly but sensitively so as not to 'flood' or overwhelm the survivor.

While some therapists believe that re-experiencing trauma is counter-productive as it may result in regression, clinical observation indicates that re-experiencing trauma is an integral part of trauma resolution. It may be necessary to forewarn the survivor that re-experiencing long hidden memories and feelings will inevitably make her feel vulnerable and as though she 'is getting worse'. It is vital to prepare the survivor for this and to point out that this is a transitory phase which will ameliorate as integration takes place.

Externalising feelings

Gestalt techniques, such as chair work or pummelling pillows to discharge anger, can be very powerful. Many survivors feel inhibited about expressing their anger or rage, and feel that if they do they will disintegrate as the anger is so overwhelming. It is essential that the survivor expresses her anger, in an environment where she is safe and in the presence of someone she trusts. Encouraging the survivor to hit a pillow releases some of the rage and anger which, once expressed, can then be worked on.

The empty chair

In chair work the survivor imagines that someone she wishes to talk to is sitting in an empty chair. The survivor then talks to that person telling them all she wants to express. This allows for the expression of anger, sadness, love and pain towards the abuser, mother, and others who played a significant role in the past. This is useful if the survivor is unable to confront the individual, or in preparation for future confrontation. This technique is particularly useful for those survivors who have difficulty processing feelings on an affective level.

Role playing

Role playing also facilitates the release of emotion and the exploration of trauma. In role playing the survivor may play the role of the child, or the abuser, or her mother, while exploring what it feels like to be in that role. This can be beneficial in encouraging an awareness of other people's perspective, motivation and actions. Role play can also be adopted cognitively to explore alternative cognitions, or behaviourally to acquire and rehearse new behaviours.

Psychodrama or dramatherapy

Psychodrama cuts through denial and intellectualisation by allowing the survivor to act out situations from the past or future, thereby giving her instantaneous access to her feelings and the opportunity to experiment with alternative and new responses. Psychodrama can be particularly useful for staging confrontations with family members and exploring whether to confront or not. Dramatherapy provides a somewhat gentler approach through the use of groupwork, role play and sculpts. However, neither psychodrama not dramatherapy should be undertaken by an untrained counsellor.

Art as healing

Some survivors who have difficulty expressing themselves verbally may find it easier to express themselves through drawing, painting, sculpture, or moulding pottery and clay. Whatever artistic expression is available to the survivor should be encouraged by the counsellor as another medium for releasing emotions and feelings. The survivor can be encouraged to bring her artistic expressions to the counselling session as a basis from which to explore feelings. One survivor would regularly draw or paint a picture to express how she felt about the previous session, which became the therapeutic focus for the following session.

Music

Music can be very evocative and emotionally arousing for many survivors. One survivor used music in a very cathartic way by playing music from the 1960s which reminded her of the period when she was being abused. Her level of dissociation was such that she could release no feelings, positive or negative. Playing music reminiscent of the abuse period prior to the therapeutic session generated potent flashbacks, and allowed powerful feelings associated with the abuse to resurface. Thus, music gave this survivor permission to discharge long repressed emotions, which could then be explored in the therapeutic session. Other survivors use music as a way to relax and choose music that has a calming effect on them.

Dance and movement

The inhibiting effects of dissociation from the abuse trauma can be alleviated through dance and movement. Many survivors report not being able to feel their bodies, or if they do, feeling very uncomfortable in them. Dance and movement therapy facilitates learning to reexperience the body and to become aware of its fluidity rather than rigidity. Survivors have found dance a particularly enjoyable way of becoming aware of their body, deriving pleasure from its versatility as an expressive form.

Bodywork

Survivors who have intellectualised their abuse experiences and dissociated from feelings benefit from learning to re-experience their bodies to access feelings. Although these survivors perform well in therapies that concentrate on verbal interaction and operate on an intellectual level, they are often petrified when asked to feel and experience their bodies. These women find it difficult to relax and often say that they cannot feel their body.

One survivor who had been in therapy for some time had been very articulate about her abuse and intellectualised to such an extent that she seemed barely affected by it and very much in control of herself. When asked to participate in body work exercises she was very frightened of relaxing and focusing on her body because she felt vulnerable in lowering her defences as her body would then be left open to invasion. After much initial resistance, she was gradually able to feel her body, usually accompanied by floods of tears and intense, raw emotional reactions which were never evident in verbal counselling sessions.

Bioenergetics, Hakomi and other physical therapies encourage the release of emotions. Grounding and breathing exercises are also valuable in preventing the survivor from dissociating from her feelings thereby increasing a sense of control and personal power. Counsellors who are not trained in these techniques should recommend body work therapy in conjunction with more traditional counselling in order to release deeply blocked emotion and feeling.

However, the cathartic nature of bodywork requires that the survivor be relatively stable and able to cope with high emotional arousal. Counsellors should not recommend bodywork until there has been some trauma resolution and the survivor has learnt breathing and desensitisation exercises which return her to a stable baseline of arousal.

The use of photographs

Looking at old photographs of the survivor as a child can elicit a variety of feelings in women who have dissociated, and also facilitate retrieval of memory and recall for specific events. Photographs taken before, after and during the abuse allow the survivor to see herself as she was prior to the abuse and to integrate these aspects of the self with the self during and after the abuse.

The use of photographs can also be used in a cognitive way. One survivor had a photograph of herself before the abuse enlarged and framed so that she could look at herself as she was, with her whole life before her and her potential undamaged. Looking at this photograph helped her to reclaim the potential of which she had been robbed, and provided the impetus to succeed through the healing process.

Some survivors have found it useful to bring photographs of the abuser to the therapeutic session in order to release emotions, both positive and negative, about the abuser. In some instances, the symbolic burning of photographs of the abuser can release a lot of the pain and anger towards the abuser.

The house

This technique also assists the retrieval of memories and feelings. Drawing the house in which the survivor was abused enables her to release many of the feelings associated with the abuse. This technique starts very gently with the survivor drawing the outside of the house followed by a floor plan of each room. The survivor is asked to describe each room and her feelings associated with the room, until she reaches the room in which the abuse occurred most frequently. Gradually the survivor is able to build up a picture not only of the family home, but also family dynamics and family routine.

Keeping a journal

Recording feelings, thoughts, dreams, experiences and insights outside therapy can be helpful to the survivor as a way to increase awareness of feelings and thoughts. A journal can also be useful after therapy has ended in charting the healing and growth process. The journal is for the survivor's benefit and should only be shared with the counsellor if the survivor wishes to do so.

Keeping a journal also has a cognitive component in enabling the survivor to monitor progress over time and chart positive outcome. Having tangible evidence of progress gives the survivor the courage to face new crises, or emerging threatening material. Reminding herself through her journal entries that she has pulled through crises before, helps her to acquire a positive belief in herself that she can do so again. This technique offers hope, optimism, and real evidence that progress is being made.

Writing letters

One way of releasing feelings of pain or anger is to externalise rather than internalise them by writing letters to others. These can be to other significant persons, living or dead, such as mother or father, the abuser, siblings or relatives. The benefit in writing letters is a cathartic one in expressing emotions and ideas although they may not necessarily be sent to the person concerned.

Although letters can be sent and used as first step in confronting the abuser, or other family members, the counsellor will need to prepare the survivor for the consequences of such confrontation, including the relative benefits gained from such action as well as any negative ramifications. The survivor should ideally be well advanced in her healing process so that she can reap the positive benefits of confrontation rather than destructive elements which could plunge her back into despair. Some therapists make a point of accompanying the survivor to the confrontation to lend much needed support.

Creative writing

Many survivors find that they express themselves best when writing creatively either in prose or poetry. A particularly cathartic method is for the survivor to write down her childhood abuse experiences. Many survivors attempt such autobiographical accounts, not necessarily for publication, but rather as a way of remembering, re-experiencing, and reprocessing their experiences. For some it is a potent mechanism for reclaiming their childhood and disclosing the secret of their abuse.

Discovering the 'Inner Child' within

Although there is no scientific evidence for the existence of the inner child, some clinicians find this concept a useful one in therapy: helping the survivor to discover her 'inner child', encouraging her to listen, to nurture and care for her child. The survivor first needs to establish communication with her 'inner child' and learn to listen to her feelings, wants and desires. By responding to the child's needs and nurturing her, the survivor will be able to integrate the child with the adult self, rather than the child's directing and initiating inappropriate behaviour.

In listening to the self the survivor will be able to monitor whether her responses and behaviours are initiated by her child or her adult. Being aware of where her responses stem from allows the survivor to freely choose her behaviour patterns and responses appropriate to any given situation. Integrating the child with the adult so that both are comfortable with each other is an important part of the healing process, and the principles of transactional analysis (TA) may be usefully employed.

The inner child needs to be nurtured and cared for and will at times be infuriatingly demanding. The survivor will need to reassure the child that the adult is now her parent and that she will protect and look after her and ensure that nothing bad happens to her. Although many survivors find the concept of the 'inner child' somewhat abstract to start with, and are nervous of establishing a dialogue with her, once they acknowledge their inner child many survivors report not only a clarity of understanding of their behaviour, but also show considerable improvement on both cognitive and affective levels.

Some survivors become so engrossed in their 'inner child' once they discover her that they become overly indulgent towards her. Allowing the child to emerge is very cathartic and survivors sometimes overidentify with the child while ignoring her adult self. This is akin to denial, in that the survivor begins to live in her past, allowing the child to direct and manipulate the adult, reducing the level of adult functioning. Although identification with the 'inner child' is important it needs to be balanced between the adult and child self so that present reality is not denied.

Parks inner child therapy (PICT)

Penny Parks (1990) has devised an innovative technique to access the inner child which overcomes its abstraction as a concept and establishes communication and dialogue. PICT consists of the exchange of letters between the adult self and her inner child. Parks notes that after some initial resistance and practise, that survivors are able to engage in a powerful dialogue. When the inner child responds to the letters from the adult self, noticeable changes in writing style, sentence construction and grammar have been observed which are reminiscent of the child's writing and level of cognitive developmental level at the time of the abuse.

Parkes reports considerable success with this novel technique which aims to resolve the trauma of child sexual abuse within six to nine months rather than more traditional therapeutic approaches which can take several years. Although PICT requires further evaluation and clinical analysis, in its present form it appears to be a highly effective cathartic technique.

Dolls and teddies

To make the inner child analogy more accessible, survivors find that holding or cuddling an old teddy or doll that they can talk to and nurture makes the concept less abstract. This makes identification with the inner child easier, and gives a more tangible focus for the kind of nurturing and care it needs. It is often useful to give the doll or teddy a diminutive version of the survivor's name in order to bond identification. Anatomically correct dolls may also be used to explore cognitive, affectual and behavioural responses to the abuse (Gil, 1989).

Clinical observation indicates that many survivors collect teddies, dolls, childhood artefacts, or are fascinated by children's toys. It is likely that such toys represent a part of the lost childhood of the survivor. Tangible objects such as toys, dolls or teddies, or childhood artefacts around the home serve an important function for survivors in reclaiming their childhood, and also to facilitate grieving for the childhood of which they feel robbed.

Playing

Another cathartic technique that fosters accessing the child within is for the survivor to re-experience what it is like to play. Many survivors report never having experienced uninhibited play as a child and feel uncomfortable around children. A common response to their own children is not knowing how to play with them. Encouraging the survivor to play with toys reduces inhibitions and defences which may release memories and emotions.

Observing children at play

Many survivors exhibit more affectual responses to children being currently abused, or seeing young children, than they do about their own abuse. Observing young children, especially children of the same sex and age when the abuse started augments the survivor's reality of her abuse. She is able to see not only size differentials but also power differentials and the innocence of the child. This is sometimes an important way of recognising that a child cannot be responsible for her sexual abuse and that she is the innocent party.

Observing children at play can be extremely painful for the survivor and may elicit powerful and violent emotions. Survivors report being able to see the reality of their abuse more clearly, being able to identify with the inner child, and being reminded of the childhood of which they were robbed. Some survivors also report feelings of jealousy that they did not have an innocent and normal childhood, while others begin to feel angry for the first time about their violation and their losses. Seeing the innocence and joy of childhood in other children releases emotions that the survivor can then explore in the therapeutic session.

Symptomatology in children

If the observation of children is combined with information about the kind of symptoms manifested by children who are currently being sexually abused, the survivor can increase awareness of her own symptoms, both in childhood and as an adult. This may also restore memories of symptoms she had as child and allow her to grieve for what happened to her. Listing the symptoms of child sexual abuse in children provides a powerful vehicle for discussing memories and associated feelings.

Dreams

The interpretation of dreams can make unconscious material and messages conscious thereby enabling the woman to understand herself and her feelings better. The counsellor should encourage the survivor to learn to interpret these dreams herself thus enhancing self awareness and insight.

Free association

Allowing the survivor to associate freely around her childhood can make previously repressed memories conscious and elicit flashbacks. It is important that the counsellor encourage the survivor to make connections between freely associated thoughts and the abuse trauma. As many survivors do not connect current affects, cognitions or behaviours with their abuse experiences, it is crucial that the counsellor enables connections to be made and discusses them with the survivor. By exploring such connections the survivor becomes more aware of the effects the abuse has had on her while gaining insight into her current cognitions and behaviour patterns.

Guided fantasy work

Guided fantasy is a very cathartic technique which elicits powerful arousal states and blocked emotions, and should not be undertaken by a counsellor without prior training. This technique is most potent when the focus of the fantasy is directed at the exploration of feelings about the body or sexuality. The counsellor will have to proceed cautiously and monitor how much the survivor can process without becoming overwhelmed. If the arousal state proves too anxiety-provoking then the counsellor will need to be flexible in terminating the fantasy, or substituting it with a less threatening one. The released emotions should form the basis for further analysis and exploration in the remaining part of the therapeutic session.

Fantasy work has another advantage in that it allows the survivor and counsellor to monitor over time the character of her fantasy world to assess progress. In addition, fantasy work also allows the exploration of possible outcomes of the initial abuse and the creation of scenarios in which the survivor is able to overpower or stop the abuse. This has great value in demonstrating to the survivor that although she was powerless and helpless as a child, as an adult she no longer is and can thus protect and empower her self in an abusive situation.

Visualisation and affirmation

Visualisation exercises can be used to explore how the survivor sees her self and how she would like to be. This technique can be used throughout therapy as visualisations change as healing takes place. One survivor asked to visualise her power in the early stages of healing remarked that it was too frightening to conjure up an image as it was overwhelmingly evil. As healing progressed she was able to visualise power as being able to defend herself. Other types of visualisations are to get the survivor to imagine and describe herself as an animal, bird or flower. Talking through and interpreting visualisations enable the survivor to reassess herself.

The counsellor must consistently validate and affirm the survivor in order to enhance positive self-image and self-esteem. The survivor can also be encouraged to affirm herself by repeating positive statements about herself such as 'I am strong; I am beautiful; I am a good person' until she believes it of herself. Another technique is to write down positive statements about herself and place them around the house where the survivor can easily see them, such as the bathroom mirror. Such affirmations and reinforcement develop positive self-image and self-esteem.

Videos

The watching of videos which contain personal accounts of other survivors and their abuse experiences can play a role in generating arousal states and empathy. This can be cathartic in permitting the survivor to re-experience her own pain and suffering by giving herself permission to feel rather than deny and repress. Watching videos also facilitates identification with other survivors reducing isolation and stigmatisation.

Books

Similar discharge can be generated through the use of first hand personal accounts by adult survivors of child sexual abuse. Books can be especially helpful if the narrator reflects a similar abuse history, or manifests similar presenting symptoms. Such accounts can be useful in allowing the survivor to identify with others and to see that healing is possible and that the resolution of abuse trauma has a positive outcome.

The counsellor will need to be careful to assess at what stage the survivor is in the healing process, as some survivors may not be able to cope with reading about other survivors and may regress as a result of reading such accounts. In addition, some survivors may overload themselves and overidentify with child sexual abuse and incest issues which can impede healing.

The range and variety of experiential/exploratory techniques is wide and diverse. Some of the techniques also have applicability in accessing cognitive distortions and in facilitating behavioural change, and can be used interchangeably across all three therapeutic approaches. In the absence of more concrete empirical evidence as to which of the experiential/exploratory techniques are most effective in the resolution of trauma, counsellors will need to experiment with the techniques they feel most comfortable with and which best suit each individual survivor. Ideally, experiential/exploratory techniques should be combined with cognitive and behavioural techniques to be most efficacious in trauma resolution. However, it should be emphasised that many of the techniques evoke strong responses, and should not be undertaken by counsellors who have not undergone training.

Cognitive techniques

Cognitive techniques aim to identify and analyse internalised distorted cognitions, while aiming to replace these with more accurate and realistic thoughts. Techniques consist of general exercises which investigate and make the survivor more aware of her automatic, habitual and distorted cognitions and how to replace these with more accurate alternatives, through cognitive restructuring.

Role playing

Role play, essentially an experiential/exploratory technique which has applications in behavioural approaches, also has a powerful cognitive component in isolating split off cognitions and internalised negative messages about the self. It also functions in merging opposing sides of her personality such as 'good girl' versus 'bad girl' or 'frightened victim' versus 'angry retaliator'. Role play allows the survivor to act out and verbalise opposing aspects of her personality which ameliorates dissociation by accommodating both ego states in the self rather than only acknowledging one side and repressing the other.

Role playing exercises may be used as an ongoing process within therapy which can be adopted regularly to establish a continuous dialogue. It may be useful to encourage the 'good girl' to act out in several sessions and then ask the 'bad girl' to rebut and comment on her. This may then be reversed with the 'bad girl' acting out followed by comments for the 'good girl'. Role play is a potent dissociative technique in facilitating access and exploration of all the components of the survivor's cognitions and the integration of the split off parts with current ego states.

The observer

In this form of role play the survivor is asked to watch herself in the session and to verbalise what she is thinking in the third person. Initially, these cognitions often reflect self-hating cognitions, but gradually the survivor becomes more objective in her self-observations and shifts to a more compassionate perspective. This exercise facilitates less threatening self-understanding as it is done in the third person and enables the survivor to substitute internalised negative cognitions with more positive self-evaluation.

Another technique using the observer, which can also be used as an experiential/exploratory technique, is to ask the adult to travel back into childhood and visit her 'child' around the time of the abuse. The adult observer is initially asked to describe the child as comprehensively as possible giving details of the room, the child's clothes, facial expression and other pertinent aspects of her. The counsellor then asks the adult how the child is feeling and other questions related to child, including how the adult feels about the child.

The survivor can also engage in a dialogue between her adult self and the child to exchange feelings and cognitions about each other. Although not all survivors are able to achieve this 'adult–child' dialogue, this exercise can elicit powerful feelings which not only access repressed memories, affects and cognitions, but also atrophied and frozen aspects of her personality. The dramatic arousal effects inherent in this exercise precludes its use until well into the therapeutic process when a strong therapeutic alliance and a firm level of trust has been established.

Good person, bad person

The essence of this form of role play is the verbalisation of opposing cognitions. A negative self-hating statement such as 'You are a bad, unlikable and unlovable person' is rebutted by a positive, self-affirming statement such as 'I am a good, likable person who deserves to be loved'. According to Briere (1989) the most effective cognitive change occurs if the disconfirming side is spoken in the second person ('You are...') which better captures the accusatory tone of introjected negativity. Self-affirming statements should be spoken in the first person to facilitate modelling and reinforcing positive self-statements. In combination such verbalisation are a powerful mechanism for disrupting the adoption of future negative cognitions.

Tape recognition

Tape recognition operates on a cognitive and behavioural level. In tape recognition the survivor is encouraged to recognise when old cognitions, behaviour patterns or responses are activated. The analogy is that primitive cognitions and behaviours which were conditioned in childhood become developmentally arrested and are recorded on tape, where they are stored in an unaltered form to be elicited whenever the individual is in the presence of the stimuli associated with the conditioned response. Some of these tapes have become maladaptive to the adult and she needs gradually to erase them.

Many of the tapes represent internalised negative messages about herself, her attributes and her abilities. The survivor may consistently play these tapes to reinforce her negative self-image and low self-esteem. The survivor will need to be aware of these negative tapes by identifying them, monitoring them when they are activated and learn to not listen to them. If the tapes are ignored they become fainter and fainter, eventually fading away which allows them to be replaced with more accurate and positive cognitions. It is unlikely that they will ever be totally erased but the less frequently they are played or listened to the more they will fade and therefore not be activated.

Reframing

In reframing, the counsellor can help the survivor to look at events, cognitions, behaviours and feelings in a different way or from alternative perspectives. This is of particular value when determining distorted cognitions and coping strategies. The counsellor can show the survivor that although some of her beliefs and coping skills were positive and adaptive in childhood, they are redundant in her adult life. Encouraging the survivor to generate alternative cognitions and coping strategies, and by emphasising that she has a choice of which ones to use, will empower her to make choices rather than being directed by rigidly ingrained habitual beliefs and behaviours.

Self-talk

In self-talk the survivor is encouraged to learn to counter and talk back to her negative cognitions. This can be particularly useful if the survivor is preoccupied with self derogatory thoughts focusing on her badness or inadequacies. The survivor can counter such thoughts by repeating positive, self-affirmative statements to herself such as 'I am a good capable person who can win through this.'

Rescue scenes

In rescue scenes the survivor visualises being abused but instead of allowing the abuse to continue she visualises alternative endings to the abuse. This may entail her rescuing herself by becoming angry at the abuser and physically attacking him, or her saying no and leaving the room. This can be empowering to the survivor in showing her that she has choices that she did not have as a child. It is also a useful way of reassuring the 'inner child' that she will not be abused again as the adult will be there to protect her.

Support scenes

As in rescue scenes, the survivor can visualise that the abuse is interrupted by the presence of all her friends in the room while the abuse is taking place. She can go on to visualise her friends support for her, their anger at the abuser, and their support in preventing the abuse from continuing. This visualisation also validates the survivor in showing her that she does have supportive friends who care for her and wish to protect her.

Metaphors

The use of metaphors can be a powerful cognitive technique for exploring the meaning the abuse experience had for the survivor, and the defences she needed to acquire. In addition, metaphors can be used to evaluate therapeutic progress. One survivor when asked for a metaphor for power at the beginning of therapy described it as a machine gun. When reassessing her feelings about power towards the end of therapy she had replaced this metaphor with one denoting power as a sword and shield.

The revised metaphor indicated that power was no longer an exclusively destructive weapon, but rather included a protective element of having a shield to protect herself with. It also revealed that the sword as weapon would primarily be used in one-to-one combat whereas the machine gun could be used at a distance and indiscriminately. The survivor felt that her healing was embedded in this by demonstrating that her anger and defensive strategy were directed against a close combatant, her abuser, and not free floating and directed at all men.

Identifying metaphors for the defences that the survivor has built around her can facilitate the dismantling of those defences. Another survivor described her defence as a steel door in the pit of her stomach that contained all the bad things that she wanted to keep locked up. Using the same metaphor, the survivor was asked to visualise and explore what would happen if she found the key that opened the door and entered this sealed chamber. Through visualisation it was possible for the survivor to begin lowering her defences, and eventually dismantle the steel door as a defence.

Groves (1987) proposes that trauma is physiologically embedded and that metaphors facilitate the description of trauma experiences and the examination of intrapsychic components which are instrumental in behavioural change.

Cognitive restructuring

Cognitive restructuring has been shown to generate statistically significant improvement in survivor's beliefs and mood states (Jehu, Gazan and Klassen, 1986). The essential components in this technique are identifying distorted beliefs and cognitions and replacing these with more accurate and realistic thoughts. Examples of some of the most common distorted cognitions observed in adult survivors of child sexual abuse are reviewed below, along with their concomitant alternative, more accurate beliefs.

All-or-nothing or dichotomous thinking

The main characteristic of this distortion is the tendency for extreme black or white categorisation such as complete failure or brilliant success. Sometimes referred to as dichotomous thinking, these cognitions focus on extremes thereby ignoring grey areas in between. This leads to low self-esteem, as even slight or imagined imperfections automatically lead to negative beliefs.

An example of all-or-nothing thinking would be 'I am completely self-centred and thoughtless. I am just no good'. The client would aim to provide an alternative, more rational response such as 'I am self-centred and thoughtless sometimes, but not at other times. I am not perfect but that does not mean that I am bad. I can work through this.'

Overgeneralisation

In overgeneralisation the survivor applies a conclusion based on isolated events to a wide range of situations. An example of such distorted thinking is 'I was abused by a man. That means that all men are abusers and not to be trusted'. An alternative cognition can be substituted here 'I was abused by my father who is a man. Many fathers do abuse their children but not all do. Not all men abuse children and some men can be trusted. I just haven't found one yet that I can trust, but I know that one day when I have finished therapy I might be able to trust some men.'

Mislabelling

Mislabelling is an extreme form of overgeneralisation in which the survivor may create a totally negative image on the basis of a single, often minor deficiency. This is unrealistic in that one cannot equate a person with one particular action or attribute. An example of mislabelling may be 'I'm a weakling who is too afraid to change'. This can be countered with 'I've shown tremendous courage in having survived my abuse and I am showing my strength by seeking counselling. If I didn't want to change then I would not be in therapy'.

Mental filtering

Sometimes referred to as selective abstraction, this distortion focuses on the filtering out of positive aspects in a situation and dwelling exclusively on minor negative details. Survivors may filter out all their positive achievements such as their survival and focus on the problems associated with the abuse. An example of this distortion is 'I have failed at everything in my life. I was hopeless at school, I made a bad marriage, I am a lousy mother, and I can never make anything work.' This can be replaced with 'I have achieved several worthwhile things in my life. I have a good career and I am a "good enough" mother and I am taking a degree course.'

Disqualifying the positive

In disqualifying the positive the survivor filters out positive experiences thereby discounting them or transforming them into negative experiences, allowing for the maintenance of distorted beliefs despite contradictory evidence. An example of such distortion was provided by one survivor upon attaining an excellent honours degree. She responded by saying that 'It was pure luck that I did so well. They must have felt sorry for me and given me extra marks'. A more realistic approach would be to say that 'I am pleased to have done so well. I deserved it as I worked hard for it and it was a struggle, but I got through it and did extremely well.'

Jumping to conclusions

This distortion, also referred to as arbitrary inference, operates by drawing a negative conclusion which is not justified by facts. A classic example of this distortion would be 'Everyone who knows me will hate me for confronting my father and disclosing the abuse. They will not want to know me any more'. This statement can be countered by 'I know that some of my friends will be shocked by my disclosure but on the whole they will support me. Those that don't aren't real friends.'

Magnification and minimisation

Both magnification and minimisation can be damaging to self-esteem. In magnification the survivor exaggerates her mistakes and deficiencies totally out of proportion leading to catastrophisation. Minimisation occurs when the survivor plays down her positive attributes or the effects child sexual abuse has had on her.

In magnification the survivor may believe that 'I will never heal from my abuse experience to lead a normal life. I have been permanently damaged.' In minimisation the survivor will argue that the effects of her abuse are imperceptible and have really not damaged or affected her in any way. Both views are distorted and can be countered with either 'I can overcome my abuse experience and I will be able to lead a healthier life. The damage can be repaired if I want it to be' or by the survivor acknowledging 'The abuse has had an effect on me and I want to explore these effects and work on them.'

Emotional reasoning

A misleading aspect of this type of thinking is that emotional feelings are taken as a reflection of reality and truth, and not seen as distorted. A pertinent example of this is when feelings of guilt about the abuse are equated with being responsible for allowing it to happen. Many survivors argue that 'I was responsible for the abuse because I feel so bad about not having said no.' A more realistic cognition would be 'I was made to feel bad by the abuse and that is what makes me feel guilty. But feeling guilty does not mean that I am guilty, or responsible.'

'Should' statements

Survivors often hold unrealistic expectations of themselves and others and believe that they should behave in accordance with these high expectations. Failure to live up to these expectations leads to guilt, low self-esteem and anger. A common should statement is 'I should have said no or kicked him where it hurts'. The alternative, more accurate statement is 'I couldn't say no because he had his hands around my throat and I couldn't kick him because he pinned my legs down on the bed'.

Personalisation

Frequently referred to as misattribution, personalisation involves assumptions of responsibility where there should be none. This is very common among survivors who assume responsibility for the abuse resulting in feelings of guilt. Personalisation commonly manifests itself in survivor's comments such as 'I must have been responsible for the sexual abuse because I enjoyed it and my body responded to it'. A more accurate and realistic statement would be 'My body responded in a normal, healthy, physiological way to sexual stimulation. That does not make me responsible for the sexual abuse.'

Provision of information

In providing the survivor with factual data to correct inaccurate information, the counsellor is fulfilling an educative role. Information may be provided verbally during the therapeutic session and also through books and articles (see Appendix A) on child sexual abuse and its impact on adult survivors.

Logical analysis

In logical analysis the counsellor reviews the logic adopted by the survivor to determine whether the evidence warrants the conclusions the survivor has drawn. In addition, it is important to develop alternative conclusions which are not distorted by the survivor's negative self-esteem.

Decatastrophising

The counsellor must broaden the survivor's perspective to take account of all pertinent information rather than being selective, in order to reduce magnification or minimisation. One example of this would be informing the survivor that although she believes herself to be permanently damaged by her abuse experience, many other survivors have achieved positive and healthy adjustments.

Distancing

Distancing involves a process of shifting the survivor's perception from a subjective focus to a more objective perspective. This allows the survivor to view her beliefs not as self evident truths but rather as hypotheses that need to be tested. To quote Beck (1976)

'Distancing involves being able to make a distinction between "I believe" (an opinion that is subject to validation) and "I know" (an irrefutable fact).'

Re-attribution

This encourages the survivor not to assume responsibility for factors that are, or were, beyond her control, such as her abuse. The counsellor and the survivor review the abuse experience and reapportion elements of responsibility in accordance with what happened, allowing the survivor to relinquish much of her self blame. Thus, the counsellor can demonstrate either that the facts of the situation do not support the survivor's self blame, or that the survivor is using double standards for her own behaviour in comparison to others, thereby challenging the survivor's degree of responsibility.

Assigned activities

One way of changing distorted beliefs is to introduce exercises designed to disconfirm distorted beliefs while confirming more accurate alternatives. Jehu, Gazan and Klassen (1986) cite an example of a survivor who believed herself to be extremely ugly. The exercise involved arriving at an agreed criteria of attractiveness which the survivor predicted at least 50 per cent of women would meet. The survivor then went to a supermarket where she and her partner monitored some 102 women coming through the entrance. As the survivor was only able to identify 15 per cent of these women as being attractive, a huge discrepancy was revealed. This discrepancy formed an empirical basis for restructuring her beliefs.

It is still unknown which active ingredients in cognitive restructuring are most effective in improving distorted beliefs and amelioration of mood disturbances. More empirical data will allow for more rigorous evaluation. Until such data is available, cognitive restructuring and more general cognitive techniques can usefully be adopted in addition to other techniques, especially behaviourally orientated ones, to resolve the trauma of child sexual abuse.

Behavioural techniques

Behavioural techniques operate in several ways. Some behavioural techniques aim to relax and desensitise the survivor to highly arousing emotions so that she does not become overwhelmed by them and is able to explore painful memories and feelings. Other techniques focus on isolating negative behaviour patterns and replacing these with more adaptive behaviours. Finally, some techniques concentrate on the acquisition of new skills which enhance behavioural change. As behaviour is inextricably linked to cognition and affect, there is some overlap in how behavioural techniques can be applied in combination with techniques which access these psychological processes.

Review of personal history

It is useful for the counsellor to get the survivor to review her past history so that a picture of behaviour patterns can be established. From this the counsellor can identify destructive or maladaptive behaviour patterns. These should be discussed with the survivor so that more adaptive alternative behaviours can be generated, and adopted into the behavioural repertoire.

Relaxation

Survivors are often so hypervigilant that they find it almost impossible to relax at all. Relaxation techniques can be an important technique in therapy by helping the woman to relax in a safe environment and allowing her to lower her defences. In addition, relaxation also helps the survivor to ground herself and to release tension.

Desensitisation

Using systematic desensitisation which combines relaxation with exposure to emotionally arousing material in a gradual, hierarchical way, can be an important technique in pacing the survivor's exposure to re-experiencing the trauma of her abuse. The survivor is taught to breathe and relax to maintain a stable baseline arousal state. When exposed to emotionally arousing material the survivor employs relaxation to return to her baseline state so that she is not overwhelmed by her arousal. This allows her to proceed to explore emotionally arousing material.

Progressively, the survivor is able to face more intense feelings and arousal states. Once the survivor is able to control and desensitise herself to painful and arousing emotions she can increase disclosure. This will allow her to explore and analyse painful material more comprehensively.

Grounding

According to Blake-White and Kline (1985) grounding '... refers to any behaviour the client can engage in to feel more in the "here and now".' Grounding is mostly indicated when the survivor begins to dissociate or is overwhelmed by affect such as a panic attack. The techniques subsumed under grounding include touching oneself or objects, focusing attention on a specific object, talking to others, self talk such as 'I am here, I am real', feeling one's feet on the floor and deep breathing. These grounding techniques are more adaptive than the quasi-grounding behaviour manifested in self-mutilation and self-inflicted pain.

Distraction

Distraction, like grounding, aims to break the cycle of self-destructive preoccupation by focusing the survivor's attention away from the psychological processes that elicit and maintain her compulsive behaviour. The survivor is encouraged to preoccupy herself with something else such as writing, painting, reading a book, playing a mentally demanding game, or taking strenuous exercise.

Time out

A common behavioural technique is 'time out' in which the survivor learns to remove herself physically from situations that are potentially dangerous to her, or which may tempt her to act out negative behaviours. This technique is useful in controlling escalating anger which may lead to violence, reducing compulsive behaviours such as binge eating, and preventing substance abuse.

'Time out' can be very empowering behavioural training for the survivor who as a child had no means of escaping her abuse. As a powerless, helpless and passive victim she was unable to flee danger. Learning that she can control situations and that she has a choice of removing herself from potentially destructive or threatening behaviour reinforces empowerment and enhances self-control over her life.

Portable therapist

The portable therapist exercise consists of the survivor asking herself in stressful or arousing situations 'What would my therapist say or do now'. This refocuses the survivor's attention away from the stressors and allows her to seek a solution with the help of the accumulated knowledge acquired during therapy.

Modelling

The counsellor plays a crucial role in modelling adaptive behaviours. In the absence of appropriate parental role models the survivor may fail to acquire certain adaptive skills and behaviours. In providing a positive role model, the counsellor can help the survivor to relearn developmentally appropriate behaviours which can then be incorporated into her behavioural repertoire.

Role rehearsal

Role rehearsal of alternative behaviours is a crucial aspect of adopting new behaviours and responses. In role rehearsal the survivor can practice her new behaviours, or roles acquired through role play, in a safe environment until she has 'fixed' the behaviour into her behavioural repertoire. This will allow her to feel comfortable about using newly acquired behaviours outside the therapeutic session in a natural, unforced way.

This is especially pertinent when the survivor becomes more self-confident and assertive. Despite having attained more confidence the survivor may feel nervous about behaving differently, and may need to practice her new assertive role, prior to adopting it outside therapy. Role rehearsal can also be a useful technique through which aspects of the survivor's personality which have been previously denied can be acted out, until she feels comfortable about integrating these with the rest of the self.

Reparenting

In reparenting the survivor learns how to parent her child and her adult self. Skills for reparenting can be modelled by the counsellor or may be generated by the survivor to reflect an ideal parent. Reparenting also allows the survivor to let go of the notion that her parents will one day change and nurture or care for her the way they should have done when she was a child. Although it is hard for the survivor to face the conclusion that she is now her own parent, once the shift in perspective is achieved the survivor begins to acknowledge the damage done to her in childhood.

Reparenting also allows for the exploration of 'good parent' and 'bad parent'. This encourages the survivor to focus on her own parents and their limitations. Such a focus has ramifications for survivors who are petrified of having children. By recognising that it is possible to be a good parent to her 'inner child' and to her adult self, the survivor may be able to approach the idea of having her own child as less frightening and more palatable.

Self-nurturing

Self-nurturing exercises include listening to inner needs, acknowledging them and aiming to satisfy them. Self-nurturing exercises may be given as homework assignments which the survivor is asked to perform between sessions. Included in these are the survivor taking time and space for herself each day in which she can totally focus on herself without being distracted. The survivor is also encouraged to spoil herself by having luxurious baths or buying herself something as a treat. This encourages the survivor to value herself, thereby increasing self respect and self-esteem which fosters a more positive self image.

Communication skills

Survivors of child sexual abuse were frequently not listened to when they were children, and their needs and desires not heard, much less respected. Such an environment also prevented the learning and development of effective communication. Many survivors thus find it difficult to communicate their needs or desires in an effective way. The survivor can reclaim her personal power and improve communication through active listening, owning her own feelings and desires, and assertiveness training. Some counsellors actively encourage the survivor to enroll in an assertiveness training course in addition to working on assertiveness in the therapy setting.

Stress management

Stress management techniques encourage the learning of new, more adaptive responses to stress. This necessitates identifying current reactions to stress, assessing their adaptiveness and substituting maladaptive responses with more adaptive and positive reactions. The survivor can practice these techniques outside sessions and learn to pre-empt stressors. Being aware of potential stressors prepares the survivor in advance to stressful situations allowing her to prepare and rehearse her responses.

Problem solving

Training in problem solving can be very beneficial to survivors, who, due to the plethora of confusing feelings, are often unable to identify problems, let alone feel able to solve them. The client will need to be systematic in (1) defining the problem, (2) selecting attainable goals, (3) selecting strategies to attain the goal, (4) implementing selected strategies, and (5) evaluating outcome. The survivor will need much support and reassurance that alternative problem solving skills are more adaptive as she may feel vulnerable adopting novel solutions to problems that previously she had always solved in what seems a much 'safer' way to her.

Assertion training

Assertion training has been shown to be particularly valuable to adult survivors of child sexual abuse. In essence assertion training fosters an awareness of and respect for one's own feelings which promotes the emergence of the true, unique self. Assertion training also aims to foster the expression of feelings more effectively through increased clarity, honesty and openness, while reducing fear of ridicule or guilt. In allowing for self-realisation, assertion training exercises provide solutions to how to avoid using excuses, manipulating, over-explaining and over apologising.

Self-confidence can also be increased through self-assertion by focusing on how to say no, how to ask for needs to be met, how to be direct to avoid manipulating others, how to avoid being a victim, how to avoid playing the role of 'rescuer', dealing with sexual harassment, how to communicate effectively on a variety of levels including communication about money, how to improve interpersonal skills, how to own her feelings, how to take responsibility for her actions while relinquishing responsibility for others, and how to set firm and clear boundaries.

Many of the exercises used in assertion training can be usefully adapted to the therapeutic session, although for some survivors, who are already well on the path to healing, it may be helpful to participate in a group training programme. Participation in such a group helps the development of interpersonal interaction and the building up of trust in relationships outside therapy. The counsellor will need to assess the readiness of each individual client before suggesting enrolment on such a programme.

Power and responsibility

It is crucial that the counsellor impress upon the survivor that at no time was she at fault, or responsible for the sexual abuse. Acknowledging this can alleviate the tremendous burden of guilt that most survivors bear. The counsellor should also emphasise that it is the abuser, and the abuser alone who is responsible for the abuse, and help the survivor to relinquish her guilt and feelings of responsibility. This provides an opportunity for the survivor to look at her own power and responsibility.

Empowering the survivor will enable her to transcend the passive victim role that she has adopted in the past, and allow her to take responsibility for her own actions. Taking responsibility for her actions and owning her own feelings allows the survivor to relinquish responsibility for others or things that are out of her control. This entails letting go of things that she has no control over and taking on things that can be controlled. Empowerment is also about being honest and direct towards others instead of adopting manipulative and devious behaviours in order to achieve goals, and respecting not only the self but also others. This is a long term process which starts gradually and the counsellor must be careful to balance this process within a realistic time frame.

Not all survivors react to the abuse experience in a passive or victim role. Some women externalise their aggression, anger and frustration by dominating or abusing others. In such cases the counsellor will need to demonstrate to the survivor that she has internalised her abuser which is why she is compelled to abuse and manipulate others. This is not the use of power, it is the acting out of unresolved trauma by imitating an abusive role model. The challenge here is to point out where such behaviours come from and to help the survivor to learn to recognise and respect the rights of others.

Educative material

Books about child sexual abuse including experiential accounts by survivors can be usefully recommended to the survivor. Experiential accounts have the advantage of reducing feelings of isolation and alienation while fostering empathy and identification with others with similar experiences.

Books and articles on child sexual abuse perform an educative function in informing the survivor of the precise nature of child sexual abuse thereby dispelling the myths that surround this subject (see Appendix A). Care should be taken by the counsellor not to introduce these too early in therapy as they might be too overwhelming for the survivor, who has only just started to deal with her own experiences and pain.

Videos which serve an educative function can also be used to increase awareness of child sexual abuse. In addition, survivors who are coming to the end of the therapy may benefit from attending short courses or conferences on child sexual abuse. These allow her to put her own experience into context and to see it in the perspective of wider issues and ramifications of child sexual abuse in society.

Diet and exercise

Promoting and fostering positive self image should include awareness of the benefits of diet and exercise, and the feeling of well being that can be generated through healthy eating and exercising the body. Restoring healthy psychological functioning can lead to restoring more healthy eating patterns and lifestyle.

Support networks

An important part of the healing process involves establishing strong support networks outside therapy. The counsellor should encourage the survivor to participate in self help groups for survivors as an essential step towards establishing support outside of therapy. Support networks ideally should also include close friends, partners, and other family members. Family members from the family of origin who are supportive of the survivor can also help tremendously in reassuring the survivor and helping her to reclaim her childhood.

Occasionally it is useful to the survivor and her support network to attend a number of therapeutic sessions in which friends, partners or family members can better acquaint themselves with the types of difficulties the survivor faces and what the treatment process entails. The counsellor may also provide constructive information and ideas on how best to support the survivor through the healing process and prepare them for the types of behavioural changes she may go through, and how they can best adapt to them.

The diverse behavioural techniques discussed all make a considerable contribution to the treatment of adult survivors of child sexual abuse. Many of the techniques, although not empirically evaluated, can when used in conjunction with experiential/exploratory and cognitive techniques, in a flexible, individualised way, result in amelioration of the effects of the impact of child sexual abuse.

CHAPTER 10

Group Treatment

Resolving the trauma of child sexual abuse through the use of experiential/exploratory, cognitive and behavioural techniques, memory retrieval and sexuality focused therapy can be very effective in the treatment of adult survivors. Although most of these techniques are primarily used in individual one-to-one counselling, many of them can also be applied to group therapy as an alternative or adjunctive treatment modality. Some survivors feel more comfortable with individual therapy, while others prefer group therapy with other survivors.

This chapter will explore some of the relative benefits and drawbacks of group therapy over individual counselling. Counsellors who wish to set up a therapeutic group for survivors, or who prefer to work in group settings, need to assess which survivors are best suited to working in a group format and are advised to consider the problems that can arise in this type of therapeutic setting.

Models for group therapy with survivors of child sexual abuse emphasise the need for co-facilitators to lead the group, the assessment and screening of survivors, structuring the group, the types of themes and issues that are commonly raised in group work and how to treat these within the therapeutic setting (Bergart, 1986; Blake-White, 1985; Gil, 1988; Gordy, 1983; Steward *et al.*, 1986; Sgroi and Bunk, 1988). Other important factors that have to be addressed include those of long term, global group therapy, or short term, time limited group work; closed or open groups; how to set up the group and the type of format that will be adopted; the type of problem behaviours that occur in group work, and how best to deal with them.

Increasingly survivors themselves are setting up self-help groups in order to resolve many of the problems associated with child sexual abuse. These groups are frequently run by survivors who have benefited from either individual or group therapy and now wish to help other survivors. Although not all these groups are facilitated, some are, and it is useful to be aware of the treatment goals of self-help groups and how survivors can benefit from them. Self-help groups can be vital in establishing a support network between survivors which individual women find enormously helpful even while involved in individual therapy, but also long after therapy has been completed.

Advantages of group treatment

There are a number of fundamental advantages to group treatment over individual counselling. One of the most crucial is that group therapy fosters interaction with other survivors who provide mutual support and understanding. This is particularly important for survivors of child sexual abuse in reducing the isolation, alienation, secrecy, shame and stigma that many survivors experience. Often survivors believe themselves to be unique in having suffered sexual abuse, and that they must be evil or bad because they were singled out.

For many survivors, to enter a room containing eight or ten women, all of whom are survivors, can generate tremendous feelings of relief and recognition that her experience is not bizarre or unique but has been experienced by other women too. Being in such a group produces feelings of not being alone while fostering identification and a sense of belonging. This encourages the survivor to not think of herself as abnormal, deviant or a freak, and to feel less responsible about what happened to her.

Group therapy also allows survivors to explore important issues of intimacy, trust and honesty in a safe environment. Many survivors struggle with a fear of intimacy and find it difficult to trust not only men but also women, often feeling threatened by them. Being in a therapeutic group setting enables the survivor to explore her interpersonal difficulties and learn to trust others again.

A further advantage of group treatment is that it fosters positive feedback and validation of the survivor's experiences. Often a survivor feels that she has idiosyncratic difficulties or bizarre behaviour patterns only to find that other women in the group have also had similar problems and are able to identify with her experiences. This provides a level of normalisation of their abuse experiences and how they survived them. A group environment also allows for the direct confrontation and exploration of alternative behaviours in a safe environment.

The participants in group therapy offer a wider variety of positive role models. These are not only provided by the facilitators or co-therapists, but also by other survivors in the group. Often survivors are better able to accept positive messages about not being responsible or blamed when they are conveyed by someone who has shared the same experience, and who, because of this bond, can validate the survivor's perceptions and feelings.

Although group participants may be at slightly different stages of the healing process, there are enormous benefits to be reaped from this. Hearing how other survivors have isolated, dealt with and resolved specific problem areas can encourage women to continue to go through the painful and extremely distressing process of recovery. Exchanging techniques which were useful to a survivor can help another survivor to experiment to find her own solution. This also provides hope and optimism that it is possible to heal, to change behaviour patterns and cognitions, and to resolve the trauma of child sexual abuse.

Finally, for professionals working for health services or statutory agencies or bodies with limited funding and tight budgets, group therapy provides the opportunity to offer therapeutic help to a larger number of women than individual counselling, which is time intensive and costly.

In evaluating the advantages of group therapy Tsai and Wagner (1978) report that '... the primary curative component was the sense of identification and emotional closeness instilled by a warm and supportive environment where a common bond was shared'. This is echoed by Gordy (1983) who cites one survivor's response to group participation who said that the '... most helpful part was comparing experiences with one another and discovering how others learned to cope with their problems'. Another survivor notes that the important aspects of group work were not having to justify oneself or one's feelings to others as they had all had similar experiences and that the validation of her as an individual helped to dispel the secrecy and her stigmatisation as a victim.

Despite these obvious advantages of group treatment for adult survivors of child sexual abuse, there are nevertheless drawbacks that should be considered.

Drawbacks of group treatment

Some survivors do not feel at all comfortable in a therapeutic group setting, and in some instances group work is counterproductive. Group work demands a certain level of interaction and verbal participation. Survivors who have never talked about their abuse find it easier to reveal their experiences to one person such as a counsellor than to a group of eight to ten women. Such survivors may also find it difficult to tolerate their feelings about the abuse and may not know how deal with them in front of others. A recurring example of this is wanting to cry but not allowing oneself to for fear that others would perceive this as a weakness.

Another common difficulty is that the survivor feels overwhelmed by the whole issue of child sexual abuse and would not be able to cope. One survivor who had had individual and family counselling expressed grave concern at her first group meeting that she would be unable to tolerate revelations about other survivors' abuse experiences. She felt that her own abuse was so overwhelming and distressing that to listen to others would be too upsetting for her.

Survivors who have had no previous group experience may have little or no knowledge about group dynamics and be afraid that the group setting could recreate dynamics which were operational during the abuse, making her feel vulnerable and threatened. Motivation to work in a group environment is also important. If the survivor is ambivalent or feels compelled to participate then group work is counterindicated.

Survivors who are narcissistic and manipulate group time and space by focusing the group attention on to themselves can be destructive to other group members. A corollary to this is the survivor who continually attempts to elicit caretaking behaviours from other group members by displaying self destructive behaviour patterns. This is unhealthy for other survivors who find themselves slipping into a caretaking role which prevents them from working on themselves.

These drawbacks to group therapy make it essential for potential participants to be screened and assessed for suitability prior to joining the group. Ideally, survivors who wish to participate in group treatment should do so in conjunction with individual counselling. This allows the survivor to combine insights from both therapeutic modalities. In addition, issues that are raised in the group setting can then be worked on in greater depth within one-to-one counselling.

Time-limited versus long term group work

Some clinicians believe that time-limited group therapy, ranging from 12 weeks to six months (Gil, 1988; Gordy, 1983; Goodman and Nowack-Scibelli, 1985) is the most efficacious in the treatment of adult survivors of child sexual abuse, with Mann (1985) proposing that 12 treatment sessions should be the minimal requirement for the dynamics of group therapy to be most effective.

Time-limited group therapy essentially provides a forum in which to explore interactional dynamics and defences of group members, and how these affect interpersonal relationships. As time-limited group therapy is by its very nature short term, it is unlikely that all survivors will be able to resolve the complexities of their abuse trauma within such a time frame. What it does provide is a safe environment in which to share mutual experiences, isolate commonalities, and increase insight into the types of difficulties survivors face, which can then be further explored in long term, individual counselling. While time-limited group therapy reduces dependency and learned helplessness, it enhances interaction with others and empowers the survivor to take more control of her life.

The advantage of time-limited group therapy is that because of imposed time constraints survivors are more motivated to address specific issues, explore them, and set goals that they want to attain. Therapeutic focus can be directed to specific experiences by setting firm and clear boundaries at the outset and delineating the issues that are to be explored. Time-limited group treatment may also minimise regression by concentrating and highlighting the strengths of the individual survivor.

Further advantages to time-limited group therapy are outlined by Sprei (1986) and include the following:

1. This format is easier for survivors who only wish to commit themselves to short term treatment.

2. Promotes goal-orientated work.

3. Focuses on common themes pertaining to child sexual abuse, while minimising focus on interpersonal relationships.

4. Limits the survivor's anxiety about joining a group.

5. Decreases level of survivor's dependency.

6. Provides a hopeful, optimistic and positive outlook for survivors.

7. Imposed time limits encourage bonding while minimising resistance to sharing.

8. Provision of clear structure in an otherwise intense and disorientating therapeutic setting.

9. Fosters surfacing of feelings and issues which can be further explored in individual therapy.

10. Best suited to needs and organisational structure of most statutory agencies or crisis intervention programmes.

Although most survivors express a sense of loss when the treatment series ends, often feeling that they would liked to have had more time, they find that they were able to begin to resolve some of their difficulties despite the limited time frame. Gil (1988) suggests giving survivors the opportunity to contract for a further series of sessions after the first series of sessions has terminated. Many survivors have found this to be beneficial, with some returning for up to three series.

Ideally, time-limited group treatment should be conducted in conjunction with long term individual counselling, in which issues that arise in group therapy can be further explored in a more global, in depth therapeutic format to aid resolution of trauma. Time-limited group therapy is highly effective when combined with individual counselling, especially if the survivor is articulate and is already in the process of recovery.

Time-unlimited group therapy

Time-unlimited group therapy resembles long term individual treatment in taking a more global, in depth approach to the resolution of trauma, and can last for six months to several years. Important components in long-term group therapy are bonding, establishing trust, the development of transference, particularly negative transference, interpersonal group dynamics which reflect family dynamics, the acting out of such family dynamics, and interactional behaviour patterns. Many of these ingredients facilitate deeper exploration of the abuse trauma which can lead to trauma resolution.

Many survivors prefer time-unlimited group therapy because of its more global approach and its focus on trust, unlimited time constraints to explore and share experiences, to examine and discuss mutual difficulties, and feel supported in the process of resolution. By participating in a long term group, survivors are more able to control the length of their stay in the group and are more empowered to leave the group when they feel ready rather than continuing for a contracted series of sessions. Taking control of their healing is important in the process towards health.

An important advantage of long term group work is that survivors have more flexibility to leave and return whenever they feel ready to address certain issues, or as more material comes into consciousness. Often survivors go through phases in which they are dealing with certain aspects of the trauma, with sometimes months or years between issues resurfacing. In time-limited group therapy not all the facets of the trauma may resurface and so any work that is done will be limited to what is current to the survivor.

A disadvantage of long term group treatment is that women may avoid dealing with specific issues through blocking, by concentrating on more general problems, particularly their current relationships, without connecting this with their early abuse experiences. To overcome this, the group needs to be structured to prevent avoidance and the facilitator needs to be directive in focusing on specific issues or topics.

To some extent the choice of whether to facilitate a time limited or long term therapeutic group will depend on the counsellors and their preferred mode of group therapy, and the range of survivors who express an interest in participating.

Role of facilitator(s)

Most clinicians who have conducted group therapy with adult survivors of child sexual abuse have found it essential to have two co-therapists facilitating the group (Bergart, 1986; Blake-White, 1985; Gil, 1988; Gordy, 1983). Two facilitators offer the opportunity of sharing the responsibility of running and directing the group, in setting goals, responding to individual survivors and planning sessions. Also, co- facilitators are able to offer two, sometimes different, perspectives and approaches as well as providing two positive role models of strong, competent and responsive women. They can also jointly increase the level of empathy and validation by reinforcing active affirmation.

A corollary to this is that group participants may find it easier to identify with and relate to one facilitator and less so to the other. Survivors tend to gravitate to either one or other facilitator with whom they establish a closer bond, identification or rapport, who the survivor can trust and is able to feel comfortable with in exploring emotionally charged material. This is important in the development of transference, or in cases of unexpressed hostility towards one of the facilitators. By having two facilitators, hostility against one can be deflected or brought out into the open by the non-affected facilitator. Counsellors must, however, guard against being split into 'good' facilitator (parent) and 'bad' facilitator (parent) and attempt at all times to present themselves as a team, without compromising their individuality.

Counsellors working in a therapeutic group setting with adult survivors of child sexual abuse need to be acutely aware of the variety of different roles in the group process that they will be required to fulfil. The myriad of roles include facilitators of the group process, observer and participant, female and parental role models, alter egos, limit and boundary setters, and educators (Courtois, 1988). In all these roles they need to remain patient, understanding, empathic, gentle, reliable and responsive to each individual group member's needs, but also to be firm in ensuring safety and preventing the infringement of boundaries and limits. Most important, they must foster the building up of trust, not only between group members, but also between individual survivor and counsellor.

It is essential that counsellors have a comprehensive knowledge base about child sexual abuse, its impact on children and its long term psychological effects on adult survivors, the dynamics involved in this form of abuse, and family dynamics before attempting to facilitate a group for survivors. To rely on developing their knowledge base through the group process from the survivors is re-creating an abusive relationship in which the 'professional' with authority and power, uses the survivor in order to gain knowledge. Counsellors will also need to have explored their own childhood and evaluated their attitudes to child sexual abuse and sexuality, and their reasons for wishing to work with adult survivors of child sexual abuse.

Group treatment is not only painful for the individual survivor but can also be extremely stressful for the facilitators. It is vital that counsellors facilitating groups for survivors of child sexual abuse have some level of support and supervision either from other professionals or their own therapist. When there are two facilitators they can offer each other mutual support on emotionally charged issues and how these have affected them, and in discussing and analysing the group process better understand the elicited dynamics, many of which can at times appear quite destructive.

Some clinicians, in particular Gordy (1983), have found it useful for one of the facilitators to be a survivor. Thus, the professional counsellor provides therapeutic input and pertinent insight, while the abused facilitator, because of her personal experience of sexual abuse, increases the potential for trust, empathy, and a potent role model for gaining mastery in learning to cope with the damaging effects of abuse. Facilitating groups jointly with a survivor has considerable advantages for group members, provided that the abused facilitator is able to remain objective despite stimulation of her own issues. It is essential that the abused facilitator separates the client's needs, issues and require-ments from her own. In addition, it is vital that the abused facilitator has extra support from her own therapist to discharge any stimulated issues or unresolved emotional conflicts.

Not all survivors respond well to a formerly abused facilitator, in that they may perceive her as being equally stigmatised, with her own problems and difficulties, and see her as less effective since she is after all a victim of sexual abuse. In contrast, other survivors believe that the abused facilitator can better understand and empathise with their experiences, making bonding and trust easier. Whatever the reaction to the abused facilitator, it is important that negative and positive feelings be discussed and explored within the group.

The issue of the sex of the facilitators is also of crucial importance. There has been some debate over whether therapeutic groups for survivors of child sexual abuse should be facilitated by both a male and a female therapist (Courtois and Leehan, 1982; Leehan and Wilson, 1985). The rationale for this is that the male therapist can provide a positive role model and also allow for the development of transference. As survivors often had negatively-experienced male models in childhood who abused their trust, it is crucial to build up trust in a male in adulthood to fully resolve the abuse trauma and to complete the healing process.

While there is considerable value in having two positive sex role models, it is not absolutely crucial to the therapeutic process (Cole, 1985) and in some instances may actually be quite destructive. Not all survivors feel able to confide in a male, even if he is a counsellor, as they frequently feel unsafe and threatened in the presence of the male sex. This would inhibit disclosure and the exploration of highly emotionally charged material, thereby impeding the therapeutic process.

Many survivors have been so traumatised by their experiences that they feel uncomfortable and vulnerable in the company of men, including a therapist. Survivors have learned to fear all members of the same sex as their abuser, and find it difficult to trust them. Another danger is that some survivors may sexualise their relationship with the male counsellor by acting out primitive and highly conditioned sexualised behaviour.

Survivors who have resolved much of their abuse trauma undoubtedly can benefit from exposure to a positive male sex role model, allowing for the recognition that not all men are abusers and that they can be empathic, understanding and can be trusted. However, the healing process needs to be well advanced for the survivor to really feel comfortable and confident in relation to a male counsellor. To insist that the survivor participate in a group which has a male co-facilitator can be counterproductive. In the case of a mixed sex group it would seem desirable to have a therapist from each sex. Counsellors should attempt different formats and combinations, to assess and evaluate their effectiveness. From this an individualised group treatment model can be devised which best suits the needs of the individual participating survivors.

Screening and assessment

It is vital to screen and make some level of assessment of survivors wishing to participate in group therapy. Assessments should ideally be made prior to the first group meeting by the co-facilitators, including detailed history taking. Courtois (1988) suggests that screening and history taking be conducted by both co-facilitators to decrease the potential for forming a pre-group alliance between survivor and therapist.

Although history-taking may be distressing to the survivor it is·useful in assessing her readiness to talk about her abuse experiences, which also serves to desensitise her to revealing her abuse history to the group. It is useful to devise a standard intake questionnaire which can be supplemented with an abuse history questionnaire plus a symptomatology checklist (Courtois, 1988) to gain a comprehensive picture of the survivor's history. Survivors should also be encouraged to ask questions of the co-facilitators such as their experience and qualifications, therapeutic orientation, what is expected of her and what the aims of the group are.

Factors that need to be screened for and assessed include preparedness of the woman to participate in group work including her goals and expectations of such work; ability to express and talk about her abuse; whether she has been in therapy, either individual or group; current situation, including general mental and physical health; self destructive behaviours, including substance dependence; how she feels about disclosing her abuse; and what stage in the healing process she feels she has reached.

Survivors who are highly volatile, aggressive, manic, disruptive or overly vulnerable and fragile would be inappropriate for a group therapeutic setting. Similarly, survivors with drug or alcohol dependency should be encouraged to enrol in an appropriate addiction programme before participating in the group process. Survivors who are actively self-mutilating or suicidal also need to be stabilised before joining the group.

Obviously psychotic, disorientated or heavily medicated survivors may interrupt the group process in eliciting caretaking behaviours or monopolising group time. Frequently, these survivors are unable to empathise with others and may prove destructive to other group members. Survivors who manifest such problems should be referred back to their therapist or clinician, and advised to join the group at a later date when they are more stabilised.

Survivors who are screened out at this stage should be informed about alternative treatment groups in the community, and if possible referred to more appropriate agencies or crisis intervention programmes. It may be necessary to refer the survivor back into individual therapy to work on resolving or containing her problem behaviours, as these may ultimately be damaging to the other group members. Although it is not always possible to screen for all problem behaviours, if these occur after the survivor has joined the group the facilitators will need to try to contain the behaviour within the group. If this fails and the survivor cannot operate within the boundaries set by the group then she must be asked to leave and referred on for individual one-to-one therapy.

Counsellors should aim to match potential group members as closely as possible for age, abuse experience, class or occupational status, race, sexual orientation, and which stage each is at in the healing process. Such matching allows for the formation of a more homogeneous group where identification, empathy and commonality of experience fosters a more effective therapeutic environment. Group size also needs to be considered with eight to ten women, plus two co-facilitators, the optimal number for the group process to be most effective.

The facilitators will also need to be clear whether they will be operating an 'open' group or a 'closed' group. In an open group new members are given access to the group and can join once the group has already been formed. In contrast, closed groups remain closed to new members and aim to function with the original constellation of the group. Thus, if a group member terminates group therapy they will not be replaced. There are advantages and disadvantages to both open and closed groups.

Open groups are best suited to long term, time unlimited group therapy which have more flexibility for group members to leave and return. The advantage of open groups is that the long standing members can provide insight and examples of how they have coped with their difficulties and faced problems. A classic example is confrontation. New members may wish to confront their abuser or family, but are concerned about the best way to achieve confrontation and the consequences. Long standing members who may have confronted their abuser as part of their healing process are able to share their experiences and the consequences of their confrontation with new members, which enables them to make a more informed choice and decision.

A major disadvantage of open groups is that with new members joining, levels of trust will constantly be questioned and need to be built up every time a new member joins. In addition, long standing members may become frustrated that extra time is given to new members to integrate them into the group. A corollary to this is repetition of material that long standing members have already worked on, or resolved, being focused on again for the benefit of new members. Although some survivors do gain extra insight from re-examining already processed material, others become angry and resentful and feel that they are not progressing but are held back from exploring other, more pertinent issues.

Closed groups avoid these drawbacks because the group members have been together from the beginning, have built up trust, and are reasonably homogeneous in terms of which treatment stage they are at. Arguably, closed groups are more effective in their therapeutic process and may represent the preferred group modality. However, one disadvantage to closed groups is that, unless there a several such groups available in the community, survivors who seek group therapy will have to be put on a waiting list until a new group is formed, which could take several weeks, or months.

Structure of the group

It is very important to structure the group so that survivors are aware of boundaries and limits. In order to provide a safe yet structured environment, it is necessary to have some basic ground rules, which should be clarified at the first session with all the participants. This session should also clarify the aims, goals and objectives of the group.

Rules that ensure safety include specifying that women can say as little or as much about their abuse as is comfortable to them and that no one will be forced to speak; that everyone has the opportunity to express her views; that while emotional discharge is encouraged, threatening behaviour, violence or abusive language is unacceptable; that whatever is discussed is confidential and will not go outside the group; and members under the influence of alcohol or drugs will be excluded from the session.

Other ground rules necessary to the group process include a commitment to regular attendance, as non attendance can be destructive to other group members; commitment to the group process to actively participate within the group by sharing experiences and not to remain a distant observer; to discuss reasons for termination of group therapy

LIBRARY
DERBY COLLEGE
OF NURSING AND
MIDWIFERY

within the group prior to leaving; and whether contact between members in between group sessions is desirable.

The times and duration of the session should also be clarified. Ideally, group treatment sessions should last between one and a half and two and a half hours. If the group meets for two and a half hours or longer then it may be useful to have a short break for about fifteen minutes, to allow time to make coffee or go to the lavatory. Time keeping should also be raised with members being encouraged to arrive promptly, and the necessity of ending the sessions on time made clear. If members arrive late this could be disruptive for the other women already present and impede the group process.

Smoking in the group should also be discussed. Some counsellors believe that smoking is often used as a crutch by clients which inhibits the discharge of emotion, and therefore actively discourage it. However, as much of the material that surfaces in the group may be very traumatic, those survivors who do smoke may need to have a cigarette in order to feel comfortable about expressing their feelings. A decision should be taken at the first meeting regarding smoking which is acceptable to both smokers and non-smokers. If the group decides to have a break in the session it might be possible to allow smokers to smoke at this time but not actually during the group work.

Other important points that need to be incorporated in the structure of the group are a list of topics for discussion, types of exercises used, the availability of paper and art materials, journal keeping, books and articles, and homework. Members will need to know what is expected of them in terms of participating in exercises and the completion of homework tasks.

Some facilitators find it useful to make themselves available in between sessions for reassurance or to answer any questions. To this effect each member should be given a written copy of both the facilitators' phone numbers. Accessibility to the facilitators between sessions is very important, especially after the first meeting as many survivors may feel hesitant about continuing in the group. Any hesitancies they may have can be discussed with the facilitator and reassurance given.

As group cohesion develops, some survivors may wish to exchange phone numbers so that they can contact each other for support in between sessions. This should be encouraged but it must be clarified that not all the participants may be happy with this and not all members may wish to reveal their phone number and should not be forced to do so. They should only be exchanged willingly.

It is useful at the beginning of each session to have a 10 minute 'check in time' per person where each woman is asked how she feels and if there is anything left over from the previous session or week that she would like to bring to the group. Women may also utilise this time to raise specific points that they feel need attention. At the end of each session it is vital to wind down so that women can leave on a positive note. Exercises in which each woman says one positive thing about herself or the group can be a very effective and optimistic way of ending the session.

Goals of the group

The facilitators need to encourage the members to express the goals they hope to achieve in the group and to ensure that their expectations are realistic. If unrealistic, it will be necessary to discuss this within the group so that all members know what they can achieve by developing realistic, measurable goals. Contracts can be drawn up with each individual woman to enable her to achieve her individual goals. These goals can be categorised into short term, medium term, and long term goals. Initially, survivors should limit their goals to two or three per time frame so that there is more likelihood of achieving them. This also focuses attention more closely on which goals are really important and need immediate attention.

It is useful to re-evaluate these goals on a regular basis and if necessary make new contracts. Facilitators can make mental notes of each individual's goals and list them for her on a record card. This is useful to keep and show the woman at the end of the series to pinpoint how much she has achieved through group therapy. The record card may then be sent to the individual survivor three months after termination. This serves to remind her of her goals and also gives her the opportunity to review how much she has achieved. Many survivors find that even after termination of group therapy, they are still working on many of their goals and have attained them outside group therapy.

Group goals in terms of required level of commitment should be discussed along with the types of techniques and exercises that will be used to achieve these goals. If there are to be homework assignments it should be made clear what is expected of each group member. Homework is a very effective way of maintaining group coherence between sessions in which women can take something from each session to work on at home. Survivors should be encouraged to complete homework tasks and then to bring them to the next meeting to share with other members, who can interpret and comment on discrepancies in perception.

Homework exercises can include drawing self portraits, focusing on parts of the body, letter writing, reading articles about child sexual abuse and its effects; watching particular videos or pertinent television programmes; listing strengths and weaknesses and sharing these with the group; replacing internalised messages with positive statements about themselves; finding childhood photographs and bringing them to the group to work on; and keeping a journal. Many of these techniques are also used in individual therapy in the resolution of abuse trauma and the reader is referred to Chapter 9 for a fuller elucidation of how the techniques are best employed.

Problem behaviours

Facilitators working with survivors of child sexual abuse need to be aware and prepared to encounter and resolve problem behaviours. Many of the problem behaviours reflect transference issues and the acting out of archaic family dynamics, in particular parental transference between survivors and co-facilitators, and sibling transference between group members. Several problem behaviours have been described by Gil (1988) including resistance, hostility, monopolising group time, avoiding the spotlight, remaining mute, and eliciting rejection.

Some members of the group may find problem behaviours frightening or intimidating. It is crucial that the facilitators respond to problem behaviours immediately and effectively. In order to gain trust from the participants the facilitators need to model appropriate conflict resolution. This is best done by explicit and direct behaviour to avoid any confusion, including reminding individuals of established and agreed ground rules.

Resistance is a protective defence mechanism which in the group process can manifest itself in a variety of ways, such as arriving late, missing sessions, feigning understanding of what is required, or forgetting or refusing to do homework exercises. The facilitators need to reduce these resistant behaviours not by applying pressure but by exploring where the resistance may be coming from. The individuals should also be given the opportunity to improve their behaviour and to try again.

In some cases the whole group may manifest collective resistance by mutually avoiding topics for discussion, overadapting to the co-facilitators or by reinforcing avoidant behaviour. These may be unconscious but nevertheless need to be brought to the surface and openly discussed in order to explore their meaning and source.

Overt hostility on the part of one individual can cause other members to withdraw and can be very intimidating for them. The facilitators need to be seen to control overt hostility so as not to lose the trust of the other members, and to model protective behaviours. In extreme cases, if hostility cannot be controlled, then the member should be asked to leave the group if she is impeding the group process.

Monopolising group time wherein one member is unable to respond to limits and will focus exclusively on herself may initially be seen as a relief for other members in deflecting attention from themselves. However, monopolising behaviours elicit learned helplessness from other members which can lead to powerful feelings of resentment. Survivors who display monopolising behaviours are often acting out primitive family dynamics which reflect many of the difficulties survivors have, such as uncertainty over boundaries and entitlements, and underlying problems related to control.

Some survivors may talk incessantly to avoid or block their own feelings or the discomfort of silence. Silence can elicit anxiety in those who fear exposure, expulsion, being put down, or being abused in some way. Problems of self-absorption or clinging, needy behaviour may also be involved. Facilitators should ensure that those individuals who monopolise group time are contained and are referred back to the ground rules drawn up at the first meeting. In addition, they may suggest that the survivor look at where this behaviour is coming from and explore ways of alternative expression.

In contrast, some survivors are terrified of having the focus of attention on them and are thus prevented from expressing affect or cognitions. Such women require gentle and sensitive encouragement to begin to speak and to talk for progressively longer periods of time, to build up their confidence and overcome their fear of being the centre of attention.

Despite encouragement to speak, some survivors will continue to remain mute. Even when not contributing to a discussion these individuals may nevertheless be making good use of the group experience through listening and observation, as well as participation in exercises or homework. The other members of the group should be consulted on whether they object to one member remaining mute. If there is no manifest resentment, then the woman may be allowed to continue in the group process with the proviso that her communication difficulties and lack of verbal input should be further explored in individual counselling.

Some survivors may consistently elicit rejection as a way of halting her anticipatory anxiety about being rejected. Such behaviour is often a defence mechanism in which the survivor aims to control the feared rejection, or it may represent an interactional deficit. If a group member constantly elicits rejection it will be necessary to demonstrate how this is manifested and get the survivor to explore why it occurs, and to generate alternative, more adaptive ways of coping with her fear of rejection.

Group themes

There are a number of recurring group themes that are raised in nearly all therapeutic groups for survivors of child sexual abuse, and therefore warrant exploration during group work. These themes are generally generated by the survivors and not the facilitators. Encouraging survivors to generate their own themes gives them some control over what is being discussed in the group, and empowers them to direct their own healing process. Facilitators may initially need to suggest a couple of the most common themes to instigate group discussion.

The most common topics or themes include low self-esteem and poor self-image; anger; intimacy; trust, or lack of trust; fear; sexuality; shyness; and depression. Other themes that frequently arise are confronting the abuser and other family members, bitterness and anger towards the non-abusing parent, often the mother, for not protecting the child; anger towards the abuser; difficulties in relationships both past and current; how to prevent further abuse and ensure personal safety; relationship to family of origin; fears about their own parenting abilities; more education and information on the nature of sexual abuse; and how to change attitudes towards child sexual abuse within society.

When a list of topics for discussion has been drawn up, group members should order them hierarchically by rating them from one to ten, with one the most threatening and anxiety provoking, and ten the least fearful and easily discussed. There should be group agreement on the rating which may necessitate a vote. Once agreement has been reached the list of topics can then be used to structure forthcoming meetings.

Themes rated ten to six can easily be discussed in the first few sessions while those rated five to one should be left for later sessions. It is important to start with the less threatening topics in the early stages of the group process as the group needs to build up a level of safety and trust among members. Once group cohesiveness is established, and women feel more comfortable about disclosure and talking about themselves, the more threatening topics can be explored.

Facilitators may ask a number of women to respond to what is being discussed to get an idea of how the group is feeling. It is also important that the facilitators encourage feedback between group members, especially when exploring such issues as self-image. This provides alternative perspectives on what is being discussed which can be further explored to change distorted cognitions and perceptions.

Stages in the group process

Mann (1973) proposes four stages of the group process, of approximately three sessions each, which operate during 12 weekly time-limited therapeutic groups. These stages manifest the following characteristics: (1) rapid symptomatic improvement; (2) return and worsening of symptoms; (3) development of resistance to change and negative transference; and (4) progress on presenting symptoms and termination. Treatment and techniques used during these four stages is similar to that of individual counselling.

During the first stage the focus is on bonding, building up trust and intimacy, and opening up and sharing abuse experiences. Goals during this stage include recovery of memories, exploring the abuse history and the effects it has had on psychological functioning, how to improve current functioning, improved self-esteem, and disclosure of the abuse to friends and family. Survivors often feel much better and manifest considerable improvement in symptomatology which may result in a 'flight into health' without actually continuing to work through the trauma (Forward and Buck, 1978).

This stage is frequently followed by a worsening of symptoms, numbing of affect, and withdrawal. Sprei (1986) proposes that this may be a fear reaction to the intensity of intimacy established during the first stage and a way to test that defences, which have been lowered, are still able to function when required. Many of these responses are defence reactions activated to regain control, and should be respected by the co-facilitators and not punished.

Stage three is characterised by significant activity in terms of working with the inner child, grieving for multiple losses, shift in apportioning responsibility and blame, exploring many of the common themes pertinent to adult survivors of child sexual abuse, setting of goals and evaluating strategies for achieving realistic goals. There is also a shift in perspective in self-image: negativity is replaced by more positive cognitions; pain gives way to anger; helplessness is replaced by initiative; the victim role is replaced by a survivor role; passivity is transmuted into activity; and the survivor begins to empower herself as a competent, strong woman.

The final stage focuses on termination of the group. Survivors often become sad and anxious about impending separation and loss. These feelings need to be explored and future plans discussed. As termination looms ever closer, some survivors experience a surge of motivation to achieve their goals and prepare for termination. The co-facilitators will need to be supportive and understanding of members' feelings of anxiety surrounding termination while retaining a positive and optimistic outlook for the future.

To aid the structure of group sessions, taking into account Mann's (1973) proposed stages, time-limited group therapy can be divided into three distinct phases. The beginning phase which establishes group cohesion, the middle phase in which core issues and themes are explored and discussed, and the termination phase which looks at letting go while reviewing individual accomplishments and positive outcome for the future.

The beginning phase

The initial phase of the group process focuses on putting the history of the formation of the group into perspective, including an overview of current knowledge about child sexual abuse. More important, early sessions should concentrate on establishing a rapport between group members and the facilitators in which all the participants feel that it is safe to explore their feelings. Learning to trust is an essential component of group therapy, and the first session should reiterate ground rules, goals of the group, safety, confidentiality, the importance of respecting each other's space, that individual pacing will be respected by others, and that no woman should feel pressured to address issues that they do not feel ready to explore.

Discussion during these early sessions will concentrate on the sharing of experiences related to the abuse, but remain relatively general and non specific until the women feel comfortable about discussing more emotionally charged issues. Exercises and homework during this phase should also be gentle and non-threatening to ease the women into the type of techniques that will be used later on. Emphasis should also be put on the availability of the facilitators between sessions, as many women will need reassurance that group therapy will be an effective healing process.

The first session is usually the most difficult for survivors. Members will need to be validated for their courage and strength in taking the decision to participate in group therapy as a way to enhance resolution of the abuse trauma. Survivors should be left under no illusions that group work is easy but should recognise that many distressing emotional feelings will surface. Preparing survivors for the group process and forewarning them that after the first few sessions they will feel elated and 'healthy', which is frequently followed by worsening of symptoms, enables her to better understand the therapeutic process and not feel overpowered or helpless in controlling her healing.

The middle phase

It is during the middle phase that the bulk of the therapeutic group work will be done. By the fourth or fifth session there should be some level of group cohesion and rapport in which the women will feel more comfortable in discussing themes and topics that have been hierarchically rank ordered as to importance and emotional threat. Exploring the least threatening of the rated themes can now begin. It is often useful if this includes a discussion about self-image which will further aid group cohesion in assisting the women in getting to know each other better. Gradually, the list can be worked through allowing for more threatening material to be explored by about session eight or nine.

This is also the period in which the survivors can begin to explore feelings through structured exercises and more in-depth homework. The facilitators need to re-evaluate individual goals and how the members feel about the group process at various stages during this phase. Members should be given the opportunity to express any doubts or fears they have about the group, and what they feel they are getting out of it. If some of the women are unhappy about aspects of the group process then these should be explored in a constructive way to find mutually acceptable solutions to the perceived problems.

It is during this middle phase that many survivors actively wish to exchange telephone numbers with other group members so that they can give each other support between sessions. This should be encouraged as the wider the support network, the more beneficial for the survivor. During this phase friendships may be formed that prove to be invaluable long after the group stops meeting.

The termination phase

Most survivors become anxious towards the end of group therapy. Feelings of sadness that the group is ending, of abandonment, rejection, loss and separation, and fear of the future may now surface. It is important that these be addressed in advance of the last session. In a twelve week time frame, these issues should be discussed by the tenth session at the latest. The more prepared the group members are for termination the better able they feel to cope with it.

Many survivors frequently feel that the contracted group series ends just as they are starting to work in depth on some of their difficulties, and beginning to explore resolution of the abuse trauma. These feelings should be discussed and positive ways of coping with them should be explored. One solution is to offer members the opportunity to contract for another series of sessions. Alternatively, they could join a self-help support group, or form their own group to discuss further issues. The facilitators can advise on the availability of other groups currently operating in the community, including self help support groups.

Some survivors have found it useful to form their own group in which they meet weekly without a facilitator to discuss progress and to explore themes as they arise. These groups usually consist of approximately four survivors who meet informally while providing support to each other. Such informal 'closed groups' can be effective in providing support and empowering the women to take control of their healing, especially if they are combined with individual counselling.

The facilitators should spend some time on reviewing the accomplishments of each individual and provide positive feedback on the changes that have been achieved. That changes have occurred should be emphasised and used as a basis for encouraging the survivors to continue evaluating their behaviour patterns in the light of their abuse experiences, and have the courage to make further changes as these become necessary. The group process can show survivors that their courage in risking individual fears has resulted in positive changes and the support of others.

Group therapy is only the first step in learning to trust again and establishing interpersonal relationships. Survivors can capitalise on what they have learned and begin to learn to trust others, establish more healthy and intimate relationships, and come to love and accept themselves. The final session should end on a note of optimism and positive outcome for the future.

Self-help support groups

More recently there has been an increase in self-help support groups for adult survivors of child sexual abuse and incest. This is welcome in offering survivors more options in which to explore and resolve their abuse trauma. As these groups are often free, survivors are more able to experiment and try the full range of options before deciding on which best suits their level of functioning, or stage of recovery.

Self-help support groups operate on a variety of levels from educating individual survivors about child sexual abuse and the impact of abuse on psychological functioning to highly organised groups which stage conferences and seminars while aiming to campaign for legislative reform and to educate the public to engender changes in society's attitudes towards child sexual abuse. In between are informal drop-in groups; regular weekly meetings on a long term, time unlimited basis; open and closed groups; crisis intervention groups often associated with rape crisis agencies; and Survivors of Incest Anonymous groups which advocate a 12 step recovery programme along the lines of Alcoholics Anonymous.

Some self-help support groups are entirely independent and voluntary, often set up by survivors who have participated in other self-help groups or who have resolved their abuse trauma through therapy. These are commonly underfunded and rely on the phenomenal commitment of individual survivors to keep them going. Other self-help groups are affiliated with more formal agencies and get some funding to provide a service to survivors in the community. Such groups often get referrals from statutory agencies or clinicians.

There are many advantages and benefits to self-help support groups for survivors (Herman, 1981). Firstly, they are free and are thus able to offer support to a much wider range of survivors than traditional psychotherapy. Secondly, self help support groups do not stigmatise survivors as patients in need of treatment, which fosters normalisation and a more positive self image in providing a sense of mental health, normalcy and competence. Thirdly, many survivors who have sought traditional psychotherapy or clinical intervention to resolve their abuse trauma have encountered negative, insensitive and occasionally destructive treatment. This has impeded effective healing and inhibited the resolution of trauma. In contrast, a self-help support group can offer a much safer and therapeutically more effective environment in which to resolve trauma, where a woman will know that she is believed, validated, supported and understood by other survivors in the support group.

Finally, self-help groups often put personal experience into a wider societal context and framework, and combine this with a wider analysis of the underlying factors which result in personal difficulties.

Self-help support groups also aim to empower the survivor to make her own choices and decisions and to take control of her life. By discouraging dependency on one particular individual (ie counsellor or therapist) the survivor recognises that she can only depend on herself, but with much support from others, which motivates her to reclaim her life herself rather than relying on advice or permission from an authority figure such as a counsellor. Self-help groups are also less directive, which allows the survivor to reach her own conclusions and insights rather than relying on the interpretations of a therapist, which make her feel more in control of her healing.

Despite these numerous advantages, self-help groups have several limitations and disadvantages. Primarily these limitations surround the types of survivors who are unlikely to do well in a self-help group and who would therefore need to be excluded from participating. Essentially, self-help support groups would find it difficult to contain the types of behaviours manifested by survivors who are in acute distress, who are suicidal or homicidal, who are substance dependent, who exhibit life threatening self-destructive behaviours such as acute anorexia or self-mutilation, or who are aggressive, violent, and impulsive. In addition, a self-help support group would be counterindicated if the survivor is unable to interact, attempts continuously to merge with others, and is overdependent.

A major disadvantage for self-help support groups is that they have no built-in safety mechanisms to contain destructive behaviours, as the individual participants have not been trained in how to contain such behaviour or how to stabilise the individual and return her to an equable baseline. Some self-help groups have recognised this limitation and now establish links with professionals or clinicians to cope with emergencies or referrals.

One way to circumvent the limitations of self-help groups is to instigate screening and assessment interviews. As Herman (1981) argues, it may be necessary for self-help support groups to screen survivors in the same way that they are screened for more formal therapeutic groups. Such screening can only benefit a group in preventing disruption while fostering mutual cooperation and support. In addition, self-help groups need to recognise that therapeutic groups do not form spontaneously but require careful organisation and structure.

Nevertheless, self-help support groups do offer tremendous support to adult survivors of child sexual abuse in demonstrating that they are not alone and that there is help available to cope with the impact of their abuse. Other survivors can provide mutual emotional support, empathy, understanding and validation of their experiences. Most important, self-help support groups can help the survivor to break the silence of her abuse and to speak out against her abuser in a safe, non-judgmental environment with other women without feeling intimated by authority figures or professionals. Support and validation from self-help support groups can give survivors the confidence to enter a more formalised treatment programme in which to fully resolve their trauma and reclaim their lives.

CHAPTER 11

Recurrent Themes

When counselling adult survivors of child sexual abuse a number of themes and issues consistently recur. These themes are almost universal among survivors and may emerge both in individual counselling or in group therapy. Counsellors should be aware of these themes as they reflect significant and pertinent issues common to survivors, and should be aware of how to respond to them when they surface.

Many of these themes crystallise the long term effects of child sexual abuse and are deeply embedded in the impact of the abuse trauma. The most potent of these themes include negative self-image, guilt and shame, anger, and fear of intimacy. Other common recurring themes revolve around unresolved feelings (especially toward the abuser and the mother), confrontation to break the silence, and sexuality.

There also certain recurring issues which are crucial to trauma resolution which should be raised and explored. These specifically relate to the need to grieve, becoming aware of coping strategies, issues of control and dependency, and empowering the survivor by offering alternative perspectives and exploring choices which the woman can make.

The emergence of these themes will vary from one survivor to another, depending on how potent they are for the individual woman, but most if not all these themes will emerge at some point in trauma resolution, and necessitate attention. This chapter looks at how recurring themes and issues manifest themselves, and how they can be explored to facilitate positive resolution.

Negative self image

The socialisation of females commonly induces negative self-image, poor self-esteem and lack of stable self-concept. When such socialisation is combined with sexual abuse experiences in childhood, the effects are exacerbated, resulting in pervasive negative feelings about the self. This poor self-image is often so deeply entrenched that, even in the light of objective evidence to the contrary, the survivor finds it tremendously difficult to validate her positive attributes or achievements.

Helen

Helen at the age of 38 was not only academically gifted, but had also spent some years running her own successful business. Although always aware of her past abuse experiences she claimed that these had had no adverse effects on her functioning. Despite her successes, Helen would always attribute her abilities and achievements to pure luck and being in the right place at the right time. She found it extremely difficult to accept praise, or to accept and validate that her achievements were a result of her abilities and hard work.

When asked to visualise her self-image she portrayed herself as a gawky, unattractive, overweight and spotty teenager who was not only clumsy but also hopeless at everything she attempted to do, and an utter failure. This image was in stark contrast to the petite, pretty, slim, well groomed and self-possessed woman who presented herself for counselling. Helen revealed that her negative self-image reflected how she looked and felt about herself at the time of the first sexual assault made by her father. She had internalised this image so deeply that despite obvious contrary evidence she was unable to view herself in anything but a negative light.

Over a period of time Helen and I explored the question of when the negative self-image first manifested itself and the kinds of negative messages her father and mother had conveyed to her, which she subsequently internalised. Helen remembered that her mother was always very critical of her, ever since she could remember, but that her criticisms became more personal and vindictive at the time the abuse started. She also found it incongruous that her father should choose this gawky, spotty teenager as a focus for his sexual attentions rather than her very elegant, self-confident and immaculate mother. Although her father insisted that he loved her deeply and that the sexual act was part of that love, she could not believe him, as it was so furtive and unpleasant.

Helen also spent some time exploring her attributes and achievements. Instead of automatically viewing these negatively, or as due to good luck, she began to recognise that she had indeed worked hard for her success and that this was not only self-generated but also self-motivated. Gradually, Helen was able to view herself more objectively and to acknowledge her many positive attributes. By re-evaluating her negative self-image, challenging her internalised distorted perceptions, and allowing herself to entertain positive components within that self-image, she was able to integrate both her negative points and her positive attributes to arrive at a more balanced and realistic self-image.

The counsellor must be careful not to overvalidate the survivor by glibly stating that it is obvious that her self-image is discrepant with the way she appears. It is essential to explore the negative messages that the survivor has internalised, discover who generated those messages, how they were transmitted, when they first became manifest, why she was particularly vulnerable to internalising them, and the level of distortion inherent in them. When these have been explored, the counsellor can encourage the woman to re-evaluate these messages and become more objective about their veracity and accuracy.

It is helpful to the survivor if the counsellor charts how and why messages become internalised or distorted. Invariably this occurs when primitive negative messages are conveyed to the child, whose cognitive developmental level prevents a full understanding of these messages. As a result they are unchallenged and become introjected without being processed, including any distortions attached to them. When they are internalised they are integrated in the primitive self-image, and because they are never altered or revised, they are transmitted into the adult self-image.

Exercises such as making separate lists of positive and negative attributes, cognitive restructuring, logical analysis, assigned activities and confirming/disconfirming can contribute to a more realistic evaluation of the components of self-image. Some components of self-image may accurately reflect genuine shortcomings, lack of ability, or negative personality traits. In this instance the survivor should be encouraged to accept these as a part of her personality and capabilities and to view them as valuable aspects of her self.

It would be inappropriate to attempt to eradicate all negative attributes as this is not only unrealistic but also undesirable. No individual is perfect and to set up an expectation of perfection may be indicative of unresolved issues related to negative self image. The counsellor should help the survivor to arrive at a realistic evaluation and recognition of all her attributes, negative, positive and neutral, to induce a balanced and integrated self that she feels comfortable and happy with.

Guilt and shame

Feelings of guilt and self-blame are almost universally manifested by adult survivors of child sexual abuse, and as a theme will recur frequently on a variety of levels within the therapeutic process. A major component in feelings of guilt is that survivors feel themselves to be responsible for their sexual abuse experiences, and tend to focus on their contribution to the abuse rather than the abuser's involvement. These feelings of guilt and responsibility become so integrated into the self that they frequently generalise to other situations in which the child, and later adult, assumes responsibility for others, and feels guilty when anything goes wrong.

This process is most evident when the child is forced to take on the responsibility of keeping the secret to protect family members, especially the mother and vulnerable siblings. Often the child is too young to understand the meaning of responsibility but assumes it nevertheless, thereby setting up a behaviour pattern that will accompany her throughout her adult life. As she invariably assumes responsibility in situations where she is not responsible, or which are not in her control, when there is negative outcome, she automatically blames herself and feels guilty.

Carina

In her late twenties, Carina entered therapy in order to seek help for relationship problems. She had had numerous, often quite long term relationships, all of which had ultimately ended in disaster. Now that she had fallen in love again she wanted to avoid yet another destructive ending. During counselling she revealed that she had been sexually abused by her stepfather from the age of four to the age of fourteen, when she left home.

Carina felt that she could have prevented the frequent sexual assaults but had complied because she could see that her mother was always grateful to her for 'taking care' of her stepfather by being 'nice' to him and playing a placatory role. Her mother also seemed to be visibly relaxed after Carina had complied with his sexual attentions, secure in the knowledge that her husband would now not force himself on her.

Not only did Carina take responsibility for keeping the secret to protect her mother from any pain but she also took responsibility for her younger siblings by protecting them and ensuring that family life ran as smoothly as possible. However, whenever there were family upsets and rows she would blame herself and feel guilty that she was the root cause of these upsets in failing in her placatory role and as provider of everyone's well being.

While discussing her adult relationships Carina revealed that she often chose weak men who she felt needed to be protected as they were incapable of taking responsibility for themselves. She would take responsibility for them and nurture them through any difficulties they encountered by taking the blame for their misfortunes. She would express this by suggesting that because she was such a bad person she was the harbinger of bad luck which resulted in these misfortunes happening to her partner. Her partners encouraged these distorted perceptions, began believing that she may indeed bring bad luck and ultimately left her.

It is essential that the counsellor explore with the survivor the ways in which she feels at fault, and the dynamics that led her to feel such inordinate guilt. More important, the counsellor must inculcate the notion that a child has no responsibility for her own sexual exploitation or victimisation. It is vital to place the responsibility firmly with the adult who took advantage of her, and to point out that it is the adult who is the offender and that she is his victim. This is especially crucial when survivors express guilt about responding to unwanted sexual attentions.

Frances

Frances felt guilty about not preventing the sexual attentions of her father, but was more concerned about the fact that she frequently enjoyed, and sometimes initiated sexual contact. In exploring her feelings she revealed that her father was the only man that had ever been able to bring her to orgasm. The fact that her body responded in such a way to his attentions created overwhelming feelings of guilt which proved to her that she must have enjoyed, and therefore encouraged her abuse. Frances believed that she must have been highly adept at seducing her father and that he had no choice but to engage in sexual contact with her.

When her father had not initiated sexual contact for some time Frances would go to him and arouse him so that he would have sex with her. In her adult relationships Frances had never been brought to orgasm by a partner, and she would often fantasise about her father and their sexual activities in order to heighten her arousal with her partner. As she was always disappointed by not being able to have an orgasm she would resort to masturbation in which she fantasied that she was being touched and aroused by her father.

It became apparent that Frances was quite naive about sex, particularly the female sexual arousal cycle, and several sessions focused on correcting sexual misinformation and demonstrating that once the arousal cycle is activated it usually culminates in orgasm. The arousal cycle is constructed in such a way that it responds to sexual stimulation without differentiating between whether the partner is appropriate or inappropriate. That her body responded to sexual stimulation was perfectly normal and healthy.

Frances also spent some time coming to terms with her culpability in initiating sexual contact, by acknowledging that even if an adult is verbally or physically solicited they should still refuse sexual contact since they know that such sexual behaviour is inappropriate. By exploring why she needed to initiate sexual contact with her father, and accepting that she was not responsible for her sexual awakening, Frances was gradually able to place the responsibility for her abuse firmly with the abuser, her father. This allowed her to accept that her responses were normal albeit to an abnormal situation thereby relinquishing much of the burden of guilt she had carried for so many years.

As Frances was also concerned about her sexual fantasies about her father, time was spent on making her aware that because she was sexually awakened at an early age that she had been sexually conditioned to certain stimuli, including her father. This conditioning was possible to extinguish but would take time and patience. By setting up new associations and using many of the techniques and exercises employed in sexuality focused therapy, Frances was able to gradually reclaim her sexuality without intrusive fantasies about her father.

A further source of guilt for many survivors is that despite their painful, confusing and frightening sexual abuse experiences, they still feel affection and love for their abuser, especially if he was a father or stepfather. The counsellor needs to validate any positive feelings the survivor has towards her abuser. By negating them, or by portraying the abuser as a monster, the survivor might feel unable to discuss these ambivalent feelings with the counsellor and feel that she should hate him, and deny her positive feelings for him. This will result in considerable emotional conflict which reinforces already deeply entrenched guilt feelings.

The survivor should be encouraged to talk about the full range of feelings that she has for the abuser, including any positive memories she holds of him. It is necessary to acknowledge these feelings as not being 'bad' or 'wrong' but as normal and under-standable given the dynamics characteristic in parent/child relationships. By integrating both good and bad aspects of the abuser, the survivor will attain a more rounded and balanced picture of her abuser, which permits a more effective resolution of the abuse trauma.

Associated with feelings of guilt are feelings of shame. The survivor may have been made to feel shameful by the abuser, by being forced to keep the secret and thereby having something awful to hide. In addition, the abuser may have shamed the child by performing particularly shameful sexual acts, for example by telling her 'Look at what you made me do', as he ejaculates into her face. Shame may also arise when the survivor is financially bribed into committing sexual acts, making her feel little more than a prostitute. Feelings of shame should be dealt with in the same way as feelings of guilt and responsibility are explored. By reattributing responsibility for the abuse and resolving associated guilt feelings, issues of shame can also be resolved.

Anger

Many survivors are unable to express rage or anger overtly. This is partly because females are socialised not to express anger, but is exacerbated in adult survivors of child sexual abuse who tend to internalise their rage rather than discharge or externalise it. Internalised anger manifests itself in self destructive behaviours, such as self mutilation, eating disorders and suicide attempts.

Anger is closely related to the responsibility and guilt that survivors feel about their sexual abuse, and the belief that they in some way encouraged or wanted it. A corollary to this are potent internalised negative messages which reinforce distorted cognitions such as 'something bad happened to me therefore I must be a bad person, so any anger I feel must be directed inwards, towards the self, and not at the abuser or non-protecting adults.'

Many survivors of child sexual abuse are terrified of their anger and frightened of expressing it. Invariably, feelings of anger are so deeply buried and controlled by the survivor, that should any of the covert anger be released, the result would be powerful, uncontrolled surge of anger which could not be channelled and would destroy everything around it, including the survivor. Most survivors describe their anger as being on a leash which they dare not let go of, for fear that the consequences would be too devastating.

One survivor likened her anger to a pressure cooker which, if even a small amount of anger were allowed to escape, would blow off the lid so that her very being would end up spattered around the room. Another survivor felt that her anger was so overwhelming that if she were to unleash it she would end up like an amorphous jelly-like mass on the floor, from which she would not be able to reconstitute herself.

Given this fear of expressing feelings of anger, the counsellor must be aware of how frightened survivors are of releasing it and provide a safe environment for its discharge. It is vital to explore what meaning anger has for the survivor and to establish its source. As many survivors believe that anger is a very negative, unacceptable emotion, which always has powerful negative consequences, it is important to reassess anger as an emotion and reframe it in a more positive light. Emphasis should be placed on the beneficial aspects of discharging anger as a release of tension, and exploring the idea that anger is a positive, healthy emotion which is a totally appropriate response to her childhood sexual abuse.

Beryl

Beryl had been sexually abused by her father from the age of four until her late teens. She had a history of self-destructive behaviours which included self-mutilation in which she would cut her face, breasts and genital areas with razor blades. Despite frequent hospitalisation an aetiological connection between self-mutilation and sexual abuse was not made. Beryl also had a history of eating problems in which she had at times been anorexic and bulimic.

After many sessions exploring the connections between her self-destructive behaviours and her sexual abuse, Beryl revealed that she sometimes felt very angry but could not pinpoint the reason why, other than that the anger was with herself rather than her father, the abuser, or her mother. It became evident that Beryl had a tremendous amount of suppressed anger which she felt she could not and *should not* externalise, but instead directed towards herself. Thus, whenever she felt angry she had the urge to cut herself or start binge eating.

Several sessions were then spent on the need to express anger and to look at how this could be done in a positive way. The analogy of the pressure cooker became a useful one in showing Beryl that, by releasing anger, in short surges at the time of anger, the anticipated explosion would be prevented. In addition,

Beryl was asked to monitor what preceded her feelings of anger and try to connect with the source of her anger.

Over several months Beryl began to recognise the connections between her anger and what had happened to her in childhood, which allowed her to start exploring her anger in a more positive way not by internalising it but by externalising it in a safe and healthy way. A more healthy discharge of anger and a recognition of its positive contribution to healing enabled Beryl gradually to extinguish her self-destructive behaviours and discard the razor blades that had been her constant companions for so many years.

As the survivor begins to shift blame and responsibility to where it belongs, on to the abuser, there may be an increase in anger and rage directed at the abuser. The survivor needs to be given permission, permission often withheld by society, to be angry with the person who violated her.

Unresolved feelings about anger can be permitted to be discharged on two levels. Firstly, the counsellor must advocate the belief that the discharge of anger in a safe and controlled environment is a positive and healthy expression of emotion, and encourage the survivor in this expression. On the second level, the counsellor must ensure that she or he does not hold unresolved, negative attitudes towards the abuser. Therapeutically, it can be very destructive if the survivor senses that the counsellor is also indirectly venting anger against the abuser. This may be threatening to the survivor and elicit protective behaviours and expressions of loyalty to defend her abuser.

The counsellor must be led to some extent by the survivor in terms of how much expression of anger she is comfortable with, and not try to force her beyond her current capabilities. In addition, the counsellor should not transmit messages of 'forgiveness'. Many survivors may eventually be able to forgive their abuser, but this must come from within themselves and should not be imposed by the counsellor.

A further focus of anger may be directed not at the self or at the abuser, but at the mother who did not protect the survivor as a child. Many survivors find it relatively easy to forgive their abuser but struggle with intense feelings of anger towards the mother. The counsellor must allow the survivor to explore these feelings towards her mother without being judgmental or by stressing the mother's perspective in the abuse dynamics. Family dysfunction theory of why sexual abuse occurs would be counterproductive in taking other family members' perspectives. It is the survivor who is attempting to heal and resolve her feelings, with emphasis placed on that, and not how other family members, in particular the mother, may feel, that is important.

Caution should also be exercised in transmitting messages that the survivor should forgive her mother because she was also a victim and was powerless. Although mothers are not responsible for the abuse, the survivor may not be ready in the early stages of her healing to accept this perspective. She may need to act out the primitive feelings and expectations she had of her mother, and her disappointment in her, prior to adopting a more realistic and accurate perspective. Acting out such feelings represents the inner child's responses to feelings of abandonment and betrayal.

As healing progresses, and primitive responses are replaced with adult understanding and cognitions, many survivors are able to achieve a perspective that acknowledges that the mother was not to blame or at fault. However, the anger and rage of the inner child towards her mother must first be explored and resolved before a more adult perspective emerges. Ignoring intense feelings of anger that a survivor may have towards her mother is to deny a large part of the impact of the abuse trauma, particularly as perceived by the child.

Integration of the inner child and the adult can only be achieved if the inner child, no matter how distorted her perceptions, is acknowledged, listened to, nurtured and understood. During integration, primitive feelings of anger can be reassessed and re-evaluated to incorporate adult cognitions. At this stage the concept of the mother as victim can be further explored and better understood, allowing the survivor, possibly for the first time, to fully blame and be angry with the only person who was solely responsible for her sexual exploitation, the abuser.

Fear of intimacy

Fear of intimacy is a very common theme which surfaces in both individual counselling and group therapy. Incorporated in the fear of intimacy is fear of physical closeness with others, both men and women, and the inability to trust others. Survivors report that being physically close to another person makes them feel threatened and vulnerable, and that they believe that trusting someone will result in being hurt again.

In fear of physical closeness, the counsellor should acknowledge that any form of physical contact with the survivor may be distressing to her, and should avoid touching the survivor; hugging her or stroking her to comfort her may be inappropriate and counter-productive. Although some survivors express a strong need for affectionate physical contact, they may feel frightened if this actually occurs, especially if they have dissociated from their body and feelings.

Given this ambivalence to physical contact it is advisable to refrain from touching or hugging the survivor in the therapeutic setting. Validation, empathic and comforting behaviours on the part of the counsellor may be better expressed through verbal dialogue. This is vital in the early stages of the therapeutic relationship to avoid eliciting anxiety in the survivor.

As healing progresses, some survivors may ask the counsellor to hug or comfort her through physical contact. If the counsellor is comfortable with this, and able to do it in a natural, positive and healthy way, then it may be appropriate to establish physical contact. However, it must at all times be initiated by the survivor and not the counsellor, and will depend very much on the individual client.

This same principle applies to group therapy. Participants in the group should be aware that not all survivors feel comfortable about being touched and that each individual woman has a responsibility to ascertain from the other women whether they wish to be hugged and if this is comfortable to them. At no time should they attempt to initiate physical contact without first having asked.

Survivors who feel comfortable about expressing themselves through physical contact may feel rejected if their request for a hug is refused, and these feelings of rejection should be further explored. It is vital to respect the survivor who prefers not to be touched, and to admire her for being able to say 'No'. This should not be seen as rejection but as a right to protect her space and boundaries, something that she was unable to do as a child.

The building up of trust is an integral part of the therapeutic relationship and is the beginning of the survivor being able to learn how to trust others outside this relationship. The counsellor can provide a potent role model to demonstrate that it is possible to trust another person in a way which does not necessarily invite exploitation. A safe environment, validation, empathy and support enables the survivor to explore what it means to trust, and learn that trust does not always precede being hurt or abused.

Once trust has been established in the therapeutic relationship, survivors begin to trust others. Building up self-esteem, confidence and self-awareness enhances trust, both trust in oneself and trust in others. Thus the survivor needs to learn to listen to and trust herself, her perceptions and feelings. Trust in herself will enable her to trust others, and lessen her fear of intimacy. Trusting is also about taking risks, and the survivor may fear that her trust will be rejected, or abused. With increased self-confidence, belief and trust in herself, the survivor can face such risks and accept the challenge.

Lois

Lois was abused by her father for most of her teenage years, and felt that he had not only raped her but had robbed her of the possibility of ever forming close relationships. While she had had a few boyfriends during adolescence, she had never been able to feel comfortable enough with a man to establish any level of intimacy. Whenever she came close to any potential intimacy she would get panic attacks, followed by severe and incapacitating depression. This would engender withdrawal and distancing herself from the man in question and the relationship would flounder.

Fear of intimacy was not exclusive to men. Lois also felt inordinately frightened and intimidated by women, whom she categorised either as ideal, perfect and so much better than herself, or as weak, silly and contemptuous like her mother. She could trust neither and had no female friends.

After much deliberation and stocktaking Lois joined a survivors' therapy group and started to establish and build up trust with other women in the group. This was enormously difficult for Lois but she persevered and formed a close bond with two of the women. She also felt able to trust the co-facilitators sufficiently to seek individual therapy with a female counsellor. Gradually Lois was able to trust herself and others, and not be crippled by her fear of intimacy.

The abuser

Feelings of anger and rage about the abuser are frequently accompanied by intense feelings of love, sympathy, understanding, and much excusing and justification by the survivor, especially if the abuser was a close family member. These ambivalent feelings are so deeply enmeshed that it is often difficult to extricate the complex and contradictory emotions. Thus, survivors veer from extreme rage against the abuser including fantasies about killing, emasculating or defiling him, to overwhelming feelings of tenderness and love.

These ambivalent feelings are also a source of guilt to the survivor in that she believes that because he damaged and harmed her, she should only have feelings of retribution and hatred for him, which preclude feelings of care and concern. The counsellor needs to be sensitive to these ambivalent feelings and be non-judgmental whichever feelings are manifest. Portraying the abuser as a monster may elicit protective responses from the survivor, requiring her to take sides and express her loyalty towards him.

It is counterproductive to project or give permission for the expression of only one extreme aspect of her many complex, and sometimes contradictory emotions. If the survivor is to integrate fully the ambivalent feelings she has, she needs to be encouraged to express both extremes, without being judged.

To assist this, time should be spent in the therapeutic session to facilitate the expression of both negative emotions and positive feelings towards the abuser. The counsellor may also need to initiate the exploration of whichever emotional pole is not manifest or acknowledged, as ignoring the full range of feeling may reinforce already activated denial and repression.

One technique to elicit positive emotional expression is to encourage the survivor to remember some of the happy times she experienced in childhood, and how she felt about those. This should include a description of how she felt when her abuser was being affectionate and attentive to her, even if this preceded an abusive episode.

Nicola

Although Nicola had been sexually abused by her stepfather she had always had very positive feelings for him. She stated that he had always been very gentle and affectionate with her, and that she had enjoyed his attentions, providing he didn't always end up wanting sex. Nicola also remembered that until she reached the age of puberty at thirteen she firmly believed that all fathers engaged in such behaviour with their daughters, and that it was a normal part of family life. This belief stemmed very much from her lack of exposure to a father figure as she had been raised singlehandedly by her mother.

Further exploration revealed that Nicola's mother found it very difficult to show any overt affection towards her daughter, who she never held, cuddled or listened to. Her mother's emotional absence was compensated for by her stepfather's overt displays of affection and interest. Nicola's desperate need to be held and cuddled was exclusively satisfied by her stepfather.

Affectionate cuddling and holding went on for a long period of time between Nicola and her stepfather before progressing to increasingly more painful and hurtful violations of her body. Nicola felt that she should hate her stepfather for these violations, but whenever she explored her feelings for him, she remembered how affectionate and caring he was and became overwhelmed by powerful feelings of love.

Nicola excused her stepfather's sexual attentions by rationalising that as her mother was also emotionally distant from him, it was not surprising that her stepfather would want to compensate for this lack of warmth by projecting all his need for affection onto Nicola. In reality Nicola felt more angry with her mother for being so cold and unaffectionate. In contrast, she believed her stepfather was basically a nice, gentle and affectionate man who simply could not control himself.

Although these rationalisations may have stemmed from internalised messages inculcated by her stepfather to exonerate himself from guilt and responsibility, it was vital to explore and validate positive emotions first to initiate the expression of negative feelings. In exploring Nicola's attribution of responsibility she was able to recognise that she had absolved her stepfather of any responsibility for the abuse.

This permitted repressed negative feelings that her stepfather did have some responsibility to her to emerge, including protecting her from his sexual appetite. Gradually Nicola was able to construct a more balanced and realistic picture of her stepfather which incorporated both positive and negative feelings, which had previously been denied and repressed.

Confrontation

An almost universal theme which underlies much of the therapeutic process, especially when focusing on the abuser, is confrontation. Once survivors begin to discharge anger and reattribute responsibility for the abuse to the abuser, they feel a need to break their enforced silence by confronting the abuser, and/or other family members. This can be a very healthy and important part of the healing process which is nevertheless often painful and disappointing.

The counsellor must ensure that the survivor is mentally and emotionally stable enough to be able to confront the abuser. The survivor must present herself as psychologically strong during confrontation to prevent the abuser trying to manipulate or destroy her through his denial. Confrontation can sometimes be extremely destructive, with unpredictable outcomes which can stimulate regression. Counsellors should be wary of recommending confrontation without first exploring the survivor's motivations and expectations of confrontation, and evaluating her ego strength.

It is vital to assess the readiness of the survivor for any type of confrontation. If this is encouraged too early on, the effect on the survivor can be extremely destructive and may undo all the therapeutic achievements that have been attained, thus inhibiting further growth. The survivor must have realistic expectations of what she hopes to gain from confrontation, and be prepared for any potential disappointment. Frequently abusers deny the abuse, and the survivor needs to be psychologically stable enough to cope with such denial. She also needs to trust her perceptions and belief in herself that despite the abuser's denial she knows, and continues to believe that, he abused her. The survivor should also be prepared for the possibility of severing all communication with the abuser, and being ostracised by the family.

If the survivor is determined to confront, the counsellor will need to support her fully in her decision. Considerable time should be spent on preparing the survivor for the confrontation through role play, role rehearsal and empty chair exercises. During such exercises the survivor can practise various scenarios and types of confrontation. In chair work exercises the survivor can take the abuser's perspective to hone her skills to counteract, for example, his anticipated denial. The survivor may also role play anticipated responses from other family members to the confrontation, to prepare herself for their potential reactions.

Some counsellors demonstrate their support by accompanying the survivor to the confrontation, which can allay her fears in knowing that she is not alone during such a painful and harrowing experience. If the counsellor is unable to accompany the survivor to the confrontation, it may be helpful to suggest that a close, supportive friend accompanies her.

Calley

During therapy Calley, who had been sexually abused by her father, decided to confront both her mother and her father. Initially she did this through letters to them which explained why she had no wish to see them. She thought this would be sufficient to exorcise the abuse experience. In the absence of any feedback to these letters, Calley felt that she had not banished her parents from her mind as they still haunted her. Although her mother had informed some of the other family members about the disclosure, she filtered this information, making Calley look reprehensible while she became the victim.

Calley finally decided that she had to face and confront her father and siblings and tell her story personally. She was extremely nervous and anticipated negative reactions from all the siblings and denial from the father. Two close friends arranged to accompany Calley to the confrontation to lend support. Calley decided not to forewarn her father that she was coming, but informed her siblings that she would visit them. Both Calley and her two friends were extremely worried that the father would turn violent and attack her, and for this reason Calley decided to inform the siblings first.

All the siblings responded with much sympathy and sensitivity to Calley's disclosure, which surprised her, since she had anticipated considerable animosity and anger towards her. Following disclosure to the siblings, Calley went with both her friends and siblings to confront her father. Although Calley's father denied the abuse, she felt supported by her friends and siblings to make a public declaration.

Since then, Calley and her siblings have become united for the first time in years and meet regularly to make up for the divisive split in the family prior to disclosure. In Calley's words: 'I lost my father and my mother through confrontation, but I regained my brothers and sisters. That has allowed me to reclaim a part of my childhood'.

Not all confrontations have such a positive outcome and the counsellor will need to warn the survivor of all the permutations of the consequences of confrontation. One survivor remembers her confrontation as one of great pain and sorrow. 'I confronted my father, who denied it; I confronted my mother who also denied it; all my family denied it and have made me the scapegoat of the family misfortune. My family is lost to me, we do not get in touch with each other, even at Christmas. I am my own parents now. That is sometimes hard for me to accept but I am getting there.'

Confrontation is not always possible, especially if the abuser is dead or uncontactable. Role playing the confrontation within the therapeutic session can be helpful, as can writing a letter to the abuser which need not necessarily be sent. The expression of feelings and emotions about the abuser through confrontation (direct or indirect) is very cathartic and can be a crucial part of healing, enabling some survivors to resolve their abuse trauma.

Confrontation, while important to some survivors, is not important to others, with some women choosing not to confront their abuser, a decision which should be respected by the counsellor. The survivor should never feel pressured to confront her abuser. Part of growth is empowering the survivor to make her own choices. The counsellor should merely accompany the survivor on her journey to self discovery and offer alternative perspectives when required to do so. The choice of whether to confront must rest with the individual survivor and it is only when she feels ready that the counsellor should encourage and actively support her.

Mothers

Another common recurring theme among adult survivors of child sexual abuse is that of mothers. This theme may emerge early in the healing process as overtly expressed anger but frequently recurs throughout the therapeutic process. Along with feelings of anger and rage, feelings of abandonment, betrayal, and expectations of care and nurturing, may also surface. Many of these feelings represent the inner child's responses to not being protected by the mother.

Children frequently believe their parents, especially their mother, to be omniscient and omnipotent and expect their mothers to be aware of their pain, hurt and anxieties. If the mother is unresponsive to these emotions the child feels she has been abandoned. Part of this belief includes the notion that, despite keeping the abuse a secret, the mother must have been aware of it, and that she chose to ignore it by not protecting her child. As a result the child and later adult feels betrayed.

Such feelings of betrayal can generalise to all women, making it difficult for the survivor to relate to other women. Often women are avoided and ignored while the focus of attention is exclusively directed at men. Other aspects of family dynamics can also become generalised, such as the belief that because the mother is weak, all women are weak. Feelings of sexual rivalry can generalise to other women, who are seen as competitors for male attention, while negative female images lead to the denial of femaleness.

Mothers are powerful role models and exert great influence on the survivor's own parenting skills. Many survivors do not want children because they are frightened of responding to their own children in the same way as their mothers did. Often, the mother presented an inadequate role model, which the survivor feels she will adopt, thereby recreating and perpetuating the cycle of abuse. Thus some survivors avoid intimate relationships, do not marry, and do not have children.

In contrast, other survivors feel a desperate need to have children in order to mother them in a much more adequate way than they were mothered. They strive to be the 'perfect' mother by giving their children everything they feel they were deprived of, such as an inordinate amount of care, love, attention, comfort, protection and nurturing. Often they have a somewhat distorted perception of what constitutes the perfect mother and find it difficult to live up to the self-imposed demands and expectations.

The perceived perfect mother may be all the things that the survivor's mother wasn't, which results in the child being overindulged and not given any boundaries within which to behave. Such mothers find it difficult to say 'no' to their child for fear that this will be interpreted as rejection and that the child may subsequently withdraw its love. Another common response is not to allow the child to cry, as the child's tears represent the many unshed, or shed but unheard, tears of her own childhood. Thus, the child is not allowed to express emotion and feelings without being immediately comforted by the mother.

Such over-protective and over-nurturing behaviour inhibit the child's sense of individuation and separateness from the mother, which prevents the acquisition of independence. The survivor may also feel resentful if the child does not appreciate how lucky it is to have such a wonderful, perfect mother. Resentment may also surface because giving the child all the things that she desperately needed from her own mother may remind the survivor how little she had in her childhood.

When faced with a survivor who is striving to be the 'perfect' mother, the counsellor must point out how her behaviours are connected to her abuse experience and that they may be equally damaging to the child. Emphasis should also be placed on the notion that the survivor may be projecting the needs of her 'inner child' onto her child, who may have very different needs. This prohibits the survivor from seeing the child as an individual by burdening it with the survivor's unresolved issues and her needs. Ideally, the survivor needs to take a step back and differentiate between the genuine needs that her child has and her own needs. Thus she can nurture each one more appropriately rather than over indulging her child while ignoring and denying herself.

Survivors who are anxious about having children may benefit from information about child rearing practices and alternative role models which may help them to re-evaluate their parenting skills. This provides a variety of choices of how to respond to the child without automatically adopting the role model behaviours they experienced in childhood. By making the survivor aware of her internalised mother, she can re-evaluate not only her own mother but also her potential for being a 'good enough' and caring mother.

Many survivors try desperately hard to protect their mothers from their pain by taking sole responsibility for keeping the abuse secret. This enforced responsibility causes considerable conflict and resentment towards the mother. Children seem to know instinctively what may prove harmful or painful to a parent and therefore develop acute protective skills to shield the adult from revealing things that may cause them pain or anger. If the sexually abused child is being exhorted to keep this secret from the mother, the child will know that to tell would not only result in repercussions from the abuser, but also upset the mother. Thus the child has responsibility imposed upon her from an early age to protect other family members, despite being unable to protect herself.

This early, enforced responsibility, once acquired, is easily elicited in many other situations causing the child, and later adult, to take responsibility for others rather than take care of herself. It is not surprising with such deeply ingrained behavioural responses that many survivors enter the caring professions. Later in adult life, the survivor may feel the weight of responsibility for her ageing mother by taking care of her, and nurturing her almost as a child needs to be nurtured.

Survivors of sexual abuse are particularly vulnerable to such role reversal as they feel they need to continue to protect their mother. This may lead to considerable confusion because, although the survivor may feel angry and disappointed in her mother for not protecting or nurturing her in childhood, she nevertheless still looks for the approval, nurturance, love and acceptance from the mother which were denied to her in childhood.

Approval from the parent is important to the child, who is totally dependent on her mother for all her needs. Seeking this eternally elusive approbation may become such a quest that the survivor will remain compliant and appeasing towards the mother in the hope that one day she will be loved and nurtured as she wanted to be in childhood. Sadly, this rarely happens and the survivor ends up expending all her caring energies and responsibility in making her mother 'happy' while not nurturing herself.

A corollary to this is the difficulty survivors have in revealing the abuse to their mothers. Frequently, survivors seem less anxious about confronting the abuser with the abuse than they are their mothers. This may be for a variety of reasons, not least that the survivor quite rightly feels that as her mother is not to blame, there is no need to hurt her by revealing the abuse.

Although the survivor knows that her mother is not to blame she nevertheless may still feel anger towards her for not protecting her. Many survivors believe that disclosure will have such devastating effects on the mother that they cannot bring themselves to tell. A very common fear is that 'It will kill her if she ever knew' or 'I will never be able to have a relationship with her again and therefore lose my family'. These fears are not as potent in relation to the abuser since many survivors would be quite happy never to see their abuser again. As many survivors are still looking for the love they feel they missed out on from their mother, they do not want to jeopardise their relationship with her.

Bonds between mothers and daughters are so complex that they frequently remain strong through all the pain and hurt of abuse. Survivors are reluctant to sever these for fear of losing this important figure in their lives who, despite perceived betrayal and abandonment, is still greatly needed. The survivor needs to explore the complexity of her feelings and emotions about her relationship with her mother, including both negative and positive feelings towards her. Permission should be granted that it is acceptable to be angry and disappointed with her mother, and giving those feelings a voice facilitates a re-evaluation of the relationship.

Stephanie

Stephanie was illegitimate and told by her mother that the only reason she had not given her up for adoption was because she was a girl; had she been a boy it would have been very different. This statement from her mother always made Stephanie feel uncomfortable but, although her mother had made many mistakes, basically she had done her best and at least had not aborted her or given her up for adoption. She had much to be thankful for.

When her mother married when Stephanie was eight, she did so because she was pregnant again. The birth of Stephanie's half brother was quickly followed by the birth of another brother. Stephanie and her stepfather initially did not get on as he resented her presence as it interfered with his access to her mother, and the amount of attention she had available for her new husband. Shortly after getting married the stepfather began abusing Stephanie, which continued until she left home at the age of fifteen, although he still attempted to rape her whenever she visited the family home.

After leaving home Stephanie would frequently visit her mother, although she felt that her mother was glad that she had left home. Stephanie made a successful career for herself and although she remembered her abuse and talked quite openly about it, she did not feel that it had affected her in any adverse way and she still loved her mother. These feelings changed quite dramatically when Stephanie got married and gave birth to a child. The day her son was born she was plagued by nightmares about her stepfather abusing her which were so intrusive and distressing that she had to be heavily sedated. Stephanie suddenly felt that she had been robbed yet again. She had been robbed of a childhood, robbed of a normal adolescence, robbed of her sexuality and robbed of rejoicing in the birth of her first child.

This generated a surge of feelings in Stephanie, feelings which she had suppressed for years, which prompted her to seek therapeutic help. It quickly transpired that Stephanie had repressed and dissociated from her feelings to such an extent that whenever she talked about the abuse, it sounded as though she was recounting someone else's story. It was evident that Stephanie needed to access her long repressed feelings and start to integrate them with her intellectual understanding of the abuse.

It became apparent that Stephanie did not feel angry with her stepfather but rather that she had a lot of repressed anger and hatred for her mother for not having protected her from the abuse. Stephanie also began to feel very forcefully that she was used as a dowry, a bride price for her mother's marriage to her stepfather. She was merely part of the bargain. 'Marry me and I will give you sexual access to my daughter.' These feelings were so deeply repressed that Stephanie was quite shocked at the vehemence of her feelings toward her mother, whom she felt she had protected, excused and loved, despite her disappointment, abandonment and betrayal.

During therapy Stephanie was able to place the responsibility for her abuse onto her stepfather where it belonged and start to feel angry with him for the first time. On the basis of this she arranged to confront him. During the confrontation she saw how weak and pathetic he really was as an individual and watched him visibly shrink in front of her, not only in physical size but also in her estimation. For the first time she saw him as any healthy adult would: weak and ineffectual, and not as a child viewing a powerful and larger-than-life violator. As she looked at him, she seemed to tower over him both in size and self-respect, and wondered why her mother, as an adult had not seen him the way she was able to for the first time.

During the months following her confrontation Stephanie started to focus more deeply on her feelings towards her mother. She still felt very angry, hurt, and resentful towards her and started to believe that her mother had seen her value as a possible dowry from the moment she was born, which is why she kept her and not had her adopted. Although she was aware of the problems her mother faced in raising her singly, Stephanie still felt that her mother had sold her. While acknowledging that her mother was probably also a victim she could not forgive her for that, and indeed despised her for it. Yet despite all her anger Stephanie felt that she could not conceive of ever telling her about the abuse.

Stephanie remembered many incidents during the abuse which convinced her that her mother must have known that it was occurring and yet did nothing about. On one holiday the family went camping and slept in a tent with two sleeping compartments divided by a flimsy sheet. Stephanie's stepfather came to her every night and performed full sexual intercourse with her while his wife was asleep on the other side of the sheet. 'How could she not have known, she must have known' was Stephanie's wail of despair.

Stephanie began to focus on whether she should ask her mother whether she had been aware of the abuse. She was, however, reluctant to approach her for two reasons. Firstly, she felt that if she were to reveal her abuse to her mother that she would have a heart attack and die. Stephanie felt that she could not carry the guilt and burden of that, and that she had to continue to protect her mother as she always had done as a child. Secondly, and more distressing to Stephanie, was that she was petrified of her mother confirming that she had known about the abuse. Despite her suspicion that her mother must have known, Stephanie was not ready to have this confirmed.

Over many months Stephanie worked on these fears and anxieties and finally decided that she must look to the future. She recognised that she could not progress further in therapy or her healing until these issues with her mother were resolved. She felt that if they remained unresolved, they would continue to haunt her and infect not only her relationship with her husband but also the future of her son, who was already perceiving and responding to her distress. Thus she decided, some eighteen months into therapy, to confront her mother.

Stephanie spent considerable time preparing herself for every eventuality of the disclosure, and used most of the therapeutic sessions to role play and rehearse.

Stephanie's mother did not die as a result of the confrontation but Stephanie suffered greatly from having her suspicions confirmed. Her mother had known about the abuse but had been powerless to stop it. She had hated herself for perpetuating it but had believed that Stephanie was strong and capable enough to cope, and that she (the mother) could not. The mother also revealed that she had been a victim of sexual abuse at the hands of her father and elder brother. Although Stephanie was able to empathise to some extent with her mother's situation she was still devastated that her mother had used her in what she perceived to be a cold and calculating way.

Gradually, Stephanie is coming to terms with her experience and her feelings towards her mother. She is beginning to understand her mother and herself better. She can empathise with her mother and forgive her for some of her involvement in the abuse, but she has not yet totally resolved all the issues associated with the way her mother manipulated and used her in her bargaining. What she is grateful for is that for the first time there is a level of honesty, no matter how painful, between her mother and herself. Being aware of her feelings makes it easier to express them so that they can finally be integrated and resolved. Stephanie also feels more positive about her healing and believes that her disclosure has allowed her to progress in the healing process rather than leaving her in the vacuum she experienced prior to disclosure. Stephanie is hopeful and takes each day at a time, knowing that she is back on the road to recovery.

The decision to confront and disclose material must always lie with the survivor, as it is part of her empowerment to decide when she is ready, and the counsellor must respect her responsibility for that.

It is crucial that counsellors be aware of their own attitudes towards mothers. Socialisation provides several conflicting messages concerning mothers ranging from the idolisation of mothers which prohibits any criticism for fear that love will be withdrawn, to mother blaming. Mother blaming is all too common in a society which excuses individual behaviour by blaming mothers and their impaired relationships with their children for innumerable social problems ranging from school failure to murder.

Counsellors should be aware of their own internal messages regarding mothers, and must ensure that any unresolved issues they may have with their own mother have been worked through. If the survivor senses that the counsellor is conveying contradictory mother related messages she may feel threatened or unable to share and explore her feelings in case the counsellor disapproves or rejects her.

Mother blaming, including seeing mothers as collusive in the abuse, should be avoided when counselling adult survivors of child sexual abuse. At the same time, the counsellor must be careful not to deny negative feelings that a survivor may have about her mother. Whether the mother colluded or not is not the issue, it is how the survivor feels about the role her mother played that is important, and these feelings must be explored and validated. The survivor must be permitted to express the full range of her feelings about her mother, including negative ones and the counsellor must support her in exploring these. To deny negative feelings towards the mother is to deny the survivor's feelings, which she may construe as denying her.

The survivor may need to blame the mother initially as a cathartic way of accessing unacceptable feelings. Once these have been discharged and explored, the survivor can re-evaluate perceived blame and responsibility of the mother. If the counsellor actively encourages mother blaming the survivor may retreat and block these feelings to replace them with protective behaviours to demonstrate her loyalty to her mother.

Sexuality

Sexuality is a common recurring theme which many survivors shy away from, but, once encouraged to explore, generate many powerful feelings and much confusion. Survivors often feel that they have been damaged sexually through their abuse. This perceived damage is not necessarily confined to attitudes to sexuality, but also encompasses physical damage to their reproductive organs, both external and internal which could prevent them from having children.

Although some survivors are psychologically and emotionally damaged in a way which makes them shy away from having children, most survivors do not suffer actual physical damage. To allay any fears the survivor may have, she should be encouraged to have a full gynaecological check-up to ascertain that there has been no damage. This will prove to the survivor that she is physically normal and healthy, and enable her to work on her perceived damage in therapy. Some survivors feel that, even if there has been no physical damage, the sexual abuse may have resulted in gross distortions.

One survivor believed that her breasts were so large because of the constant massaging and attention they had received since puberty, while another felt that all her outer genital organs were grossly enlarged because of the early manipulations forced on her. Self exploration with mirrors together with medical information and pictorial examples may help the survivor to see that physically she is perfectly normal and has not been damaged.

The emotional damage is much less easily identified and resolved. Many survivors begin to make connections between their promiscuous behaviour in late adolescence and early adulthood and their sexual abuse in childhood. In trying to reclaim their sexuality they need to explore how they see their sexuality and sexual behaviour. It is common for survivors to feel that certain aspects of their sexual behaviour is abnormal and conditioned by their abuse experiences. This includes not only the aspects of the sexual act which they enjoy, but also those aspects which generate anxiety and fear.

Focusing on how they perceive their sexuality and exploring what is pleasurable allows the survivor to reclaim her sexuality and integrate this with her adult self rather than eliciting primitive, childhood responses. This can be achieved through reading books on female sexuality, becoming aware of the complexity of the sexual response cycle and the diversity of sexual behaviour and its expression. The notion that sexuality is about feelings, good feelings, may usefully be explored, including the enjoyment of pleasure for pleasure's sake. Demystifying societal attitudes about sexuality and what sexual behaviour is may also be invaluable.

Some survivors may, in reclaiming their sexuality, wish at this point to experiment with their sexuality. One survivor who had had misogynist tendencies, and only ever cultivated heterosexual relationships during her adult life, was able for the first time to develop deep friendships with other women, and allow her sexuality to be released. Survivors may want to explore their sexuality in relation to women and form close lesbian attachments. However, this is by no means the choice of all survivors. Research has shown that there is no significant correlation between child sexual abuse and lesbianism, or that survivors automatically turn against all men and become lesbian. However, some survivors feel that they have always been lesbian, but that their sexual abuse diverted their sexuality into heterosexuality and, by exploring their sexuality as an adult, feel more comfortable about their lesbianism.

Reclaiming sexuality involves empowering the survivor to feel more comfortable about her sexuality, giving her the confidence to explore what is most enjoyable for her, and allowing her to express her sexuality in the way she would have had she not been sexually abused as a child. This includes enjoying her body, exploring her feelings and how she wants to share these with her partner, and delighting in pleasurable sensations of which she was robbed as a child. Some survivors see this stage in the therapeutic process as a reawakening of the sexuality which was denied her in adolescence, and experience great joy in experimenting with their bodies and enjoying the feelings that her body can give her.

Related to reclaiming sexuality is the reclaiming of the survivor's body. She begins to protect her body against violation by others and starts to love her body. This includes accepting her body for what it is and nurturing it rather than constantly abusing it or trying to change it. Many survivors have eating problems such as anorexia and bulimia which relate to a need to change body image, and a need for self-punishment to expiate feelings of pleasure.

The anorexic survivor is often trying to show that she is still an asexual child by denying her femaleness. In bulimia, many survivors recreate the abuse of their body experienced in childhood. The pleasure derived from eating and bingeing must be expiated through punishment. To this effect the bulimic survivor induces vomiting immediately after eating, sometimes as frequently as forty times after a bingeing session.

With her body wracked with pain from vomiting, the survivor is able to punish herself for the pleasure her body experienced during the consumption of food. It is easy to see how this is connected with the abuse in which the survivor may have experienced pleasure during sexual stimulation to which her body responded, which she believes needs to be punished.

In contrast, some survivors become obese as a way of hiding behind their body. These women feel that their obesity makes them so unattractive that no man, or woman, will be interested in them sexually. Extra weight and a massive frame also provides a stark contrast to the childhood body and is therefore a way of avoiding memories of what happened to her as a child. In addition, some survivors believe that their body mass will be interpreted as strength and power to ward off any attack.

Vanessa

Vanessa was a slim, attractive 33-year-old who had had a ten year history of child sexual abuse. As a child, Vanessa was extremely thin, to the point of anorexic. She remembered feeling that her thinness made her look asexual, as she had no curves at all but could not understand why her grandfather was sexually interested in her. As a young adult Vanessa acquired a few more curves but still had a boyish shape.

When Vanessa started to remember her incest she began to abuse her body through binge eating. In a short period of time she would put on four stone which, as she was so petite, made her look massive. In exploring this she revealed that being slim reminded her of her physique as a child and her abuse. This daily reminder was so painful that she had to hide behind extra weight to ward off any sexual interest from men.

It became evident that whenever Vanessa felt she was progressing in therapy and healing from the incest, she would lose weight but as soon as she entered a crisis or began blocking material, this would be followed by bingeing and considerable weight gain. Gradually, Vanessa began to make a connection with her body image, her incest and her sexuality.

Vanessa began to explore what her body meant to her and how she felt about her sexuality. Increasingly, she realised that she was abusing her body in the same way that it had been abused in childhood and began to want to take care of it by nurturing it and valuing it. She lost weight and started to exercise and found that she was soon the same weight as she had been before remembering the incest. The difference was that she now accepted her body, was happy that she looked good and began to enjoy her reawakened sexuality.

Grieving

One survivor described her abuse as 'Child sexual abuse is not only about being violated but also about being robbed. Robbed of sexuality, robbed of childhood, robbed of feelings'. This woman felt that she had lost all these things and that she would never be able to regain them. Such losses need to be mourned, yet many survivors feel that they have no right to grieve and that they should put their experiences behind them. The literature on bereavement (Murray Parkes, 1972) stresses that it is crucial to mourn losses and that if grieving is suppressed this can lead to pathological grief, which can impede the healing process, and the integration of the loss. Similarly, in healing from child sexual abuse it is important for survivors to be encouraged to go through a period of mourning in which to grieve for their multiple losses.

Losses that survivors encounter include not only the loss of the loved parent who either abused them or abandoned them by not protecting them, but also the loss of innocence, childhood, loss of the real self, loss of the inner child, loss of spontaneity, loss of sexuality, and loss of joy and delight in being alive. The survivor of child sexual abuse has a right to grieve for these myriad losses which have been wrenched from her, and should be encouraged to do so.

Yet, many survivors find it difficult to feel grief and equally hard to express it, in particular through mourning or crying. They feel that they have no right to cry about their experiences and, even if they did, it would be futile because they would not be heard. Another fear is that if they were ever to cry this would open a floodgate which could never be closed again. Stress should be placed on the importance to the healing process of grieving, and reassurance given that to cry will not mean that she will never be able to stop, but rather that crying is a cleansing process which allows healing to take place.

The wounds of child sexual abuse must be cleansed with the survivor's tears. The survivor must not be afraid of her tears but must see them as a cleanser which will stop further infection of the wound. While the counsellor and supportive friends can provide the salve for these wounds, it is the survivor who needs to cleanse them first with her tears, before the salve can be applied.

Grieving may take many months and the survivor will need much support during this period. Survivors may feel they are getting worse or regressing during the grieving process since they seem to be constantly crying. It must be emphasised that this is normal and that tears must be shed before healing can progress. Stressing that tears are not equated with weakness, but reflect her strength and courage, will validate the survivor in her crying and make her feel more positive towards her grief. From her grief will emerge integration and new strength from which to grow and resolve her abuse trauma.

Coping strategies

Survivors often first enter counselling or therapy because their usually adaptive coping strategies suddenly appear to be counterproductive and maladaptive. The counsellor will need to help the survivor to identify which strategies she has employed in the past and their adaptive value in the present. It should be emphasised that these coping strategies, while often highly creative and normal reactions to sexual abuse, are essentially primitive and conditioned responses which need to be reviewed in adulthood.

Once the survivor is able to identify her coping strategies she can begin to monitor her responses and start to consider more adaptive alternative responses and coping strategies. The counsellor's role is to encourage the survivor to explore alternative coping strategies and to support her in her experimentation and validate her in her final decisions. Established coping strategies and responses feel safe to the survivor as they have been activated over many years, and she knows what to expect. Although the survivor may recognise that they are maladaptive, she may be reluctant to relinquish them for fear of adopting novel behaviours and their consequences. Adopting new strategies involves taking risks, but these risks are a part of the healing process which empower the survivor to make choices.

Practising new coping strategies is essential and can be achieved in the counselling session through role play and role rehearsal until the survivor feels confident about adopting new strategies outside therapeutic sessions in a natural, assured way. Survivors can benefit from increased insight into their coping strategies to feel more in control of their responses and behaviours. Knowing that the survivor has a choice over which responses to activate, encourages her to take control of her life and behaviour, rather than being directed by primitive responses which are often confusing and frequently destructive in her adult life.

Control and dependency

Issues of control and dependency are recurring themes for almost all survivors. Dependency on the victim role can be so crippling that many women feel unable to take control of their lives, causing them to seek relationships which reinforce both their perception of themselves as a victim and their dependency needs. Dependency needs stem from childhood in which children, by definition, are dependent on their parents to provide, nurture and care for them. This dependency is questioned in the abuse experience wherein the survivor was forced to comply with the demands made on her but in which she had no choice to do things that were painful to her.

Some survivors also struggle with the issue of control. Many make attempts at controlling their abuse experiences through dissociation and selective psychogenic amnesia. Another form of control may be to use their abuse as a form of blackmail towards the abuser by exacting financial or attentional rewards. One survivor would exchange sexual demands made by her father for money or special dispensation or privileges. This made her feel that at least she was exercising some control and retribution over her father. However, it was also a great source of guilt as she felt that since she had struck a bargain with him, which perpetuated the abuse, she was equally responsible for maintaining it.

The counsellor will need to show the survivor that she was not responsible for the abuse, and that given the limited resources available to her, extracting such secondary gains were one of the few ways in which she was able to exact any level of control over it. This is not wrong but merely indicative of her powerlessness and a strategy to gain some level of control which helped her to survive and cope with the abuse. Exploring the survivor's need for control is a useful way for her to re-evaluate the usefulness of controlling behaviours in adult life, to find more direct, less manipulative ways of achieving satisfaction of needs and goals.

A further issue of control is that many survivors feel the need to take tight control over their environment, relationships and interactions. To this effect, survivors become very controlling over what they allow themselves to experience and how they allow others to behave. Many survivors feel anxious and uncomfortable about change or being in novel situations in which they feel they have no control. This often inhibits them from seeking new experiences and leads them to keep a tight rein on what activities they allow themselves to indulge in.

One survivor found that she knew her immediate environment extremely well but realised that she had never explored outside it. Thus she limited herself and her experiences to a very narrow area over which she had control. Part of the healing process should encompass the survivor's exploration of new environments, activities, feelings and relationships by taking the risk of putting herself in novel situations and seeing how she feels about them. This can provide considerable release for the survivor as she feels she is escaping her self-imposed prison by relinquishing her need to control her environment and to enjoy a wider range of life experiences.

Not all situations and experiences can be controlled, and the survivor must learn to evaluate which aspects of the environment she has control over and which she cannot control. Such evaluation enables her to exercise control actively when she has it but to let go when she cannot exert any influence. This is also true of relationships and aspects of her abuse experience. Letting go of controlling behaviour in situations outside her control will diminish the survivor's frustration.

Powerlessness

A fundamental goal of therapy for adult survivors of child sexual abuse is to empower the survivor. Integral to child sexual abuse are overwhelming feelings of powerlessness in not being able to prevent or stop the abuse. This powerlessness reinforces victim role behaviours which prevent the survivor from recognising that as an adult she has choices and can say no.

In the absence of any real power, the survivor learns to manipulate others in the search for gratification of her needs. Survivors are invariably unable to express themselves or ask for anything directly, and develop highly acute skills for manipulation and deception, often learned from the abuser and the abuse experience. Manipulation becomes a conditioned behavioural response which is difficult to extinguish in adulthood. Being aware of manipulative behaviours enables the survivor to refrain from activating them. When combined with therapeutic techniques which encourage direct expression of feelings and emotional needs, such as assertion training, and learning to say no, the survivor can relinquish her reliance on manipulation for the gratification of her needs or in attaining goals.

Resolving the abuse experience includes a re-evaluation of powerlessness by assisting the survivor to take control of her life through more adaptive behavioural responses, and to apprise her of the fact that she has choices over how to live her life. The notion of having choices is alien to many survivors and the counsellor should explore and illuminate the range of choices available to the client. The counsellor can accompany the survivor on her journey to empowerment, not by directing and controlling her, but by encouraging exploration and experimentation. Choices should be made by the survivor and not imposed by the counsellor. Making her own choices and feeling happy in her choice, reinforces the survivor in many ways and gives her the confidence to continue to adopt healthy psychological and emotional functioning outside therapy.

Emphasis should also be placed on the survivor's courage, power and strength to survive, which was invaluable to her in the healing process, and should be capitalised after termination of therapy. The counsellor does not have the answers, nor can the counsellor provide the survivor with the power or strength to make choices. The power and strength is within the survivor herself and only she can decide how she will use it. The healing process is the survivor's journey to discovery; the counsellor is merely a fellow traveller. Empowerment is the culmination of the healing and growth process in which the survivor is able to make choices and decisions, can take control of her life, and can express both her strengths and weaknesses without feeling vulnerable. Trauma resolution allows the survivor not just to survive, but to live and enjoy being alive.

CHAPTER 12

The Role of the Counsellor

As child sexual abuse and incest are increasingly discussed in the media it is likely that more and more adult survivors of child sexual abuse will seek some form of counselling or therapy to resolve their abuse trauma. As more survivors come out of isolation and hiding, mental health workers need to prepare for such an increase by acquainting themselves with the unique long term psychological and emotional effects associated with child sexual abuse. As we have seen, survivors face a variety of difficulties and long term effects, many of which are specific to their sexually abusive experiences, which the counsellor will need to be aware of to offer effective treatment.

There are several issues that the counsellor should consider, irrespective of therapeutic orientation, before attempting to treat adult survivors of child sexual abuse. The role of therapist is always crucial to the therapeutic dyad, but in the case of survivors of child sexual abuse the counsellor needs to be even more sensitive to the client's needs and areas of conflict by validating her voice, a voice which may never previously have been heard. Traditional hierarchical approaches to therapy are less successful than those which stress a more equal relationship between counsellor and client based on empathy, validation and empowering the survivor.

It is essential that counsellors are consciously aware of their own socialisation and family history, including attitudes to child sexual abuse, their own possible abuse experiences, and their sexuality. Part of psychotherapeutic training involves the trainee therapist addressing and exploring their psychodynamic world in therapy to work on any unresolved traumas and conflicts. The importance of this self-exploration for counsellors of sexual abuse survivors cannot be stressed enough. The counsellor's own therapy is almost a prerequisite if the therapeutic relationship is to be a positive one in which the survivor can heal. Without it, much damage and destruction may ensue not only for the survivor but also for the counsellor.

Other crucial issues that need to be considered are the gender of the counsellor and how this may affect the therapeutic relationship, the impact of the abuse material on the counsellor, and the need for counsellors to have access to supervision and a support network in which to work through some of the traumatic material that is revealed to them in the counselling session. Without this support, the counsellor may become ineffective in the therapeutic relationship. The counsellor also needs to be prepared for transference and countertransference during the therapeutic process.

On a more practical level, the counsellor will need to ensure that the therapeutic session is conducted in a safe environment so that the survivor feels comfortable about building up trust. The survivor needs to feel safe to explore and release painful and emotionally disturbing feelings without being violated. This will entail establishing clear boundaries in which the client and counsellor can work, validating the survivor and her feelings as she expresses them, and adopting a positive prognosis and outcome.

Although the healing process is painful and lengthy, ultimately it will empower the survivor in her choice to lead a more healthy, less frightened and inhibited life. The emerging self, awakened through growth and healing, will be able to embrace life, its joys and pleasures as well as its sadness, instead of being deeply repressed and in a state of constant anxiety and fear.

Attitudes towards child sexual abuse

It is vital that, before any counsellor or therapist attempts to include adult survivors of child sexual abuse in their caseload, or if existing clients reveal a history of incest or child sexual abuse during therapy, they engage in some consciousness-raising about child sexual abuse. This will include not only addressing issues of socialisation and deeply entrenched attitudes towards children, but also accessing information on the incidence and prevalence of child sexual abuse, the myths surrounding it, issues of responsibility, collusion and seductiveness, theories which purport to explain why child sexual abuse occurs, the long term effects, and prevailing societal attitudes towards child abuse.

Child sexual abuse often elicits violent reactions, ranging from complete denial that such a dreadful thing could happen, to horror and fear which threatens fundamental assumptions about the world and childhood. Both extremes may result in distortions of perception which influence how we see the problem of child sexual abuse, and may necessitate questioning our own mental health, well being and safety. Many attitudes and responses to child sexual abuse are unconscious and therefore some exploration will need to take place through examining attitudes towards sexuality in general, including individual sexuality, the counsellor's own history of socialisation, family background and childhood experiences within which to evaluate possible abuse experiences.

Any counsellor with survivors in their caseload should undertake consciousness and unconsciousness raising to ascertain what their own fears are about this issue and what they think and feel about the subject. It is essential that the counsellor explore the whole issue so that unconscious or hidden messages are not conveyed to the survivor in the therapeutic process which may be detrimental to the client.

Thus, the counsellor needs to be clear about the prevalence of child sexual abuse, the myths that surround it (in particular abuser and victim profiles), and where the responsibility for child sexual abuse lies. It is imperative that the counsellor recognises that the responsibility of abuse can lie only with the abuser rather than with the child. Theories of collusion by other family members, in particular the mother, may describe some of the manifest family dynamics, but are essentially a way of justifying and excusing the abuser. Irrespective of whether there was collusion or not, the choice to abuse is made by the abuser and therefore is his responsibility.

Whether the child was perceived to be seductive or behaved in a seductive way, the choice to act upon perceived seductiveness lies with the abuser. Counsellors need to be quite clear whether they themselves have internalised any of these myths and ascertain how they feel in relation to these issues. If, for instance, the counsellor concludes that because so many survivors blame their mother for not protecting them from the abuse, mothers must be collusive, the hypervigilant client will sense that the counsellor is also blaming the mother. Such recognition can elicit the survivor's protective behaviours and prompt her to express her loyalty to her mother and abuser by blocking those negative feelings she has about them. This impedes the healing process as the survivor again feels that she needs to hide and not express certain feelings in case she may be rejected or criticised by the counsellor.

If the counsellor believes that all abusers are monsters and beasts, and projects this in the counselling session, the survivor may feel threatened when she senses that it is unacceptable for her to discuss the positive feelings of love and affection she may have felt for the abuser in between episodes of abuse. Counsellors need to be aware of what their feelings towards child sexual abuse are so as not to project their own attitudes, beliefs and thoughts onto the client, who may perceive this as critical, harsh and rejecting and consequently not trust the counsellor with the full range and complexity of her feelings and emotions.

The counsellor also needs to convey to the survivor an understanding of the long term effects that child sexual abuse can have on the adult and make connections between the abuse and her present behaviour patterns, cognitions and psychological functioning. This necessitates believing in the reality of the survivor's abuse experience, even when the survivor doubts her own memories and perceptions, and emphasising that the survivor is not abnormal, insane or mad, but rather that her behaviour and feelings are perfectly normal reactions to an abnormal traumatic experience.

As far as possible the counsellor will need to retain an empathic, positive regard for the survivor during therapy without judging any of the participants in the sexual abuse, or projecting any biases about responsibility, or personal fears and conflicts onto the client. This does not preclude the counsellor having their own fears and conflicts but these should be shared with a therapist or supervisor outside the counselling session. To project these onto the survivor will render the therapeutic relationship not only ineffective but also highly detrimental and destructive to both survivor and counsellor.

Attitudes towards own sexuality

Sexuality is often associated with complex and confusing emotions that many people struggle to come to terms with throughout their lives. Counsellors and therapists are not immune from or inoculated against these conflicts. It is of prime importance that any unresolved feelings or conflicts around the counsellor's own sexuality should be examined and worked on.

This exploration should include an examination of how males and females are differentially socialised to express their sexuality and to obtain sexual gratification. Counsellors may also inquire to what extent they have internalised these socially stereotyped roles and their feelings about them. Traditionally, males are socialised to satisfy their needs at all costs and to take what they desire. Many men also find it difficult to maintain close intimate relationships with the opposite sex without some level of sexual interest. The socialisation of males often includes the message that if they are thwarted in attaining their goal it is permissible to externalise anger or frustration and discharge this through violence and force.

In contrast, females are invariably socialised to be passive, compliant and yielding in their sexuality and to their role of needing to please men. Females learn early that they have no power in their relationships with men but that they do have a commodity that men crave – sex. In the absence of any real power, women learn to manipulate and exploit their bargaining power by exchanging sex for love, security, marriage and children. Women are also discouraged from expressing their sexual needs and desires lest they be seen as sluts or whores.

It is vital that counsellors are aware of how differently sexuality is expressed by men and women, and how their own socialisation has moulded them. According to Russell (1983) a woman has a 44 per cent chance of being raped. Knowing this may make the female counsellor feel very vulnerable in relation to men and remind her that she, like the survivor, is powerless and a potential victim. If such realisation occurs during disclosure of traumatic and horrific descriptions pertaining to child sexual abuse, the female counsellor may begin to feel unsafe, causing her to manifest fear and anxiety in much the same way as the survivor.

To prevent this, the female counsellor needs to look at her own sexuality and be careful not to project her own fears and anxieties onto the survivor. She may also identify with the survivor on certain aspects of sexuality and victim role which need to be acknowledged and dealt with so that over-identification and counter-transference can be worked through.

Acknowledging own history

Many survivors of child abuse, including child sexual abuse, enter the helping or caring professions (Briere, 1989; Gil, 1989). It is highly likely that a certain percentage of therapists and counsellors may themselves have been victims of child abuse, including sexual abuse. Briere (1989) predicts that one third of all female and between 10 per cent and 15 per cent of male therapists have a history of sexual abuse and that a larger percentage may have been physically or emotionally abused. Thus, there may be considerable personal relevance when working with survivors of abuse.

If counsellors are aware of their abuse history, they may bring high levels of empathy and understanding to the therapeutic relationship in a way in which a non-abused therapist may not be able. This can be very effective for the therapeutic process provided that the abused counsellor has addressed, explored and resolved the abuse trauma. However, if there are unresolved conflicts and trauma, it is essential that the counsellor undergo therapy in order to avoid inappropriate counter-transference and projection on to clients.

Some counsellors may not remember or be aware of their own possible abuse history. As many survivors enter therapy unaware that they have been sexually abused in childhood, or have dissociated from their abuse experience, some counsellors may have repressed their own abuse experiences. To establish the likelihood of an abuse history it is necessary for counsellors to attempt to reconstruct their own childhood history and explore any potential abuse experiences.

This exploration should include the examination of family dynamics, the socialisation process, feelings of inadequacy, powerlessness, victimisation, issues of dependency and control, and the relationship to both parents. While the counsellor may not have been abused, or at least not sexually, in re-examining their childhood and family history, the counsellor may be able to increase levels of empathy and understanding of what it might have felt like for the survivor as a child being sexually violated, and this understanding will enhance the therapeutic relationship.

The counsellor's own needs as a child should also be investigated including an assessment of to what extent these were met. If needs were not met, the counsellor will benefit from exploring whether they are being met now and how this is being achieved. For example, if the counsellor felt powerless as a child and was never heard or paid attention to, this may be a reason for choosing to enter the caring profession as a counsellor. As counsellors, individuals may feel the power and control of which they were deprived in childhood in that they represent an authority figure to clients. In helping others, the counsellor may be displacing personal archaic needs by fulfilling the needs ' of others.

Part of this re-evaluation of the counsellor's childhood may include acknowledging strengths and weakness and being aware of limitations. There may be certain aspects of the abuse trauma that the counsellor feels are too uncomfortable or traumatic to face. If this becomes evident the counsellor should refer survivors to another clinician or agency until these issues have been resolved. To continue to work with survivors in the knowledge that it is restimulating uncomfortable childhood memories is destructive of the treatment process and detrimental to the counsellor. Admitting limitations should not be seen as weakness but rather as strength, the strength to acknowledge the influence of childhood on the counsellor.

The survivor as counsellor

Some survivors who have resolved the trauma of child sexual abuse may be drawn to becoming therapists or counsellors themselves to help other survivors. This may be a form of displacement in that the survivor as therapist helps another as a symbolic representation of the self, in which the client's catharsis becomes the therapist's catharsis. Although abused therapists frequently make excellent counsellors, there are some mental health professionals who question their therapeutic value. Certainly the abused therapist has many advantages over the non-abused counsellor, but there are also problem areas that need to be considered.

A major contribution that the abused counsellor can bring to the therapeutic relationship is an increased level of empathy and a deeper understanding of the abuse and the survivor's experience of it. The abused therapist may also more easily crystalise how these experiences affected the survivor, not only as a child, but the kind of influence it exerts on current functioning. The abused counsellor is likely to have had first hand experience of many of the difficulties that survivors face, and will have worked through these during her own healing process.

In contrast to non-abused counsellors, the abused counsellor may be more able to believe not only that sexual abuse occurred, but also be more attuned to the survivor's descriptions of the abuse. Many non-abused counsellors question whether sexual abuse did in fact occur, or was merely a product of fantasy. This is in part due to difficulty in believing some of the accounts provided by survivors about their abuse. Descriptions can sometimes appear so horrifying and incredible that the counsellor questions how such abuse can have taken place, and how the child managed to survive it.

Counsellors may also find disclosed material unbelievable as it is threatening to their assumptions about the world being a safe and just place. Also non-abused counsellors may find the survivor's experiences far outside their own terms of reference and experiences, making them incredulous. The abused therapist, however, may find abuse related descriptions entirely believable because they resemble her own experiences. Thus the abused counsellor can enhance a crucial aspect of the therapeutic relationship by conveying to the survivor that her abuse is credible and its validity is not questioned, as others may have in the past.

Despite these very real positive contributions there are some pitfalls. One aspect that may endanger the efficacy of such a therapeutic dyad is that abused counsellors may project their own unresolved issues and internalised fears on to the client. This might include highly subjective and personal opinions about child sexual abuse, such as that all men are potential abusers, that abusers must be confronted for healing to take place, negative prognosis for the outcome of healing, and that the survivor will always remain a victim.

All counsellors, whether abused or not, must guard against imposing their own personal views and unresolved issues, but the abused therapist must be especially careful not to direct the client along the same path that he or she may have travelled. It is essential that the survivor clarifies her unresolved trauma and the issues involved and how she wants to work on it. To have these imposed may be important and gratifying to the counsellor, but will not foster the healing process. Timing is also important and the survivor must be allowed to work at her own pace.

Any survivor who wishes to become a therapist or counsellor must ensure that her healing has been such that she has resolved many, if not all, of her unresolved trauma before embarking on counselling adult survivors of incest. They must be aware of not projecting their needs and gratifications on to the client, and not use the therapeutic relationship as a mechanism for undertaking further work on themselves. In addition, they must guard against advocating or reinforcing their own defence mechanisms such as intellectualisation, sublimation, denial, dissociation, or displacement. Abused counsellors also need to be aware that the impact of the material they encounter may re-stimulate their own abuse, and that this can affect their own healing and healthy functioning. The problems of transference and counter-transference, and the primacy of the survivors's needs over the counsellor's own should also be fully addressed.

The abused therapist should also consider the relative merits of disclosing her/his abuse to the survivor, or of remaining silent. Some survivors report that they have benefited from such disclosure and felt more able to respect the counsellor, saw her/him as being more credible, felt better understood, validated, and more able to trust. They also feel more able to share their abuse experience with an abused counsellor, feel safer with them, and believe that they are less likely to be abused in such a therapeutic relationship.

Another positive aspect is that abused counsellors can give the survivor a sense of hope and optimism that it is possible to heal, and that once healing has taken place they can help others. As one survivor said 'It showed me that it was possible to heal and that good could come out of all those negative and painful experiences that I had when I was a child. Seeing my therapist healed and still able to help me, gave me the courage to continue with the painful process of healing.'

In contrast, some survivors report feeling less able to respect the abused therapist and less able to trust him or her with their feelings. Often they feel more vulnerable and under pressure to compare themselves with the counsellor, resulting in the client feeling less healthy and therefore a failure in that she has not resolved her trauma yet. Some survivors also report that they tended to focus more on the counsellor and her or his problems and how he or she resolved them rather than focusing on their own, which can elicit pronounced care-taking behaviours. This permits them to avoid resolving their own issues, or deny the therapeutic focus that they need. There is a danger that the therapeutic focus is diluted for the survivor when faced with an abused counsellor, which makes the survivor feel less important and worthy of counselling.

Ultimately the decision to self-disclose lies with the abused counsellor. Ideally, the abused counsellor should make this decision at the outset so that all potential clients are aware that he or she is a survivor. To self-disclose during the therapeutic contract will undoubtedly change the therapeutic relationship, often for the worse, and as such is not to be recommended. Some mental health professionals have strong reservations about self disclosure (Gil, 1989) while others believe that to not disclose reflects secrecy and dishonesty which is seen as yet another violation against the survivor.

This view cannot be ignored and has some validity. It can be overcome by abused counsellors advertising themselves as such so that both survivors and the referral services know this and utilise this information when making the choice to enter therapy with an abused counsellor. Those abused counsellors who choose not to reveal their own abuse history are entitled to do so.

Some survivors may question the counsellor whether they were abused in childhood which may make it difficult for the therapist to respond truthfully. In such a situation Gil (1989) recommends asking the client what it would mean to her if the counsellor had been abused, and how she would feel if he or she had not been abused. Exploring the meaning of this to the survivor may generate a deeper understanding of what her abuse experiences mean to her and the sort of unresolved issues the client is struggling with. This approach allows for the reinforcement of the primacy of the survivor's needs by focusing on her needs and not those of the therapist.

Impact of the material on the counsellor

The trauma of child sexual abuse generates many powerful, painful emotions and feelings in the survivor. The counsellor is not immune to these potent and painful feelings and may often feel emotionally involved. In addition, some of the material brought into the counselling session can elicit feelings of pain, anger and sadness in the counsellor. The counsellor can prepare herself for the nature and content of such material by reading some of the excellent first hand accounts by survivors that have been published in the last few years (see Appendix A).

However, reading such accounts is not the same as facing a survivor displaying so much anguish, fear and distress and the counsellor will on occasion have to muster all the resources available to her in order to remain focused on the client and to respond to her appropriately. To counteract the high emotional intensity it is essential for the counsellor not only to have a satisfactory support network and supervision, but also to have alternative activities in which to relax and regenerate depleted reserves of energy and emotion to prevent therapist burnout.

It is counterproductive to live and breathe child sexual abuse by reading exclusively around the topic. Some counsellors report becoming so obsessed with the whole issue that they begin to categorise individuals into either survivors or abusers by making assessments wherever they go, out in the street, on trains and in supermarkets. To avoid this the counsellor is advised to take frequent mental breaks from the topic.

Briere (1989) also advises that the counsellor should arrange the caseload in such a way as to not consist exclusively of survivors but to intersperse them with non-abused clients. This will achieve a better balance between clients and maintain a level of objectivity towards survivors. Briere also stresses the value of taking regular physical breaks as well as mental breaks from counselling by arranging time away from the counselling environment (1989).

Counsellor support network and supervision

Given the traumatic and intensely emotional content of the impact of child sexual abuse counsellors need to ensure that they have their own support network that they can turn to to discuss and evaluate their counselling. Ideally this support network should include the counsellor's own therapist if they are in therapy, and a supervisor who has some experience of child sexual abuse and its effects.

While maintaining the role of confidentiality, it is sometimes helpful to be able to discuss particularly distressing cases with a supervisor who may offer advice or at least support to the counsellor to remain effective in the counselling sessions. Regular meetings with such a supervisor, at least once a week or once a fortnight, can be extremely beneficial in clarifying material that has surfaced and how this can best be acted upon. More important, it is an opportunity for the counsellor to relieve the emotional effects this material has on them which allows them to work it through. Supervision also allows the counsellor to assess and process levels of transference and countertransference, allowing for more objectivity in the therapeutic setting.

It may also be useful to establish a network of other counsellors who specialise in the area of child sexual abuse, not only to exchange latest research findings but also as a way of maintaining contact. Such a network can foster the exchange of ideas on techniques that have proven to be particularly effective or cathartic, while allowing for a re-evaluation of those which are less effective or counter-productive.

Some counsellors may also wish to become involved in programmes that aim to educate both the public and other professional workers about the nature and effects of child sexual abuse on children and its lasting effects on adults. Others may wish to become involved in projects which work towards the prevention of child sexual abuse, or to conduct further research in the field. Whatever the counsellor chooses to do, a network of support can be generated to foster the sharing of knowledge and validation for work that is being achieved.

Our understanding of child sexual abuse is still in its infancy and thus requires a constant exchange of ideas, conceptualisation and treatment methods. This exchange can make valuable contributions not only to the enhancement of our understanding of the problems associated with child sexual abuse but also to the improvement of treatment methods which are effective in the healing process.

Gender of the counsellor

The gender of counsellors working with survivors of child sexual abuse is considered by some mental health professionals, and survivors, to be extremely important. Several writers, including the present author, argue that the most effective therapeutic relationship is that between a female survivor and female counsellor (Blake-White and Kline, 1985; Herman, 1981). This view does not deny that male counsellors can make a valuable contribution to the therapeutic relationship with female survivors. Many do, and are able to represent a positive male role model to the survivor which can encourage the formation of healthy and valid relationships with men. It is essential to recognise that the gender of the counsellor does exert an influence on the therapeutic dyad, which can be positive to treatment, but may also be counter-productive and destructive to some survivors. Counsellors, irrespective of gender, should be aware of the advantages and disadvantages of which therapeutic dyad is most effective.

Female counsellors

Most survivors if offered the choice, or asked to state a preference, find they choose a female counsellor or therapist. For the female survivor who was abused by a male, a female counsellor is seen as more appropriate in that the survivor is more able to trust the counsellor and feel that she will not be seen as a sexual object to be abused again. In the case of female survivors who were abused by another female, a female counsellor may be counter indicated and a male therapist may be more appropriate.

Female counsellors are frequently seen by the survivor as being more empathic and attuned to how the survivor may be feeling. Generally the female survivor also feels more comfortable and safe with a female counsellor when sharing and revealing painful memories and experiences. There is some identification with the female therapist as a woman, who, because of her sex, will not abuse or victimise her. Survivors may also feel that a woman counsellor will be more attuned, sensitive and gentle in her treatment of the survivor.

Although generally the same sex counsellor forms the preferred therapeutic dyad, there are some problems that may occur in such a dyad which need to be addressed. The positive attitudes most survivors invest in a female counsellor are essential in the initial phase of the therapeutic relationship when the focus is on establishing trust and creating a safe environment, but as therapy progresses difficulties may arise which may be worse if the gender of the counsellor is female.

Some survivors may reject certain aspects of being female as a result of having internalised abuser or male values, and will consequently devalue all females. Such women commonly express great disappointment at being assigned to a female counsellor as they believe a female will not be as good as a male. Survivors who project such views are probably the most likely to benefit from a female counsellor, but may not be able to entertain this possibility until considerably advanced in the treatment process. It may be more productive to work initially with a male counsellor, and then go on to a female counsellor when ready.

Some survivors may also perceive the female counsellor as a potential competitor and display hostility and aggression towards her. If the survivor's incest experience incorporated aspects of rivalry between mother and daughter for the father's sexual attention, and the counsellor is perceived as being attractive to other men, then primitive responses may be elicited. Such dynamics should be explored to prevent the therapeutic process being impeded if the survivor feels she has no respect for the counsellor and views her as someone to be annihilated and removed from competition.

Survivors who have pronounced negative self-image, in which they see themselves as weak, pathetic, powerless victims, may generalise this to other women including the female counsellor. Some survivors may also begin to see the female counsellor as a symbolic representation of other important females in their lives, especially the mother.

Projecting a mother figure onto the counsellor may cause severe disruption in the therapeutic relationship. One survivor saw her counsellor as her mother who was cold, rejecting and unloving. The counsellor also physically resembled the survivor's mother to such an extent that the survivor could not look at her without seeing her mother. She also began to see this mother-figure as the embodiment of maternal failure. The counsellor was seen as harsh, cold, distant, rejecting and uncaring. The survivor felt that she was unable to trust the counsellor as she would undoubtedly betray her as her own mother had done. Rather than wait for her to be abandoned yet again, the survivor left therapy.

Although the counsellor cannot prevent the survivor from abandoning therapy, it is important that the survivor be encouraged to continue, to resolve such transference. When unresolved feelings about the survivor's mother, such as anger for not having protected her, rage because she is still with the abuser and has chosen him over her, are transferred onto the counsellor it is essential to point out to the survivor that it is her inner child that is generating these projections. Making this conscious will give the survivor permission to explore this further on a child level, providing fruitful insights into unresolved areas, but also make her aware that she has the choice to relate to the counsellor on an adult level.

Gradually the survivor will find she is able to relate on an adult level more frequently, and as transference lessens, she will be able to see the female counsellor as an individual, separate, adult woman, who is not her mother or an internalised negative image of femaleness. By offering reassurance, support and clarification the counsellor will be able to provide a positive female role model with which the survivor will be able to identify. A strong, caring, responsive female role model can go some way to affirm the value of being a woman which will allow the survivor to relinquish any distorted perceptions that she has about being female, so that she can reclaim her femaleness and become a woman.

This is a fundamental part of healing, allowing the survivor to feel good about being a woman rather than seeing herself as a victim to be exploited. A same sex counsellor will assist the survivor in re-evaluating her status as a woman. If the survivor prefers a male counsellor this should be recognised as important to the survivor at particular stages of the healing process. Seeing a male counsellor should not prevent her from making a later choice to see a female counsellor to explore other issues that she has been unable to resolve with a male counsellor. Both therapeutic dyads have their merits and their associated problems but may have value at specific stages of the healing process.

The male counsellor

The male counsellor faces more difficulties than the female counsellor when treating female survivors of child sexual abuse. Fundamental requirements for male counsellors are to explore their own attitudes towards child sexual abuse, feelings about the meaning of gender roles including an understanding of how females are socialised, a clear comprehension of male hierarchical role structures which operate in socialisation and society, especially male power and dominance, and sexuality.

The male counsellor may have to work harder to create a safe environment in which the survivor feels able to disclose her sexual abuse history, and be more sensitive in both establishing trust and conveying empathy. In many respects the male counsellor is asking the survivor to forget that he is a man, who will not wield the power bestowed upon his gender. This may be difficult to convey to the survivor but needs to be achieved to enable the counsellor to make crucial therapeutic connections with the survivor.

One hazard facing the male counsellor is that the female survivor may have generalised her fear, anger, rage and aggression towards all men, and bring these potent feelings into the therapeutic setting. The survivor may see him as a potential abuser who will abuse his power by dominating her and forcing her to behave in a sexual way. Alternatively, the survivor may see him as an authority figure who has the power to make her better and as such is dependent on him for his approval which may elicit archaic behaviour patterns of compliance.

The male counsellor will need to reassure the female survivor that he is not an abuser and that he will not exploit or victimise her in any way, especially in a sexual way. This fear on the part of the survivor may be so great that she will seek to avoid talking about the sexual abuse for fear that this may be perceived as a 'turn on' on the part of the counsellor, and that he may then sexualise his relationship with her.

Briere (1989) suggests that there are a number of principles to which the male counsellor must attend when helping female survivors of child sexual abuse. Of primary importance is that the male counsellor be crystal clear about the boundaries within the therapeutic relationship in which he will not abuse her in any manner either through voyeuristic titillation, or flattery, or in initiating physical contact. The male counsellor must ensure that he is healthy enough, both sexually and interpersonally, so as not to view the survivor as an object for his own gratification either in exerting his power, control and dominance, or for his erotic and sexual needs.

A corollary to this is that the therapist must make clear to the survivor that he does not subscribe to or condone male sexual aggression or privileges. He must be specific in his reassurance to the survivor that although he is a male that he does not collude with such male behaviours as rape and child sexual abuse, and that he finds such expression of male sexuality dysfunctional and unacceptable.

Several researchers (Holroyd and Brodsky, 1977; Briere, 1989; Gil, 1989) report that there is a shockingly high preponderance of counsellors who do abuse their relationship with their clients by initiating and manipulating them into sexual activity. This is morally indefensible as they are abusing their position of trust by exploiting the client at her most vulnerable.

When the therapeutic relationship between a female survivor and a male counsellor becomes sexualised the survivor will experience this as a recreation of her childhood abuse. As such she will find it difficult to extricate herself from such manipulations because she is still unable to say no, and will feel that she has to comply to this affirmation of her role as victim. Even if the counsellor does not initiate sexual activity he must be aware that some of his behaviours may be perceived as sexual by the survivor.

One survivor who had been seeing a male counsellor for some period of time found that the therapeutic relationship became increasingly sexualised. She found it extremely difficult not to be aware that her counsellor was a man which she perceived as a potential threat. She was drawn to watching each movement he made in fear that he might try to move too close to her. She was also conscious of how he sat and whenever he uncrossed his legs and spread them out, she interpreted this as a form of sexual display and invitation. She found it impossible to focus on anything during the counselling sessions because '... the air was permeated with sexuality. Wherever I looked I was aware of his manhood which meant I was unable to concentrate on anything other than when will he make the first move'.

If this occurs the male counsellor must attempt to contain this perceived sexualised behaviour, and reassure the survivor that she is safe and that he will under no circumstances exploit her. Only then can the therapeutic process continue by exploring the feelings that the maleness of the counsellor has elicited in the survivor. In such a situation it is not the adult survivor that is responding to the counsellor but her inner child. Working with the inner child to resolve her feelings about the threatening nature of male sexuality will enable the survivor to understand where these feelings stem from, and allow her to express them. Progressively the survivor will be able to relate to the male counselor on an adult level and not perceive his presence or behaviour as sexualised.

In contrast to the female counsellor, the male counsellor must work much harder to prevent such transference while being careful to reinforce positive, independent and self-affirming behaviours in the survivor. Females are socialised to be dependent on males, to be compliant and passive. The male counsellor should stress that he does not adhere to such male hierarchical socialisation by not reinforcing her for such behaviours but rather by encouraging the empowerment of the survivor and reinforcing less gender stereotypical role behaviours.

Male counsellors can also provide a positive male role model to the survivor from which she can learn that not all men are like her abuser but are capable of caring, supportive behaviours that do not lead to sexual exploitation. Recognising this is a crucial component of healing in that the survivor can re-evaluate her perception of men allowing her to form healthy relationships with healthy men. The male counsellor may be the first man that the survivor has encountered who is non-exploitative, sensitive, and emotionally responsive in a non-sexual way. Such an alternative model enables the survivor to be less frightened of trusting other men outside therapy.

While many survivors benefit from a therapeutic relationship with a male counsellor, not all will be able to establish this when first entering therapy. It may be pertinent to enter therapy with a male counsellor once the survivor has progressed in her healing with a female counsellor. Female counsellors may find it pertinent to encourage certain survivors to see a male counsellor for a period of time, either as an adjunct or concurrently to their existing counselling. This will enable the survivor to address some of the unresolved issues around her abuser and as a way of exploring the possibility of a non-exploitative and caring relationship with a healthy male.

Transference

The therapeutic relationship involves a highly personal interaction between the client and the counsellor during which the survivor may perceive the counsellor not only as a powerful authority figure, but also as a psychologically important person that the survivor has become dependent on. The powerful nature of this interaction, together with the survivor's vulnerability may remind the survivor of similar psychologically important figures in her childhood, causing her to see the counsellor as a symbolic manifestation of these figures.

This investment will distort the survivor's perception of the counsellor so that she begins to respond to her as if she were responding to that psychologically important figure in childhood. The female counsellor may begin to represent the survivor's mother, while the male counsellor will come to represent the abuser. Once this process of transference has taken place, old feelings, thoughts and behaviours will be reactivated and directed at the counsellor. These invariably include anger, hurt, betrayal and rage.

The counsellor will need to deal with this transference by not feeling personally attacked but recognising that primitive responses have been reactivated and that it is the survivor's inner child who is responding. Transference can provide useful insights into the therapeutic issues that are current for the survivor which need to be fully explored to be resolved. Thus the counsellor should, without denying the validity of the feelings generated, point out to the survivor that her inner child is responding by expressing her long buried and deeply repressed feelings. Reassurance should be given that it is permissible to act out these feelings within the therapeutic session. Counsellors should also ensure that they remain objective during transference and not feel personally threatened or attacked.

Releasing these feelings in a safe, supportive environment is healthy and cathartic, and facilitates trauma resolution. To deny or leave these feelings buried will only impede the healing process. The survivor should be encouraged to act out her transference, especially if this is interspersed with sessions in which the survivor explores her adult feelings towards the counsellor, rather than seeing her merely as a primitive important figure. This shows the survivor that she has a choice to respond with her inner child or to respond on an adult level, and to integrate both responses into the self.

The counsellor must at all times be aware of the transference process and not feel threatened psychologically by any acting out behaviours. It is vital to retain an objective perspective and to validate the survivor in allowing her child a voice. The counsellor must be wary of not showing her own emotional reaction to destructive onslaughts. Even if the counsellor experiences feelings of anger, hurt, rage, disappointment or irritability, it is crucial to remain impassive but sensitive.

Counter-transference

The counsellor not only needs to be prepared for the survivor's transference, but must also be cautious of the possibility of counter-transference through which the counsellor reacts to the client with her own primitive behaviour patterns based on her own childhood experiences. This is especially the case for the survivor counsellor who finds that client material restimulates childhood abuse experiences. However, non-abused counsellors are just as vulnerable to counter-transference.

Disclosed material may sometimes strike chords in the counsellor which can restimulate a childhood memory or feeling which has been repressed. Although this may not be an abuse related memory, it may nevertheless reactivate archaic feelings and behaviour patterns which the counsellor must not allow to infect the therapeutic session. These require immediate attention and need to be dealt with swiftly outside the therapeutic setting during supervision so as not to impede the healing process.

Being aware of the possibility of counter-transference can help counsellors to prepare for it by making contingency plans such as arranging their own therapist or supervision. Knowing that there is a support network will remind the counsellor that she has not failed in her reaction to the material, but has prepared for this by being able to work it through with someone else rather than transferring reactions onto the client.

Creating a safe environment

It is crucial that the therapeutic setting takes place in a safe environment in which the survivor feels comfortable and is able to share her painful and fear inducing memories and feelings. This will mean using a quiet room that will not be subject to too much noise or interruptions. Ideally, the room should not have a telephone in it, or if it does, it should be unplugged as incoming telephone calls can be very distracting.

The room should also exude comfort and warmth and should have a moderate temperature, adjusted to prevailing weather conditions. Many counsellors work from their home rather than a clinic environment. There are some advantages to this in generating a more warm, personal atmosphere in contrast to a more formal clinical or medical setting. If the counsellor does work from home, she must ensure that there is quiet, and that there will be no family interruptions.

Although there are advantages to being in a neutral room with few distractions, some survivors have expressed a preference in being in an informal room with books and family artefacts around them. Such informality normalises and destigmatises their abuse trauma so that they do not feel they are medically ill or clinically insane. An informal setting is not only less clinical but also allows the survivor to view the counsellor as more human, with a life of their own. Other survivors have felt intimidated in a room full of books, feeling that they are in the presence of an intellectual which reinforces the power and authority of the counsellor in relation to the weak, ineffectual and pathetic figure of the survivor.

Having personal possessions and family photographs prominently displayed may also elicit negative responses from some survivors. Often personal artefacts give the survivor an excuse to distract herself from the therapeutic session by looking around the room and focusing on these rather than on what is being explored in the counselling session. This allows some survivors to dissociate more easily from painful material which may arise during the session.

Other survivors have felt jealous of the counsellor, especially if family photographs are happy ones involving children and partners. This is particularly true for survivors who are totally alienated from their own family, and who feel extremely isolated. As many survivors find it difficult to form, let alone maintain relationships, seeing such happy family snaps may highlight her own loneliness and despair.

A balance should be struck between the informality of a room in the counsellor's house which reflects the counsellor's human qualities and the stark formality of the clinic consulting room. It will not be possible to please each individual client and so a gentle, harmonious balance that is palatable to the majority of clients will be the most apt.

Seating is also very important. Seating that creates a hierarchy and power differential between the client and counsellor should be avoided. Survivors are highly sensitised to expressions of power and authority and seating the client in a lower chair or on the other side of a desk will convey to the survivor that she is of less importance than the counsellor.

Ideally, the survivor and counsellor should sit on a comfortable sofa facing each other allowing the client ample room to move around to make herself most comfortable. It is helpful to be seated on the same level and to be close enough to reflect intimacy, without being so close as to be perceived as violating the survivor's space. Some clients may prefer to sit on cushions on the floor. Providing the counsellor is comfortable about sitting on the floor she should preferably follow suit and join the survivor on the floor.

The counsellor should face the survivor and be able to see all of her so that all physical responses, or nervous habits can be observed. Sometimes such responses may be the only indicators the counsellor has that the material being explored is painful to the survivor who may be unable to cry but may manifest her agitation or arousal through non-verbal communication. By observing physical responses, the counsellor will be able to tune in with how the survivor is feeling and conduct the counselling session with more sensitivity.

Some counsellors believe that dress is important in making statements about them-selves to the survivor which may influence their perceptions of the counsellor. Fairly informal, yet clean, tidy and co-ordinated dress helps to present a relaxed approach in which survivors feel most comfortable. If the counsellor is overdressed the survivor may again perceive a power differential, while the counsellor who looks untidy may transmit the message to the survivor that she is not important enough to make an effort for.

Setting clear boundaries

The setting of clear boundaries is fundamental to counselling adult survivors of child sexual abuse because they have a history of boundaries being violated and so need to know what the boundaries are and that these are respected by both parties. Implicit in any counselling relationship is the confidentiality of the material discussed in session. Even though this may be implicit to the counsellor, it will need to be made explicit right at the beginning of the first session, so that the survivor is quite clear that the information she imparts will go no further.

Clear boundaries must also be established as to the length of the counselling session. If the session is to be fifty minutes or an hour it must be made clear to the survivor that this is so even if painful and distressing material arises immediately prior to the end of the session. It is helpful if the counsellor warns the survivor that they are coming to the end of the session about ten minutes beforehand to give her an opportunity to raise anything else she wishes to. In addition, the counsellor should strive to ensure that the survivor is relatively calm when the session ends so that she does not leave in an overwrought state, and attempt to end the session on a positive note.

The question of payment must also be quite clear. The survivor should know before she attends her first counselling session not only how long each session will be, but also how much it will cost, and the method of payment. Some counsellors operate a sliding scale of fees so that survivors with limited financial resources are not excluded from therapy. It is essential to negotiate a mutually acceptable fee and be clear about how this will paid prior to the first session.

To ensure safety it is essential to impress upon the survivor that she will not be violated in any way during the counselling session either physically, sexually or emotionally. To make boundaries absolutely clear, some counsellors draw up a contract between the survivor and the counsellor in which such issues as confidentiality, length of session, payment, and making of appointments are clearly stated and this is signed by both parties. A contract can also include conduct issues such as smoking, the use of alcohol and drugs, and unacceptable behaviours which will not be tolerated such as violence.

Some counsellors prefer clients not to smoke during the counselling session as this can inhibit the flow of feelings and be used as a crutch to avoid talking about distressing material. Other counsellors believe that if the client smokes and finds it helpful to her when discussing emotionally charged issues, then she should not be prevented from doing so. This decision will have to be mutually agreed between the counsellor and the survivor, and if smoking is permitted, the counsellor should encourage the survivor to cut down for health reasons as well as reducing addictive and dependency behaviours.

It is vital that neither the counsellor or the client are intoxicated or under the influence of drugs, as this could impede the effectiveness of the counselling session. If the client arrives under the influence of either alcohol or drugs it may be necessary to cancel the counselling session and arrange another time. If this happens repeatedly, the counsellor should encourage the survivor to enroll in a substance abuse programme as part of her therapy so that she can come to counselling sessions sober.

Counsellors should be discouraged from socialising with the survivor or establish a relationship with her outside therapeutic sessions. Some counsellors have strict rules about contact between sessions including restricting telephone contact. However, occasionally a survivor may go into crisis in between sessions and may need to contact the counsellor in order to talk through what has precipitated this. In such instances it may be reassuring to her to know that she can ring her counsellor.

Providing the facility of telephone contact is not abused, it can be important for the survivor to feel that she can ring in between sessions if she needs reinforcement or reassurance. If this is abused, the counsellor will need to curb this swiftly by discussing it with the survivor in the next session as a way of exploring current issues and problems that the survivor is not bringing into the session but prefers to discuss on the telephone. This can sometimes provide vital therapeutic insight which can be further explored.

Physical contact

Some survivors are very anxious about physical contact, even between women. For this reason physical contact should be kept to a minimum and the counsellor will need to emphasise this when setting boundaries. It is possible to give reassurance and show empathy without physically touching the survivor through eye contact and verbal affirmation. Some counsellors believe that when a survivor is crying that they should touch or reassure her by stroking or holding her. Physical contact should not be advocated for all survivors; some see this as an invasion.

However, there are survivors who do express a desire to be hugged in order to feel safe and comforted. This is especially so with a female counsellor where the survivor wishes to be held by her mother in the way she never was as a child. The counsellor must explore how she feels about physical contact and assess how the individual survivor wishes to be comforted or reassured.

If the counsellor feels that there are positive contributions to be made by hugging the survivor or if the survivor has specifically asked to be held, then this should be considered and provided. It must be stressed, however, that it is the survivor who should initiate such contact and not the counsellor. It may be that, as trust is established, survivors may ask to be held and will not be afraid of such physical closeness. In the early stages of counselling it may be detrimental and anxiety provoking to make any physically demonstrative gestures.

Validating the survivor

Most survivors do not know what it is like to be validated or valued, and feel that they were not heard when they tried to express themselves to significant others in childhood. It is essential that counsellors give survivors total attention and validation as an individual who has feelings and thoughts which she has a right to express and be heard. Counsellors should ensure that they do not convey feelings of boredom, irritation, disbelief, tiredness or inattentiveness. Many survivors are hypervigilant to such responses and highly sensitised to even the slightest expression of such emotions. If the counsellor expresses overt boredom, the survivor will feel rejected, yet again, and believe that she is not important enough to warrant the counsellor listening to her.

Counsellors should also emphasise to the survivor her importance in the therapeutic relationship, that she is a valuable individual who is worthy of help and has a right to heal. Caution should be exercised in conveying to the survivor that the abuser or the mother is more important or worthy of therapy than she is. The therapeutic focus of attention must be on the survivor and not on the abuser, or the mother, valuable therapeutic time must not be spent analysing their motives or behaviour. The survivor must be clear that it is she who is in therapy and it is her healing that is vital, not that of her abuser or mother.

A common difficulty survivors face is doubting the truth of her memories and perceptions. This is especially so for survivors who have dissociated or suffer from psychogenic amnesia, but can also occur in survivors who have no memory deficits. As children, many survivors frequently pretended to be asleep to avoid, or prevent the abuse. This twilight state leads many survivors to question whether the abuse really did happen or whether she dreamt it. When this is combined with denial and repression it is not surprising that many survivors occasionally doubt their abuse experiences. It is crucial that the counsellor believes what the survivor remembers. The therapeutic relationship is not a court of law which seeks to establish the absolute truth of what to place, but a safe, supportive environment in which to explore the truth as the survivor experienced it.

The counsellor will need to consistently affirm, believe and validate the material that is brought into consciousness without being judgmental or disbelieving, no matter how bizarre it may appear to be. To heal, the survivor will need to feel that she can trust her perceptions and memories, and that this trust is reinforced by the counsellor's belief in her. If she senses that the counsellor doubts the veracity of her disclosures, she will begin to doubt herself and her experiences. Any perceived doubts will generate feelings of rejection in the survivor and reinforce her in her belief that she should never have revealed her secret. For some survivors this will be seen as valid grounds for terminating therapy.

Equally, the counsellor must be wary of not presenting a hierarchy of sexual abuse, in which some forms of sexual violation are considered more traumatic than others. Child sexual abuse does not just consist of acts of rape, digital penetration or oral sex, but also includes non-touching behaviours such as voyeurisim, titillation and the viewing of pornographic material in which the abuser does not actually physically touch the child. It is not necessary for the abuser to have touched or raped the survivor for her to experience this as a violation of her body and as sexual abuse. What is important is how the survivor perceived her violation and how she believes it has affected her.

All forms of child sexual abuse have the potential to a elicit negative effects on the child and the later adult. To convey that it 'wasn't that bad' or that cuddling, tickling or inappropriate touching are a 'figment of the survivor's imagination' or just 'normal' affectionate behaviours between adults and children is damaging to the survivor. The counsellor must also ensure against dismissing such 'trivial' forms of violations by comparing them with the more overt sexual behaviour experienced by other survivors. It is the violation of boundaries, trust and the psychological meaning that it has for the survivor that is crucial no matter what form the abuse took.

Similarly, the counsellor must guard against constructing a hierarchy of severity of abuse based on the relationship of the abuser to the child. To convey that it is less traumatic or painful if the abuser is a stepfather, or friend of the family will invalidate the survivor's experience and make her feel that she has no right to feel the way she does about her abuse. This can cause her to deny the effects the abuse has had on her and prevent her from resolving the abuse trauma.

It is largely irrelevant what blood ties existed between the child and the abuser; the fact remains that she was violated, and this violation should be the therapeutic focus of attention. Survivors already have the propensity to negate or minimise their abuse, and are often heard to say 'Well my abuse was not as bad because at least it was my stepfather rather than my real father'. If the counsellor concurs with this view she will reinforce existing denial and rationalisation which will render the treatment process ineffective.

Adopting positive prognosis

As well as normalising the effects of child sexual abuse on the adult survivor, it is necessary to emphasise that her response patterns are normal and creative in the presence of an abnormal and traumatic experience. It is paramount that the counsellor conveys to the survivor that she can heal from these experiences and that she is capable of forming healthy relationships, taking control of her life, relinquishing her victim role, and that archaic and conditioned behaviour patterns can be re-evaluated to become more adaptive to her adult self.

There are a number of techniques that the counsellor can use to help convey a positive prognosis. These include the use of books and articles, including first person accounts of survivors who have been through the healing process and feel themselves to be more healthy adults. The counsellor can also remind the survivor how courageous and strong she has been not only in surviving but also by entering therapy to heal from the abuse trauma.

As therapy progresses the counsellor can remind the survivor how much she has grown and how much healing has taken place. This will validate the survivor and give her the strength to continue through the process of healing. The emphasis should be on how much she has already achieved and that this achievement is an indication of her hard work, determination and strength, and is not due to the counsellor. It is her own strength and courage that have produced these changes and she will continue to heal and grow until she no longer feels contaminated by her abuser and her sexual abuse experiences.

It is worth reminding the survivor that while it is unlikely that she will be able totally to erase or exorcise all her abuse experiences, healing will integrate many of these experiences and childhood trauma with her adult self, allowing her to make choices about her life and take control over it, rather than the abuse controlling her. This will release energies which have previously been devoted to suppressing her experiences. These can now be channelled into areas that bring her happiness and enjoyment rather than pain and despair. The process of empowerment is within all survivors. The journey is painful and hard but leads to self discovery and a fuller appreciation and enjoyment of life. It is possible to heal and the rewards and benefits of treatment are enormous.

CHAPTER 13

Recovery

The healing process for adult survivors of child sexual abuse is complete when the woman no longer feels contaminated by her abuse experiences and the trauma ceases to influence her thoughts and behaviour patterns. Instead of the abuse exerting control over the survivor's life in eliciting unconscious, maladaptive archaic behaviour patterns, the survivor is able to take control of her life and make her feelings and thoughts conscious, enabling her to make choices rather than being internally driven or directed. She has learnt to trust herself and her perceptions and not be fearful of taking risks in expressing and exploring her new self.

Survivors for the first time feel able to embrace life by reclaiming their childhood, their sexuality, and the unpolluted self which has been in hiding since commencement of the abuse. For many survivors this is accompanied by the release of tremendous energy reserves and previously unacknowledged creativity. Survivors frequently want to engage in activities that previously they were too frightened to contemplate or attempt, and actively seek new experiences and challenges. As one survivor remarked 'It is like waking up and finding I have a whole new life to live and experience. I am not afraid of attempting new tasks or meeting new challenges. I am enjoying exploring the self, the me, that has been hidden for the last thirty years. I am enjoying the childhood I never had at the age of thirty four.'

Judging when the survivor has reached this stage of healing can sometimes be difficult for the counsellor but it helps if empowerment of the survivor has been fostered throughout the therapeutic process. If the survivor has been encouraged to empower herself gradually and learnt to trust her feelings, she will be more likely to recognise and decide when she is ready to leave therapy. The counsellor must also be prepared for termination and let go of the survivor by encouraging her in her decision. It may also be pertinent to emphasise to the survivor that there is always an opportunity to return to therapy, if necessary, at a later date.

While the therapeutic relationship facilitates growth and healing the survivor may still find it difficult to face certain issues without the support of the counsellor. To ease this transition the counsellor should ensure that the survivor has a strong support network outside therapy. If a support network has not been established in conjunction with individual counselling, the counsellor will need to emphasise the inestimable value of support networks.

Counselling sessions in the termination phase should focus on establishing a support network, including friends and colleagues, plus the availability of self-help support groups local to where the survivor lives. Some time should also be spent on the support available to the survivor from her partner. This may include seeing the partner separately or together with the survivor to acquaint him or her with the healing process through which the survivor has been. Some survivors undergo tremendous changes during therapy and many partners have difficulty in accepting the newly emerged self. The survivor and the partner will need to be prepared for this prior to the termination of therapy so that any fears or anxieties can be worked through in the counselling sessions.

Terminating therapy

It is crucial, if the survivor is genuinely ready to terminate therapy, that the counsellor encourages her to do so. Exploring the survivor's feelings about ending therapy and how she feels about letting go of the therapeutic relationship is vital to ensure that the survivor is ready to relinquish her dependence and reliance on the counsellor. If there are any unresolved issues surrounding dependency and control they will manifest themselves at this stage, and should be explored. The survivor will undoubtedly be nervous about terminating therapy which is entirely normal. Validating the survivor's anxieties is important to reassure her that these are natural and not an indication that she is not ready to terminate therapy.

One problem counsellors face is that some survivors may try to flee into health as soon as particularly emotional or traumatic material begins to surface. The survivor may begin to intellectualise or minimise her experiences, and suggest that the counselling sessions to date have been sufficient as she 'feels so much better now'. Although the counsellor cannot prevent the client from terminating therapy, it should be pointed out that many survivors do use 'flight into health' as a mechanism to avoid and deny the expression or exploration of more traumatic material.

Letting go of the client and encouraging her in her decision to leave therapy is crucial if the survivor is to feel comfortable in ending therapy. The counsellor will need to congratulate the survivor on her hard work and her achievement by emphasising that the survivor is the one who did all the hard work while the counsellor merely accompanied her on her journey. The counsellor may also suggest that the survivor explore other forms of therapy for particular issues in the future, or indeed come back if she is in crisis.

The counsellor should not feel threatened if a survivor decides to leave therapy but feel encouraged and delighted that one of her clients has healed from her trauma. Some survivors decide to leave therapy in order to explore other forms of therapy that focus on issues that the survivor has not resolved such as body awareness or massage rather than more traditional 'talking' therapy. Again this should not be seen as threatening to the counsellor, or as failure. Healing from the trauma of child sexual abuse is not a linear process and some survivors benefit from diverse therapies depending on the stages they are at in their healing.

Cathie

Cathie had been in therapy for over two years and had also attended a self-help support group on a weekly basis for the last year. She felt that she had progressed considerably during what was essentially 'talking therapy' in understanding and coming to terms with her abuse experiences. However, despite her growth she was aware that she was still not able to entirely integrate her feelings and cognitions to the level that she wanted to. She felt that many of her new, more adaptive responses were not natural but contrived.

Finally Cathie decided that she needed to take space away from talking through her abuse experiences and seek to reduce her readiness to dissociate by seeking alternative therapy which would focus specifically on the body by employing techniques of body awareness and body massage. Initially she was frightened about how she would respond to such forms of therapy as she still frequently felt dissociated from her body and feelings. During her last counselling session she discussed the fact that for her, dissociation was the last block that she felt she needed to work through and that talking about it was not sufficient, she actually had to feel it.

The decision Cathie made was a valid one which reflected the stage of healing she was at, and not dismissive of the work she had done in the last two years. It was suggested that, should she wish to return at any stage to a more 'talking' therapy, the counsellor would be available to her. Cathie appreciated this as an option, which to date she has not needed to exercise.

Counselling adult survivors of child sexual abuse necessitates a unique approach which incorporates many therapeutic techniques, and it is essential that the counsellor tailors techniques and approaches to each individual client. If the survivor can benefit from alternative forms of therapy or therapeutic orientations, the counsellor should encourage the survivor to explore these. Body-focused therapies can be particularly valuable to survivors in the later stages of healing as they become less frightened of their body and are able to cope with more physical contact.

Such therapies as body-focusing and massage are not mutually exclusive to more traditional counselling, and many survivors are able to do both in conjunction. This can be very beneficial as the feelings generated by body focused therapy can provide useful insight which can be further explored in counselling. One survivor, who benefited from weekly sessions of both counselling and body massage therapy, said 'During body-focused therapy I am in the present and just let myself feel and be. When I go to counselling I use those feelings to explore not only the present but also the past and the future'.

If the survivor is genuinely ready to terminate therapy, emphasis should be placed on how positive her decision is and how much she has to look forward to. To leave therapy is a courageous decision which reflects the survivor's strength, determination and growth. Although her abuse experience may always be with her, she is no longer a victim of it as she has now cleansed the wound which may throb from time to time, but is well enough healed not to become infected again.

Returning to therapy

Some survivors prefer to leave therapy knowing that they have the option to return if certain crises occur or when new issues arise. It may be invaluable to the survivor to know that she can resume therapy when she feels she needs it most. Terminating and then resuming therapy does not reflect failure for the client or the counsellor. As healing from the trauma of child sexual abuse is not a linear process, women may enter and leave therapy during certain phases of growth with some issues not entirely resolved but becoming less important.

Occasionally, material may resurface many years later and although the survivor is better equipped to deal with these because of her therapeutic experience, specific issues may arise which she feels unable to deal with by herself. To return to therapy should be seen as a positive step rather than as an expression of failure, and may be a more effective way for some survivors to resolve the abuse trauma.

One survivor used counselling to address specific issues as they arose. When she felt that a certain issue or painful experience had been fully resolved she would take a break from therapy knowing that she could return in the future if other issues arose. As she was predominantly stable and had a strong support network she found that she could function well without therapy in many areas related to her abuse experiences, and only needed to return to therapy when she or her support network could not cope.

For her this was very valuable as she felt she had more control over her healing process in terms of making decisions about being in therapy and she got tremendous satisfaction from being able to work on much of her trauma by herself with only occasional input from her counsellor. Not all survivors benefit in this way, and the counsellor should assess the viability of such options for the individual woman, and her current ego-strength and circumstances.

Support networks

Support networks outside counselling are invaluable to survivors and should be encouraged and cultivated from the beginning of therapy, throughout the healing process, and particularly when the survivor feels ready to terminate therapy. Although the support network does not have to be vast in terms of numbers, it needs to be strong and reliable. Survivors find it difficult to trust others and if they have even one or two friends whom they can trust this can make all the difference in fostering the healing process, even after counselling has been terminated.

In some cases it can be helpful for members of the support network to see or talk to the counsellor; not to talk specifically about the survivor, but more as a way of increasing their awareness in general of child sexual abuse, its effects and the problems encountered during the healing process. Reading material may be helpful to increase levels of empathy and encourage a deeper understanding of what it means to be a survivor of child sexual abuse (see Appendix A).

Time may also be spent focusing on the kinds of difficulties survivors face and how they have tried to cope with these. Members of support networks often become concerned that there are phases in the healing process in which the survivor seems to regress and get worse rather than better. The counsellor can prepare friends and members of the support network for the kind of phases that the survivor may encounter and what these mean. The counsellor may also give advice on the most effective ways to support the survivor when in particular phases.

In this respect the counsellor is fulfilling not a therapeutic role but more of an educative or informative, advisory role. Some therapists may feel that this should not be their function. However, the dearth of support groups for friends and partners of survivors in Great Britain indicates that until more resources and groups become available, this function can be usefully fulfilled by the professional counsellor, especially if it will enhance and facilitate healing and support for the survivor.

Self-help support groups for partners and friends provide an invaluable adjunct to the survivor's support network. Survivors often reveal in counselling that although they feel a great deal of support from friends and partners, sometimes the fact that they are survivors can impose a tremendous strain on their relationships. In turn, friends and partners feel that they want to support the survivor but often do not know how best to do this, especially when the survivor is behaving in negative and self-destructive ways, which often includes rejection of the support that is being offered.

Much can be achieved by preparing friends and supportive individuals for the effects of child sexual abuse trauma and the changes the survivor may undergo during healing. Emphasising the need to validate, believe, comfort and listen to the survivor is sometimes not enough. The supporting partner or friend also needs to know the origin of any self destructive behaviour which threatens the relationship between themselves and the survivor, and understand that this is a form of acting out that the survivor needs to explore before she can accept and acknowledge the value of that relationship.

A great deal of patience and self restraint on the part of friends may need to be exercised. The support network may sometimes feel rejected by the survivor, or threatened by her behaviour, leading them to question whether this is all worth it, and consider withdrawing their support. The counsellor can impress upon them that, although their feelings are totally understandable, they need to view the survivor's behaviour not as a rejection but rather as symbolic acting out of previous significant relationships. Preparing the support network for these hazards can strengthen their willingness and ability to continue to support the survivor. The counsellor must, however, ensure the survivor's confidentiality by not revealing the details of the counselling sessions but merely talking in general terms.

Partners

Many of the difficulties that survivors face such as fear of trust, intimacy and sex, are augmented when they are in a stable relationship. This can have quite severe implications for partners of survivors. Without fully understanding the reason why, the partner may have to cope with depression, anger and rage leading to self destructive behaviour including suicide threats. The partner may feel impotent in containing such behaviours, and not know how to help the survivor, especially if the survivor is not sure what her own feelings are.

Partners may react in a number of ways when they find out the person they love has a history of child sexual abuse. Some partners block the implications of such trauma from their mind, and exhort the survivor to do the same. As one partner stated 'This is all in the distant past. Leave it alone and forget about it and get on with living now'. This is not only very harsh but denies the effect the abuse has had on the survivor.

Some partners desperately want to help the survivor and are very sympathetic and understanding but feel inadequate because they do not know what to do in order to undo the trauma. Other partners may feel guilty because they feel unable to give 100 per cent support during the sometimes long process of healing. That healing can take a long time can become a source of irritation to the partner who may believe that the survivor will never heal and has a negative prognosis.

Annabel

Annabel's husband expressed his frustration surrounding the many sexual problems in their relationship by arguing that Annabel had now been in therapy for over a year which was not only a financial strain for the family, but more important, had not produced any results. He felt that their sexual difficulties had, if anything, worsened. He could not see that there would ever be any improvement and exerted tremendous pressure on his wife to terminate therapy as he felt it was like 'throwing money into a bottomless pit which was forever hungry for more'.

Needless to say, this attitude did very little for Annabel's healing as she felt dependent on her partner financially to restore her well being and mental health. His reluctance to continue to pay for her therapy made her feel that she was not important or worthy enough to invest in. As a result Annabel withdrew into herself, became increasingly depressed and reactivated her self-mutilatory behaviour of slashing herself with razor blades.

Partners with this sort of approach can have disastrous effects on the survivor's healing. It would have been useful for Annabel's husband to have been prepared for the length of the healing process and the kind of problems and difficulties she was facing, and had some clearer idea of how he could best facilitate her healing. It is crucial that partners realise that healing is a lengthy process which can take many months, if not years, of very hard work.

During this process the survivor may appear to be selfish in needing support and inordinate amounts of attention. The partner may become resentful of this and feel rejected by the survivor, especially if her or his needs are not met. Although Annabel's husband agreed to put their sexual relationship on hold while Annabel was dealing with certain traumatic issues engendered in the impact of her sexual abuse, he felt that he could not wait forever, and that Annabel was being selfish in expecting him to refrain from sex.

The counsellor may find it helpful to see the survivor's partner at some point during therapy to explain the process of healing and how it can best be facilitated. It is essential to clarify that healing is a long term process so that neither the partner or survivor are under false illusions of 'being able to sort this out quickly'. Some survivors have had to cope with the impact of their abuse for over thirty years in isolation; therapy is unlikely to rectify this overnight.

Partners should be encouraged to respect the amount of time and space the survivor needs for her healing process. Healing can be a very slow and painful process for some survivors. If the partner is able to respect the amount of time this will take and not hurry her through it, the survivor will feel that she is being supported by her partner and recognise that her partner believes in her and that she is worth taking whatever time she needs to heal.

Essentially, the partner will need to understand the effects of child sexual abuse in order to validate the damage that has been done. Partners will also need to be aware that child sexual abuse is never, under any circumstances, the child's fault and must believe the survivor's story of what happened. To this effect it is counterproductive to sympathise with or justify the abuser. This can sometimes be difficult if the partner knows the survivor's family and has formed a good relationship with them as this may create divided loyalties.

The survivor needs to feel that her feelings about her family are validated by her partner and that her partner supports her rather than trying to be objective and to justify the abuser's behaviour. Similarly, if the survivor expresses problems with other family members, such as the mother, it is essential that the partner validates these feelings and encourages the survivor to express and explore them.

Emphasis should also be placed on the importance of communication and the partner must make time available to listen to the survivor and believe what she has to say. Survivors often feel that they were not listened to or heard when they were children, and this becomes a crucial issue for some survivors. To avoid recreating such dynamics, the partner will need to ensure that channels of communication are kept open and that, if the survivor needs to talk, she will be heard.

The isolation that many survivors suffer from is related to an inability to communicate effectively. Many survivors remember that the family itself was very isolated in terms of not encouraging social activities or inviting friends to their home. This has inhibited channels of communication. In addition, survivors were frequently socialised to not express any needs of any kind as children. Parental messages may convey that they know what is best for the child, while ignoring how the child feels about their decisions and what is right for them. Such parents rarely ask their children how they feel about certain things, or allow them to express dissatisfaction or discomfort. Such children find it difficult as adults to ask for things for themselves, believing that they would either be ignored or their need denied.

Partners may need to ask the survivor constantly what her needs are and how they can best be met. Initially, the survivor may find it difficult to express her needs, desires and wants. For years her needs may have been denied and to find suddenly that someone actually wants to know what those needs are and to satisfy them can be quite frightening for the survivor. But gradually she will be able express her needs more clearly and be aware of how they are best satisfied.

There may be occasions when the partner cannot cope or be supportive to the survivor, and in this case the partner will need to set limits on how much help can be given. Setting limits is helpful both to the survivor and the partner. The survivor will recognise that ultimately it is she who has the power over her healing and that this process is dependent on how much work and time she wants to invest in her healing. In contrast, the partner is not totally overwhelmed by the survivor's need for help.

Partners should not feel a failure if they have been unable to help in a crisis that the survivor is going through. The partner only has limited emotional resources in how much s/he can deal with the survivor's emotional trauma, which should be respected. There will be times when the partner is unable to respond to the survivor in an ideal or sensitive way, or finds it difficult to deal with the material that is emerging. When this happens, partners will have to learn to say no and express their discomfort without the survivor feeling rejected. It is easier to do this if limits are set, and to do so before resentment builds up.

One major problem that partners face is that the survivor may change as a result of the healing process. She may become more assertive, more selfish in expressing her needs rather than suppressing or displacing them on to the partner by attending to her or his needs while denying her own. The partner may feel ignored, rejected or unloved because the survivor is less attentive, compliant and dependent on her or him. Such changes can be very damaging to the relationship causing resentment and re-evaluation of the partnership.

Maggie

When Maggie was first married she was extremely compliant and very attentive to her husband's needs and desires, to the extent that she would often anticipate his needs and fulfill them without him even having to express them. She behaved in a similar way with her three children, paying them an inordinate amount of attention and doing everything for them. In her early thirties, Maggie entered therapy complaining of being listless and not having enough energy to satisfy everyone's needs. She felt that she was splitting herself into four so that none of her family felt left out.

During counselling Maggie revealed that she never gave any time to herself and never listened to the needs that she had. In exploring her natal family background she disclosed that she had been abused by her father for ten years and that she had not only taken over the role of wife in bed, but also became mother to her siblings. Even as a child she put all her family's needs and requirements first, never having time to think for herself.

Through therapy Maggie became more confident and more assertive in expressing her needs and relinquishing many of the tasks that she had always carried out for her family. She recognised that she was trying to be a superwife and supermother and that she no longer had the energy to do this. She began taking time for herself and delegated more household chores to the rest of the family. This met with much resistance and accusations that she wasn't performing the duties a wife and mother should. Maggie refused to be swayed by their displeasure believing for the first time that she had rights and that she needed time and space for herself. As Maggie began to value herself more and more she found that she was eliciting more respect from others.

Maggie also became more assertive and more self confident in expressing her opinions and disagreeing with her husband. Her husband found this extremely frustrating, saying that 'She is no longer the woman he had married' and he wasn't sure whether this change in her was at all positive. He failed to recognise that Maggie was merely expressing herself as an individual with needs, independent thoughts and ideas which she had previously sublimated. Instead of being the family doormat, Maggie showed that she valued herself enough to attend to her needs, express opinions and pursue her own interests.

Survivors may change so dramatically that they appear unrecognisable. The dynamics which first caused her to fall in love with her partner, and vice versa, may no longer operate, which will necessitate a re-evaluation of both individuals, and the relationship.

Sadly, this may result in terminating the relationship. Change is often interpreted as threatening by partners because they feel unable to understand what is happening and do not know how to cope with the changes taking place. This is particularly difficult if the partner refuses to change or accommodate changes in the survivor. The survivor may feel that the partner has remained static in holding a certain image of her which has been remodelled. This can lead to bitter arguments and severe problems, including in some cases separation or divorce.

If partners are aware of these kinds of pitfalls, they may be able to minimise the negative effects of such change. This may entail the partner seeking counselling as well, or both undertaking couple therapy. This may be useful in allowing the couple to communicate their feelings about each other, the changes that have taken place, and how they both feel. The partner may then be able to recognise that the survivor is not threatening and that the relationship can continue, albeit in a modified way, which takes into account the survivor's growth.

For some survivors being in counselling may reactivate many memories and associations with the abuse to the extent that this may adversely affect her relationship with the partner, particularly their sexual contact. Some survivors in reclaiming their sexuality may re-evaluate their sexual relationship, decide to become celibate or not indulge in certain sexual activities. Many survivors feel able to give relief to their partners through regular masturbation, but feel uncomfortable if they are touched in a sexual way at all.

Often these reactions are reflective of the stage of healing that the survivor is at, and providing the partner is able to be supportive, empathic and patient with the survivor, they can be resolved. It is essential that the survivor reclaim her sexuality and her expression of it. This may take some time, but does not mean that she will never return to enjoying or desiring sex. The more supportive and understanding the partner is, and the less pressure he puts on her, the more effective resolution will be.

Partners may become frustrated and angry with the survivor, feeling that 'I am not only living with you but also with your abuser'. The partner will need to express the anger and discharge it in some way that will not be destructive to the survivor, but will allow for the release of very potent feelings. This can be achieved in counselling sessions, or alternatively by talking to other partners of survivors.

Sadly, there are few resources for partners of survivors which provide a forum to discuss these types of feelings. Although the counsellor can answer questions and help partners to understand and learn how to cope with the survivor's healing process, it can sometimes be more cathartic to actually talk to other partners of survivors to share experiences and useful coping mechanisms. Therapy, or self help support groups would provide such opportunity, and it is hoped that as partners' needs are recognised, that such groups will become more widely available.

Siblings

Child sexual abuse affects the whole family, even if only one child was abused. The non-abused sibling may disbelieve the survivor if they are confronted with her experiences, or alternatively slot into place some of the feelings and memories that they have never been able to understand. Non-abused siblings who disbelieve that abuse occurred may try to block or deny what happened to ward off threatening feelings. This may prompt them to call the survivor a liar, deny her disclosure, and refuse to have anything to do with her by severing all contact. This is a defensive reaction which the survivor will need to respect and accept.

Not all siblings are able to be supportive to the survivor and many are very destructive. The survivor may need to let go of her ties to her siblings and explore her feelings about this in counselling while giving herself permission to grieve for the loss of her siblings and family.

For other survivors, non-abused siblings may become very supportive to the survivor in exploring their own memories and concurring with the survivor's disclosures. Some siblings may also be able to provide vital clues or missing pieces of the jigsaw puzzle which the survivor needs to complete the picture of her abuse. Supportive siblings may prove invaluable to the survivor in her healing by confirming her abuse experiences, or by recognising that the family and abuser did behave in an abnormal way. This will validate the survivor's experience by showing her that her perceptions were not distorted, that she is not insane and that she did not make it all up.

Some non-abused siblings may feel guilty because they did not protect the survivor, or hurt that the survivor never confided in them. By disclosing the abuse to siblings the survivor both brings the secret out into the open and allows for bridges to be built between siblings. Many survivors felt that they never had a relationship with their siblings because they felt so different, but are now able to have a positive relationship with them.

It is an extremely valuable means of reclaiming the survivor's childhood if they can enhance childhood reminiscences and remember positive aspects of their childhood rather than focusing exclusively on the negative abuse trauma. The survivor no longer feels that she has been robbed of her childhood because she is able to explore it with her siblings and exchange experiences. This can prove very releasing for the survivor in validating her perceptions and interpretations of events realistically.

In some cases the siblings may also have been abused but have no memory of it. It may be helpful for the sibling(s) also to enter therapy to explore memories and recollections. Even if the sibling was not abused, it may be useful for the counsellor to spend some time exploring how the sibling feels about the disclosure, the effects this has on them, and how to extend the best support to the survivor.

Survivors can greatly benefit from rebuilding relationships with siblings and receiving their support. This is especially so for survivors who have terminated all contact with the abuser and seldom see their mother, and who feel isolated, and without family ties.

Sometimes such family ties are too difficult and painful to re-establish. Knowing that there are siblings who are supportive gives the survivor a link to the family which diminish her feelings of abandonment and alienation from her blood ties.

Mothers

Mothers who react positively towards the survivor on disclosure of the abuse can also prove to be very supportive to the survivor. If the mother acknowledges that the abuse has taken place and is empathic towards the survivor, she can give valuable support to the survivor and greatly assist her in her healing process. Supportive mothers may also benefit from counselling to explore how they feel about their daughter's revelations, and how they can best cope with what has happened to her.

Some mothers decide to leave the abuser and may need counselling and support in this decision, which will include assessing her means of coping without her partner both financially and emotionally. Other mothers will feel that their loyalty is to the abuser and will effectively renounce the daughter. In such cases the survivor will need to work on this in therapy, and grieve for the loss.

If the mother is supportive and caring, a new, deeper relationship may be established between her and her daughter. The hostility and resentment between mother and daughter can then be seen in the context of the abuse experiences. This can be further explored in joint counselling, allowing the mother and daughter to re-evaluate their relationship. This can create deeper bonds between them in which they recognise that they were both victims who suffered at the hands of the abuser. The supportive mother can be very influential not only in the healing process but also for maintaining health; if the potential is there, it should be nurtured and fostered.

The abuser

Most survivors do not re-establish contact with the abuser once healing has taken place other than to confront him. Little is known about survivors who wish to re-establish a relationship with the abuser, and how therapeutic this is. Family therapy does attempt to reunite the family when working with children. In my experience, family therapy for adult survivors is frequently destructive to the survivor, and commonly fails in its goal of reuniting the family. Should the survivor have the unification of the family as her goal, then it would be pertinent to suggest family therapy in conjunction with individual counselling. Most survivors do not have reunification with the abuser as their goal and the counsellor should refrain from imposing this on the survivor. The healed adult self usually has the strength to let go of the abuser and the abuse experience without needing to re-establish a relationship with him.

Letting go

The healed adult self has resolved the trauma of her abuse so that it no longer contaminates her life. The survivor is now free to take control of her life rather than being directed and driven by her abuse trauma. Although the abuse experience will always remain a part of her, the survivor can now let go of those aspects over which she has no control or influence. Through mourning her multiple losses, she can let go of them and only reclaim those that she can realistically regain. The survivor begins to recognise which situations or factors she has control over and take responsibility for them, while relinquishing control and responsibility for things that she cannot influence. This allows the survivor to take control of her life and to make choices and decisions. She is no longer a victim of her abuse but a strong, competent, responsive woman who enjoys life to the full and is prepared to take risks and meet new challenges.

Healing also allows the survivor to form new intimacies and relationships which reduce her isolation and stigmatisation. The survivor not only trusts herself and her perceptions but can now also trust others. The healed self is confident about expressing her needs, thoughts, opinions and feelings without fear of rejection or ridicule. Through healing, the true self can now come out of hiding and realise her potential and abilities before they were polluted by the abuse. The healed self can face new challenges and take risks in pursuing her goals. She no longer carries the burden of guilt and secrecy and is able to respond to others more honestly and directly, yet with more warmth and empathy. Her scars have healed and she has let go of her victim behaviours by believing in and valuing herself. She no longer survives, but lives.

Appendix A

Suggested Further Reading

1. Personal accounts (autobiographical, biographical and fictional)

Angelou, M., (1984), *I know why the caged bird sings*, Virago, London.

Armstrong, L., (1979), *Kiss Daddy goodnight*, Pocket Books, New York, NY.

Bass, E., and Thornton, L., (1983), *I never told anyone*, Harper and Row, New York, NY.

Brady, (1979), *Fathers days*, Dell, New York, NY.

Danica, E., (1989), *Don't: A woman's word*, The Women's Press, London.

Evert, K., and Bijkerk, I., (1987), *When you're ready: A woman's healing from childhood physical and sexual abuse by her mother*, Launch Press, Walnut Creek, CA.

Fraser, S., (1989), *My father's house*, Virago, London.

Galey, I., (1988), *I couldn't cry when Daddy died*, Settle Press, London.

Gallagher, V., and Doods, W. F., *Speaking out, fighting back*, Madrona, Seattle, WA.

Hart, T., (1979), *Don't tell your Mother*, Quartet, London.

Hill, E., (1985), *The family secret*, Dell, New York, NY.

Janssen, M., (1983), *Silent scream*, Fortree Press, Philadelphia, PA.

McNarron, T., and Morgan, Y., (1982), *Voices in the night: Women speaking out about incest*, Cleis Press, Pittsburgh, PA.

Moggach, D., (1983), *Porky*, London, Cape.

Morgan, L., (1987), *Megan's secret*, Papers Inc, Auckland, NZ.

Morris, M., (1982), *If I should die before I wake*, Souvenir Press, London.

Portwood, P., Gorcey, M., and Sanders, P., (1987), *Rebirth of power*, Mother Courage Press, Racine, WI.

Randall, M., (1987), *This is about incest*, Firebrand, Ithaca, NY.

Saadawi, N., El, (1980), *The hidden face of Eve*, Zed Press, London.

Spring, J., (1987), *Cry hard and swim*, Virago, London.

Tasane, S., and Dreyfuss, C., (1989), *Bird of prey*, Clubman Books Ltd, London.

Walker, A., (1983), *The colour purple*, Women's Press, London.

Wisechild, L. M., (1988), *The obsidian mirror*, Seal Press, Seattle, WA.

Women's Research Centre, (1989), *Recollecting our lives: Women's experiences of child sexual abuse*, Press Gang Publishers, Vancouver.

Wynne, L. E., (1987), *That looks like a nice house*, Launch Press, Walnut Creek, CA.

2. Books about incest and child sexual abuse for survivors

Baldwin, M., (1988), *Beyond victim: You can overcome childhood abuse... even sexual abuse*, Rainbow Books, Moore Haven, FL.

Bass, E., and Davis, L., (1988), *The courage to heal*, Harper and Row, New York, NY.

Butler, S., (1985), *Conspiracy of silence: The trauma of incest* Volcano Press, San Francisco, CA.

Daugherty, L. B., (1984), *Why me? Help for victims of child sexual abuse (even if they are adults now)*, Mother Courage Press, Racine, WI.

Gil. E., (1983), *Outgrowing the pain: A book for and about adults abused as children*, Launch Press, Walnut Creek, CA.

Lew, M., (1988), *Victims no longer: Men recovering from incest and other child sexual abuse*, Nevraumont Publishing, NY, NY.

Nelson, S., (1987), *Incest: Fact and myth*, Stramullion Co-operative, Edinburgh.

Poston, C., and Lison, K., (1989), *Reclaiming our lives: Hope for Adult survivors of incest*, Little Brown, Boston.

Rush, F., (1980), *The best kept secret: Sexual abuse of children*, McGraw Hill, New York.

Sisk, S. L. and Hoffman, C. F., (1987), *Inside scars: Incest recovery as told by a survivor and her therapist*, Pandora Press, Gainesville, FL.

Tower, C. C., (1988), *Secret scars: A guide for survivors of child sexual abuse*, Penguin, NY, NY.

Turner, J., (1989), *Home is where the hurt is: Guidance for all victims of sexual abuse in the home and for those who support them*, Thorsons, Northampton.

Utain, M., and Oliver, B., (1989), *Scream louder: Through hell and healing with an incest survivor and her therapist*, Health Communications Inc, Deerfield Beach, FL.

Walsh, D., and Liddy, R., (1989), *Surviving sexual abuse*, Attic Press, Dublin.

Ward, E., (1984), *Father–daughter rape*, The Women's Press, London.

Wood, W., and Hatton, L., (1989), *Triumph over darkness: Understanding and healing the trauma of child sexual abuse*, Beyond Words Publishing Inc, Hillsboro, CA.

3. Useful books and articles and on child sexual abuse for counsellors working with adult survivors

Baldwin, M., (1988), *Beyond victim: You can overcome childhood abuse... even sexual abuse*, Rainbow Books, Moore Haven, FL.

Bass, E., and Davis, L., (1988), *The courage to heal*, Harper and Row, New York.

Bergart, A. M., (1986), Isolation to Intimacy: Incest Survivors in Group Therapy, *Social Casework* 67, 266–275.

Blake-White, J., and Kline, C. M., (1985), Treating the dissociative process in adult victims of childhood incest, *Social Casework* 66, 394–402.

Braun, B. G., (1986), *Treatment of multiple personality disorder*, American Psychiatric Press, Washington.

Briere, J., (1989), *Therapy for adults molested as children: Beyond Survival*, Springer, New York.

Cole, C. H. and Barney E. E., (1987), Safeguards and the therapeutic window: a group treatment strategy for adults incest survivors, *American Journal of Orthopsychiatry*, 57, 4, 601–609.

Courtois, C. A., (1988), *Healing the incest wound: Adult survivors in therapy*, Norton, New York.

Daugherty, L. B., (1984), *Why me? Help for victims of child sexual abuse (even if they are adults now)*, Mother Courage Press, Racine, WI.

Deighton, J., and McPeek, (1985), Group treatment: Adult victims of childhood sexual abuse, *Social Casework* 65, 403–410.

Faria, G., and Belohlavek, N., (1984), Treating female adult survivors of childhood incest, *Social Casework*, 465–471.

Forward, S., and Buck, C., (1979), *Betrayal of innocence: Incest and its devastation*, Penguin, New York.

Gelinas, D. J., (1981), Identification and Treatment of Incest Victims, in Howell, E., and Bayes, M., (ed), *Women and mental health*, Basic Books, New York.

Gil, E., (1988), *Treatment of adult survivors of childhood abuse*, Launch Press, Walnut Creek, CA.

Gil, E., (1983), *Outgrowing the pain: A book for and about adults abused as children*, Launch press, Walnut Creek, CA.

Goodman, B., and Nowak-Scibelli, D., (1985), Group treatment for women incestuously abused as children, *International Journal of Group Psychotherapy*, 35, 4, 531–544.

Goodwin, J. M., (1989), *Sexual abuse: Incest victims and their families*, 2nd Edition, Year Book Medical Publications Inc, Chicago.

Hall, L., and Lloyd, S., (1989), *Surviving child sexual abuse: A handbook for helping women challenge their past*, Falmer Press, Lewes.

Herman, J.l. and Schatzow, E., (1984), Time limited group therapy for women with a history of incest, *International Journal of Group Psychotherapy*, 34,4 605–616.

Howell, E., and Bayes, M., ed., (1981), *Women and mental health*, Basic Books, NY.

Hunter, M., (1990), *Abused boys: The neglected victims of sexual abuse*, Lexington Books, Lexington, Mass.

Jehu, D., (1988), *Beyond sexual abuse: Therapy with women who were childhood victims*, Wiley, Chichester.

Kane, E., (1989), *Recovering from incest: Imagination and the healing process*, Sigo Press, Boston, Mass.

Kennedy, J., (1989), *Touch of silence: A healing from the heart*, Cosmoenergetics Publications, San Diego, CA.

Lew, M., (1988), *Victims no longer: Men recovering from incest and other child sexual abuse*, Nevraumont Publishing, NY, NY.

Maltz, W., and Holman, (1987), *Incest and sexuality: A guide to understanding and healing*, Lexington Books, Lexington, MA.

McGuire, L. S., and Wagner, N. N., (1978), Sexual dysfunction in women who were molested as children: One response pattern and suggestions for treatment, *Journal of Sex and Marital Therapy*, 4, 1, 11–15.

Parks, P., (1990), *Sexual abuse – rescuing the inner child*, Souvenir Press, London.

Poston, C., and Lison, K., (1989), *Reclaiming our lives: Hope for adult survivors of incest*, Little Brown, Boston.

Salter, A. L., (1988), *Treating child sex offenders and their victims: A practical guide*, Sage, Newbury Park, CA.

Sgroi, S. M., (1988), *Vulnerable populations vol.1: Evaluation and treatment of sexually abused children and adult survivors*, Lexington Books, Lexington, MA

Sgroi, S. M., (1982), *Handbook of clinical intervention in child sexual abuse*, Lexington Books, Lexington, MA.

Sisk, S. L. and Hoffman, C. F., (1987), *Inside scars: Incest recovery as told by a survivor and her therapist*, Pandora Press, Gainesville, FL.

Stein, R., (1973), *Incest and human love*, Spring Publications, Dallas, Texas.

Tower, C. C., (1988), *Secret scars: A guide for survivors of child sexual abuse*, Penguin, NY, NY.

Trepper, T. S. and Barrett, M. J., (1986), *Treating incest: A multiple systems perspective*, Haworth Press, New York.

Tsai, M., and Wagner, N. N., (1978), Therapy groups for women sexually molested as children, *Archives of Sexual Behaviour*, 7, 5, 417–427.

Turner, J., (1989), *Home is where the hurt is: Guidance for all victims of sexual abuse in the home and for those who support them*, Thorsons, Northampton.

Utain, M., and Oliver, B., (1989), *Scream louder: Through hell and healing with an incest survivor and her therapist*, Health Communications Inc, Deerfield Beach, FL.

van Buskirk, S. S. and Cole, C. F., (1983), Characteristics of eight women seeking therapy for the effects of incest, *Psychotherapy Theory, Research and Practice*, 20, 503–514.

Walsh, D., and Liddy, R., (1989), *Surviving sexual abuse*, Attic Press, Dublin.

Wood, W., and Hatton, L., (1989), *Triumph over darkness: Understanding and healing the trauma of child sexual abuse*, Beyond Words Publishing Inc, Hillsboro, CA.

4. Other useful books for counsellors working with adult survivors

Barbach, L., (1975), *For yourself: The fulfilment of female sexuality*, Doubleday, NY.

Barbach, L., (1982), *For each other: sharing sexual intimacy*, Anchor Press, NY.

Carnes, P., (1983), *Out of the shadows: Understanding sexual addiction*, CompCare Publishers, Minnesota.

Chodrow, N., (1978), *The reproduction of mothering: Psychoanalysis and the sociology of gender*, University of California Press, Berkley, CA.

Dickson, A., (1982), *A woman in your own right: Assertiveness and you*, Quartet, London.

Dickson, A., (1985), *The mirror within: A new look at sexuality*, Quartet, London.

Ernst, S., and Goodison, L., (1981), *In our own hands*, The Women's Press, London.

Figley, C. R., (1985), *Trauma and its wake: The study and treatment of post-traumatic stress disorder*, Bruner/Mazel, NY.

Jackson, S., (1982), *Childhood and sexuality*, Basil Blackwell, Oxford.

Masson, J. M., (1985), *The assault on truth:, Freud's suppression of the seduction theory*, Faber, London.

Miller, A., (1981), *The drama of being a gifted child*, Basic Books, NY.

Miller, A., (1984), *Thou shalt not be aware: Society's betrayal of the child*, Farrar, Strauss and Giroux, NY.

Welldon, E. V., (1988), *Mother, madonna, whore: The idealisation and denigration of motherhood*, Free Association Books, London.

Weeks, J., (1985), *Sexuality and its discontents*, Routledge, London.

Whitfield, C. L., (1987), *Healing the child within*, Health Communications, Inc, Deerfield beach, FL.

5. Longterm effects of child sexual abuse on adult survivors

Browne, A., and Finkelhor, D., (1986), Impact of child sexual abuse: A review of the research, *Psychological Bulletin*, 99, 1, 66–77.

Ellenson, G. S., (1986), Disturbances of perception in adult female incest survivors, *Social Casework*, 67, 149–159.

Ellenson, G. S., (1985), Detecting a history of incest: A predictive syndrome, *Social Casework*, 66, 525–532.

Gelinas, D. J., (1983), The persisting negative effects of incest, *Psychiatry*, 46, 313–332.

Herman, J. L., (1981), *Father–daughter incest*, Harvard UP, Cambridge, MA.

Kilpatrick, A. C., (1987), Childhood sexual experiences: problems and issues in studying long-range effects, *Journal of Sex Research*, 23, 2, 173–176.

Mayer, A., (1985), *Sexual abuse: Causes, consequences and treatment of incestuous and paedophilic acts*, Learning Publications, Inc. Holmes Beach, FL.

Meiselman, K. C., (1978), *Incest: A psychological study of causes and effects with treatment recommendations*, Jossey-Bass, San Francisco.

Russell, D. E. H., (1986), *The secret trauma: Incest in the lives of girls and women*, New York, Basic Books.

Wheeler, B. R. and Walton, E., (1987), Personality disturbances of adult incest victims, *Social Casework*, 68, 597–602.

Wyatt, G. E. and Powell, G. J., (1988), *Lasting effects of child sexual abuse*, Sage, Newbury Park.

6. Exploding the myths of child sexual abuse

Ash, A., (1984), *Father–daughter sexual abuse: The abuse of paternal authority*, University College of North Wales.

Butler, S., (1985), *Conspiracy of silence: The trauma of incest*, Volcano Press, San Francisco.

Crewdson, J., (1988), *By silence betrayed: Sexual abuse of children in America*, Harper and Row, NY.

Dominelli, L., (1986), Father–Daughter Incest, *Critical Social Policy*, 16.

Driver, E., and Droisen, A., (1989), *Child sexual abuse: Feminist perspectives*, Macmillan, Basingstoke, Hants.

Fairtlough, A., (1982), *Responsibility for incest: A feminist view*, UEA Social Work Monograph, University of East Anglia, Norwich.

Feminist Review, (1988), *Family secrets: Child sexual abuse*, Feminist Review, London.

Herman, J., (1981), *Father–daughter incest*, Harvard UP, Cambridge, MA.

London Rape Crisis centre, (1984), *Sexual violence: The reality for women*, Women's Press, London.

Macleod, M., and Saraga, (1987), *Child sexual abuse: Towards a feminist professional practice*, Report of the conference held at the Polytechnic of North London, April 1987, PNL Press, London.

Miller, A., (1984), *Thou shalt not be aware: Society's betrayal of the child*, Pluto Press, London.

Nelson, S., (1987), *Incest: Fact and myth*, Stramullion Co-operative, Edinburgh.

Rhodes, D., and McNeil, S., ed., (1985), *Women against violence against women*, Onlywomen Press, London.

Rush, F., (1980), *The best kept secret: Sexual abuse of children*, McGraw Hill, New York.

Ward, E., (1984), *Father–daughter rape*, The Women's Press, London.

7. Books for parents and professionals working with children

Bagley, C., and King, K., (1990), *Child sexual abuse: The search for healing*, Tavistock/Routledge, London.

Braun, D., (1988), *Responding to child abuse: Action and planning for teachers and other professionals*, Bedford Square Press/Community Education Development Centre, London.

Burgess, A. W., Groth, A. N., Holmstrom, L. L. and Sgroi, S. M., (1978), *Sexual assault of children and adolescents*, Lexington Books, Lexington, Mass.

Burgess, A. W., (1984), *Child pornography and sex rings*, Lexington Books, Lexington, Mass.

Doyle, C., (1988), *Sexual abuse: Giving help to children*, National Children's Bureau.

Everstine, D. S. and Everstine, L., (1989), *Sexual trauma in children and adolescents: Dynamics and treatment*, Brunner/Mazel, NY.

Family Rights Group, (1989), *Child sexual abuse after Cleveland – alternative strategies*, Family Rights Group, London.

Finkelhor, D. Williams, L. M. and Burns, N., (1988), *Nursery crimes: sexual abuse in day care*, Sage, Newbuy Park, CA.

Giarretto, H., (1982), *Integrated treatment of child sexual abuse: A treatment and training manual*, Science and Behaviour Books, Inc, Palo Alto, CA.

Glaser, D., and Frosh, S., (1988), *Child sexual abuse*, British Association of Social Workers/Macmillan, London.

Hagans, K. B. and Case, J., (1988), *When your child has been molested: A parent's guide to healing and recovery*, Lexington Books, Lexington, MA.

Herbert, C. M. H., (1989), *Talking of silence: The sexual harassment of schoolgirls*, Falmer Press, London.

Hillman, D., and Solek-Tefft, J., (1988), *Spiders and flies: Help for parents and teachers of sexually abused children*, Lexington Books, Lexington, Mass.

Illsley, P., (1989), *The drama of Cleveland*, CPBF/SCOSAC., London.

James, B., and Nasjleti, M., (1989), *Treating sexually abused children and their families*, Consulting Psychologists Press, Inc, Palo Alto, CA.

Janus, M. D., McCormack, A., Burgess, A. W. and Hartman, C., (1987), *Adolescent runaways: Causes and consequence*, Lexington Books, Lexington, Mass.

Jones, D. P. H. and McQuiston, M. G., (1988), *Interviewing the sexually abused child*, Royal College of Psychiatrists, London.

Mayer, A., (1983), *Incest: A treatment manual for therapy with victims, spouses and offenders*, Learning Pub. Inc, Holmes Beach, FL.

Milner, J., and Blythe, E., (1989), *Coping with child sexual abuse: A guide for teachers*, Longman, London.

O'Hagan, K., (1989), *Working with child sexual abuse*, Open University Press, Milton Keynes.

Riches, P., ed, (1989), *Responses to Cleveland: Improving services for child sexual abuse*, National Children's Bureau, London.

Sandberg, D. N., (1989), *The child abuse-delinquency connection*, Lexington Books, Lexington, Mass.

Schetky, D. H. and Green, A. H., (1988), *Child sexual abuse: A handbook for health care and legal professionals*, Brunner/Mazel, NY.

Smith, S. B., (1985), *Children's story: Sexually molested children in criminal court*, Launch Press, Walnut Creek, CA.

Useful Organisations and Contacts

Organisations

Centre for the Development of Feminist Theory and Practice. Current activities: training, research resource centre and networking. Publications list and annotated bibliographies.

Child Abuse Studies Unit. Polytechnic of North London, Ladbroke House, 62–66 Highbury grove, London N5 2AD. Tel: 0171 607 2789 ext. 5014.

ISICSA (Information Service on Incest and Child Sexual Abuse). 24 Blackheath Rise, London SE13 7PN. Tel: 0181 852 7432.

ISN (Incest Survivors Network). Tel: 0171 385 2617. Provides information on self help support groups available throughout the country, networking, resource centre and training.

SACCS (Sexual Abuse Child Consultancy Service). Mytton Mill, Montford Bridge, Shropshire SY4 1HA. Tel: 01743 850015. Provides individual therapeutic work with children and young people, groupwork, consultation, conferences and training workshops to both statutory and voluntary agencies.

SCOSAC (Standing Committee on Child Sexual Abuse). 73 St Charles Square, London W10 6EJ. Tel: 0181 960 6376.

Spectrum Incest Intervention Project. 7 Endymion Road, London N4 1EE. Tel: 0181 341 2277, Judy Keshet-Orr. Training in sexual abuse and related issues, staff supervision and support groupwork.

Women's Therapy Centre. 6 Manor Gardens, London N7. Tel: 0171 263 6200. Workshops for therapists and counsellors working with survivors of child sexual abuse.

Helplines

Childline. 0171 239 1000. Although primarily for children they do have a information on groups and counsellors for survivors throughout the country.

Survivors of sexual abuse. 0181 890 4732 Service available to both males and females by male and female counsellors. Also run three groups in London area in Hounslow, Harrow, Teddington (see below).

Rape Crisis Centres. (see local telephone directories).

Support groups and counselling services for survivors

Due to lack of funding many self help support groups find it difficult to sustain groups, and suffer from a constant threat of folding. The groups and services listed below are ones that have been operating for some considerable time, and the details are correct at time of going to press. The list is not exhaustive as it cannot include all local self help support groups. Local Rape Crisis Centres generally have information about survivors groups that operate in their area, as do local mental health offices such as MIND. Telephone numbers for Rape Crisis Lines or Centres and MIND should be in your local area telephone directory.

London

Deptford Women's Advice and Counselling Service. The Albany, Douglas Way, Deptford, SE8. Tel: 0181 692 6268.

Fulham ISN (Incest Survivors Network). Tel: 0171 385 2617.

Hackney Hackney Women's Group. 20 Dalston Lane, London E8. Tel: 0171 254 2980. Thurs. 7–9pm.

Harrow Survivors of Sexual Abuse. Tel: 0181 890 4732.

Hounslow Survivors of Sexual Abuse. Tel: 0181 890 4732.

Kingston Kingston Women's Centre. 169 Banbury Park Road, Kingston-on Thames, Surrey. Tel: 0181 541 1964. Women's groups and girls' group. First Wednesday in each month, 7.30pm.

London Rape Crisis Line. PO Box 69, London WC1X 9NJ. Tel: 0171 837 1600, 24 hour service.

Teddington c/o Survivors of Sexual Abuse. Tel: 0181 890 4732.

Waltham Forest Incest Survivors. c/o Waltham Forest Women's Centre, 109 Hoe Street, London E17. Tel: 0181 520 5318.

Women's Counselling Project. The Blenheim Project, 321 Portobello Road, London W10 5SY. Tel: 0181 960 5599. Offers free, confidential counselling.

The Women's Therapy Centre. 6 Manor Gardens, London N7. Tel: 0171 263 6200. Occasionally run group workshops.

England

Avon Sexual Abuse Centre. PO Box 665, Bristol. Tel: 0117 935 1707 or 0117 941 2194. Have their own magazine called *Taboo*.

Birmingham Rape Crisis. PO Box 558, Birmingham B3 2HL. Tel: 0121 766 5366. 24 hours.

Cambridge. Choices. 7c Station Road, Cambridge CB1 2JB. Tel: Counselling line (01223) 467897. Tues. 11–2pm. Offers a counselling service, individual counsellors, group work and telephone counselling currently with female survivors and others affected by sexual abuse, carers and siblings etc.

Cambridge Incest Survivors. c/o Cambridge RCC, Box R, 12 Mill Road, Cambridge. Tel: Cambridge (01223) 358314. Wed. 6pm–12 midnight; Sat. 11am–5pm.

Chelmsford Rape Crisis Line. PO Box 566, Chelmsford, CM2 8YP. Tel: (01245) 492123. Tues. and Fri. 7.30pm–9.30pm.

Essex Child Abuse Advisory Service. Hurlingham Chambers, 61 Station Road, Clacton-on-Sea, Essex, CO15 1SD. Tel: 01255 435000.

South Essex Rape and Incest Crisis Centre. The Hall, West Street, Grays, Essex, RM17 6LL. Tel: 01375 380609 Crisis Line. Tues. 8–10pm; Thurs. 12–4pm; Fri. 10–noon. HIV and AIDS information line. Wed. 12–4pm. there is a Sexual Health Worker

Luton Rape Crisis Centre 12 Oxford Road, Luton, Beds LU1 3AX. Tel: 01582 33426. Offer individual, one-to-one counselling.

Stockport Taboo. 2 Fiveways Parade, Hazelgrove, Stockport. Tel: (01625) 859264. Tues and Thurs 9–8pm; Mon, Wed and Fri 9–5.30pm.

Norwich Adult Survivors Of Incest. PO Box 100, 17–19 St Maddermarket, Norwich. Tel: (01603) 630777.

Sheffield Incest Survivors Group. c/o Sheffield Rape Crisis Line, PO Box 34, Sheffield S1 1UD. Tel: 0114 244 7936. Mon-Fri 11am–4pm; Tues 7.30–9.30; Thurs, 7–9pm.

Suffolk Positive Change Association, Mount Pleasant, Debenham, Stowemarket, Suffolk IP14 6PT. Tel: (01728) 860490. Mainly individual counselling (PICT – Parkes Inner Child Therapy).

Scotland

Aberdeen Incest Survivors Group. c/o Aberdeen Rape Crisis Centre, PO Box 123, Aberdeen. Tel: (01224) 620772. Thurs. 7–9pm.

Central Scotland Incest Survivors Group. c/o Central Scotland Rape Crisis Centre PO Box 28, Falkirk, FK2 9BJ. Tel: (01786) 471771.

Dundee Women's Aid, 2 Union Street, Dundee, DD1 4BH. Tel: (01382) 202525.

Edinburgh Incest Survivors Group. c/o Edinburgh Rape Crisis Centre, PO Box 120, Brunswick Road, Edinburgh, EH7 5XX. Tel: 0131 556 9437. Mon, Tues, Wed. 6–8pm; Thurs. 1–8pm.

Kircaldy Incest Survivors Group. c/o The Volunteer Centre, 18 Brycedale Avenue, Kircaldy. Tel: (01333) 428878.

Glasgow Incest Survivors Group. c/o Strathclyde Rape Crisis Centre, PO Box 53, Glasgow G21 YR. Tel: 0141 221 8448. Mon, Wed, Fri. 7–10pm.

Ireland

Belfast Rape Crisis Centre. PO Box 46, Belfast BT2 7AR, Northern Ireland. Tel: (01232) 249696. Mon-Fri. 10am–2pm; Sat-Sun. 11am–5pm.

Clonmel Rape Crisis Cente. 33 Parnell Street, Clonmell, Republic of Ireland. Tel: (052) 24111 or freephone 1800 340340.

Cork Rape Crisis Cente. 27 McCurtain Street, Cork, Republic of Ireland. Tel: (021) 968086 or freephone 1850 478478.

Dublin Rape Crisis Cente. 70 Lower Leeson Street, Dublin 2, Republic of Ireland. Tel: (01) 661 4911 or freephone 1850 788888.

Galway Rape Crisis Cente. 3 St Augustine Street, Galway, Republic of Ireland. Tel: (091) 64983 or freephone 1800 355355.

Kerry Rape Crisis Cente. 2nd Floor, 33 Denny Street, Tralee, Kerry, Republic of Ireland. Tel: (066) 23122 or freephone 1850 633333.

Limerick Rape Crisis Cente. 17 Upper Mallowe Street, Limerick, Republic of Ireland. Tel: (061) 311511 or freephone 1850 311511.

Waterford Rape Crisis Cente. 33 George Street, Waterford, Republic of Ireland. Tel: (051) 73362 or freephone 1850 296296.

Groups for men

Breakthrough. London N1. Tel: 0171 359 2884. Young gay and bisexual men and women. One-to-one counselling 16–21 year olds.

Survivors. PO Box 2470, W2 1NN. Tel: 0171 833 3737 Helpline 7pm–10pm Tues, Wed, and Thur. Individual, face to face counselling offered. Also training for external agencies.

Groups for mothers of sexually abused children

Tavistock Centre. Child and Family Department, 120 Belsize Lane, London NW3 5BA. Tel: 0171 435 711.

Bibliography

SCAN, (Sexual Child Abuse Newsletter), March, 1989.

Adams-Tucker, C., (1985) Defense mechanisms used by sexually abused children, *Children Today*, Jan/Feb 1985, 9–12.

Allen, C. M., (1990) Women as perpetrators of child sexual abuse: Recognition barriers in: Horton et al (eds) *The Incest perpetrator*. Newbury Park, CA: Sage.

American Psychiatric Association, (1987) *DSM-III*, 3rd Edition, American Psychiatric Press, Washington, DC.

Angelou, M., (1984) *I know why the cage bird sings* London: Virago.

Ash, A., (1984) *Father–daughter sexual abuse: The abuse of paternal authority*. University College of North Wales.

Atha, B. P., (1986) Child sexual abuse, *Health at School*, 1, 123–124.

Bagley, C., and King, K., (1990) *Child sexual abuse: The search for healing* London: Tavistock/Routledge.

Baker, A. W., and Duncan, S. P., (1985) Child Sexual Abuse: a study of prevalence in Great Britain. *Child Abuse and Neglect*, 9, 457–467.

Baldwin, M., (1988) *Beyond victim: you can overcome childhood abuse... even sexual abuse* Moore Haven, FL: Rainbow Books.

Bannister, A., (1985) Monster Man Has Gone, *Community Care*, 28/11/85, 20–21.

Barbach, L., (1975) *For yourself: The fulfilment of female sexuality*, New York: Doubleday.

Barbach, L., (1982) *For each other: Sharing sexual intimacy*, New York: Anchor Press.

Bark, P., and Sheehy, N. P., (1986) An empirical review of judicial proceedings in cases of child sexual abuse, *Early Child Development* and Care 26, 19–27.

Bass, E., and Davis, L., (1988) *The courage to heal*. New York, NY: Harper and Row.

Bass, E., and Thornton, L., (1983) *I never told anyone*, New York: Harper and Row.

Becker, J. V., Skinner, L. J., Abel, G. G., and Treacy, E. C., Incidence and type of sexual dysfunction in rape and incest victims, *Journal of Sex and Marital Therapy*, 8, 65–74.

Benedek, E. P., (1985) Children and psychic trauma in: Eth, S., and Pynoos, R. S., *op. cit.*.

Benward, J., and Densen-Gerber, J., (1975) Incest as a causative factor in anti-social behaviour, *Contemporary Drug Problems* 4, (3), 323–340.

Bergart, A. M., (1986) Isolation to intimacy: incest survivors in group therapy, *Social Casework*, 266–275.

Berliner, L. and Loftus, E. (1992) Sexual abuse accusations: Desperately seeking reconciliation, *Journal of Interpersonal Violence* 7, 4, 570–178

Bixler, R. A., (1981) The incest controversy, *Psychological Reports*, 49, 267–283.

Blake-White, J., and Kline, C. M. Treating the dissociative process in adult victims of childhood incest, *Social Casework*, 394–402.

Bliss, E., (1988) Multiple personalities, *Archives of General Psychiatry*,, 37, 1388–1398.

Boor, M., (1982) The multiple personality epidemic, *Journal of Nervous and Mental Diseases*, 170, 302–304.

Borgman, R., (1984) Problems of sexually abused girls and their treatment, *Social Casework*, 182–186.

Bradbury, A., (1986) A model of treatment, *Community Care*, 627, 24–25.

Brady, A., (1979) *Fathers days.* New York: Dell.

Brant, S. T., and Tisza, V. B., (1977) The sexually misused child, *American Journal of Orthopsychiatry*, 47(1), 80–90.

Brassard, M. R., Tyler, A. H., and Kehle, T. J., (1983) School programs to prevent intrafamilial child sexual abuse, *Child Abuse and Neglect*, 7, 241–245.

Braun, B. G., (1986) *Treatment of multiple personality disorder*, American Psychiatric Press, Washington.

Braun, D., (1988) *Responding to child abuse: action and planning for teachers and other professionals* London: Bedford Square Press/Community Education Development Centre.

Brayne, E., and Chandler, T., (1986) Overcoming guilt, loss: Difficulties of telling, *Social Work Today*, 4/8/86, 10–12.

Briere, J. (1992) *Child Abuse Trauma.* Newbury Park, CA: Sage.

Briere, J. (1992) Studying delayed memories of childhood sexual abuse, *The APSAC Advisor*, Summer 1992, 17–18

Briere, J. and Conte, J. (1993) Self-reported amnesia for abuse in adults molested as children, *Journal of Traumatic Stress* 6 (1) 21–31

Briere, J., (1989) *Therapy for adults molested as children: Beyond survival.* New York: Springer.

Browne, A., and Finkelhor, D., (1986) Impact of Child Sexual Abuse: a review of the research, *Psychological Bulletin*, 99, 1, 66–77.

Browning, D., and Boatman, B., (1977) Incest: Children at risk, *American Journal of Psychiatry*, 134, 69–72.

Burgess, A. W., (1984) *Child pornography and sex rings.* Lexington, Mass: Lexington Books.

Burgess, A. W., and Grant, C. A, (1988) *Children traumatised in sex rings*, National Centre for Missing and Exploited Children, Pennsylvania.

Burgess, A. W., Groth, A. N., Holmstrom, L. L., and Sgroi, S. M., (1978) *Sexual assault of children and adolescents.* Lexington, MA: Lexington Books.

Byres, J., (1986) Films for child sexual abuse prevention and treatment: a review, *Child Abuse and Neglect*, 10, 541–546.

Byrne, K., and Bloxham, R., (1986) When sensitivity is on trial, *Social Services Insight*, 20/4/86, 20–21.

Calof, D.L. (1993) Facing the truth about false memory syndrome, *The Family Therapy Networker* Sept/Oct 1993

Calof, D.L. (1994) A Conversation with Pamela Freyd, Ph.D: Co-founder and Executive Director, False Memory Syndrome Foundation, Inc., *Part I Treating Abuse Today*3, 3 25–39

Calof, D.L. (1994) A Conversation with Pamela Freyd, Ph.D: Co-founder and Executive Director, False Memory Syndrome Foundation, Inc., *Part II Treating Abuse Today* 3, 4 26–33

Campbell, B., (1987) The skeleton in the family's cupboard, *New Statesman*, 31/7/87.

Carnes, P., (1983) *Out of the shadows: Understanding sexual addiction,* Minnesota: CompCare Publishers.

Ceci, S.J. and Bruck, M. (1993) Suggestibility of the child witness: A historical review and synthesis, *Psychological Bulletin*, 113, 3, 403–439

Chasseguet-Smirgel, J., (1976) Freud and female sexuality: the consideration of some blind spots in the exploration of the 'dark continent', *International Journal of Psycho-Analysis*, 57, 275–286.

Childline, (1990) *The second year,* Childline, London.

Children's Legal Centre, (1986) Child sexual abuse – the law, *Childright*, 25, 11–14.

Children's Legal Centre, (1986) Prevention and restraint of child sexual abuse, *Childright*, 26, 14–16.

Chodrow, N., (1978) *The reproduction of mothering: Psychoanalysis and the sociology of gender* Berkley, CA: University of California Press.

Cole, C. H., and Barney, E. E., (1987) Safeguards and the therapeutic window: a group treatment strategy for adult incest survivors, *American Journal of Orthopsychiatry*, 57, 4 601–609.

Conte, J. R., (1984) Progress in treating the sexual abuse of children, *Social Work*, 29, 3, 258–263.

Conte, J. R., (1987) Programs to prevent sexual abuse: what outcomes should be measured? *Child Abuse and Neglect*, 11, 169–172.

Conte, J. R., and Schuerman, J. R., (1987) Factors associated with an increased impact of child sexual abuse, *Child Abuse and Neglect*, 11, 201–211.

Conte, J. R., Rosen, C., Saperstein, L., and Shermack, R., (1985) An evaluation of a program to prevent the sexual victimisation of young children, *Child Abuse and Neglect*, 9, 319–328.

Courtois, C. A., (1988) *Healing the incest wound: adult survivors in therapy.* New York: Norton.

Cowburn, M., (1986) Keeping the family together, *Community Care*, 21/8/86 22–23.

Creighton, S. (1993) Organised Abuse: The NSPCC Experience, *Child Abuse Review* 2, 4.

Crewdson, J., (1988) *By silence betrayed: Sexual abuse of children in America.* New York: Harper and Row.

Danica, E., (1989) *Don't: a woman's word.* London: The Women's Press.

Deighton, J., and McPeek, (1985) Group treatment: adult victims of childhood sexual abuse, *Social Casework*, 403–410.

DeJong, A. R., Hervada, A. R., and Emmett, G. A., (1983) Epidemiologic variations in childhood sexual abuse, *Child Abuse and Neglect*, 7, 155–162.

DeYoung, M., (1981) Siblings of Oedipus: Brothers and sisters of incest victims, *Child Welfare*, LX 8, 561–568.

DeYoung, M., (1987) Disclosing sexual abuse: the impact of developmental variables, *Child Welfare*, LXV 3, 217–223.

Dominelli, L., (1986) Father daughter incest: patriarchy's shameful secret, *Critical Social Policy*, Summer 1986.

Donaldson, N. A., and Gardner, R., (1985) Diagnosis and treatment of traumatic stress around women after childhood incest, in: Figley, C. R., *op. cit.*.

Doyle, C., (1988) *Sexual abuse: Giving help to children*. London: National Children's Bureau.

Dreiblatt, I. S., (1982) *Issues in the evaluation of the sex offender*, Presented at The Washington State Psychological Association Meeting, May 1982.

Driver, E., (1984) *Incest and the role of the professional*, Presented at Teeside Polytechnic, Middlesborough, 25/5/84.

Driver, E., and Droisen, A., (1989) *Child sexual abuse: Feminist perspectives*. Basingstoke, Hants: Macmillan.

Dunning, N., (1985) Child sexual abuse, *The Scottish Child*, 6, 7, 4–7.

Edwards, S. (1984) *Women on Trial: A study of the female suspect, defendant and offender in the Criminal Law and Criminal Justice System*. Manchester: Manchester University Press.

Eisenberg, N., Owens, R. G., and Dewey, M. E., (1987) Attitudes of health professionals to child sexual abuse and incest, *Child Abuse and Neglect*, 11, 109–116.

Eiser, J. R., (1980) *Cognitive social psychology: a guidebook to theory and research*. London: Mcgraw Hill.

Ellenson, G. S., (1985) Detecting a history of incest: a predictive syndrome, *Social Casework*, 525–532.

Ellenson, G. S., (1986) Disturbances of perception in adult female incest survivors, *Social Casework*, 149–159.

Elliot, M. ed. (1993) *Female Sexual Abuse of Children: The Ultimate Taboo*. Essex: Longman.

Elliot, M., (1985) I never taught him to scream. He might be alive if he had screamed, *Community Care*, 9/5/85 11–14.

Ernst, S., and Goodison, L., (1981) *In our own hands*. London: The Women's Press.

Eth, S., and Pynoos, R. S., (eds) (1985) *Post traumatic stress disorder in children*, American Psychiatric Press, Washington, DC.

Everstine, D. S., and Everstine, L., (1989) *Sexual trauma in children and adolescents: Dynamics and treatment*, Brunner/Mazel, NY.

Evert, K., and Bijkerk, I., (1987) *When you're ready: a woman's healing from childhood physical and sexual abuse by her mother*, Launch Press, Walnut Creek, CA.

Fairtlough, A., (1982) *Responsibility for incest: a feminist view*, UEA Social Work Monograph.

Faller, K. C., (1984) Is the child victim of sexual abuse telling the truth? *Child Abuse and Neglect*, 8, 473–481.

Faller, K.C. (1987) Women who sexually abuse children, *Violence and Victims*, Vol 2 263–76

Family Rights Group, (1989) *Child sexual abuse after Cleveland – Alternative strategies*, Family Rights Group, London.

Faria, G., and Belohlavek, N., (1984) Treating female adult survivors of childhood incest, *Social Casework*, 465–471.

Ferenczi, S., (1949) Confusion of tongues between the adult and the child: the language of tenderness and of passion, *International Journal of Psycho-Analysis*, 30, 225–230.

Ferguson, P., (1985) Child sexual abuse – can the legal system cope? *The Scottish Child*, 6, 7 13–16.

Figley, C. R., (1985) *Trauma and its wake: The study and treatment of post-traumatic stress disorder*, Bruner/Mazel, NY.

Finkelhor, D. and Russell, D. (1984) Women as Perpetrators in D. Finkelhor (ed) *Child Sexual Abuse: New Theory and Research*, Free Press, NY.

Finkelhor, D. Williams, L. M., and Burns, N., (1988) *Nursery crimes: sexual abuse in day care*, Sage, Newbury Park, CA.

Finkelhor, D., (1979) *Sexually victimised children*, Free Press, NY.

Finkelhor, D., (1982) Sexual abuse: a sociological perspective, *Child Abuse and Neglect*, 6, 95–102.

Finkelhor, D., (1983) Removing the child – prosecuting the offender in cases of sexual abuse: evidence from the national reporting system for child abuse and neglect, *Child Abuse and Neglect* 7, 195–205.

Finkelhor, D., (1984) *Child sexual abuse: new theory and research*, Free Press, NY.

Finkelhor, D., (1984) How widespread is child sexual abuse? *Children Today*, July-August 1984.

Finkelhor, D., (1984) Sex among siblings: a survey in prevalence, variety and effects, *Archives of Sexual Behaviour*, 9, 3 171–194.

Finkelhor, D., (1984) What's wrong with sex between adults and children?: Ethics and the problem of sexual abuse, *American Journal of Orthopsychiatry*, 49, 4, 692–697.

Finkelhor, D., (1986) *A sourcebook on child sexual abuse*, Sage, Beverly Hills, CA.

Finkelhor, D., and Browne, A., (1985) The traumatic impact of child sexual abuse: a conceptualisation, *American Journal of Orthopsychiatry*, 55 530–541.

Fontana, V. J., (1984) When systems fail: protecting the victim of child sexual abuse, *Children Today*, 7/84, 14–18.

Forseth, L. B., and Brown, A., (1981) A survey of intrafamilial sexual abuse treatment centres: Implications for intervention, *Child Abuse and Neglect* 5, 177–186.

Frank, E. Anderson, C., and Rubinstein, D., (1979) Marital role strain and sexual satisfaction, *Journal of Consulting and Clinical Psychology*, 47, 6, 1096–1103.

Fraser, S., (1989) *My Father's House*, Virago, London

Freeman-Longo, R., (1986) The impact of sexual victimisation on males, *Child Abuse and Neglect*, 10, 411–414.

Freud, S., (1933) The aetiology of hysteria, in: Strachey, *The complete works of Sigmund Freud*, Hogarth Press, London.

Freyd, J.L. (1994) Personal Perspective on the Delayed Memory Debate, *Treating Abuse Today*, Vol 3, No 5 13–20

Friedrich, W. A., (1987) Behaviour problems in sexually abused children, *Journal of Interpersonal violence*, 2, 381–390.

Fromuth, M. E., (1985) The relationship of child sexual abuse with later psychological and sexual adjustment in a sample of college women, *Child Abuse and Neglect*, 10, 5–15.

Frosh, S., (1988) Issues for men working with sexually abused children, *British Journal of Psychotherapy*.

Frosh, S., (1988) No Man's Land: the role of men working with sexually abused children, *British Journal of Guidance and Counselling*, 16, 1, 1–10.

Frude, N., (1982) The sexual nature of sexual abuse: a review of the literature, *Child Abuse and Neglect*, 6, 211–223.

Furniss, T., (1983) Family process in the treatment of intra-familial sexual abuse, *Journal of Family Therapy*, 5, 4, 263–278.

Furniss, T., (1984) Mutual influence and interlocking professional-family process in the treatment of child sexual abuse and incest, *Child Abuse and Neglect*, 7, 207–223.

Furniss, T., (1984) Organising a therapeutic approach to intra-familial child sexual abuse, *Journal of Adolescence*, 7, 309–317.

Garbarino, J., (1987) Children's response to a sexual abuse prevention program: a study of the Spiderman comic, *Child Abuse and Neglect*, 11, 143–148.

Gardner, R. (1992) *True and False Accusations of Child Sexual Abuse*, Creative Therapeutics, Cresskill, N.J.

Garrett, T. B., and Wright, R., (1975) Wives of rapists and incest offenders, *Journal of Sex Research*, 11, 2, 149–157.

Gebhardt, P. Gagnon, I. Pomeroym, W., and Christenson, C., (1965) *Sex offenders: an analysis of types*, Harper and Row, NY.

Gelinas, D. J., (1981) Identification and Treatment of Incest Victims, in: Howell, E., and Bayes, M., (ed) *Women and mental health*, Basic Books, New York.

Geller, M., Devlin, M., Flynn, T., and Kaliski, J., (1985) Confrontation of denial in a father's incest group, *International Journal of Group Psychotherapy*, 35, 4, 545–567.

Gentry, C. E., (1978) Incestuous abuse of children: The need for an objective view, *Child Welfare*, LVII 6 355–364.

Giarretto, H., (1976) The treatment of father–daughter incest: a psycho-social approach, *Children Today*, 7/8/76 2–5.

Giarretto, H., (1982) *Integrated treatment of child sexual abuse: a treatment and training manual*, Science and Behaviour Books, Inc, Palo Alto, CA.

Giarretto, H., (1982) A comprehensive child sexual abuse treatment program, *Child Abuse and Neglect*, 6, 263–278.

Gil, E., (1983) *Outgrowing the pain: a book for and about adults abused as children*, Launch Press, Walnut Creek, CA.

Gil, E., (1988) *Treatment of adult survivors of childhood abuse*, Launch Press, Walnut Creek, CA.

Goldstein, E. (1992) *Confabulations*, Sirs Books, Boca Raton, FL

Goodman, B., and Nowak-Scibelli, D., (1985) Group treatment for women incestuously abused as children, *International Journal of Group Psychotherapy*, 35, 4, 531–544.

Goodwin, J. M., (1989) *Sexual abuse: incest victims and their families*, 2nd Edition, Year Book Medical Publications Inc, Chicago.

Goodwin, J., (1982) Use of drawing in evaluating children who may be incest victims, *Children and Youth Services Review*, 4, 269–278.

Goodwin, J., (1985) Post traumatic symptoms in incest victims, in: Eth, S., and Pynoos, R. S., *op. cit.*.

Goodwin, J., Cormier, M. P. H. L., and Owen, J., (1983) Grandfather–granddaughter incest: a trigenerational view, *Child Abuse and Neglect* 7, 163–170.

Goodwin, J., McCarthy, T., and DiVasto, P., (1981) Prior Incest in mothers of abused children, *Child Abuse and Neglect*, 5, 87–95.

Goodwin, J., Simms, M., and Bergman, R., (1979) Hysterical Seizures: a sequel to incest, *American Journal of Orthopsychiatry*, 49, 4, 698–703.

Greaves, G. G., (1980) Multiple personality 165 years after Mary Reynolds, *Journal of Nervous and Mental Diseases*, 168, 577–597.

Gross, M., (1979) Incestuous rape: a cause for hysterical seizures in four adolescent girls, *American Journal of Orthopsychiatry*, 49, 4, 704–708.

Gruber, K. J., (1981) The child victim's role in sexual assault by adults, *Child Welfare*, LX 5, 305–311.

Hagans, K. B., and Case, J., (1988) *When your child has been molested: a parents guide to healing and recovery*, Lexington Books, Lexington, mass.

Hagedorn, J., (1985) Learning to kiss and tell, *The Times Educational Supplement*, 28/6/85.

Hall, L., and Lloyds, (1989) *Surviving Child Sexual Abuse: a Handbook for helping women challenge their past*, Falmer Press, Lewes.

Hames, J. (1993) Child Pornography: A Secret Web of Exploitation, *Child Abuse Review* 2, 4

Hanks, H.G.I. and Saradjian (1991) Women who abuse children sexually: Characteristics of sexual abuse of children by women, *The Journal of Systemic Consultation and Management*, 2, 247–262

Harrison, P. A, Lumry, A. E., and Claypatch, (1984) *Female sexual abuse victims: Perspectives on family dysfunction, substance abuse and psychiatric disorders,*, Paper presented at the second National Conference for Family Researchers, Durham, NH.

Hart, T., (1979), *Don't Tell Your Mother*. London: Quartet.

Helfer, R. E., (1982) A review of the literature on the prevention of child abuse and neglect, *Child Abuse and Neglect*, 6, 251–261.

Henderson, J., (1983) Is incest harmful? *Canadian Journal of Psychology*, 28, 34–39.

Herbert, C. M. H., (1989) *Talking of Silence: The sexual harassment of schoolgirls.* London: Falmer Press.

Herbert, C. P., (1987) Expert medical assessment in determining probability of alleged child sexual abuse, *Child Abuse and Neglect*, 11, 213–221.

Herman, J. L., (1986) Histories of Violence in an outpatient population: an exploratory study, *American Journal of Orthopsychiatry*, 56, 1, 137–141.

Herman, J. L., and Schatzow, E., (1984) Time-limited group therapy for women with a history of incest, *International Journal of group Psychotherapy*, 34, 4, 605–616.

Herman, J.L. (1992) *Trauma and Recovery.* New York: Basic Books.

Herman, J.L. and Schatzow, E. (1987) Recovery and verification of memories of childhood sexual trauma, *Psychoanalytic Psychology* 4 (1) 1–14

Hester, B., (1986) Incest in families: its effects and help from counselling, *Marriage Guidance*, 22, 3, 3–7.

Hill, E., (1985) *The Family Secret.* New York: Dell.

Hillman, D., and Solekolek-Tefft, J., (1988) *Spiders and Flies: Help for parents and teachers of sexually abused children.* Lexington, MA: Lexington Books.

Hirsch, M., (1986) Narcissism and partial lack of reality testing (denial) in incestuous fathers, *Child Abuse and Neglect*, 10, 547–549.

Hollingsworth, J., (1986) *Unspeakable Acts.* Chicago; Congdon and Weed Inc.

Hooper, C. A., (1987) Getting him off the hook, *Trouble and Strife*, 12, 20–25.

Hoorwitz, A. N., (1983) Guidelines for treating father–daughter incest, *Social Casework*, 515–524.

Horowitz, M. J., (1976) *Stress response syndromes.* New York: Aronoson.

Hudson, W. W., Harrison, D. F., and Crosscup, P. C., (1981) A short-form scale to measure sexual discord in dyadic relationships, *Journal of Sex Research*, 17, 2, 157–174.

Hunt, I, (1990) Surely a woman couldn't be guilty of such an act, *The Independent*, 23.5.90.

Illsley, P., (1989) *The Drama of Cleveland.* London: CPBF/SCOSAC.

Ireland, K. (1993) Sexual Exploitation of Children in International travel and Tourism, *Child Abuse Review* 2, 4

Jackson, S., (1982) *Childhood and Sexuality.* Oxford: Basil Blackwell.

James, B., and Nasjleti, M., (1989) *Treating Sexually Abused Children and their Families.* Palo Alto, CA: Consulting Psychologists Press, Inc.

James, J., and Meyerding, J., (1977) Early sexual experiences as a factor in prostitution, *Archives of Sexual Behaviour*, 7, 31–42.

Jampole, L., and Weber, M. K., (1987) An assessment of the behaviour of sexually abused and nonsexually abused children with anatomically correct dolls, *Child Abuse and Neglect*, 11, 187–192.

Janoff-Bulman, R., (1979) Characterological versus behavioural self-blame, *Journal of Personality and Social Psychology*, 37, 1798–1809.

Janssen, M., (1983) *Silent Scream.* PA: Fortree Press.

Janus, M. D. McCormack, A., Burgess, A. W., and Hartman, C., (1987) *Adolescent Runaways: Causes and Consequence.* Lexington, Mass: Lexington Books.

Jehu, D. Gazan, M., and Klassen, C., (1984) Common therapeutic targets among women who were sexually abused in childhood, *Journal of Social Work and Human Sexuality*, 3, 25–45.

Jehu, D. Klassen,C., and Gazan, M., (1986) Cognitive restructuring of distorted beliefs associated with childhood sexual abuse, *Journal of Social Work and Human Sexuality*, 4, 49–69.

Jehu, D., (1988) *Beyond Sexual Abuse: Therapy with women who were childhood victims.* Chichester: Wiley.

Jones, D. P. H., (1986) Individual psychotherapy for the sexually abused child, *Child Abuse and Neglect*, 10, 377–385.

Jones, D. P. H., and McQuiston, M. G., (1988) *Interviewing the Sexually Abused Child.* London: Royal College of Psychiatrists.

Justice, B., and Justice, R., (1979) *The broken taboo: Sex in the family.* New York: Human Sciences Press.

Kane, E., (1989) *Recovering from Incest: Imagination and the healing process.* Boston, Mass: Sigo Press.

Kelly, L., (1985) The things they say and unfortunately believe, in: Rhodes, D., and McNeil, S., (ed.) *Women Against Violence Against Women* Onlywomen Press.

Kennedy, J., (1989) *Touch of Silence: a Healing from the Heart.* San Diego, CA: Cosmoenergetics Publications.

Kilpatrick, A. C., (1987) Childhood sexual experiences: problems and issues in studying long-range effects, *Journal of Sex Research*, 23, 2, 173–196.

Kirsta, A. (1994) *Deadlier Than the Male: Violence and Aggression in Women.* London: Harper-Collins.

Langevin, R., Paitich, D., Freeman, R., Mann, K., and Handy, L., (1978) Personality characteristics and sexual anomalies in males, *Canadian Journal of Behavioural Science*, 10, 3, 222–238.

Langmade, C. J., (1988) The impact of pre and post-pubertal onsetting incest experience in adult women as measured by sex anxiety, sex guilt, sexual satisfaction and sexual behaviour, *Dissertation Abstracts International*, 44, 917B.

Laurance, J., (1986) Bentovim's technique, *New Society*, 28/11/86.

Lew, M., (1988) *Victims No Longer: Men recovering from incest and other child sexual abuse.* New York: Nevraumont Publishing.

Lindberg, F. H., and Distad, L. J., (1985) Post-traumatic stress disorders in women who experienced childhood incest, *Child Abuse and Neglect*, 9, 329–334.

Lloyd, J., (1982) The management of Incest: an overview of three inter-related systems – the family, the legal and the therapeutic, *Journal of Social Welfare Law*, January 1982, 16–28.

Loftus, E.F. (1993) The reality of repressed memories, *American Psychologist* 48 95, 518–537

London Rape Crisis Centre, (1984) *Sexual Violence: The reality for women.* London: Women's Press.

Lustig, N. Dresser, J. W. Spellman, S., and Murray, T. B., (1966) Incest: A family group survival pattern, *Archives of general psychiatry,* 14, 31–40.

Lutz, S. E., and Medway, J. P., (1984) Contextual family therapy with the victims of incest, *Journal Adolescence,* 7, 319–327.

Lynn, S.J. and Nash, M.R. (1994) Truth in Memory: Ramifications for psychotherapy and hypnotherapy, *American Journal of Clinical Hypnosis* 36: 3 194–208

MacFarlane, K., and Korbin, J., (1983) Confronting the incest secret long after the fact: a family study of multiple victimisation with strategies for intervention, *Child Abuse and Neglect,* 7, 225–240.

MacFarlane, K., Waterman, J., Conerly, S., Damon, L., Durfee, M., and Long, S., (1986) *Sexual abuse of young children: evaluation and treatment.* London: Holt, Rinehart and Winston.

MacLeod, M., and Saraga, E., (1987) *Child Sexual Abuse: Towards a Feminist Professional Practice,* Report of the conference held at the Polytechnic of North London, April 1987. London: PNL Press.

MacLeod, M., and Saraga, E., (1987) Abuse of Trust, *Marxism Today,* 8/87 10–13.

Maltz, W., and Holman, B., (1987) *Incest and sexuality: a Guide to Understanding and Healing.* Lexington, MA: Lexington Books.

Manchester, A. H., (1979) The law of incest in England and Wales, *Child Abuse and Neglect,* 3, 679–682.

Mannarino, A. P., and Cohen, J. A., (1986) A clinic-demographic study of sexually abused children, *Child Abuse and Neglect,* 10, 17–23.

Masson, J. M., (1984) *Freud: The assault on truth. Freud's suppression of the seduction theory.* New York: Farrar, Strauss and Giroux.

Mathews, R., Matthews, J.K. and Speltz, R. (1989) *Female Sexual Offenders.* Orwell, Vermont: The Safer Society Press.

Matthews, J.K. (1993) Working with Female Sexual Offenders, in M. Elliott (ed) *Female Sexual Abuse of Children.* Essex: Longman.

Mayer, A., (1983) *Incest: a treatment manual for therapy with victims, spouses and offenders.* Holmes Beach, FL: Learning Pub. Inc.

Mayer, A., (1985) *Sexual abuse: Causes, consequences and treatment of incestuous and paedophilic acts.* Holmes beach, FL: Learning Publications, Inc.

Mayhall, P. D., and Norgard, K. E., (1983) *Child abuse and neglect: Sharing responsibility,* New York, John Wiley and Sons.

McCann et al, (1988) Trauma and victimisation: a model of psychological adaptation, *The Counselling Psychologist,* 16: 4, 531–594.

McCarty, L. M., (1981) Investigation of incest: Opportunity to motivate families to seek help, *Child Welfare,* LX 10, 679–689

McDonough, H., and Love, A. J., (1987) The challenge of sexual abuse: protection and therapy in a child welfare setting, *Child Welfare,* LXVI 3, 225–235.

McGuire, L. S., and Wagner, N. N., (1978) Sexual dysfunction in women who were molested as children: One response pattern and suggestions for treatment, *Journal of Sex and Marital Therapy*, 4, 1, 11–15.

McHugh, (1992) Memory and reality: Emerging Crisis Historical perspectives on Recovered memories, Paper presented at FMSF Conference April 1992

McIntyre, K., (1981) Role of mothers in father–daughter incest: a feminist analysis, *Social Work*, 11/81 462–466.

McNaron, T., and Morgan, Y., (eds) (1982) *Voices in the Night: Women Speaking about Incest*. Pittsburg: Cleis Press.

Meiselman, K. C., (1978) *Incest: a psychological study of causes and effects with treatment recommendations*. San Francisco: Jossey-Bass.

Metropolitan Police and Bexley Social Services, (1987) *Child sexual abuse: Joint investigative programme*, Bexley Experiment London: HMSO.

Miller, A., (1981) *The drama of being a gifted child*. New York: Basic Books Inc (Pluto Press).

Miller, A., (1984) *Thou shalt not be aware: Society's betrayal of the child*. New York: Farrar, Strauss and Giroux.

Milner, J., and Blythe, E., (1989) *Coping with child sexual abuse: a guide for teachers*. London: Longman.

Mitra, C. L., Father–daughter incest: a paradigm of sexual exploitation, *Justice of the Peace*, 22/5/82 312–313.

Moggach, D., (1983) *Porky*. London: Cape.

Moore, B. E., (1976) Freud and female sexuality: a current view, *International Journal of Psycho-Analysis* 57, 287–305.

Moore, J., (1985) *The ABC of child abuse work*. Aldershot: Gower Publishing.

Morgan, L., (1987) *Megan's secret*. Auckland, NZ: Papers Inc.

Morris, M., (1982) *If I should die before I wake*. London: Souvenir Press.

Mrazek, D. A., (1983) Long term follow up of an adolescent perpetrator of sexual abuse, *Child abuse and neglect*, 7, 239–240.

Mrazek, P. B., and Kempe, C. H., (1981) *Sexually abused children and their families*. Oxford: Pergamon Press.

Mrazek, P. J., Lynch, M. A., and Bentovim, A., (1983) Sexual Abuse of children in the United Kingdom, *Child abuse and neglect*, 7, 147–153.

Nash, M.R. (1992) Retrieval of childhood memories in psychotherapy: Clinical utility and historical verifiability are not the same thing. Paper presented at the Annual Convention of the American Psychological Association, Washington, DC

Nasjleti, M., (1980) Suffering in silence: the male incest victim, *Child welfare*, LIX., 5 269–275.

Nelson, S., (1987) *Incest: fact and myth*, Stramullion Co-Operative Ltd, Edinburgh.

NSPCC, (1990) *Research Briefing No 11*. London: NSPCC.

O'Connor, A. A., (1988) Female sex offenders, *British Journal of Psychiatry*, 150, 615–620.

O'Connor, A. A., (1988) Sex offences committed by women, *British Journal of Sexual Medicine*, February.

O'Donnell, C., and Craney, J., (1982) *Family violence in Australia.* Cheshire: Lonfman.

O'Hagan, K., (1989) *Working with child sexual abuse.* Miton Keynes: Open University Press.

Oates, K., (1986) *Child abuse and neglect: What happens eventually.* New York: Brunner/Mazel.

Ofshe, R. and Watters, E. (1993) Making Monsters, *Society,* 30, 3, 4–16

Olio, K.A. and Cornell, W.F. (1993) Making Meaning Not Monsters: Reflections on the Delayed Memory Controversy

Orbach, S. (1994) *What's Really Going On: Making Sense of our emotional lives.* London: Virago.

Orbach, S. (1994) False Therapy Syndrome, *The Guardian Weekend,* 11/6/94

Osborn, J., (1990) Effect of child sexual abuse on women, *Social work monographs.* Norwich: UEA.

Parks, P., (1990) *Sexual abuse – rescuing the inner child.* London: Souvenir Press.

Pauncz, A., (1951) The concept of adult libido and the Lear complex, *American Journal of Psychotherapy,* 5, 187–195.

Pauncz, A., (1954) Psychopathology of Shakespeare's 'King Lear', *American Imago,* 9, 59–78.

Pauncz, A., (1954) The Lear complex in world literature, *American Imago,* 2, 51–83.

Perlmutter, L. H., Engel, T., and Sager, C. J., (1982) The incest taboo: Loosened sexual boundaries in remarried families, *Journal of Sex and Marital Therapy,* 8, 2, 83–96.

Perry, R., (1985) Child abuse: procedures and practice, *The Scottish Child,* 6, 7, 10–12.

Peters, J. J., (1976) Children who are victims of sexual assault and the psychology of offenders, *American Journal of Psychotherapy,* 30, 398–421.

Peters, S. D., (1984) *The relationship between childhood sexual victimisation and adult depression among Afro-American and white women,* unpublished doctoral dissertation, University of California, CA.

Phelan, P., (1986) The process of incest: Biologic father and stepfather families, *Child Abuse and Neglect,* 10, 531–539.

Pierce, R. L., (1984) Child pornography: a hidden dimension of child abuse, *Child Abuse and Neglect* 8, 483–493.

Pierce, R., and Pierce, L. H., (1985) The sexually abused child: a comparison of male and female victims, *Child Abuse and Neglect,* 9, 191–199.

Pincus, L., and Dare, C., (1978), *Secrets in the family.* London: Faber and Faber.

Portwood, P., Gorcey, M., and Sanders, P., (1987) *Rebirth of power.* Racine, WI: Mother Courage Press.

Poston, C., and Lison, K., (1989) *Reclaiming our lives: hope for adult survivors of incest.* Boston: Little Brown.

Prins, H., (1980) *Offenders, deviants or patients: an introduction to the study of socio-forensic problems.* London: Tavistock.

Putnam, F. W., (1985) Dissociation as a response to extreme trauma, in: Kluft, R. P., (ed) *Childhood antecedents of multiple personality*, American Psychiatric Press, Washington, DC

Randall, M., (1987) *This is about incest*. Ithaca, NY: Firebrand.

Renvoize, J., (1982) *Incest: a family patterns*. London: Routledge and Kegan Paul.

Rhodes, D., and McNeil, (1985) *Women against violence against women*. London: Onlywomen Press.

Riches, P., (ed) (1989) *Responses to Cleveland: Improving services for child sexual abuse*, National Children's Bureau.

Rist, K., (1979) Incest: Theoretical and clinical views, *American Journal of Orthopsychiatry*, 49, 4, 680–691.

Rogers, C. M., and Tremaine, T., (1984) Clinical intervention with boy victims of sexual abuse, in: Stuart, I. R., and Greer, J. G., (eds) *Victims of sexual aggression: treatment of children, women and men*. New York: Van Nostrand Reinhold.

Rush, F., (1980) *The best kept secret: Sexual abuse of children*. New York: Mcgraw-Hill.

Russell, D. (1984) *Sexual Exploitation: Rape, child sexual abuse, and sexual harassment*. Beverly Hills, CA: Sage.

Russell, D. E. H., (1983) The incidence and prevalence of intrafamilial and extrafamilial sexual abuse of female children, *Child Abuse and Neglect*, 7, 133–146.

Russell, D. E. H., (1986) *The secret trauma: Incest in the lives of girls and women*. New York: Basic Books Inc.

Ryan, G., (1986) Annotated bibliography: adolescent perpetrators of sexual molestation of children, *Child Abuse and Neglect*, 10, 125–131.

Saadawi, N. E., (1980) *The hidden face of Eve*. London: Zed Press.

Sagarin, E., (1977) Incest: problems of definition and frequency, *Journal of Sex Research*, 13, 2, 126–135.

Salter, A. C., (1988) *Treating child sex offenders and victims: a practical guide*. Beverly Hills: Sage.

Salter, A.C. (1993) *Accuracy of expert testimony in child sexual abuse cases: a case study of Ralph Underwager and Hollida Wakefield*. Monograph commissioned by New England Commissioners of Child welfare Agencies

Saltman, V., and Solomon, R. S., (1982) Incest and multiple personality disorder, *Psychological reports*, 50, 1127–1141.

Sandberg, D. N., (1989) *The Child Abuse-delinquency Connection*. Lexington, Mass: Lexington Books.

Sanderson, C., (1988) How the public construe child sexual abusers, In: *Inner London probation service conference papers 1988*. ILPS.

Saphira, M., (1985) *The sexual abuse of children*. Auckland: Papers Inc.

Scavo, R. R., (1989) Female adolescent sex offenders: a neglected treatment group, *Social casework*, February.

Schetky, D. H., and Green, A. H., (1988) *Child sexual abuse: a handbook for health care and legal professionals*, Brunner/Mazel, NY.

Schover, L. R., Friedman, J. M., Weiler, S. J., Heiman, J. R., and LoPiccolo, J., (1982) Multiaxial problem-oriented system for sexual dysfunctions: and alternative to DSM-III *Archives of General Psychiatry*, 39, 614–619.

Schultz, L. G., and Jones, P., (1983) Sexual abuse of children: Issues for social service and health professionals, *Child Welfare*, LXII 2, 99–108.

Schultz, R., Braun, B. G., and Kluft, R. P., (1985) Creativity and imaginary companions phenomena, in: Braun, B. G., *Proceedings of Second International Conference on Multiple Personality Dissociative States*. Chicago: Chicago Rush University.

SCOSAC, (1990) *Newsletter*, Issue no., 12, July.

Sedney, M. A., and Brooks, B., (1984) Factors associated with history of childhood sexual experiences in a non-clinical female population, Journal of American Child Psychiatry, 23, 215–218.

Seligman, M. E. P., (1975) *Learned helplessness: on depression, development and death*. San Francisco: Freeman and Co.

Server, J. C., and Janzen, C., (1982) Contra-indications to reconstitution of sexually abusive families, *Child Welfare*, LXI 5 279–288.

Sgroi, S. M., (1982) *Handbook of clinical intervention in child sexual abuse*. Lexington, MA: Lexington Books.

Sgroi, S. M., (1988) *Vulnerable populations, Vol.1: Evaluation and treatment of sexually abused children and adult survivors*. Lexington, MA: Lexington Books.

Silbert, M. H., and Pines, A. M., (1983) Early sexual exploitation as an influence in prostitution, *Social Work*, 28, 4, 285–289.

Sinason, V. (ed) (1994) *Treating Survivors of Satanist Abuse*. London: Routledge.

Sisk, S. L., and Hoffman, C. F., (1987) *Inside scars: Incest recovery as told by a survivor and her therapist*. Gainesville, FL: Pandora Press.

Smith, G., (1986) Child sexual abuse: the power of intrusion, *Adoption and Fostering*, 10, 3, 13–18.

Smith, H., and Israel, E., (1987) Sibling incest: a study of the dynamics of 25 cases, *Child Abuse and Neglect*, 11, 101–108.

Smith, S. B., (1985) *Children's story: Sexually molested children in criminal court*. Walnut Creek, CA: Launch Press.

Smith, S.E. (1993) Body memories: and other pseudo-scientific notions of "Survivor Psychology". Paper presented at the False Memory Syndrome Foundation Conference May 1993

Snowden, R., (1982) *Working with incest offenders: Excuses, excuses, excuses*, Aegis, Summer 1982.

Spring, J., (1987) *Cry hard and swim: The story of an incest survivor*. London: Virago Press.

Stern, C. R., (1984) The aetiology of multiple personality, *Psychiatric Clinics of North America*, 7, 149–160.

Summit, R. C., (1983) The child sexual abuse accommodation syndrome, *Child Abuse and Neglect* 7, 177–193

Summit, R., and Kryso, J., (1978) Sexual abuse of children: a clinical spectrum, *American Journal of Orthopsychiatry*, 48, 2, 237–251.

Tasane, S., and Dreyfuss, C., (1989) *Bird of prey*. London: Clubman Books Ltd.

Taubman, S., (1984) Incest in context, *Social Work*, 29, 1, 35–40.

Taylor, R. L., (1984) Marital therapy in the treatment of incest, *Social Casework*, 195–202.

Terr, L.C. (1991) Child traumas: An outline and overview, *American Journal of Psychiatry 148 (1) 10–20*

Terr, L.C. (1994) *Unchained Memories*. London: Harper-Collins.

Tower, C. C., (1988) *Secret scars: a guide for survivors of child sexual abuse*. New York: Penguin.

Trepper, T. S., and Barrett, M. J., (1986) *Treating incest: a multiple systems perspective*. New York: Haworth Press.

Trowell, J., (1985) Working with families where incest is actual or feared, *Health Visitor*, 58, 189–191.

Trowell, J., and Castle, R. L., (1981) Treating abused children: Some clinical and research aspects of work carried out by the national advisory centre of the National Society for the Prevention of Cruelty to Children in the United Kingdom, *Child Abuse and Neglect*, 5, 187–192.

Tsai, M., and Wagner, N. N., (1978) Therapy groups for women sexually molested as children, *Archives of Sexual Behaviour*, 7, 5, 417–427.

Tufts New England Medical Centre, (1984) *Sexually exploited children*, Final Report for the Office of Juvenile Justice and Delinquency Prevention, US Report of Justice, Washington DC.

Turner, J., (1989) *Home is where the hurt is: Guidance for all victims of sexual abuse in the home and for those who support them*. Northampton: Thorsons.

Tyler, R. P. T., and Stone, L. E., (1985) Child pornography: perpetuating the sexual victimisation of children, *Child Abuse and Neglect*, 9, 313–318.

Utain, M., and Oliver, B., (1989) *Scream louder: Through hell and healing with an incest survivor and her therapist*. Deerfield Beach, FL: Health Communications Inc.

Van Buskirk, S. S., and Cole, C. F., (1983) Characteristics of eight women seeking therapy for the effects of incest, *Psychotherapy Theory Research and Practice*, 20, 503–514.

van der Kolk and Kadish, W. (1987) Amnesia, dissociation and the return of the repressed, In B.A. van der Kolk *Psychological Trauma*. Washington, DC: American Psychiatric Press.

Van der Kolk, B. A., (1989) The compulsion to repeat the trauma: reenactment, revictimisation and masochism, *Psychiatric Clinics of North America*, 12, 2, 389–411.

Vitaliano, P. P., James, J., and Boyer, D., (1981) Sexuality of deviant females: adolescent and adult correlates, *Social Work*, 26, 6, 468–472.

Vizard, E., (1984) The sexual abuse of children, *Health Visitor*, 57, 234–236.

Vizard, E., (1985) The problem of child sexual abuse and approaches to prevention, *Early Child Development and Care*, 19, 133–149.

Vizard, E., (1987) Interviewing young sexually abused children – assessment techniques, *Family Law*, 17, 28–33.

Vizard, E., and Bentovim, A., (1985) Incest – the role of the general practitioner, *Maternal and Child Health*, 2/85 55–59.

Wakefield, H. and Underwager, R. (1993) Interview with Hollida Wakefield and Ralph Underwager, *Paidika The Journal of Paedophilia* Winter 1993, 3, 1, 3–12

Walker, A., (1983) *The colour purple*. London: Women's Press.

Walker, C. E., Bonner, B., and Kaufman, K. L., (1988) *The physically and sexually abused child: Evaluation and treatment.* Oxford: Pergamon Press.

Walsh, D., and Liddy, R., (1989) *Surviving sexual abuse.* Dublin: Attic Press.

Ward, E., (1984) *Father–daughter rape.* London: The Women's Press.

Weeks, J., (1985) *Sexuality and its discontents.* London: Routledge.

Welldon, E. V., (1988) *Mother, madonna, whore: The idealisation and denigration of motherhood.* London: Free Association Books.

Wells, J., (1985) Bruises are more obvious, *Community Care*, January 10, 1985, 14–17.

Werman, D. S., (19) On the occurrence of incest fantasies, *Psychoanalytic Quarterly*, 245–255.

West, N., (ed) (1985) *Sexual victimisation.* Aldershot: Gower.

Wheeler, B. R., and Walton, E., (1987) Personality disturbances of adult incest victims, *Social Casework*, 597–602.

White, S., Strom, G. A., Santilli, G., and Halpin, B. M., (1986) Interviewing young sexual abuse victims with anatomically correct dolls, *Child Abuse and Neglect*, 10, 519–529.

Whitfield, C. L., (1987) *Healing the Child Within.* Deerfield Beach, FL: Health Communications Inc.

Wilbur, C. A., (1985) The effects of child abuse on the psyche, in: Kluft, R. P., (ed) *Childhood antecedents of multiple personality.* Washington, DC: American Psychiatric Press.

Wilbur, C. B., (1984) Multiple personality and child sexual abuse, *Psychiatric Clinics of North America*, 7, 3–8.

Wilk, R. J., and McCarthy, C. R., (1986) Intervention in child sexual abuse: a survey of attitudes, *Social Casework*, 20–26.

Will, D., (1983) Approaching the incestuous and sexually abusive family, *Journal of Adolescence*, 6, 229–246.

Williams, L.M. (1992) Adult memories of childhood abuse: Preliminary findings from a longitudinal study, *The APSAC Advisor*, Summer 1992, 19–20

Williams, L.M. (1994) Recall of childhood Trauma: A prospective Study of women's memories of child sexual abuse, *Journal of Consulting and Clinical Psychology*

Williams, L.M. (1994) Recovered memories of abuse in women with documented child sexual victimisation histories, *Journal of Consciousness and Cognition*

Wilson, G., (1987) Male–female differences in sexual activity, enjoyment and fantasies, *Personality and Individual Differences*, 8, 1, 125–127.

Wilson, G., (1988) Measurement of Sex Fantasy, *Sexual and Marital therapy*, 3, 1, 45–55.

Wilson, G., and Cox, D. N., (1983) Personality of paedophile club members, *Personality and Individual Differences*, 4, 3, 323–329.

Wisechild, L. M., (1988) *The obsidian mirror*. Seattle, WA: Seal Press.

Women's Research Centre, (1989) *Recollecting our lives: Women's experiences of child sexual abuse*. Vancouver: Press Gang Publishers.

Wood, W., and Hatton, L., (1989) *Triumph over darkness: Understanding and healing the trauma of child sexual abuse*. Hillsboro, CA: Beyond Words Publishing Inc.

Wyatt, G. E., and Peters, S. D., (1986) Issues in the definition of child sexual abuse in prevalence research, *Child Abuse and Neglect*, 10, 231–241.

Wyatt, G. E., and Peters, S. D., (1986) Methodological considerations in research on the prevalence of child sexual abuse, *Child Abuse and Neglect*, 10, 241–251.

Wyatt, G. E., and Powell, G. J., (1988) *Lasting effects of child sexual abuse*. Newbury Park: Sage

Wynne L. E., (1987) *That looks like a nice house*. Walnut Creek, CA: Launch Press.

Yapko, M.D. (1994) *Suggestions of Abuse: True and False Memories of Childhood Sexual Abuse*. New York: Simon and Schuster.

Yapko, M.D. (1994) Suggestibility and repressed memories of abuse: A survey of psychotherapists' beliefs, *American Journal of Clinical Hypnosis* 36; 3

Index